BOOK PARTS

BOOK PARTS

EDITED BY

DENNIS DUNCAN & ADAM SMYTH

OXFORD
UNIVERSITY PRESS

OXFORD

UNIVERSITY PRESS

Great Clarendon Street, Oxford, OX2 6DP,
United Kingdom

Oxford University Press is a department of the University of Oxford.
It furthers the University's objective of excellence in research, scholarship,
and education by publishing worldwide. Oxford is a registered trade mark of
Oxford University Press in the UK and in certain other countries

Published in the United States of America by Oxford University Press
198 Madison Avenue, New York, NY 10016, United States of America

British Library Cataloguing in Publication Data

Data available

Library of Congress Control Number: 2019931134

ISBN 978–0–19–881246–3

Printed and bound by
CPI Group (UK) Ltd, Croydon, CR0 4YY

Book Parts is dedicated to Philippa Jevons (indexer), Marten Sealby (cover designer), Dawn Preston (copyeditor), Anna Scully (text designer), the SPi typesetting team, Jacqueline Norton (Senior Commissioning Editor), Aimee Wright (Senior Assistant Commissioning Editor), Catherine Owen and John Smallman (Editorial Assistants), Elakkia Bharathi (Project Manager), Jack Lynch (blurb writer), Stephen Orgel (Reader 2), and an anonymous Reader 1

❧CONTENTS❧

LIST OF FIGURES

LIST OF PLATES

CONTRIBUTORS

TAMARA ATKIN is Senior Lecturer in Late Medieval and Early Renaissance Literature at Queen Mary University of London. She is the author of *The Drama of Reform: Theology and Theatricality, 1461–1553* (2013) and *Reading Drama in Tudor England* (2018). With Laura Estill, she is co-editing a collection of essays on *Early British Drama in Manuscript*.

SIDNEY E. BERGER has published more than fifteen books and more than sixty articles in such fields as bibliography, the book arts, printing history, medieval literature, twentieth-century literature, and book history. He was editor for six years of *Rare Books and Manuscripts Librarianship*, and he is currently Associate Editor of *Preservation, Digital Technology and Culture*. He was the Ann C. Pingree Director of the Phillips Library at the Peabody Essex Museum; he is now Director Emeritus at that library. He was also Director of the California Center for the Book (University of California, Los Angeles) and Head of Special Collections and University Archivist at the University of California, Riverside. *Rare Books and Special Collections* won the ABC Clio/American Library Association award (2015); his most recent book is *The Dictionary of the Book* (2017).

CLAIRE M. L. BOURNE is Assistant Professor of English at Pennsylvania State University, where her teaching and research focus on early modern plays and book history. She is currently completing a book entitled *Typographies of Performance in Early Modern England*. Her writing has appeared or is forthcoming in *English Literary Renaissance*, *Papers of the Bibliographical Society of America*, *Shakespeare*, and *Shakespeare Bulletin*, as well as several edited collections, including ones that examine Christopher Marlowe at the intersection of print and performance; Shakespeare in print after 1640; and early modern marginalia.

MEAGHAN J. BROWN is Digital Production Editor at the Folger Shakespeare Library, where she is working on Miranda, Folger's new digital asset platform. She holds a PhD in the History of Text Technologies from Florida State University and an MSIS from the University of Texas at Austin. Meaghan's research interests include how early modern printers present the act of printing to their readers, citation practices in early modern studies, and digital humanities. She swears these are related. Her work has appeared in *Book History*, *Papers of the Bibliographical*

Society of Canada, and *Archives Journal*. Meaghan is also Managing Editor of the *Papers of the Bibliographical Society of America*.

RACHEL SAGNER BUURMA is Associate Professor of English Literature at Swarthmore College, where she works on eighteenth- and nineteenth-century literature and print culture, the history of the novel, twentieth-century Anglo-American literary criticism, literary informatics, and book history. Her work has recently appeared in *Representations*, *Victorian Studies*, and *New Literary History*. She is finishing a book on the material history of narrative omniscience, beginning one on the research practices of Victorian novelists, and is working on a history of English studies titled *The Teaching Archive* with Laura Heffernan. Along with Jon Shaw, she co-directs the *Early Novels Database*.

LUISA CALÈ is Senior Lecturer at Birkbeck, University of London. Luisa has published on Romantic literature, visual, and material culture. Her current project, entitled *The Book Unbound*, explores practices of reading, collecting, and dismantling the book, with chapters on Walpole, Blake, and Dickens.

NICHOLAS DAMES is Theodore Kahan Professor of Humanities at Columbia University, and the author of *Amnesiac Selves: Nostalgia, Forgetting, and British Fiction, 1810–1870* (Oxford, 2001) and *The Physiology of the Novel: Reading, Neural Science, and the Form of Victorian Fiction* (Oxford, 2007). A specialist in the novel, with particular attention to the novel of the nineteenth century in Britain and on the European continent, his interests also include novel theory, the history of reading, and the aesthetics of prose fiction from the seventeenth century to the present. His current project is a history of the chapter, from the textual cultures of late antiquity, particularly the editorial and scribal practices of early Christianity, to the modern novel.

JENNY DAVIDSON is Professor of English and Comparative Literature at Columbia University in New York. Her most recent book is *Reading Jane Austen*. She is currently at work on a book about Edward Gibbon and the ruins of Rome.

DENNIS DUNCAN is a writer and translator based in London. His publications include *The Oulipo and Modern Thought* (2018), *Babel: Adventures in Translation* (2018), and *Tom McCarthy: Critical Essays* (2016). Another monograph, *Index, A History of the*, is due out with Penguin in 2020.

ALEXANDRA FRANKLIN is Co-ordinator of the Bodleian Libraries Centre for the Study of the Book at Oxford University. As a rare books librarian she helped to create the Bodleian Broadside Ballads online resource (ballads.bodleian.ox.ac.uk), compiling a subject index of the woodcut illustrations on ballad sheets. She has published articles on the woodcut illustrations in popular prints and continues to research the history of reading and uses of printed imagery while managing educational and fellowship programmes within the Bodleian's Department of Special Collections.

JOSEPH A. HOWLEY is Associate Professor of Classics at Columbia University. His first book, *Aulus Gellius and Roman Reading Culture: Text, Presence and Imperial Knowledge in the Noctes Atticae* (2018), considers the second-century Roman essayist Aulus Gellius in light of the reading culture and literary trends of the Roman imperial world. He has published on topics including book-burning, study abroad, and intellectual culture in ancient Rome. His current project concerns the role of enslaved labor in the book culture of ancient Rome. He received his PhD in Classics from the University of St Andrews in 2011 and held a 2014–16 Mellon Fellowship in Critical Bibliography from the Rare Book School in Charlottesville, Virginia.

GILL PARTINGTON is Munby Fellow at Cambridge University and works at the intersections of literature, visual culture and media. Her research concerns the material page and its unorthodox histories, forms, uses, and abuses. She has published work on the altered books of artists Tom Phillips and John Latham, and is currently working on a project about the genealogies of the non-codex book.

SEAN ROBERTS is Associate Professor of Art History at Virginia Commonwealth University in Qatar and President of the Italian Art Society. His research is concerned with the interactions between Italy and the Islamic lands, the cultural history of maps, and with the place of prints in the histories of art and technology. He is the author of *Printing a Mediterranean World: Florence, Constantinople and the Renaissance of Geography* (2013) and is co-editor with Tim McCall and Giancarlo Fiorenza of *Visual Cultures of Secrecy in Early Modern Europe* (2013). Sean's essays on cartography, diplomacy, and printmaking have appeared in journals including *Imago Mundi*, *Print Quarterly*, *Renaissance Studies*, *Journal of Early Modern History*, and *Intellectual History Review*.

SHEF ROGERS is Associate Professor at the University of Otago, where he co-directs the university's Centre for the Book. He is Editor of *Script and Print: Bulletin of the Bibliographical Society of Australia and New Zealand* and President of the Society for the History of Authorship, Reading and Publishing (SHARP). He has published essays on eighteenth-century travel books, royal licences for publishing, copyright payments to authors, and books with free supplements.

DANIEL SAWYER is Postdoctoral Research Assistant in the Faculty of English and Junior Research Fellow at Corpus Christi College, University of Oxford. He studies medieval English literature using a combination of literary and textual criticism alongside quantitative and qualitative codicology. He is currently writing the first book-length history of the reading of later Middle English verse, and is editing parts of the first complete English Bible translation, the Wycliffite Bible, for a major new edition. He has also published on unnoticed Middle English verse, rediscovered manuscript fragments, and perplexing medieval bookmarks; his most recent article is a study of 1,511 lost manuscripts.

HELEN SMITH is Professor in Renaissance Literature and Head of the Department of English and Related Literature at the University of York. She is author of *Grossly Material Things: Women and Book Production in Early Modern England* (Oxford, 2012) and co-editor of *Renaissance Paratexts* (with Louise Wilson, 2011), *The Oxford Handbook of the Bible in Early Modern England, c. 1530–1700* (with Kevin Killeen and Rachel Willie, 2015), and *Conversions: Gender and Religious Change in Early Modern Europe* (with Simon Ditchfield, 2016). Helen has published widely on early modern material texts, publishing, and women's cultural work.

ADAM SMYTH is Professor of English Literature and the History of the Book at the University of Oxford. He is the author of, among other things, *Material Texts in Early Modern England* (2018) and *Autobiography in Early Modern England* (2010). He is currently editing *Pericles* for Arden Shakespeare, and he writes regularly for the *London Review of Books*.

TIFFANY STERN Professor of Shakespeare and Early Modern Drama at The Shakespeare Institute, University of Birmingham. Her monographs are *Rehearsal from Shakespeare to Sheridan* (2000), *Making Shakespeare* (2004), *Shakespeare in Parts* (with Simon Palfey, Oxford, 2007; winner of the 2009 David Bevington Award for Best New Book in Early Drama Studies), and *Documents of Early Modern Performance* (2009; winner of the 2010 David Bevington Award for Best New Book in Early Drama Studies). She has co-edited a collection of essays with Farah Karim-Cooper, *Shakespeare's Theatres and the Effects of Performance* (2013), and edited the anonymous *King Leir* (2001), Sheridan's *The Rivals* (2004), Farquhar's *Recruiting Officer* (2010), and Brome's *Jovial Crew* (2014). She is General Editor of New Mermaids and Arden Shakespeare 4, and is author of over fifty chapters and articles on sixteenth- to eighteenth-century dramatic literature.

WHITNEY TRETTIEN is Assistant Professor in the Department of English at the University of Pennsylvania. She has written on a wide range of text technologies, from Renaissance textiles and Samuel Pepys' shorthand writing to John Bagford's scrapbooks and electronic literature. She is currently composing a hybrid print/digital monograph on the recycling of fragments in seventeenth-century book projects.

HAZEL WILKINSON is Fellow and Lecturer in Eighteenth-Century Literature in the Department of English at the University of Birmingham. She is the author of *Edmund Spenser and the Eighteenth-Century Book* (2017) and the principal investigator on *Fleuron*, an online database of printers' ornaments. She is currently editing Alexander Pope's *Ethic Epistles* with Marcus Walsh for the *Oxford Edition of the Writings of Alexander Pope*.

ABIGAIL WILLIAMS is Professor of Eighteenth-Century Studies at the University of Oxford. She is the author of *The Social Life of Books* (2017), *Poetry and the Creation of a Whig Literary Culture* (Oxford, 2005) and the editor of Jonathan Swift's *Journal to Stella* (2013). She has also led the creation and development of the Leverhulme-funded *Digital Miscellanies Index*. She is currently working on wilful misreading in eighteenth-century literature and in digital culture, and starting work on *Between the Sheets*, a history of reading in bed.

A NOTE ON THE TYPE

The typefaces used in *Book Parts* are Caslon or Caslon variants, based on the type designed by William Caslon (c.1692–1766) and widely used in Britain in the eighteenth century. The fleurons are FCaslon Ornaments or Adobe Caslon Pro; the book in the divider was drawn by Anna Scully.

INTRODUCTIONS

CHAPTER 1

Dennis Duncan and Adam Smyth

When we asked Pooh what the opposite of an Introduction was, he said 'The what of a what?' which didn't help us as much as we had hoped, but luckily Owl kept his head and told us that the Opposite of an Introduction, my dear Pooh, was a Contradiction.

A. A. Milne, *The House at Pooh Corner*

This introduction, like A. A. Milne's, will be something of a Contradiction, and yet we hope that it will not be the Opposite of an Introduction. The balancing act here will be to write a history of the book part known as the introduction while at the same time writing an introduction to a history known as *Book Parts*. Rather like chapter X of volume IV of *The Life and Opinions of Tristram Shandy, Gentleman* (1761)—'being my chapter upon chapters', Tristram declares, 'which I promised to write before I went to sleep'—this introduction will be both part of the body of the book, while also being a gazing in on that body from without.[1] Introductions are paradoxical forms: they come before the main text, but often (as with this present chapter) they are written after it. An introduction frames the work that follows, but the term does not distinguish whether that framing is being done by the author or by someone else—the editor, perhaps, or a literary celebrity (T. S. Eliot introducing *The Moonstone*, say, or Will Self on the book of Revelation).[2] In these cases, the introduction occupies a sort of indeterminate space, supplementary to the text it introduces, but also crucial in setting certain interpretative wheels in motion; a self-effacing text that is also a document of control. Some book parts are purely programmatic: we click a button and page numbers appear throughout our document with no further intervention. Others are created, written, but still anonymous: the lawyer does not sign the copyright statement, nor the indexer their index. The introduction is rather different. Only with the blurb do we find another instance of a specific, identified voice other than the author's and, like the blurb, the introduction tells us what we should think about the book we have in our hands. The introduction is the curious space where someone else, the named interloper, is allowed first say.

Should we read the introduction or not? Maybe save it till last. May contain spoilers. As *L'Organiste athée* (1964), an experimental novel entirely composed of prefaces, points out, readers are wont to treat prefatory material as optional. Indeed,

---

[1] Laurence Sterne, *The Life and Opinions of Tristram Shandy, Gentleman*, ed. Ian Campbell Ross (Oxford: Oxford University Press, 2009), pp. 225–6.

[2] Wilkie Collins, *The Moonstone, with an Introduction by T. S. Eliot* (Oxford: Oxford University Press, 1928); *Revelation, with an Introduction by Will Self* (Edinburgh: Canongate, 1998).

the introduction often declares its subordinacy on the page, using roman numerals for its pagination so as not to intrude into the sequencing of the main attraction. On the other hand, it may serve as an advertisement for wavering readers, unsure whether to commit to the rest of the work. This was the case made by Bonaventure d'Argonne at the turn of the eighteenth century: 'The Italians call those Prefaces which authors put at the start of their books "la salsa del libro". A good preface, in effect, is like a fine-tasting sauce: it whets the appetite of the reader, and disposes them to devour the book.'[3]

'I have observed,' wrote Isaac D'Israeli of introductions, 'that ordinary readers skip over these little elaborate compositions'; two centuries later, e-book devices often leap over paratexts to land directly on page one of the main text.[4] But since you've read this far, and are thus not ordinary, we'd like to introduce *Book Parts*. *Book Parts* is an intervention in the growing field of the history of the book, and it aims to give a history to the constituent material components that make up, or that often make up, the physical book. *Book Parts* is an attempt to conceive of the book not as a single stable object, but as a coming together or an alignment of separate component pieces, each possessed of particular conventions and histories, each enjoying a different relationship to the main text, and each the product of distinct kinds of labour. *Book Parts* is an attempt to think and write about the book through the mechanism of the blazon: like Spenser's *Epithalamion* (1595) which records 'Her goodly eyes like sapphires shining bright, / Her forehead ivory white, / Her cheeks like apples', *Book Parts* is an attempt to consider a whole (in the form of a book) as a set of distinctly conceived, analysed, and even celebrated parts. *Book Parts* crumbles the wholeness of the book in order to see more clearly the workings and changing histories of each piece: this is book history as anatomy, a sense of the book (to switch metaphors) as a teeming collection of atoms, each jostling to perform a role, rather than as a singular bibliographical fact. In *Book Parts*, we read books as things incorrigibly plural, to quote Louis MacNeice.[5]

Each of the twenty-two chapters of this book considers a particular constituent part of the physical book, organized in the order a linear reading might encounter them: from dust jacket to blurb. Each chapter is short, so avoids over-reaching for a definitive historical account: what we hope to present is a lively analysis of the form that is grounded in the particular moment when that form came into prominence (for dust jackets, the late nineteenth century; for errata lists, the sixteenth), but which also looks out to later and sometimes earlier instances, too. Given the rise to

[3] M. de Vigneul-Marville [Bonaventure d'Argonne], *Mélanges d'histoire et littérature*, vol. 1 of 3 (Paris: Claude Prudhomme, 1701), p. 332.

[4] Isaac D'Israeli, *Curiosities of Literature*, ed. Benjamin Disraeli (Widdleton, 1872), vol. 1, p. 128; Ellen McCracken, *Paratexts and Performance in the Novels of Junot Díaz and Sandra Cisneros* (Basingstoke: Palgrave Macmillan, 2016), p. 40, noted and discussed in Rachel Sagner Buurma, Chapter 13, 'Epigraphs'.

[5] Louis MacNeice, 'Snow', in *Collected Poems* (London: Faber and Faber, 1979), p. 30.

cultural prominence of printing from the late fifteenth to the seventeenth centuries, the early modern period is well represented, but contributors find other moments of book part significance, too. Each chapter has a period mooring, but also a view of the longue durée: we hope readers will, as a result, feel some pleasure in seeing the book, an object we thought we knew, through a new lens.[6] Our geographical focus is broadly on England, but there are regular forays into other national bibliographical cultures, too. We've tried to find a balance between the exact (bibliography's natural mode) and the expansive (the current direction of travel for the history of the book).

Work on paratexts has become an important feature of the history of the book.[7] Such work usually draws inspiration from Gérard Genette, whose *Seuils* appeared in 1987, and was translated as *Paratexts* in 1997.[8] The French title—meaning *thresholds*— reminds us that paratexts are instruments at the edge. Of the twenty-two chapters here, only those on stage directions and illustrations are concerned with paratexts that share the space of the main text. A paratext is, by definition, a literally marginal form. Whether at the edge of the page or at the ends of the book, paratexts surround the main text like the glosses of medieval religious commentary (Plate 1). Hemmed in by page numbers, catchwords, introductions, indexes, endleaves, the main text—the masterpiece the author proudly submits as a manuscript to the print shop or, today, as a Word file to her publisher—is only one piece of the finished book. To consider paratexts then—recalling them from the margins, letting them take centre stage—is to be reminded that no book is the sole work of the author whose name appears on the cover; rather, every book is the sum of a series of conventions and collaborations. Speaking of dust jackets, the bibliographer Charles Beecher Hogan declared, rather magnificently, 'It's a piece of wrapping with which the author had nothing to do'.[9] To consider the paratexts of a book is also to be reminded that not everything is intended for us, the readers. There are sections that are solely directed at others— binders, librarians, lawyers—parts of the book that, if they are working well, are working discreetly, like a theatrical prompt, whispering out of the audience's earshot.

While Genette's book, in its careful attention to the conceptual and material edges of books, has been a great catalyst for paratextual scholarship, it is not without its problems, not least in terms of its almost exclusive focus on the nineteenth- and

---

[6] For recent, playful attempts to analyse the book as an assemblage of parts, see *The Thing the Book: A Monument to the Book as Object*, ed. John Herschend and Will Rogan (San Francisco, CA: Chronicle, 2016), which includes meditations on book parts by artists and writers including Martin Creed, Miranda July, Ed Ruscha, and Jonathan Lethem; and Kevin Jackson, *Invisible Forms: A Guide to Literary Curiosities* (London: Picador, 1999).

[7] See, for instance, Helen Smith and Louise Wilson (eds), *Renaissance Paratexts* (Cambridge: Cambridge University Press, 2011).

[8] Gérard Genette, *Seuils* (Paris: Seuil, 1987); *Paratexts: Thresholds of Interpretation*, trans. Jane E. Lewin (Cambridge: Cambridge University Press, 1997).

[9] Charles Beecher Hogan, *A Bibliography of Edwin Arlington Robinson* (New Haven, CT: Yale University Press, 1936), iii. Noted in Gill Partington, Chapter 2, 'Dust Jackets'.

twentieth-century novel and its consequent lack of historical, generic, and material range. And while the concept of paratext is crucial for our book, the title *Book Parts* is indicative also of an important difference of approach, a reflection of our commitment to a consideration of material form, as well as genre. The book parts we discuss are types of writing with literary conventions, but they are also physical parts of the book, like the errata list glued in after publication, or the wrapper, or the hand-altered index.

For all this, however, *Book Parts* is not, at base, concerned with the construction, the engineering, of the book. So no chapters on bindings, paper, or indeed type (which have in any case all been the subject of numerous excellent and detailed academic treatments already).[10] The architecture of the codex-as-machine receives some discussion in certain chapters—it would be perverse not to mention the function as well as the appearance of endpapers, say, or dust jackets—but, loosely, we are principally concerned here with word and image. At the same time, it is worth saying at the outset that the *book* in *Book Parts* is narrowly defined. The trajectory of much current academic book history is outwards, away from bibliography's historical focus on the Western codex, towards a global study of the materials and practices of reading and writing from scrolls and tablets to inscriptions on shells and bones. And certainly, one or two of our paratexts—the table of contents, for example, or the epigraph—can trace their origins back to the era of the scroll. Nevertheless, our aim when we were compiling the chapters that follow was to describe the type of book you are probably holding now—the modern codex (with a nod to the e-book)—and the sections into which it divides itself, the parts known in the trade as 'front matter' and 'back matter', along with a few additional elements like page numbers and illustrations that don't quite fit these broader categories. There is more work to be done. Even by our own crude rubric some readers will feel that there are omissions to be addressed (should we have included a chapter on lists of abbreviations? On glosses? On the tissue sheets traditionally tipped in to protect plate images?); others with expertise in the global history of the book will notice oversights that could have been avoided had we cast our net beyond the Western codex. We hope that scholars will feel moved to take up the gauntlet, writing the stories of parts unfamiliar to us, anatomizing the book in all its varieties.

❧ 📖 ❧

The Introduction to the Work, or Bill of Fare to the Feast.
Henry Fielding, Tom Jones (1749), I. 1. i. 1

Prologue, dedicatory epistle, preface, textual note, address to the reader, isagoge, proem, preamble, exordium: whether we consider the many pieces of text that come

---

[10] See, for example, David Pearson, *English Bookbinding Styles, 1450–1800* (London: British Library; New Castle, DE: Oak Knoll, 2005); Dard Hunter, *Papermaking: The History and Technique of an Ancient Craft* (New York: Knopf, 1943); Robert Bringhurst, *The Elements of Typographic Style* (Vancouver: Hartley and Marks, 1992).

before the main text as mechanisms of deferral, as arduous little tasks that postpone (and earn) the pleasure in store, as forces that create the context in which we should approach the work, as supplements that legitimize the main text, or as a collective environment in which we adjust our eyes to the new light of the work in hand, the history of the introduction is, among other things, the story of the emergence of one prefatory form out of a minestrone soup of many.

The line between the introduction and other forms of prefatory address tackled in this volume (Meaghan Brown on addresses to the reader; Helen Smith on acknowledgements and dedications) is often blurred. Might we wish to propose a general rule: that a preface will be by the book's primary author, while an introduction will be by somebody else? History will not back us up. Philemon Holland's translation of Pliny includes two sections labelled as 'Preface', one by Pliny, and one by himself, riding roughshod over the distinction we were trying to draw.[11] And when the wags of the Scriblerus Group took aim at prefaces in the early eighteenth century, they refused to discriminate between those appended by critics to editions of the classics and those, like Dryden's, provided by the author of the work.

William Tyndale, writing in exile in 1526, hedges his bets. The title page to his commentary on Paul's letter to the Romans identifies the work as *A compendious introduccion, prologe or preface*.[12] The book's running head, nevertheless, settles on Introduction, jettisoning the other terms—a compositor's early foray into genre definition?—and Tyndale's text bears many of the hallmarks of a modern 'introduction' (though, with a Borgesian touch, the book does not actually include the text it introduces). When Tyndale uses the term again in his translation of the Book of Jonah—this time the main text does follow the introduction—he gives an extensive gloss of what his introduction sets out to achieve. The title page runs as follows:

> The prophete Jonas with an introduccion before teachinge to vnderstande him, and the right vse also of al the scripture, and why it was written, and what is therin to be sought, and shewing wherewith the scripture is locked vp that he whiche readeth it, can not vnderstonde it, thoughe he studye therin never so muche: & againe with what keyes it is so opened, that the reader can be stopped out with no sotiltie or false doctryne of man, from the true sense & vderstandynge therof.[13]

As a title, it's certainly a mouthful. Of its time, we might offer, if we were being generous. But as a description of the purpose of the introductory essay, it is rather modern, in the sense that it would surely strike a chord with any scholarly editor working today. That contemporary editor would no doubt quibble with the notion

---

[11] Pliny the Elder, *The History of the World, Commonly called, The Naturall Historie of C. Plinius Secundus*, trans. Philemon Holland (London: Adam Islip, 1601).

[12] William Tyndale, *A Compendious introduccion, prologe or preface vp on the pistle of Paul to the Romaynes* (Worms: Peter Schöffer, 1526).

[13] William Tyndale, *The Prophete Jonas* (Antwerp: Merten de Keyser, 1531?).

that they could provide the 'true sense' of the work they were introducing—but providing readers with a sense of why it was written, and giving them the keys to understand it? These things have not changed much in 500 years of introductions.

In English literature, we can find introductions or prefaces as far back as we could possibly want to go. Alfred the Great, in the last decade of the ninth century, composes a preface—or *fore-spræc*: fore-speech—to be included before his own translation of Pope Gregory's *Pastoral Care*. It outlines his translation strategy (the famous formulation: 'hwilum word be worde, hwilum andgit of andgite' ['sometimes word for word, sometimes sense for sense']), and explains the context in which a work like this was urgently needed. Alasdair Gray's *The Book of Prefaces* (2000) presents a chronological survey of excerpted prefaces—a broad term Gray uses to include introductions—running from Caedmon in the mid-seventh century to Wilfred Owen in the early twentieth. Some are by the author of the work being introduced, others are not, but, either way, Gray (drawing, as so many writers on paratext do, on architectural metaphors) sees the preface as a 'verbal doorstep to help readers leave the ground they usually walk on and allow them a glimpse of the interior'. For Gray, prefaces are caught between a twin pull of selling the work, on the one hand, and preparing the reader for the task of reading: prefaces are both 'advertisements and challenges', when we might expect those rhetorical burdens to be opposed. Gray identifies certain 'pleasures' that he hopes readers will experience when reading these introductions, including 'seeing great writers in a huff'; observing 'the biographical snippet' ('we discover Shelley writing and sunbathing on a platform of green turf'); and 'the pleasure of hearing writers converse'.[14]

While early modern books usually carried some kind of introductory statement, for books published after about 1800, the introduction serves often to signal, or to make the case for, cultural significance or even canonicity. The presence of the introduction in a modern edition is a way of tagging a set of literary judgements and institutional affirmations. The publication history of John Milton's *Paradise Lost* shows the relatively late emergence of the 'introduction' as a stable literary and bibliographical concept. Appearing first in 1667 with no prefatory materials, the 1668 issue added seven prefatory leaves, conveying a note of 'The Argument' (a plot summary) for each of the two books, introduced by printer Samuel Simmons ('for the satisfaction of many that have desired it, I have procur'd it'), plus Milton's defence of unrhymed verse, and a list of thirteen corrections under the heading 'Errata'.[15] The 1674 second edition broke the poem into twelve books, not ten, and included an engraving of Milton by Walter Dolle and commendatory verses by Samuel Barrow, in Latin, and Andrew Marvell, in English; and in 1688 a first attempt was made at an illustrated edition, with a frontispiece carrying Robert White's engraved portrait followed by

---

[14] Alasdair Gray, *The Book of Prefaces* (London: Bloomsbury, 2000), pp. 7–9.

[15] John Milton, *Paradise Lost* (1668), pp. [3–16].

engraved plates accompanying each book. In the eighteenth century, editions cluster paratextual materials before and sometimes after the poem: Thomas Newton's 1757 edition includes a ten-page dedication to the Earl of Bath; a 'Preface' which provides the history of the text and an editorial rationale; an eighty-five-page 'Life of Milton'; and Joseph Addison's 'Critique upon the Paradise Lost'. In the nineteenth century, editions continue to include a life of Milton (sometimes separated out into biographical facts, and a discussion of the poet's 'moral character'), along with a sampling of criticism by Samuel Johnson, and others—as seen, for example, in the 1821 edition printed by John Bumpus. None of these editions cited use the term 'introduction', but it starts to be deployed around this time: David Masson's 1874 edition includes within the introduction materials 'bibliographical, biographical, and expository'. In doing so, Masson's edition highlights the ways in which modern (that is, post-1800) introductions gather and make coherent earlier, more dispersed paratextual framings. By the late twentieth century, a new edition that did not organize its opening discussion as an 'Introduction' would be unusual. For Barbara Lewalski's 2007 text, the introduction is a space to rehearse the history of the composition and publication of the poem, with a nod to Milton's biography; to outline the generic tradition and the historical context in which the poem rather restlessly sits; to make connections with other Miltonic texts; and to declare the central questions that the poem addresses. The relative weighting of these components will vary across editions, but their presence, and the overall shape of the scholarly introduction, is remarkably stable.

The presence of an introduction is also a reliable marker of canonicity, or at least of some considerable critical standing. An even surer sign of cultural renown is the appearance of book-length introductions, separated from the text, like John Broadbent's *Paradise Lost: Introduction* (1972), designed for schools and colleges. In recent years—since the late 1980s—the terms 'Companion' or 'Guide' have come to occupy this terrain, the shift in terminology suggesting a model of back-and-forth pedagogy, the joint enterprise of reading a difficult poem, and an unease with Broadbent's more hierarchical relationship with his readers.

At the start of the eighteenth century, the 'Battle of the Books' saw a great harumph against scholarly apparatus on the part of the so-called 'Ancients', one of the two sides in the controversy. The *Grub Street Journal* would approvingly translate the comments of the French churchman, Pierre Daniel Huet, who looked back ruefully to a time when literary works came with few paratextual appendages: 'the works of the antients were forced to be read in manuscripts…[and] those methodical appendages…such as *Translations, Prefaces, Arguments, Sections, Notes, Commentaries* and *Indexes, Grammars* and *Dictionaries*, the keys of Learning, were then very scarce'.[16] The preface, one of many book parts in Huet's grumbling litany,

---

[16] *Grub Street Journal*, no. 322 (26 February 1736), p. 2. Originally, 'Il falloit lire les ouvrages des anciens dans des Manuscrits…[et] tous ces accompagnemens méthodique…de traductions, de prefaces, d'avertissemens, de divisions,

is singled out for specific abuse by a number of English writers of the period. Alexander Pope sees it as a sign of intellectual decline: 'Prologues into Prefaces decay', he writes in his *Dunciad* (I.277), seeing a poetic form atrophied into a prosaic one.[17] In the *Grub Street Journal* again, the history of the preface is linked not to the prologue but to another paratext, the index. When the latter shifted to the back of the book, it claims, publishers felt that their frontmatter appeared scanty and the preface, pure filler, was born:

> The *Preface* can boast of an invention no antienter [ancienter] than Printing. The publishers of the *Classics* seldom ventured any further than a touch of the Author's life, and an *Index*, which, in most of the books I ever saw printed before 1600, stood in the same place where our *Preface* does now. But when the custom grew up of placing the *Index* at the end, then people begun to think that the book looked naked, they therefore filled up the place, where the *Index* had been, with a set of words, which, like that, had no more sense nor meaning in the place where they stood.[18]

Meanwhile, Jonathan Swift complains simultaneously that eighteenth-century readers pay prefaces not enough attention and too much:

> it is lamentable to behold with what a lazy scorn many of the yawning readers in our age do now-a-days twirl over forty or fifty pages of preface and dedication (which is the usual modern stint), as if it were so much Latin. Though it must be also allowed, on the other hand, that a very considerable number is known to proceed critics and wits by reading nothing else.[19]

Do many people *really* read nothing else? Surely this is the even worse mirror image of D'Israeli's claim that the common reader doesn't bother with introductions. We hope in this volume that neither will be the case. One of the usual staging posts of a modern academic introduction is to trumpet the wares on offer. In a volume of this size, however, it would be tiresome to summarize every chapter, and Swift's warning, that the *précis* might serve in place of the real thing, has introduced a new anxiety to our introduction. So we will finish our chapter promptly, rather as Tristram finishes his—'[s]o much for my chapter upon chapters'—and turn from bill of fare, to feast.[20]

---

de notes, de commentaires, & de tables. Les Grammaires & les Dictionnaires qui sont les clefs d'érudition, étoient alors fort rares', Pierre Daniel Huet, *Huetiana, ou Pensées diverses de M. Huet, evesque d'Avranches*, ed. P.-J. T. d'Olivet (Paris: Jacques Estienne, 1722), pp. 171–2.

[17] In fact, the two terms were at one stage interchangeable, as when Caxton announces, 'Here begynneth the preface or prologue of the fyrste book of Esope', *Aesop's Fables* (Westminster, 1484), sig. d5r.

[18] *Grub Street Journal*, no. 318 (29 January 1736).

[19] Jonathan Swift, *A Tale of a Tub* (London: John Nutt, 1704), pp. 121–2.

[20] Sterne, *Tristram Shandy*, p. 226.

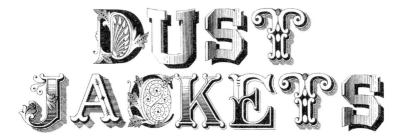

DUST JACKETS

Gill Partington

CHAPTER 2

In what sense is the dust jacket a book part? It is stamped with the book's title and in that sense belongs to it, yet it remains a separate and separable entity. It is an anomaly: a part apart. The jacket's strange on-off relationship with the book is its defining feature, as this chapter shows, and one that can be traced throughout its history, from its first appearance. Its precise moment of origin can be hard to determine. It has a long pre-history in the makeshift wrappers fashioned by readers from at least the early modern period to protect their books.[1] It also has a host of close relations in the shape of slip cases and cardboard sheaths, which narrowly pre-exist it.[2] Nevertheless, dust jackets as specially made, 'printed detachable coverings' mark a distinct innovation in book design, and it seems clear they emerged as a response to the advent of publishers' bindings in the 1820s.[3] Previously sold either unbound or in temporary covers awaiting the owner's choice of binding, books were now issued as standard in permanent, cloth-covered boards.[4] Publishers were keen that these bindings reach customers' shelves in pristine condition, so began to encase them in paper coverings.

Historical evidence of the jacket's early history in this period is elusive, however. The accolade of oldest dust jacket was held for many years by one that was not only separated from its book, but missing entirely. It was Heath's *The Keepsake*, a literary annual published in 1833, and identified almost exactly a century later by the antiquarian John Carter as the earliest specimen of a book encased in a bespoke paper covering. But, during a visit to the Bodleian Library in Oxford in 1951 to exhibit this prize volume to the Society of Bibliophiles, its most notable feature was somehow detached and misplaced.[5] *The Keepsake* itself now sits in the Bodleian in a watered silk binding, but the whereabouts of the jacket remains a mystery. It continued to hold its record *in absentia* for another half a century, a strange situation that was at least partially resolved when an attempt to locate *The Keepsake*'s missing jacket instead uncovered one that was older still. And this, belonging to another literary annual entitled *Friendship's Offering* of 1829, currently remains the earliest

[1] Recycled texts were sometimes used as wrappers for books, like the copy of Richard Stanyhurst's *The First Fovre Bookes of Virgils Æneis, Translated into English Heroicall Verse* (1583), contained in a wrapper made from a twelfth-century manuscript of the *Aeneid* (Oxford: Bodleian, Wood 106).

[2] Both Tanselle and Godburn point out the difficulty of identifying the first book jacket and discuss the overlap with other kinds of protective outer layers already being manufactured by publishers.

[3] G. Thomas Tanselle, *Book-Jackets: Their History, Forms and Use* (Charlottesville, VA: Bibliographical Society of the University of Virginia, 2011), p. 11.

[4] This innovation was in turn linked to the transition to the technique of 'case binding', which allowed covers to be produced separately to the book and then glued to the text block, speeding up production considerably.

[5] Mark Godburn, *Nineteenth-Century Dust Jackets* (New Castle, DE: Oak Knoll, 2016), p. 32.

recognized specimen. It, too, has been detached from its book, this time archived in a different location, and held carefully under a separate call mark.[6]

However, these early artefacts are not exactly dust jackets in the modern sense. Examination of the covering to *Friendship's Offering*, along with the photographic record of the missing *Keepsake* jacket, reveals that they are all-over wrappings. The placing of the title text, along with the pattern of creases and discolouration, shows they initially encased the book entirely and the former was even sealed with wax. According to Mark Godburn, the similarity with gift-wrapping paper is not accidental, since literary annuals such as *The Keepsake* and *Friendship's Offering* were—as their names suggest—primarily intended as gift books. Sealed wrappings invited readers to tear open the paper, and nearly all 'would have been damaged or discarded when purchasers opened them'.[7] Yet these particular examples have been retained by their early readers, and *The Keepsake*'s has clearly been re-folded around the bindings in order to create a supplementary outer cover. This early, ad hoc book jacket demonstrates not only the resourcefulness of nineteenth-century book hackers, but also the ambivalence of this object, right from its inception. With its confusing palimpsest of folds and uses, it points to a fundamental uncertainty about what a book jacket is: a disposable wrapper, or an integral part of the book?

Publishers may indeed have assumed that these sealed wrappings would be discarded once the book reached the shelf, but it seems readers were not quite so sure. Clearly, if their disposability was taken for granted, then no examples would remain. The eventual transition to modern jackets, with flaps folding inside the book's covers, may have been in part a bid to catch up with the behaviour of some readers, who were already adapting, rather than throwing away their wrappings. There are even instances of a kind of 'hybrid' wrapping, incorporating dotted lines and instructions to cut and fold the paper around the bindings into a jacket, if the reader so wished. John E. Wheelock's *In Search of Gold* (1884), for instance, was printed with the instruction 'cut open at this line and use wrapper for outside cover', demonstrating not only that sealed wrappings were the direct precursors of modern, flap-style jackets, but that there was even a degree of crossover between them.[8] Nevertheless, the transition from one to the other is not seamless, since what we might call the material affordances of the two are different: custom-made flap jackets did not have to be torn off, and permitted the book to be read with the covering *in situ*. They suggested—or at least allowed for—a greater degree of permanence. But, as they came to be the norm from the 1860s onwards, they raised a new set of questions about the relationship of jacket and book.[9]

---

[6] Michelle Pauli, 'Earliest-Known Book Jacket Discovered in Bodleian Library', *Guardian*, 24 April 2009: https://www.theguardian.com/books/2009/apr/24/earliest-dust-jacket-library.

[7] Godburn, *Nineteenth-Century Dust-Jackets*, p. 30.

[8] Tanselle, *Book-Jackets*, p. 69.

[9] According to Thomas Tanselle, several examples of flap jackets exist from the 1860s, and after this point they became standard. *Book-Jackets*, p. 68.

The range of different approaches to design and format shows that there was initially no consensus about even basic features. Evidently, when Lewis Carroll made a special request for the title to be printed on the spine of his book jackets, this was not yet common practice. Carroll took a particular interest in the physical presentation of his books, writing to his publishers, Macmillan, in the mid-1870s, with detailed instructions about arrangements for the forthcoming *Hunting of the Snark* (1876). With the title on the spine of the jacket, he argued, 'it can stand in bookstalls without being taken out of the paper and so can be kept in a cleaner and more saleable condition'.[10] Carroll's intervention illustrates the extent to which books were exposed to the soot and grime of Victorian London, especially on its many street bookstalls. It also shows that the flap jacket was at this stage considered *more* disposable than the sealed wrapping, not less, since it was frequently discarded even earlier. Jackets were routinely removed by booksellers, who regarded them as an obstacle to the easy identification and display of books. They were issued as part of the book by publishers, but customers may seldom have seen them.

By the end of the century, this had changed. Printing the title on both spine and front became standard, along with other developments indicating that jackets were being retained rather than removed by sellers. What had previously been a largely plain protective layer began to fill with text and illustration. The jacket now displayed the price and the various binding options available (buyers could sometimes choose between cheaper 'illuminated board' or a deluxe, more expensive cloth edition). It trumpeted the book's popularity: 'Fifty thousand copies sold!' It became a space for promotional quotes and endorsements (the term 'blurb' emerged around this time, as discussed in Chapter 22 of the present volume by Abigail Williams, giving a name to new kinds of jacket text). It was a sales pitch for the book beneath, but also for other books from the same publisher. Publishers' lists had featured on all-over wrappings, too, but flapped jackets went for the hard sell. William Hamilton Gibson's *Highways and Byways* was issued by Harper Brothers in 1883 in a jacket that did not carry the volume's own title, but instead reprinted a glowing review of a different book by the author. Printed in two lengthy, dense columns and set horizontally so it wrapped around the book, it resembles a separate single-page broadside or advertising leaflet rather than a jacket.[11] Some publishers even printed advertisements for other commodities, too. The back of an 1885 edition of *Paul and Virginia* was emblazoned with advertisements for pianos and miracle nerve cures.[12] Dust jackets represented premium advertising space, 'hoarding[s] that did not sit still, but travelled into the very homes of potential customers'.[13] Where they had once been apologetic

[10] Godburn, *Nineteenth-Century Dust-Jackets*, pp. 101–2.

[11] Godburn, *Nineteenth-Century Dust-Jackets*, p. 120.

[12] Godburn, *Nineteenth-Century Dust-Jackets*, p. 117.

[13] Sean Jennett, *The Making of Books* (London: Faber and Faber, 1951), p. 452.

and austere, they now competed for attention alongside newspapers, magazines, and posters in the noisy, visual world of late nineteenth-century print.

The innovation of flapped jackets even provided a brand new kind of space, folded inside the cover yet not inside the book itself. These were at first blank, as if publishers were not sure what use to make of them, but in the 1890s promotional text began to migrate onto the flaps. Other uses were tried, too. Harper Brothers gave the back flap of its jackets over to detailed guidance on 'How to Open a Book', instructing readers to '[l]ay the book back downward, on a table or smooth surface' to avoid damage. Within the space of a few years, the new conventions and layout of the dust jacket were sufficiently familiar to be the subject of parody. The front of the 1906 jacket for Gelett Burgess's *Are You a Bromide?* spoofed the hyperbolic clichés of the blurb, along with its then customary accompanying image of a woman, dubbing her 'Belinda Blurb' (see Fig. 22.1). On its front inside flap, Burgess's jacket satirized Harper's instructions, comically confusing the position of the reader with the book itself, resulting in a series of physical contortions: 'Lay on your back, on a table or smooth surface. Place your feet on the chandelier, then, holding the Book in one hand, look it over with the other.'[14]

The front of the dust jacket, previously minimal—featuring only the title or else a reproduction of the title page—gradually became a space for illustration. Here, though, it entered into a fraught relationship with what lay underneath. Its ostensible purpose was to protect rather than compete with cloth bindings, which had grown increasingly ornate over the second half of the nineteenth century, featuring expensive gilt decoration, coloured illustration, and embossed designs. Jackets, by contrast, were made of cheap, buff-coloured paper. Their illustrations at first tended merely to replicate the binding, careful not to upstage it. Some designs even allowed the binding itself to be seen directly. Kipling's *Jungle Book*, published in 1894, has a handsome navy cloth cover with a gilt engraving of elephants, visible through a jacket made of semi-transparent glassine. Margaret Turnbull's *Looking after Sandy* (1914) has holes cut in the jacket revealing the cover illustration beneath.[15] Similar windows were sometimes cut in the jacket's spine, too, making titles visible and allowing the identical jacket design to be used for an entire series. By the end of the nineteenth century, however, the jacket's increasingly prevalent promotional function meant that slavish fidelity to what was underneath was largely abandoned. It began to carry quite different illustrations, showing publishers' willingness to experiment with different aesthetic strategies. Where the cover art may be relatively restrained, the outer jacket needed more eye-catching and instant appeal. The relationship between ornate cloth cover and plain paper jacket gradually reversed itself, and by the interwar period the golden age of illustrated bindings had come to an end.

---

[14] Godburn, *Nineteenth-Century Dust-Jackets*, p. 152.

[15] Tanselle, *Book-Jackets*, p. 77.

With the visual emphasis now on jackets, publishing houses invested in their design and impact. Victor Gollancz's bright yellow jackets, designed by typographer Stanley Morison, were instantly recognizable and stamped the books with a uniform house style in the interwar period. Faber and Faber also broke new ground in the same period, commissioning emerging artists Rex Whistler, Graham Sutherland, and Ben Nicholson to produce designs, and over the following decades the jacket became a vehicle for more established figures, indicating its rising cultural status. Sidney Nolan provided the artwork for C. P. Snow's novels in the early 1960s, endowing the books with the cachet of artist as well as author. On occasion these two roles overlapped: Evelyn Waugh designed his own jacket art for his early comic novels in the 1920s and 1930s. Usually, though, the jacket design was beyond the creative jurisdiction of the author. Ernest Hemingway was famously unhappy with the jackets for *The Sun Also Rises* and *A Farewell to Arms*. The ensuing wrangles with his publisher confirmed the jacket as the province of marketing departments rather than writers.[16] The jacket had selling power, and publishers sought to maximize its potential in a variety of ways. Simon and Schuster published Alexander King's *Mine Enemy Grows Older* in 1958 with not one but two jackets, advising readers that if they didn't like the top one, they could take it off to reveal a more 'conservative' one underneath.[17] And while the author may not have control of this branding strategy, he or she nevertheless became frequently represented on it, as the rear and back flap began to carry author biography and image.

In the era of the paperback, dust jackets may no longer be an unavoidable part of the reading or book-buying experience but it's arguable that their function as advertising space has given way to a different kind of marketing role. Trade books now commonly have two incarnations, published initially in more expensive hardback, then later in a cheaper paperback edition. This two-stage publication model not only allows the paperback to carry the reviews and blurb from the first edition, but it also elevates the hardcover—complete with its jacket—to the status of a premium product. The jacket has become either a sign of luxurious expense or else a fussy excess, as its ubiquity wanes. Its decline has not been universal, though. In some publishing contexts, notably Japan, the dust jacket has not disappeared but migrated onto the paperback, creating a peculiar double paper wrapper. Japanese books are also typically sold wrapped not only in a dust jacket but in an *Obi* or 'belly band', a strip of paper encircling the book to keep it closed. And in France, another kind of hybrid between the paperback and hardback can be found. The so-called 'French fold' incorporates the dust jacket's flapped design into the paperback cover.

---

[16] Leonard Leff, *Hemingway and His Conspirators: Hollywood, Scribners, and the Making of the American Dream* (Lanham, MD: Rowman and Littlefield, 1999), p. 115.

[17] Tanselle, *Book-Jackets*, p. 61.

This range of approaches shows shifting, often conflicting attitudes to the jacket throughout its history. If it is no longer simply a disposable wrapping, then what exactly is the function of this paper covering? The term 'jacket', which entered popular usage in the 1890s, doesn't so much define its object as question its status. In the first place it oscillates awkwardly between two interchangeable compounds: 'book jacket' and 'dust jacket'. The first positions the jacket in relation to the book, and continuous with it. The second suggests something outward-facing rather than inward-facing: its defining relationship is with the dust which it repels. In the second place, the metaphor pulls in different directions. A jacket is a particular kind of garment. Not quite a coat, it can be worn inside as well as out. It is nevertheless an outer layer, which can be taken off without actually being in a state of undress. But this clothing metaphor has been developed in other ways. In 1929, *Publishers' Weekly* dismissed these 'mere overalls for the book', implying that they are rough temporary clothes and not proper attire.[18] Jacob Schwartz described them as 'chemises', suggesting a different, more lightweight and intimate garment, part of the wearer's outfit rather than an outer protection for it.[19] The artist Rockwell Kent (himself a notable designer of book jackets) declared in 1930 that 'the real purpose of the paper jacket is to conceal the drab cloth cover of the book...to dress up a sorry article. Its function is exactly that of clothes, rouge and powder to plain women.'[20] The emphasis switches here from covering to disguise. Books are not only dressed in jackets but 'dressed up'.

Underlying these varying images are questions about the nature of the jacket's relationship to the book. Is it an extension of the book or an advertisement for it? Is its function to protect, conceal, decorate, or reveal what is underneath? Should it be worn or taken off? To put things in theoretical terms, how does the jacket work as a paratext? Gérard Genette defines this concept as the 'threshold' that frames a text and governs its interpretation. A paratext is made up of the 'accompanying productions [enabling] a text to become a book and to be offered as such to its readers'.[21] However, these accompanying productions come in two distinct forms. The peritext exists as a physical part of the book, as with the title page, colophon, or index. The epitext, meanwhile, is outside the book's covers but still shapes its reading, as with the reviews and advertising that surround a book. The jacket makes this distinction a difficult one to maintain. It is both inside and outside. It can be physically contiguous with the book or it can be separate. As both an advertisement *for* the book and part *of* it, it conflates peritext and epitext. It is conventionally outside the

---

[18] John T. Winterich, *Publishers' Weekly* 116 (21 December 1929): 2885.

[19] Jacob Schwartz, *1100 Obscure Points* (London: Ulysses Bookshop, 1931), p. ix.

[20] Rockwell Kent, *News-Letter of the American Institute of Graphic Arts* 26 (December 1930): 2. Quoted in Tanselle, *Book-Jackets*, fn. 57.

[21] Gérard Genette, *Paratexts: Thresholds of Interpretation*, trans. Jane E. Lewin (Cambridge: Cambridge University Press, 1997), p. 1.

space of the literary text, yet the words of authors are found all over it in the form of blurb and review quotations. Sometimes the book's internal content even spills over onto the jacket. E. E. Cummings' play *Him*, published in 1927, used the inner flaps of its jacket for a drama in miniature, entitled 'Imaginary Dialogue between an Author and a Public' (see Plate 2). In the 1881 edition of Disraeli's *Endymion*, published by Belford Clarke, the front of the jacket includes a key to the characters of the novel so that a paratext usually found within the covers is positioned outside them.[22]

Where to draw the boundaries of the book, then? This is not merely an abstract point of principle, but shapes the practices of book collecting and archiving. For libraries, the status of the dust jacket is a long-running and unresolved issue. It is ironic that the jacket to *The Keepsake* was misplaced in the Bodleian, but also symptomatic of an institutional blind spot. While the precise details of its disappearance remain a mystery, one hypothesis is that it was simply discarded by someone who saw it as worthless.[23] This was common practice. Up until the 1970s the Bodleian, like most research libraries, simply discarded jackets.[24] This part of *The Keepsake* could not be kept because there was no place for it, and even today, it isn't always clear what the correct place for jackets is. The Bodleian continues to separate books and jackets on acquisition. Books belong on the shelves, jackets are flattened out and placed in boxes, where they occupy an institutional limbo; retained, but no longer part of the book.[25] Moreover, they are not catalogued individually, but in batches according to acquisition date, so it is no simple matter to reunite book and jacket. The British Library similarly separates its jackets, as do other research and university libraries.[26] One resulting irony is, of course, that G. Thomas Tanselle's *Book-Jackets*, which argues for the central importance of jackets as bibliographic data, must itself be encountered in its naked, unjacketed state by those researching the topic. To see the two together in the Bodleian, readers must find its acquisition date, call up the appropriate box file, and retrieve the jacket from a pile of others. In the British Library, it is (at the time of writing) pinned to a notice board at the entrance to the Rare Books reading room, publicizing recent acquisitions. Tanselle's readers can—just—glimpse book and jacket simultaneously, but not physically unite them.

Clearly, the reasons for this practice involve practicalities of storage and maintenance of books. Removing the jackets allows space for one more book per

---

[22] Tanselle, *Book-Jackets*, p. 58.

[23] Mark Godburn, 'The Earliest Dust-Jackets: Lost and Found', *Script and Print* 32, no. 4 (2008): 233.

[24] Julie Anne Lambert, 'Dustjackets in the Bodleian Library' (unpublished paper, revised from a talk given at a conference on dust jackets convened by Sotheby's at the University of London, 2017).

[25] Lambert, 'Dustjackets in the Bodleian Library'.

[26] Rosner reports that the library (the then British Museum) began to retain its jackets rather than discarding them in 1923, 'not, however, in the books to which they related, but in separate bundles'. Less than a decade later, however, the question of what to do with them, and where to keep them, became an issue, and officials at the British Museum decided that there was space for only a selection to be preserved. Charles Rosner, *The Growth of the Book Jacket* (London: Sylvan, 1954), p. xiii.

forty others, according to one calculation.[27] But there is another assumption at work, too. The jacket is not part of the book proper, and perhaps there is even something about it that does not belong in the august surroundings of the research library. Even in the twenty-first century such institutions still bear the traces of earlier archival policies, which viewed the jacket as a tawdry trace of the bookshop, removed in order that the book could assume the sober appearance appropriate to the library shelves. The jackets of scholarly texts may carry illustration but the binding underneath is often notable for its lack of adornment, puritanically guarding against anything so crass as judging a book by its cover. The jacket's superficial charms must be discarded in order for an authentic encounter with the book to occur, in other words. According to such institutional logic, the book starts on page 1, or with the colophon or title page. If Harper's used to include instructions on 'How to Read a Book' on their jacket flaps, this absence of jackets implies a less explicit but equally emphatic reading lesson. Reading does not—or *should* not—involve perusal of the jacket or blurb. The removal of the jacket is when consumers become readers.

In the policies of public libraries, by contrast, blurbs, plot teasers, and jacket illustrations are retained, precisely because they are what readers need in order to make a choice. The issue is one of genre as much as location, in that the jacket is considered a legitimate or even necessary aspect of fiction reading. Cambridge University Library, while it removes jackets from scholarly books, stores its 'supplementary' material (its non-academic books) in their jackets, suggesting there is a different logic at work for different kinds of books. But the matter is more complicated still, since public libraries not only retain jackets but then often encase these in the extra protection of transparent mylar sleeves. And if the jacket is given a jacket, does this mean it is considered to be the book's *de facto* cover rather than merely an outer layer? The trial of the playwright Joe Orton and his lover Kenneth Halliwell indicates this is indeed the case. The pair were jailed in 1962 after spending years doctoring books from Islington libraries, the jackets of which they would alter with surreal collaged additions, before returning them to the shelves. Agatha Christie's *The Secret of Chimneys* has giant cats looming over a Venetian scene (Plate 3), and a biography of John Betjeman replaces the cover portrait of its subject with a heavily tattooed man in his underwear. They would also replace the blurb text, pasting over the jacket flaps with outrageous and lewd alternatives. The plot of Dorothy L. Sayers' *Clouds of Witness* becomes hilariously smutty, involving a lost pair of knickers and a phallus. From a historical perspective, their harsh six-month sentence undoubtedly reflects the persecution of homosexuality in the period, but from a bibliographic one, it constitutes what is probably the one and only legal ruling on the status of the jacket. The pair's crime of defacing books incorporated what they did to dust jackets. Jackets must therefore be a part of the book.

[27] Henry Petroski is quoted to this effect in Tanselle, *Book-Jackets*, p. 41.

Bibliographers and book collectors, meanwhile, have been surprisingly reluctant to think about dust jackets at all.[28] What Tanselle characterizes as a 'general neglect' is based on the assumption that jackets were 'somehow unworthy of serious attention—that in fact they were not bibliographical objects at all'.[29] Yet 'neglect' seems too weak a word to describe the kind of visceral distaste shown by many collectors and dealers in the first half of the twentieth century. They 'should be discarded the moment a book is received', according to the collector Morris Parrish.[30] Richard de la Mare, despite commissioning some of the century's most iconic jacket art while at Faber and Faber, nevertheless dismissed the jacket as 'that wretched thing, of which we sometimes deplore the very existence'.[31] 'It's a piece of wrapping with which the author had nothing to do,' declared the bibliographer Charles Beecher Hogan.[32] Even as late as 1970, the bibliographer Edwin Gilcher insisted the dust jacket 'can in no sense be considered an integral part of the book they serve to protect'.[33] A rare defence came from Ralph Strauss in *T. P. Cassell's Weekly*:

> Don't throw away these gay covers in which they are generally encased. One day they may be of considerable value...I am convinced the jacket in some form or another will be required at future book sales, and perhaps some ingenious collector will devise a plan for its preservation.[34]

Strauss's prediction was correct, as the sums paid for rare books in more recent decades testify. In 1986, when Kipling's *Just So Stories* sold with its jacket for £2,600, Sotheby's declared it 'the highest auction price...for a dust-jacket', based on the logic that the unjacketed version was worth a mere 100 pounds.[35] In 1998, Conan Doyle's *The Hound of the Baskervilles* in a rare 1902 jacket sold for £72,000, 'more than one hundred times the price of an average copy without one'.[36] For collectors—or at least investors—the book without the jacket is not the complete article. 'The unjacketed copy is...a defective copy,' and the higher price is required for a 'perfect copy'.[37]

[28] Tanselle observes that while descriptive bibliographies are the place one might expect to find this detail, 'there has been a peculiar resistance to the inclusion of jacket descriptions'; *Book-Jackets*, p. 24.

[29] Tanselle, *Book-Jackets*, p. 7. This observation is borne out by the fact that Phillip Gaskell's still standard textbook, *New Introduction to Bibliography*, devotes only a single paragraph to jackets.

[30] Quoted in Tanselle, *Book-Jackets*, p. 7.

[31] Richard de la Mare, 'A Publisher on Book-Production', 1935, quoted in Rosner *The Growth of the Book Jacket*, p. xiii.

[32] Charles Beecher Hogan, *A Bibliography of Edwin Arlington Robinson* (New Haven, CT: Yale University Press, 1936), p. iii.

[33] Edwin Gilcher, *A Bibliography of George Moore* (Dekalb, IL: Illinois University Press, 1970), p. xiii.

[34] Rosner, *The Growth of the Book Jacket*, p. xiii.

[35] Tanselle, *Book-Jackets*, p. 53.

[36] Anthony Rota, *Apart from the Text* (Ann Arbor, MI: University of Michigan, Private Libraries Association, 1998), p. 139.

[37] Tanselle, *Book-Jackets*, p. 54.

Here, the jacket begins to operate less like a paratext and more as what Jacques Derrida calls a 'supplement' which 'adds in order to replace'.[38] In other words, it is an addition, but one which paradoxically indicates a lack in the original object. Auction prices manifest this logic in bald numerical terms, but they also reflect a wider sense that the jacket's absence renders the book somehow incomplete. Its illustration and design, blurb and author biography are now considered part of the experience of the book. It provides something indispensable to the book's meaning yet not present inside its covers. As in the earlier examples, readers of Disraeli's novel *Endymion* would be in the dark without the jacket's key to the characters, and to take away E. E. Cummings' jacket would be to subtract part of the work of the author.

However, this logic has a further twist, since the supplement comes to achieve a kind of autonomy from the book. The dust jacket also now has value in its own right. It was first accorded institutional recognition at the Victoria and Albert Museum exhibition 'The Art of the Book Jacket' in 1949. When it belatedly entered the academy and the cultural canon, it was under the aegis of art history (or the 'decorative arts') rather than bibliography or literature. And since then, with only a few exceptions, scholarship has approached dust jackets in aesthetic terms, so that they have become significant as part of the story of graphic design, rather than the story of the book.[39] The jacket has acquired cultural status as an artwork, but also as a sought-after collectors' item. The Bodleian, though it consigns new jackets to obscurity in storage, archives rare and notable nineteenth-century examples in the John Johnson collection of Printed Ephemera. They belong to a set of disposable printed paraphernalia and curios archived because of their rarity and historical interest. As ephemera, they have value precisely *because* of their disposability, placed alongside visiting cards, bookmarks, postcards, and matchboxes. Whether they are categorized as art or ephemera, however, the effect is the same. They are pronounced worthy of attention while detached (conceptually and physically) from books.

While they were once taken off for disposal, jackets are now just as likely to be removed for display. Those vandalized by Orton and Halliwell are now framed and proudly put on show by the same Islington libraries that once retained them as evidence of wrongdoing. At a 2017 exhibition, Finsbury Library marketed postcards of all the designs, celebrating them as 'unique and rare artworks'.[40] Like other notable jacket illustrations by famous artists, these peculiar subversions of the originals have become iconic and recognizable examples of the form. Meanwhile, the books they protected—and which Orton was imprisoned for damaging—have long disappeared into obscurity. It seems dust jackets are given most attention when they

---

[38] Jacques Derrida, *Of Grammatology* (corrected edition; Baltimore, MD: Johns Hopkins University Press, 1998), p. 144.

[39] Martin Salisbury's *The Illustrated History of the Dust Jacket: 1920–1970* (London: Thames and Hudson, 2017) is the latest example, but there are numerous other book-length treatments of jacket illustration.

[40] The copyright of these jacket images now belongs to the Islington Local History Centre.

part company from the book, as demonstrated by the industry of merchandise that trades lucratively on their iconic, retro aesthetic. Their images adorn posters, t-shirts, mugs, tote bags, pillows, and a host of other non-book objects. Jackets might not be easy to find in the Bodleian Library reading rooms, but in the gift shop they are everywhere. Children's book jackets are depicted on gift-wrapping paper, 1940s pulp jacket illustrations adorn notecards, and repurposed or 'upcycled' jackets enclose blank notebooks.[41]

The jacket has acquired a life of its own, and its relationship to the book has shifted yet again. Debates have previously centred around whether or not it is 'integral' to the book, but this now seems the wrong question. Rather than acting *as* a frame for the text, it is often found *in* one, displayed in isolation on gallery and museum walls. Instead of asking whether the jacket really belongs to the book we might just as well pose the question the other way around, enquiring if the book is a necessary part of the jacket. Beyond this, however, this supplementary element disturbs the idea of the book as a self-contained and self-evident whole. In its absence, the book is missing something. But its presence makes things complicated, since book-plus-jacket add up to something more than a single, complete entity. The jacket subtly changes the book's identity, confusing boundaries and muddying the issue of what is inside and outside. It constitutes an uncertain border of both the physical object and the literary work, confronting us with the question of where the book begins and ends.

---

[41] Bodleian Libraries, University of Oxford: https://www.bodleianshop.co.uk/christmas-797/gift-wrap/winter-playtime-giftwrap.html; Bodleian Libraries, University of Oxford: https://www.bodleianshop.co.uk/gifts/bookshelf/the-devastating-man-notecard.html

CHAPTER 3

FRONTISPIECES

Luisa Calè

The frontispiece provides a face to the book. From a medieval Latin word meaning 'looking at the forehead', the *Oxford English Dictionary* (*OED*) attests the term at the end of the sixteenth century referring to 'the front of a building', but it soon takes a bibliographical inflection to indicate 'the first page of a book or pamphlet'. Like the façade of a building, the paper frontispiece marks the threshold between the space outside and inside the book. Elaborate architectonic forms abounding in the iconography of early frontispieces reference classical architecture as well as more ephemeral models such as theatrical backdrops, commemorative arches, and temporary architectural structures erected in the sixteenth century for triumphal entries to celebrate heroes.[1] This iconography activates the trope of the book as a monument and connects the codex to the architectural structure of the art of memory, which arranged invention, composition, and elocution into distinct parts of a building for mnemonic recall. The act of reading thus becomes a journey into the interior of the text. This metaphor is powerfully visualized in William Blake's frontispiece to his illuminated prophetic poem *Jerusalem*, which shows a traveller holding a lantern seen from behind in the act of entering the door of the text.

The emergence of the frontispiece is associated with the age of printing, and the publication of books in print runs of multiple copies. Unlike manuscripts made in individual copies, which might be bound at the time of production, copies of a printed book lying unbound in booksellers' shops were hard to differentiate given that 'a blank leaf at the beginning of the book served to protect it during the interval between printing and sale'.[2] The frontispiece is an essential component of the paratext, for it delimits and identifies the book, separating it from other book specimens. Antony Griffiths has pointed out that 'engraved title pages lay on top of sewn gatherings of unbound books as they lay "en blanc" on the shelves of booksellers, and so drew attention to them much better than letterpress'.[3] The Goncourt brothers proclaimed the seventeenth century 'the century of the frontispiece'.[4] Seventeenth-century examples of 'frontispiece' collected by the *OED* identify a range of uses that have since been differentiated as distinct book parts: 'The first

[1] Margery Corbett and Ronald Lightbown, *The Comely Frontispiece: The Emblematic Title Page in England 1550–1660* (London: Routledge and Kegan Paul, 1979), pp. 7–8; Alistair Fowler, *The Mind of the Book: Pictorial Title Pages* (Oxford: Oxford University Press, 2017), pp. 16–18.

[2] Fowler, *The Mind of the Book*, p. 5.

[3] Antony Griffiths, *The Print before Photography: An Introduction to European Printmaking 1550–1820* (London: British Museum, 2016), p. 185.

[4] Michael F. Suarez and H. R. Woudhuysen, *The Book: A Global History* (Oxford: Oxford University Press, 2013), p. 235.

page of a book or pamphlet, or what is printed on it; the title page including illustrations and table of contents; hence, an introduction or preface'. Part of this process of differentiation involved distinguishing the frontispiece from the engraved title page as verso and recto of the first page opening respectively. According to the *OED*, their position and function in the book's paratext was accomplished between the late seventeenth and early eighteenth century.[5]

While its paratextual role suggests that the frontispiece had a stabilizing function in defining the identity of a book, its production and distribution highlight the division of labour involved in the production of the codex as a composite object. The frontispiece was printed in a different workshop on an extra leaf that often came from a different paper stock from the rest of the book, and stood out for its different materiality. As an unbound object printed separately, signed by the engraver, and offered as a separate plate by print publishers, the frontispiece belonged to the practice of engraving.[6] The frontispiece's identity as an engraving is enhanced by the practice of adding tissue to avoid offset of ink onto the facing page. As a separate plate the frontispiece had a bibliographic function as a marketing specimen: book publishers would send it out with the book's prospectus, while also pasting it in windows and in the street for advertising purposes. Yet while these options emphasized the bibliographic properties of the frontispiece as a book part that could stand for the whole, its physical characteristic as an unbound object separated from the book made it easy for it to become a collectible.[7]

The frontispiece's ambiguous role as a detachable book part is illustrated by the library of Samuel Pepys. In itemizing his collection for his library catalogue, Pepys described two albums as 'My Collection of Frontispieces of Books Put together Anno Domini 1700'.[8] Pepys's collection identifies specific bibliographic functions performed by the unbound frontispiece. His albums document and supplement the contents of his library, taking on the role of a virtual paper surrogate, while organizing it into distinct subjects, and perhaps a mnemonic system of knowledge, as Jan van der Walls has argued.[9] The bookseller and antiquarian John Bagford (1650–1716), who had a part in forming great libraries such as those of Robert Harley and Hans Sloane, collected frontispieces as well as title pages, initials, borderpieces, and other book fragments as specimens for a history of the art of typography, which he never completed. (Bagford is also discussed in Chapter 4 of the present volume.) These materials, incorporated in the Harleian manuscripts at his death and transferred to

---

[5] *OED*, 3 and 4.

[6] Roger Gaskell, 'Printing House and Engraving Shop: A Mysterious Collaboration', *Book Collector* 53 (2004): 213–51.

[7] Griffiths, *The Print before Photography*, pp. 185–6.

[8] *Catalogue of the Pepys Library at Magdalen College Cambridge*, gen. ed. Robert Laham (Woodbridge: D. S. Brewer, 1980), III, compiled by A. W. Aspital, pp. 87–175.

[9] Jan Van Der Waals, 'The Print Collection of Samuel Pepys', *Print Quarterly* 1, no. 4 (1984): 236–57, esp. 238 and 252.

the British Museum, were recorded in 'several paste-board covers with loose papers' in 1759, then as 'several loose papers, now bound together in four volumes' in 1808.[10] Collections such as Pepys's and Bagford's document the circulation of frontispieces as prints mounted in albums or loose papers, also suggesting their alternative lives inside other books or outside books altogether. For instance, as Roger Gaskell points out, copies of frontispiece portraits would be printed out for distribution among friends and patrons.[11] New or additional frontispieces could mark a presentation copy as part of a gift economy that customized a book reclaiming it from its status as a commodity. As a detached book part, the frontispiece was an 'itinerant form'.[12]

As an 'illustration', the frontispiece provides an image that can stand for the book. It presents its contents in one synthetic image that shapes the act of reading; it raises generic expectations that inscribe the text within literary genres, and it defines its subject areas by scenes that illuminate how reading translates into action, forms of sociability, and domains of practice. In what follows, I will explore a range of frontispiece genres, moving from the portrait of the author to narrative frontispieces, from polyscenic to allegorical representations of the book.

The emergence of the engraved portrait frontispiece anchors the figure of the author to the act of writing as a technology of communication at a distance. By supplementing the author's name on the title page with a facing portrait, such a choice of frontispiece marks the intersections between book production and the field of art. As separate plates, representations of the author could be sourced from existing portraits engraved from a range of media, including coins, busts, and paintings produced for other purposes, sometimes engraved as part of independent series, then repurposed as frontispieces tipped into the book. The bibliographic forms taken by Shakespeare's likeness illustrate the emergence of the portrait frontispiece. Consider the transfer of Martin Droeshout's engraved portrait from the title page of the first and second folios to the frontispiece in the third folio, with Ben Jonson's epigraph printed as a caption underneath. As Margreta de Grazia notes, comparison between the frontispiece of the Shakespeare folios and the imposing architectonic title page of Ben Jonson's 1616 edition points out the divergence between Shakespeare's nature and Jonson's art. A different canonizing claim is made with the Chandos portrait engraved by Martin van der Gucht for Nicholas Rowe's edition of Shakespeare published by Jacob Tonson in 1709, which includes a decorative frame copied from the

---

[10] Anthony Griffiths, 'The Bagford Collection': https://www.bl.uk/picturing-places/articles/the-bagford-collection, accessed 11 December 2017; A. W. Pollard, 'A Rough List of the Contents of the Bagford Collection', *Transactions of the Bibliographical Society* 1st series, 7 (1902–4): 143–59; Milton McC. Gatch, 'John Bagford, Bookseller and Antiquary', *British Library Journal* 12, no. 2 (Autumn 1986): 150–71.

[11] Gaskell, 'Printing House and Engraving Shop', p. 217.

[12] Volker R. Remmert, '"Docet parva pictura, quod multae scripturae non dicunt": Frontispieces, Their Functions, and Their Audiences in Seventeenth-Century Mathematical Sciences', *Transmitting Knowledge: Words, Images, and Instruments in Early Modern Europe*, ed. Sachiko Kusukawa and Ian Maclean (Oxford: Oxford University Press, 2006), pp. 239–70, 268.

1660 Rouen edition of the dramatic works of Pierre Corneille: 'by appropriating its ornate apparatus in order to crown Shakespeare, the engraving resolved the contest between French regulated Art and the English natural genius: the modern portrait of the English contender had usurped the classical bust of his French co-rival'.[13] As well as negotiating Shakespeare's place in a cosmopolitan classical canon of drama, de Grazia notes that the portrait also represented the publishing house; indeed, the commercial significance of Tonson's copyright to Shakespeare from 1709 to 1767 is reflected in the adoption of the Chandos portrait as a sign for his shop located at Shakespeare's Head in the Strand.[14] While the portrait anchors the work to the author function and its publishing nexus, as a multi-volume enterprise, Rowe's Shakespeare differentiates its overall frontispiece from frontispieces that mark the threshold to individual plays. Narrative frontispieces are chosen for the plays to isolate key moments in the action: placed next to the title page, with no indication of act and scene, no title, nor excerpt, these scenes shape the reading to come.[15] The shift from the authorial statement made by the frontispieces to the Shakespeare Folios towards a corpus identified with performance on the stage is signalled in the frontispieces to John Bell's acting edition of Shakespeare, published in 1774, the year of the lapse of perpetual copyright, which marks the rise of cheap reprint publications that had a significant role in shaping the English canon.[16] Alongside a version of the Chandos portrait engraved by John Hall used as a frontispiece for the whole venture, followed by a portrait of the actor David Garrick, the frontispieces to individual volumes feature key actors arrested in dramatic poses inspired by theatrical portraiture pioneered by Garrick.[17] In 1802 a stipple engraving of *Shakespeare attended by Painting and Poetry* after the Alto-Relievo sculpted by Thomas Banks above the entrance of the Boydell Shakespeare Gallery in Pall Mall functions as a frontispiece to Boydell's nine-volume edition of Shakespeare's *Dramatic Works*, presenting the edition as part of the exhibition complex of the gallery.

Sculptural busts and profile heads in coins and medallions show the impact of classical iconography and the monumental ambition of frontispiece portraits evident in Alexander Pope's works. The frontispiece to Pope's translation of *The Iliad of*

[13] Margreta de Grazia, *Shakespeare Verbatim: The Reproduction of Authenticity and the 1790 Apparatus* (Oxford: Clarendon, 1991), p. 82.

[14] De Grazia, *Shakespeare Verbatim*, 81; David Piper, *The Image of the Poet: British Poets and Their Portraits* (Oxford: Clarendon, 1982), p. 52.

[15] Stuart Sillars, *The Illustrated Shakespeare* (Cambridge: Cambridge University Press, 2008), p. 62; on the narrative frontispieces, see Stuart Sillars, 'Defining Spaces in Eighteenth-Century Shakespeare Illustration', *Shakespeare* 9, no. 2 (2013): 149–67.

[16] Mark Rose, 'The Author as Proprietor: Donaldson v. Becket and the Genealogy of Modern Authorship', *Representations* 23 (Spring 1988): 51–85; Thomas F. Bonnell, *The Most Disreputable Trade: Publishing the Classics of English Poetry 1765–1810* (Oxford: Oxford University Press, 2008), pp. 32–4.

[17] Shearer West, 'Shakespeare and the Visual Arts', in *Shakespeare in the Eighteenth Century*, ed. Fiona Ritchie and Peter Sabor (Cambridge: Cambridge University Press, 2012), pp. 223–53, 232.

Homer features George Vertue's engraved bust of Homer 'ex marbore antiquo in aedibus Farnesianis' ('from an antique marble in the Farnese Palace'). Pope himself posed for a series of terracotta and marble busts produced by Louis-François Roubiliac between 1738 and 1741, later reproduced in a bust portrait frontispiece for the first volume of William Roscoe's edition of the *Works of Alexander Pope* (1824). Coin-style profiles of Pope engraved by Jonathan Richardson (1738) and minted by Jacques Antoine Dassier (1741) outlined a model used in allegorical compositions. In the frontispiece of William Warburton's octavo edition of Pope's *Works* (1751), a medallion portrait of Pope is inscribed in a pyramidal structure above the more eye-catching portrait of his editor William Warburton surrounded by putti and allegorical figures, marking the competing claims to authority inherent in the production of a posthumous edition.[18]

While the portrait frontispiece anchors the book to its author function, other frontispiece genres offer different solutions to the problem of representing disciplinary practices and their objects. Catalogues of collections can be presented as an arrangement of objects in an interior, as exemplified in Ole Worm's arresting view of the *Museum Wormianum* (1654). Polyscenic models of composition allow for the choice and display of a number of key scenes in the field of the frontispiece, such as in an English translation of Giambattista della Porta's *Natural Magick* (1658), which shows images of 'Fire', 'Chaos', and 'Ayre' on top, allegorical statues of 'Art' and a multi-breasted 'Nature' to the sides of the title, and 'Earth' and 'Water' to the sides of a small profile portrait of the author under the title. In addition to showcasing objects, elements, and topics, frontispieces can offer models for the mediation of knowledge. Consider the English edition of Bernard Le Bovier de Fontenelle's *Conversations on the Plurality of Worlds* (1715), whose bipartite frontispiece shows an image of the cosmos above, with a caption identifying the relevant celestial bodies, and a male tutor pointing their marvels to a female disciple below it. These figures provide exemplary attitudes, which indicate how the book can be put into practice as a rational recreation by the readers turned viewers. Other frontispieces gender the dissemination of science by way of classical references and compositional devices. The frontispiece to Voltaire's *Elémens de la Philosophie de Neuton* (1738) brings together different iconographies of the frontispiece (Fig. 3.1). The composition is divided in two areas: the author is represented at his writing desk in his study, with books and scientific instruments lying on the ground; a cloud-like shape hovering above his head marks out the boundaries between the real and tangible interior below and the imagined world above. This cloud composition evokes uses of clouds as a medium for the manifestation of supernatural beings, from the intervention of gods in human affairs in classical epics to architectural forms such as baroque apotheosis ceilings in Christian churches

[18] W. K. Wimsatt, *The Portraits of Alexander Pope* (New Haven, CT: Yale University Press, 1965); Malcolm Baker, *The Marble Index: Roubiliac and Sculptural Portraiture in Eighteenth-Century Britain* (New Haven, CT: Yale University Press, 2015), pp. 261–75.

Fig. 3.1 *Jacob Folkema after Louis-Fabricius Dubourg, frontispiece, François-Marie Arouet, Voltaire, 'Elemens de la Philosophie de Neuton' (Amsterdam: Ledet, 1738), Wikimedia Commons*

and the more recent apotheosis of William and Mary painted by James Thornhill in the Great Hall at Greenwich Hospital in 1710. Just as Thornhill had repurposed the iconography of the ascension to the secular purposes of national identity, in representing Newton in Voltaire's thought cloud, the frontispiece produces an apotheosis of science. Newton's physiognomy can be identified by comparison with portraits by Sir Godfrey Kneller and Roubiliac as well as through his astronomical attributes (a planet on which he points compasses), while his features are reflected by a mirror held up by a bare-breasted female. This act of reflection conveys and contains a gendered figure of mediation: Gabrielle Émilie le Tonnelier de Breteuil, Marquise du Châtelet, philosopher, scientist, and translator of Newton, is cast in the role of a scientific muse, who refracts his light downward enabling Voltaire to write.[19]

Allegories of arts and sciences would be summed up in emblematical frontispieces representing the soul of the subject supplemented by attributes that point to their domain of practice.[20] Consider the frontispiece of John Evelyn's *Sculptura: or the History and Art of Chalcography and Engraving in Copper* (1662), which presents a female allegory identified by the instruments of her trade lying next to her. Emblematical embodiments can be mobilized to elevate or satirize more ephemeral subjects. Drawing on the emblematical tradition, Henry Fuseli produced simple, stark compositions featuring one central figure and a satirical caption for the frontispieces to William Seward's *Anecdotes of Some Distinguished Persons* (1795–6), a collection of articles that had previously appeared in the *European Magazine*. The frontispiece to the first volume singles out the image of a witch, an element of composition that seems sourced from his depiction of Macbeth, Banquo, and the witches exhibited at Boydell's Shakespeare Gallery since 1789 (Fig. 3.2). Fuseli's triangular composition presents the witch crouching, bent, and writing on a scroll inscribed with the Horatian motto 'UNDE UNDE EXTRICAT' (Hor., Sat. I, 3, 88: 'unless he procures the interest or capital by hook or by crook').[21] An embodiment of the secret lore of gossip, this modern sibyl presents anecdotes as unbound fragments, intimating that she might be disseminating her papers to the winds.[22] For the third volume Fuseli drew 'The Figure of Memory', as Seward's advertisement clarifies, with the inscription 'Dies Praeteritos!' ('the days gone by'), suggesting the biographer's role in storing the memories of times past. The painter showcases his mannerist skills by choosing a contorted pose that brings attention to her shapely form, while also

---

[19] Patricia Fara, 'Images of Émilie dû Châtelet', *Endeavour* 26, no. 2 (2002): 39–40; Gerald L. Alexanderson, 'About the Cover: Voltaire, Du Châtelet, and Newton', *Bulletin of the American Mathematical Society* 52, no. 1 (2015): 114–18. On Châtelet, see Mary Terrall, 'Émilie du Châtelet and the Gendering of Science', *History of Science* 33 (1995): 283–310.

[20] Corbett and Lightbown, *The Comely Frontispiece*; Fowler, *The Mind of the Book*, pp. 42–53.

[21] Horace, *Complete Works*, ed. John Marshall (London: Dent, 1953), 39; *Satires, Epistles and Ars Poetica*, trans. H. Rushton Fairclough (Cambridge, MA: Harvard University Press, 1928), p. 39.

[22] For a very similar depiction of a sibyl, see Charles Grignion after Henry Fuseli, illustration to Johann Caspar Lavater, *Essays in Physiognomy* (1793), British Museum, Department of Prints and Drawings, 1863,0509.77.

alluding to the allegory of Theory painted by Sir Joshua Reynolds for the new premises of the Royal Academy at Somerset House in 1779–80. Finally, for the fourth volume Fuseli opted for 'the figure of Discretion', a half-clad, muscular, seated male figure inscribed with the motto 'Decoro inter verba silentio' (Hor., Carm., IV, I, 35–6), which skilfully selects words from Horace's line about 'unbecoming silence' so as to read 'dignified silence between words', commenting on the challenge of writing about distinguished people, while readers might remember the love context and potential opposite meaning in the original text.[23] From the secret gleanings of the witch to the figure of Discretion Fuseli uses the frontispieces to trace a playful and satirical iconographical trajectory that elevates Seward's *Anecdotes* as modern biographical allegories. Seward repays him in his Advertisements, celebrating 'the playfulness of Correggio with the chastity of the Antique' (IV, 'Advertisement').

To conclude, I would like to return to the notion of the 'itinerant frontispiece' to think about its possibilities as a book part that is cut loose from its original context and inserted in another book. Consider the frontispiece engraved by William Blake

---

[23] 'Cur facunda parum decoro / inter verba cadit lingua silentio' ('Why halts my tongue, once eloquent, with unbecoming silence midst my speech'), Horace, *The Odes and Epodes*, trans. C. E. Bennett (Cambridge, MA: Harvard University Press, 1988), p. 285. For the bibliographic history of these frontispieces, see D. H. Weinglass, *Prints and Engraved Illustrations by and after Henry Fuseli* (Cambridge: Scolar, 1994), pp. 174–7, nos. 136–8.

ΓΝΩΘΙ ΣΑΥΤΟΝ

🥀 **Fig. 3.3** *William Blake after Henry Fuseli, frontispiece to Johann Caspar Lavater, 'Aphorisms on Man' (London: Johnson, 1788), © British Museum*

after a design by Fuseli for Johann Caspar Lavater's *Aphorisms on Man*, translated by Fuseli and published by the radical publisher Joseph Johnson in 1788 (Fig. 3.3).[24] A man sits at his desk with writing matter in front of him, his torso twisted upwards towards a female figure hovering in the top-right corner, her finger enjoining him to read the Greek words engraved on what looks like a tablet: 'γνωθι σεαυτον' ('know thyself'). This scene of self-knowledge is mediated by feminine intervention. Attributed to the Pythia, the motto was inscribed on Apollo's temple in Delphi to greet those who enter, and discussed by Socrates in Plato's dialogues (Charm. 164d–e; Laws, XI, 923a). The architectural reference of the original is missing from Fuseli's frontispiece, which brings to view a scene of writing in an interior. The female priestess seems to have been substituted by a muse cast in the role of mediator of supernatural knowledge. An epigraph from Juvenal inscribed in the facing title page, '—e coelo descendit γνωθι σεαυτον. | Juv. Sat. IX' ('The saying "Know Thyself" comes from heaven'),[25] explains the spatial orientation for self-knowledge coming from the sky in Fuseli's composition, suggesting a supernatural visitation, such as in

---

[24] Weinglass, *Prints and Engraved Illustrations by and after Henry Fuseli*, pp. 90–2, no. 80.

[25] Juvenal, Satire XI, 27, in *Juvenal and Persius*, ed. and trans. Susanna Morton Braund (Cambridge: MA: Harvard University Press, 2004), p. 403 (the reference on the title page erroneously indicates 'Sat. IX').

Caravaggio's *The Inspiration of St Matthew*. The frontispiece invites the reader to identify with the author and the translator, and put the motto into practice through the act of reading. Given the iconography of engraving a book's title on a tablet in early frontispieces, the motto can operate as an alternative title. Fuseli's iconography places *Aphorisms on Man* within a classical tradition of self-knowledge extending from Plato's philosophical dialogues to Juvenal's satires. This scene is complicated when the plate is abstracted from its original textual anchoring and repurposed in an alternative prophetic context.

The itinerant possibilities of the frontispiece are explored in William Blake's frontispiece to *Visions of the Daughters of Albion* (1793). As a full-plate illustration etched on a page printed on one side only, it is easy to move around. As a frontispiece, it has a proleptic function in shaping the reading to come, presenting the three main characters bound back-to-back in a desperate scene of bondage; yet in one copy the plate is inserted as a full plate illustration after the title page, to be read after the title and its motto 'The Eye sees more than the Heart knows', inviting the reader to take in the bondage scene as articulating more than what words can express, casting a knowing shadow on the initial scene of same-sex enthusiasm.[26] In another copy the bondage scene is placed last, repurposed as a book ending.[27] As an unbound full-plate illustration, it also has a life outside the illuminated book in the so-called *Large Book of Designs*, a collection of plates separated from the texts of the illuminated books as a collection of specimens of colour printing offered to the Royal Academician and miniaturist Ozias Humphry.[28] In Blake's *Book of Designs* the relationship between frontispiece and full-plate illustration is reversible because of the freedom of combination that characterizes Blake's illuminated printing. Blake's bookmaking subverts the units of composition of the codex, because his books are not made out of quires and gatherings: each page is printed individually as a relief etching, as opposed to what happens in letterpress printing, where one sheet of paper will host four, eight, or sixteen pages pulled in one session depending on the format of the book. Blake's units of composition are inherently moveable book parts.[29]

While illuminated printing is mobile in its units of composition, in challenging the distinction between frontispiece, illustration, and text all unified by the same mode of production, this uniform medium might discourage the addition of extraneous materials. Yet a copy of the frontispiece to Lavater's *Aphorisms on Man* is inserted at the end of another copy of *Visions of the Daughters of Albion*, which is thus bookended by two frontispieces: while Blake's bondage frontispiece marks the

[26] William Blake, *Visions of the Daughters of Albion*, Copy G, plate 2. Cambridge, MA, University of Harvard, Houghton Library, Lowell 1217.5F.

[27] William Blake, *Visions of the Daughters of Albion*, Copy A, plate 11. London, British Museum, 1847,0318.116–21.

[28] Martin Butlin, *The Paintings and Drawings of William Blake* (New Haven: published for the Paul Mellon Centre for Studies in British Art by Yale University Press, 1981), 85.5.

[29] Gaskell, 'Printing House and Engraving Shop', p. 220.

beginning of the text, Fuseli's scene of male self-knowledge concludes it.[30] This inserted plate blurs the boundaries between the two books, showing how the frontispiece functions as a book part that can be repurposed as an illustration inside another book, or as a tail vignette, an opening turned into an ending, which suggests that the ending can be a new beginning, opening the entrance to another book. How does this frontispiece mobilize Lavater to reread *Visions*? Looking back at the opening of the book, the seated male figure looking up to the Greek motto seems echoed by the figure of a woman who seems to step out of the title page to look up to the title of *Visions of the Daughters of Albion*. The motto below—'the Eye sees more than the heart knows'—chimes with the Socratic motto in the Lavater frontispiece. That the two frontispieces mark the beginning and ending of the text suggests a trajectory from the female focus of the *Visions of the Daughters of Albion* to the male scene of Socratic self-reflection suggested by the frontispiece to Lavater. Yet how does reading Blake's book revise the Lavaterian scene of self-knowledge presented at the end? Is the female muse suggesting that the tablet bearing the Socratic injunction to self-knowledge should invite male self-reflection after reading the daughters' visions, and bring Lavater's behavioural maxims to bear on the reader's thinking about rape, pleasure, and the rights of women articulated in Blake's illuminated book?

What is the logic of this act of collecting? The stark contrast of medium indicates that this plate does not belong to the illuminated book; it has been added as a separate specimen. Is it inviting the reader to think about Blake's illuminated book within a coterie including Fuseli, Lavater, and Blake? As a repository of engravings, Blake's book responds to a different dynamic of authorship, which privileges the visual properties of the frontispiece. Seen as an engraving, it can be abstracted from the letterpress and turned into a specimen of Blake's corpus as an engraver. The frontispiece becomes a different object of knowledge subjected to different orders and rules of dissemination. Unlike Pepys's album, which assembles frontispieces according to subjects subsuming them under the name of the owner and his library, Bagford's frontispieces are relocated to the British Museum's Department of Prints and Drawings as part of the disciplinary division of the art of typography from the art of engraving. The frontispiece's status as a separate plate that shares a mode of production with illustration comes back to the fore. Its role as a book part is deemphasized as it is archived as a specimen of engraving and arranged in portfolios under the name of the artist.

[30] William Blake, *Visions of the Daughters of Albion*, Copy O, plates 1 and 12. London, British Museum, 1940, 0713.27.1; 1940,0713.27.12.

CHAPTER 4

TITLE PAGES

WHITNEY TRETTIEN

In 1891, the bibliographer A. W. Pollard published his ambitiously titled *Last Words on the History of the Title Page*.[1] Needless to say, his words were not the last. Since then, a wide range of typographers, book historians, and literary critics have written monographs and articles on the title page and its close kin the frontispiece.[2] Indeed, it is perhaps no exaggeration to suggest that more has been written about the title page than any other part of the book. This fascination stems in part from the sense that it neatly illustrates the impact of print. Simply put, before the advent of movable type, books did not have title pages; within fifty years of print's emergence, they did. The story of how books developed from medieval manuscripts with no title page, to incunables with a simple label-title, to printed books coming with a title page as standard, seems to index every significant technological shift in the history of printing. As the typographer Stanley Morison writes, in a quote that has become canon in the research, 'the history of printing is in large measure the history of the title page'.[3]

Yet even as the title page chronicles the development of printing technologies, it also shows those technologies to be inextricably entwined with the social life of the texts they reproduce. The title page is the site of a book's self-presentation to its potential audience, where it informs readers about a text by in-forming—moulding into structured information—the facts of its production. This process of bibliographic encoding is full of friction. On the one hand, the book trade needs readers (and authorities) to trust its products, and the architecture of the title page serves a critical role in generating confidence in a text. On the other, precisely because it functions in this way, the title page is susceptible to manipulation by printers and publishers eager to advertise a book's contents, skirt regulations, and bypass censors. Even when the publication facts on a title page are true, they are not for all that neutral. As Jeffrey Masten points out, inscriptions like 'at the Ben Jonson's Head' are not just data points on a map but are 'located more thickly within the cultural codes' of a particular moment, implicating a broader array of literary and textual practices.[4] Situating the title page historically thus requires a parallax perspective that tracks these shifting contexts, both technological and human.

---

[1] A. W. Pollard, *Last Words on the History of the Title Page* (London: Nimmo, 1891).

[2] See, for example, Theodore Low De Vinne, *Title Pages as Seen by a Printer* (New York: Grolier Club, 1901); Ronald McKerrow, *Title Page Borders Used in England and Scotland 1485–1640* (Oxford: Oxford University Press, 1932); Margery Corbett, *The Comely Frontispiece* (Chicago, IL: University of Chicago Press, 1979); Margaret Smith, *The Title Page: Its Early Development 1460–1510* (London: British Library, 2000); and Alastair Fowler, *The Mind of the Book: Pictorial Title Pages* (Oxford: Oxford University Press, 2017).

[3] Stanley Morison, *First Principles of Typography* (Cambridge: Cambridge University Press, 1967), p. 11.

[4] Jeffrey Masten, 'Ben Jonson's Head', *Shakespeare Studies* 28 (2000): 160–8, 163.

This chapter aims to offer a set of strategies for doing just that. Although the transition from manuscript to print is an important part of the title page's history, I also hope to nudge us beyond this as the primary schema for understanding its emergence by introducing overlapping and even resistant frameworks. As the book enters newly networked spaces—and we ourselves do, too—such histories not only expose something of the past but give us new models for managing the emerging information infrastructures of today.

The very concept of a title—a short, usually illustrative label for a text—seems natural to readers today, but it only emerged after a change in textual reproduction and circulation. Before print, copyists marked the beginnings of a text with an incipit, Latin for 'here begins', or 'it begins'. The incipit is a narrative statement briefly identifying the subject and possibly author of a particular work or section of a work. For instance, books of the Bible and parts of the liturgy are often known simply by their first words, as in the Apocalypse of St John, or the 'Agnus Dei' chant. Incipits changed according to the contexts in which a particular manuscript was being produced; copyists might add or remove them, depending on whether a section needed marking, or they might not use an incipit at all. Visual markers like large display scripts, elaborate illuminations and borders, or rubrication were also used to signpost the beginnings of texts. Sometimes these decorations were so lavish as to take over the whole page, known today as an 'incipit page'. Information about the copyist or the specific circumstances of a manuscript's production were not often part of the incipit but instead were included separately in a colophon, a note at the end or beginning of a manuscript including details about the name and location of the scribe. Colophons can be notoriously grumpy. As the end of one late fourteenth-century manuscript at Leiden University reads, 'hoc opus est scriptum magister da mihi potum; dextera scriptoris careat grauitate doloris' ('This work is written, master, give me a drink; release the right hand of the scribe from the oppressiveness of pain').[5]

Because visual markers often accompanied the incipit, they can seem to the modern eye like a proto-title page, but it would be wrong to think of these decorative beginnings as its direct precursor. The incipit is not just a half-formed title—an argument that assumes the latter as its telos.[6] Rather, as D. Vance Smith has suggested in an extended reading of *Piers Plowman*, the use of incipits gestures toward an entire theory of reading that sees texts less as objects to be marked in space and more

[5] Giulio Menn, ' "Give me a drink!": Scribal Colophons in Medieval Manuscripts', *MedievalFragments* (blog), 28 September 2012, https://medievalfragments.wordpress.com/2012/09/28/give-me-a-drink-scribal-colophons-in-medieval-manuscripts/.

[6] Smith, *Title Page*, p. 25.

as processes unfolding in time.[7] The emphasis on beginnings is also a function of the particular contexts of scribal production in which medieval texts circulate. Books were, for the most part, made to order and might contain many texts bundled together in a single volume. Thus the material book and a discrete text were more fluid in their relations than they would be after the advent of moveable type: a bound manuscript might contain many texts, and thus many incipits. Furthermore, medieval libraries were small by today's standards, and the physical appearance and location of a book were more than enough to distinguish one volume from another. In those instances where it was not, as in larger monastic libraries, catalogues of incipits served to locate texts within volumes, which also may have been chained to their place and thus immobile. In such an environment, a title page would seem an unthinkable appendage, completely mismatched with the structure, purpose, and social circulation of material texts.

This point must be made because it helps explain why title pages, or something like them, *do* seem to become necessary after the invention of movable type. With print came the mass reproduction of texts and thus a new need to label individual copies. While such rubrics are inevitably reductive, we might think of this for convenience's sake in terms of token and type. When every material text is a more or less unique copy, there is no type, only tokens, each expressing—again, to a greater or lesser degree—some aspect of its circumstances of production: the elaborate illuminations of a particular monastery, the functional utility of texts copied for students in the commercial scriptorium of a university town. Once reproduction is mechanized, there begin to appear multiple near-identical tokens of a given text, giving rise to a cultural sense for the overarching category of the physical book as a kind of type. It is no longer feasible to identify texts by narrating the subject of each token in its opening lines, nor are elaborate incipit pages or illuminated initials practical; the sheer proliferation of copies of texts seems to necessitate a shorter, more convenient label. That is, it urges on the shift from a textual ecology steeped in narrative—beginnings, openings, texts as unfolding in time—to one of metadata. Books were becoming coterminous with texts.

Many incunables stage this transition, as early printers attempted to work out the relationship between their texts and the new technologies. For instance, the titles that most readers use now for incunables, like *Aesop's Fables* for William Caxton's 1484 printing of Aesop, are in fact conventional; the book itself contains something more like an incipit paired with information that might be found in a colophon, reading in larger type at the top of the first page: *Here begynneth the book of the subtly historyes and fables of Escope whiche were translated out of Frensshe in to Englysshe by wylham Caxton at westmynstre in the yere of oure Lorde M. CCC. Xxxiij.* Other incunables

[7] D. Vance Smith, *The Book of the Incipit: Beginnings in the Fourteenth Century* (Minneapolis, MN: University of Minnesota Press, 2001).

leave the text's initials blank for hand illumination and rubrication—a nod to the customization possible with manuscripts and evidence of readers' expectations. One particularly striking example shows how self-conscious the trade was of developing new book labels for the new medium of print. It is a copy of Aristotle's works now at the Morgan Library and printed on vellum by Nicholas Jenson around 1483 (Plate 4). On the opening page, an illuminator has richly decorated the text in trompe l'oeil, rendering the printed words as manuscript written on tattered fragments of parchment. Of course the substrate really *is* a kind of parchment, an irony that has the effect of aging a technology that is in fact anxiously new. This point is emphasized in the illuminations that adorn the trompe l'oeil manuscript: some sit atop the parchment, while others exceed its torn edges, intentionally blurring the line between the old 'manuscript' and the new printed vellum. More, the illuminations are themselves done realistically to appear as bejewelled pendants set atop a manuscript and so stand in for an elaborate border—a mixing of media that looks back to earlier manuscript traditions while echoing and anticipating the use of engravings as both printers' borders and metalwork or plasterwork designs. The mingling of cameos with metal putti and realistic-looking but clearly iconic human figures on the pendant—as well as the inclusion of Aristotle's iconized face in the illuminated initial—further plays on the tension between media and representation.

For our present purposes, though, the most intriguing aspect of this opening page peeks out from behind the tattered parchment. Along the top of the page, almost—but not quite—sitting atop the fake tattered manuscript, is a depiction of Aristotle conversing with Averroes. They seem to be in the midst of a dispute over an open book at their feet, and the book is crucial, for it hinges together these two figures who are in fact separated by over a millennium of time. Here, the physical object enables an ongoing dialogue over the longue durée. At the bottom of the page is a competing image, out of balance visually with the scene above. It is an architectural frontispiece etched with the phrase 'VLMER ARISTOTILEM PETRUS PRODUXEAT ORBI' ('Peter Ulmer brought [this] Aristotle to the world'). Peter Ulmer likely refers to Peter Ugelheimer, a well-known Venetian bookseller. If the scene at the top treats Aristotle as a figure haunting texts, in dialogue with future authors, the image below conflates Aristotle with *this* Aristotle, this physical copy of Aristotle's text, newly brought to the world by a particular individual. The book as a stage for transtemporal conversation, always beginning again with each new reading, is becoming the book as a historically specific physical copy, identified by a kind of title page. That the top image looks like a medieval illumination and the bottom like a printed frontispiece only elevates the tension between the old and the new ways of managing textual metadata.[8]

---

[8] Alastair Fowler briefly discusses a similar example, known as the Ugelheimer Justinian and now at the Gotha Research Library, in *The Mind of the Book*, pp. 18–20. There was a trend in Venice for trompe l'oeil illuminations of tattered parchment in illuminated incunables.

Clever and beautiful as they are, such illuminations were not scalable for mass reproduction, and within a decade we see printers beginning to devise new ways of identifying texts in circulation. Margaret Smith outlines these stages in her monograph on the title page's early development. First, printers added label-titles, short titles printed on the otherwise blank leaf at the beginning of the text block. As Smith persuasively argues, the blank pages were probably intended as protective coverings during shipment, but once there, they made it hard to distinguish one text from another, especially since most printers would use the same basic stock of paper and typefaces for all their jobs. Manuscripts easily recognized by colourful initials and decorated incipits had become monochrome blocks of text. Thus short titles—many of them closer to an incipit in their grammar, like the Caxton example above—were added to these protective leaves in order to identify individual copies. These label-titles were simple aesthetically; printers did not have to hand large display fonts yet and so had to use the same basic type size as the main text. Few of the early label-titles were accompanied by woodcuts (only one in five during the incunable period), but at least one image—the so-called Accipies woodcut showing St Gregory instructing two scholars—seems to have circulated as a kind of visual mark-up language indicating schoolbooks.[9] Although the label-title responds to the circulation of mass-reproduced texts in sheets, printers seem not to have immediately seen these marked-up covers as a title page. As Smith points out, some printers continued to refer to this leaf as the 'alba', or white (blank) sheet.[10]

Although the label-title probably served multiple purposes in its earliest days, once known among printers, its presence spurred further experimentation with decorative borders and woodcuts. The colophon also moved from the back of the book to merge with this newfound space at the beginning, where texts were introduced and situated within their own metadata. By the end of the first fifty years of printing, then, a part of the book that we might reasonably recognize as a title page had established itself as a familiar and standard feature of every new printed text. At minimum, it might include a title, the name of the author, the place and date of publication, and the name of the printer or publisher; but the title page was also a flexible space that swelled at various points to absorb other materials both textual and visual, including classical mottos, epigraphs, printers' marks, and illustrations. For instance, one of the most famous title pages in the history of English printing, that of Shakespeare's first folio, includes the publisher's comment on the veracity of the text ('Published according to the True Originall Copies') as well as a large engraved portrait. It is, I want to emphasize—against the work of early bibliographers like Pollard—neither possible nor desirable to track a path of evolution amongst the

---

[9] Smith, *Title page*, p. 87. On the Accipies woodcut, see Robert Proctor, 'The Accipies Woodcut', *Bibliographica* 1 (1894): 52–63.

[10] Smith, *Title Page*, p. 68.

various elements. Decorative woodcuts appeared, disappeared, and reappeared at various times in the early decades of printing, as did the use of an author's name, a publication date or place, and a printer—even, as Smith points out, within a single shop.[11] Title pages today look vastly different than those of the eighteenth century; there is no 'progress' between then and now, only a series of technological, cultural, economic, and aesthetic pressures that shape any given instance. Cutting across this variety is the title page's utility as a site to encode bibliographic metadata and so turn texts into books, discrete objects devised to circulate within certain legal or social frameworks.

One eighteenth-century pamphlet gestures at the title page's function with brilliant irony. It is titled *The First of April: A Blank Poem, In Commendation of the suppos'd Author of a Poem lately publish'd, call'd, Ridotto, or Downfal of Masquerades*, and it is indeed a 'blank poem', published *circa* 1723 (Fig. 4.1). There is no text, only paratext: a title page and a dedicatory letter 'To No Body', followed by several pages with page numbers, a running title, and footnotes floating at the edges of an otherwise empty field. Of course, for the absence of text the book is nonetheless full; information about the non-existent poem encrusts its edges, crowding out

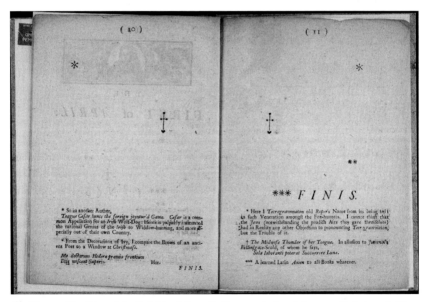

Fig. 4.1 *The First of April: A Blank Poem, In Commendation of the suppos'd Author of a Poem lately publish'd, call'd, Ridotto, or Downfal of Masquerades' (1723). Image courtesy of Rare Book Collection, Kislak Center for Special Collections, Rare Books and Manuscripts, University of Pennsylvania*

[11] Smith, *Title Page*, p. 132. On the development of title page borders in England and Scotland, see McKerrow, *Title Page Borders*.

the space where literature would do its work. And this is, of course, the joke. The framing mechanisms of print have overtaken verse, such that the poem's primary 'meaning' resides not in the poem itself but in the mechanisms that enable it to circulate: the epitaph on the title page, the fact that the printer advertises it there as a response to another poem 'lately publish'd'. Printed shortly after the passage of the Statute of Anne in 1710, considered the first law providing government-regulated copyright protection, *The First of April* plays on, even mocks, its audience's desire to read books, not poems. Here, the apparatus has overwhelmed all else.[12]

Even as readers (and censors) came to expect a certain truth in title pages, it is important to emphasize that the metadata that they present—like all metadata—is not neutral. Title pages lie.[13] Printers might use a false imprint to protect an author or themselves, as the Protestant printer John Day did under the reign of Mary, when he seems to have printed religiously radical pamphlets under the name 'Michael Wood', with 'Rouen' as the place of publication.[14] Some of William Tyndale's tracts claim to be printed by 'Hans Luft' in Marburg, a university town in Hesse known for its connection to Martin Luther, even though they were printed in Antwerp. Later, during the French Revolution, many politically or socially subversive books printed in France were labelled 'Londres' on their title pages to protect their printers, whose names may also have been fictionalized.[15] False imprints could also be used to promote a book, making it seem more foreign or 'exotic', as Mitch Fraas has shown in a visualization of Continental books bearing an American imprint.[16] Sometimes, though, false imprints were simply playful. At least three seventeenth-century English books claim to be printed in Utopia; in a copy of one, Francis Godwin's *Nuncius inanimatus* (1629), now at the Folger Shakespeare Library, a sober reader has crossed out 'Utopia' and written above it 'Londini' and, for good measure, 'Anglia'.[17]

That some printers chose to lie rather than simply omitting incriminating facts altogether suggests the extent to which the title page is bound up in—and

---

[12] This book has been the subject of two blog posts: Whitney Trettien, 'A Blank Poem (1723); or, the Present of Absence', *diapsalmata* (blog), 29 August 2010; Sarah Werner, 'Reading Blanks', *Wynken de Worde* (blog), 10 October 2010.

[13] Jacob Blanck, *The Title Page as Bibliographical Evidence* (Berkeley, CA: University of California, 1966).

[14] Elizabeth Evenden, *Patents, Pictures and Patronage: John Day and the Tudor Book Trade* (Burlington, VT: Ashgate, 2008), pp. 32ff.

[15] James Mitchell, 'The Use of the False Imprint 'Londres' during the French Revolution, 1787–1800', *Australian Journal of French Studies* 29, no. 2–3 (1992): 185–219.

[16] Mitch Fraas, 'Don't Believe that Imprint,' *Mapping Books* (blog), 14 June 2013, http://mappingbooks.blogspot.com/2013/06/dont-believe-that-imprint.html.

[17] Godwin, *Nuncius inanimatus* (1629), STC 11944, Folger Shakespeare Library. The other two books claiming to be printed in Utopia are John Taylor's *Odcombs complaint* (1613), STC 23780 and *A copie of quaeries, or A comment upon the life, and actions of the grand tyrant and his complices* (1659).

contributed to the development of—the emergent data technologies of modernity. Religious and state authorities needed to know where and when things were printed so that they could censor and control their circulation. Publishers and authors did, too, in order to track piracy. In the first century of printing, a regulatory apparatus of licenses and guilds developed and with it laws enjoining printers to name the author and publisher of a text on the title pages of their books.[18] That apparatus had the effect of further ensconcing the title page as a crucial, indeed legally necessary part of any printed book, enabling the eventual rise of copyright laws. Those laws in turn necessitated the copyright page, sometimes known as the 'edition notice' (see Chapter 5 of this volume). These developments can only be illustrated with broad brushstrokes here, but the crucial point is this: while the appearance of title pages is a function of movable type and mass reproduction, those technologies are also intertwined with the rise of systemic censorship and surveillance; they enabled and contributed to it. The metadata monitoring that marks today's globally net-worked technological infrastructure has its roots in the title page's function in con-trolling the capitalist book trades of early modernity.

One figure neatly evinces these changing relationships: John Bagford, a shoemaker-turned-bookseller living at the end of the seventeenth century (also discussed in Chapter 3 of the present volume). Bagford gathered scraps of texts—print, manuscript, seemingly everything he could get his hands on—and assembled them into note-books. Some of these he sold to wealthy collectors like Samuel Pepys and Sir Hans Sloane; others, though, he kept for himself, building from them a vast personal archive that he intended to illustrate the history of print. In this archive is an enor-mous collection of printed title pages, including exemplars from all periods and across Europe, and some 3,600 items in English alone. Later bibliophiles like Thomas Frognall Dibdin named him the 'most hungry and rapacious of all book and print collectors'—even Pollard disparages him in his book on title pages—but, as Milton McC. Gatch has shown, the reputation is unjust.[19] Bagford seems to have been collecting scraps that otherwise might have been discarded. In doing so he did history a service, saving for us around 800 titles not attested in short-title catalogues, including 544 pre-1701 items.[20] As Bagford well knew, in saving title pages, he was saving for us the human history of printing: evidence that a book existed, even if it has been lost to us.

[18] Adrian Johns, *Piracy: The Intellectual Property Wars from Gutenberg to Gates* (Chicago, IL: University of Chicago Press, 2009), pp. 8–9.

[19] Thomas Frognall Dibdin, *Bibliomania; or Book-Madness; a Bibliographical Romance* (London, 1842), p. 326; Milton McC. Gatch, 'John Bagford as a Collector and Disseminator of Manuscript Fragments', *Library* 7, no. 2 (June 1985): 95–114.

[20] Gatch, 'Bagford as Collector', p. 96; Milton McC. Gatch, 'John Bagford, Bookseller and Antiquary', *British Library Journal* (1986): 150–71.

As we begin to digitize the past, the title page once again enters new territory. Search the term 'title page' in a library catalogue and you are likely to find not just articles about title pages, but also actual title pages entered as articles, now with their own metadata describing the metadata they themselves presented in printed form. The paratextual apparatus that once conceptually tied discrete bundles of printed material together has itself become a text, floating free in the digital database. It is a vestigial organ that points to an earlier media ecology. As we move into a new technological regime, one vastly more complicated in its capacities and use of metadata than what came before, the history of this book part might serve as a guide.

BOOK PARTS

Imprints, Imprimaturs, and Copyright Pages

Shef Rogers

Chapter: 5

The printed codex celebrated its 500th birthday in the middle of the last century. While printed books may appear to have fossilized a whole set of structures and reader expectations, closer examination reveals a history of change. Nowhere is this variation more evident than in the elements of a book that govern the business of publishing. This chapter examines the imprint or copyright page in printed books: a feature present in manuscript books prior to print, in the earliest incunabula and in all books since. The copyright page (often the verso of the title page) has continued to evolve in response to changes in bookselling, conceptions of ownership, taxonomies of knowledge, and publishers' business needs. This chapter offers a chronological survey of the elements that attest to the history of a title's creative origins, its commercial production, its public distribution, and its place in the world of knowledge:

colophons;

imprints;

licences;

copyright and moral rights;

edition statements;

quality and standards statements; and

cataloguing information.

Another way to organize these elements would be to arrange them under the most appropriate user of the information. These users include printers, publishers and booksellers, cataloguers, government officials, and, much less frequently, readers. Where possible, I have connected the emergence or disappearance of particular elements with changes in printing technology or distribution methods to demonstrate that the history of the copyright page epitomizes the history of the European printed book.

Figures 5.1–5.3 provide a visual index to most of the features discussed in this chapter, with the exception of a creative commons licence.[1]

COLOPHONS

Clay tablets and manuscript books often included a brief note at the end. These statements might indicate the structure of the work or could be of a more personal nature, recording the scribe's name and perhaps a particular occasion or location. Such notes, particularly those appended to religious texts, might express gratitude to God, or might simply represent a sigh of relief at having completed the work. This statement became known as the colophon, derived from the Greek word for summit.

---

[1] For full details about Creative Commons licences, see https://creativecommons.org/.

Regiſtrum.

Huius operis diligēter impꝛeſſi Lugduni
a magro Johāne Trecbſel alemāno.anno ſa⸗
lutis noſtre. Ƕcccccxcvij.ad nonas Aprilis.
chaꝛæ cōſignate buiuſcemodi characteribus.
a.b.c.d.e.f.g.b.i.k.l.m.n.o.A.B.C.D.E.Ff.G.
H.et J.connectēde ſunt.o.ꝛ.J.quine.B. ter⸗
ne.relique autem quaterne.

❧ **Fig. 5.1** *Robert Holkot, 'Quaestiones super IV Libros Sententiarum' (Shoults FC/1497/H) by kind permission of the Shoults Collection, Special Collections, University of Otago, Dunedin, New Zealand*

From the mid-fifteenth century, as Europeans developed printed books, the colophon became a more formal collocation of essential information to indicate who had published a work, where it could be purchased, and, because the book was normally sold unbound in sheets, a statement called the register that told the binder the order of the sheets for binding. Fig. 5.1 includes all three of these details, adding a visual icon known as a printer's device to brand the publisher's productions. The first printer's device appeared in the Mainz Psalter of 1457. It was not until 1476 that a printer decided to include a full imprint on the title page, in Regiomontanus's *Calendar*. By 1496, the title page imprint had become fairly common because the number of continental printers and publishers had increased rapidly.[2] During the sixteenth century, publishers gradually stopped including printed registers, as the practice of printing signatures at the foot of selected recto leaves became conventional and binders no longer required separate instructions.[3] By the mid-seventeenth

[2] See 'Printer's device' and 'Imprint', *The Oxford Companion to the Book*, ed. Michael F. Suarez, S. J. and H. R. Woudhuysen (Oxford: Oxford University Press, 2010).

[3] See Daniel Sawyer's discussion of signatures in Chapter 11.

century, as presses developed larger platens and papermakers made larger sheets of paper that could be folded to make a gathering (rather than having to nest folio sheets inside each other), the number of leaves in gatherings also became standardized, further reducing the need for a register to indicate exceptions to the pattern. Colophons were also gradually supplanted by imprints, migrating to the front of the book at the foot of the title page. They have, however, remained a feature of fine press printing, to acknowledge the book's makers, to highlight the quality of the materials used to make the book, and, in limited editions, to record the book's place in the numbered series.

IMPRINTS

In modern usage, 'imprint' may refer either to the statement identifying the publisher of a work, or to a subsidiary editorial group of a larger publishing firm. The latter type of imprint only emerged in the twentieth century, while the basic publisher imprint was the logical development from the colophon. It retains that function essentially unchanged today, though the publisher's address and sometimes the place or even date of publication may appear on the copyright page rather than on the title page. In the *Chicago Manual of Style* example (Fig. 5.2), the university press's name and

The University of Chicago Press, Chicago 60637
The University of Chicago Press, Ltd., London
© 1969, 1982, 1993 by The University of Chicago
All rights reserved
First edition published 1906. Twelfth edition 1969
Thirteenth edition 1982. Fourteenth edition 1993
Printed in the United States of America
02 01 00 99 98   10 9 8 7 6 5

ISBN (cloth): 0-226-10389-7

Library of Congress Cataloging-in-Publication Data

University of Chicago Press.
   The Chicago manual of style — 14th ed.
    p. cm.
  Includes bibliographical references and index.
   1. Printing, Practical—United States—Style manuals.
2. Authorship—Handbooks, manuals, etc.   3. Publishers and
publishing—United States—Handbooks, manuals, etc.   I. Title.
Z253.U69   1993
808'.027'0973—dc20   92-37475
                                                           CIP

∞ The paper used in this publication meets the minimum
requirements of the American National Standard for
Information Sciences—Permanence of Paper for Printed
Library Materials, ANSI Z39.48-1992.

Fig. 5.2 *A representative copyright page from the 'Chicago Manual of Style', 14th edition*

date of publication appear on the title page, while the actual postal address of the publisher is on the verso.

The imprint traditionally consisted of several essential pieces of information: the publisher's name and the location of the shop, the names of other booksellers involved in a book's distribution (joint publication shared the risk and increased market reach), and the place and date of publication.[4] At different times and in different countries, the amount of information required varied by law, but for much of the handpress period, the imprint was directed primarily to wholesalers rather than to retail purchasers.[5]

From 1799 in Britain, legislation mandated that the printer's name be recorded in books,[6] either—in an echo of the colophon—at the end of the book or on the back of the title page. As technology shifted from wooden or iron handpresses to much larger, faster, and more expensive steam and mechanical presses, the printer became a more visible figure in the process of publication, and therefore one worth being able to identify.

The other significant technological shift in the nineteenth century was the development of decorated cloth and printed paper bindings. By then, books were much less frequently sold in unbound sheets, with publishers' bindings the norm. The ability to display information on the boards and spine saw the publisher's name or imprint shift to the cover. The development of the dust jacket in the later nineteenth century further extended this trend (see Chapter 2 of the present volume). But an imprint or name did not enable a reader or magistrate to locate a publisher, and so further details such as the publisher's address, the printing history of the book, and other production and legal technicalities shifted to the verso of the title page. Once that location became conventional in the later nineteenth century, the book trade came to refer to the verso of the title page as the copyright page.

In the twentieth century, publishers further specialized and the meaning of imprint as subsidiary specialty publisher came into use. Often these imprints represented formerly independent firms subsequently bought out by a larger publisher, as was the case with Viking, acquired by Penguin in 1975. But imprints could also be created by particularly successful editors: in 1935 Michael Joseph (1897–1958) established his own imprint under Victor Gollancz Ltd, then took over the larger firm in 1938. The Michael Joseph imprint in turn became a subsidiary of Penguin in 1985. Imprints may also represent a particular focus within a larger enterprise: in 2017 a leading editor, Alex Clarke, left the Michael Joseph imprint to establish Wildfire, a

---

[4] For English books, David Foxon very effectively parses the details of the imprint at the turn of the eighteenth century. His careful distinctions among the terms 'publisher', 'bookseller', and 'printer' are applicable to both the previous and following centuries. D. F. Foxon, *Pope and the Early Eighteenth-Century Book Trade*, rev. and ed. James McLaverty (Oxford: Clarendon, 1991), pp. 1–12.

[5] Peter W. M. Blayney, *The Stationers' Company and the Printers of London, 1501–1557*, 2 vols (Cambridge: Cambridge University Press, 2013), p. 76.

[6] See 'Imprint', *Oxford Companion to the Book*.

division within the Headline company to publish books that 'spread like wildfire'. Such imprints nearly always have a distinctive logo—a distant and usually smaller cousin of the printer's device—that adorns the spine of the book and dust jacket and may also be printed on the title page to brand the imprint's collection. One of the most familiar examples of imprint evolution is Penguin's creation in 1940 of the Puffin imprint for its children's books.

LICENCES

Throughout the middle ages and early modern periods, many aspects of the book trade were controlled by trade guilds that managed production and marketing according to guidelines developed by their members. Such methods worked adequately so long as places of printing were dominated by and concentrated in a few urban centres. Legal restrictions on the number of printers limited the spread of printing and thus assisted guild control. Under such conditions, determining who had the right to print any particular text was a matter of negotiation within the guilds. However, no legal system was able to exercise authority beyond its own borders, and since Latin was the *lingua franca* of Europe, with French not far behind, books published in one country were often reproduced in others without permission, while books regarded as potentially threatening to either the religious or political order tried to pass themselves off as the products of another country through false imprints. And as competition among printers increased, the right to print particularly lucrative titles such as prayer books and almanacs became highly contested. Throughout Europe, printers then turned to the ruling authorities for licences granting a monopolistic right to print either a particular title or whole classes of titles such as Bibles and law books. At times the laws required that these licences be printed in the works, but even if not legally compelled, many publishers found it useful for marketing to imply a royal endorsement. From 1538, books printed in England under royal auspices had to state that they were published not only 'cum privilegio regali', but also 'ad imprimendum solum'. 'What needed to be explained, therefore, was that a royal privilege was not the Henrician equivalent of "By appointment to Her Majesty the Queen" but only a commercial monopoly…"For printing only" was intended to explain that the printer's monopoly did not *in any way* imply royal endorsement of the book's contents'.[7] Despite this attempt at clarification, publishers continued to try to bask in the glow of royal approval and to seek royal licences for significant or expensive titles through much of the eighteenth century.[8]

---

[7] Blayney, *Stationers' Company*, pp. 484–5; his italics.

[8] For a full discussion of British royal licences from 1695 to 1760, see Shef Rogers, 'The Use of Royal Licences for Printing in England, 1695–1760: A Bibliography', *The Library*, 7, no. 1 (2000): 133–92. Other jurisdictions awarded licences to titles of similar cultural significance, such as works of scientific discovery, or to works at high risk of piracy, such as tables of interest rates or volume measures.

The sole European body with authority across multiple countries was the Papacy, and the Catholic Church was a steady issuer of book licences. The ecclesiastical imprimatur ('let it be printed') attested to a work's doctrinal appropriateness rather than to its commercial value or national significance. Before an imprimatur was granted, a church censor, frequently a bishop or other learned theologian, would issue a 'nihil obstat' attesting that 'nothing [of doctrinal concern] stands in the way' of the book's publication. Such testimonies to a work's credibility were not limited to the church, however. Samuel Pepys, as President of the Royal Society in England, issued an imprimatur for Newton's *Principia* (1687) and university chancellors also issued imprimaturs for major or controversial scholarly books. Ordinarily printed facing a title page or on a leaf preceding the title page, imprimatur and nihil obstat statements are nonetheless best considered within the constellation of attempts to assert control over the book.

All of these licences were intended to attest to certain positive qualities in books. The Catholic Church and various governments in Europe, most notably in England in the second half of the seventeenth century, also exercised their power in various ways to restrict publication or declare illegal books already published. The Catholic Church first published an index of forbidden books in 1559 and only formally abolished the index in 1966. Governments more often required publishers to submit work for review prior to publication. In England, the laws governing such a review were termed Licencing Acts, and resulted in each approved book bearing a statement of permission, usually on a leaf preceding or facing the title page. John Milton penned his famous *Areopagitica* (1644) arguing against pre-publication censorship, a position that the British parliament eventually accepted when it allowed the Licencing Act to lapse in 1695, replacing it in 1709 with copyright requirements to identify authors and publishers.

COPYRIGHT AND MORAL RIGHTS

Copyright is a complex legal concept that evolved slowly as an extension of licensing, and that evolved somewhat differently in different jurisdictions.[9] However, its general purpose was consistent (to promote the diffusion of new knowledge) and a variety of international agreements beginning with the Berne Convention for the Protection of Literary and Artistic Work in 1886 have aimed to increase consistency. Peter Blayney regards copyright as an eighteenth-century invention,[10] and in Britain it is possible to date it more precisely to the 1710 Statute of Anne. That legislation, like patents and licences, afforded an author sole control of a text for a period of fourteen years, renewable for a further fourteen years if the author were still alive.

---

[9] *Primary Sources on Copyright (1450–1900)*, http://www.copyrighthistory.org.

[10] Blayney, *Stationers' Company*, p. 861.

However, booksellers, long accustomed to treating titles as tradable stock and managing their own affairs through the Stationers' Company, were very reluctant to cede ownership to authors. The question was decisively put to rest in 1774 in favour of authors. Ever since, copyright has primarily been a story of the extension of the term of protection, the ability of heirs to renew protection, and the precise types of material eligible for protection.

The Berne Convention had made copyright automatic in 1886, meaning that authors or publishers no longer needed to register their work with a copyright authority such as the Stationers' Company in Britain (registration legislated in 1710) or the US Copyright Office (registration legislated in 1790). Continued debate about protection for non-verbal creations, such as pictures and sculptures, led to the introduction in the United States in 1909 of the familiar copyright symbol, ©, for these other media. In 1954, the symbol's use was extended to denote copyright in all kinds of works. Although publishers do not legally have to include the symbol or a claim of copyright, the presence of a copyright claim on the verso of the title page has become almost universal.

Copyright protects property rights to particular expressions of ideas, but not the ideas themselves. Because ideas and expression cannot always be easily separated, and because ideas and the person who has the ideas are similarly entangled, the notion of moral rights has also gradually developed. Three moral rights are enshrined in law in most jurisdictions:[11]

1. the right of disclosure (the author decides whether to publish or not) and withdrawal (the author may retract a publication if the author's views change). Because few violations of this right have been taken to court, this right is 'largely an example of symbolic legislation' (363);
2. the right of attribution (prevents others from claiming a work or failing to give credit to the original author); and
3. the right of integrity (prevents modification of an author's work, even if the change is an improvement, without authorial permission).

These rights, unlike copyright, cannot be assigned to others. In the United Kingdom, authors must assert their moral rights by means of a formal statement in the publication rather than enjoying the right automatically as they now do with copyright. Moral rights were first widely enacted by the Berne Convention of 1928.

Complex issues of personality also arise in relation to books of memoirs or historical narratives, where the interpretation of a person's motivations might not paint a flattering picture. As a consequence, copyright pages, particularly for works of historical fiction, now often include a statement that any resemblance to particular

---

[11] Cyrill P. Rigamonti, 'Deconstructing Moral Rights', *Harvard International Law Journal* 47, no. 2 (2006): 353–412.

persons, living or dead, is coincidental. First appearing in the credits of motion pictures following a defamation lawsuit in 1934 against Metro-Goldwyn-Mayer's film *Rasputin and the Empress*,[12] the legal value of such a disclaimer was upheld in later cases, leading to its extension to print works. The disclaimer need not follow any prescribed wording, but should attempt to indicate the extent to which an author has taken liberties with facts. In the example from *Vanessa and Her Sister* (Fig. 5.3), the statement not only distinguishes historical figures from imagined characters, but also disclaims any likeness to persons living in 2015. The second disclaimer included in Parmer's novel acknowledges the publisher's efforts to comply with copyright constraints when citing earlier works that inform the historical fiction. Such portmanteau caveats are very common in anthologies, where it may be impossible to trace authors or heirs who could authorize reproduction of a text. Both types of disclaimers may be helpful in legal claims against an author or publisher, though neither affords guaranteed protection. Like some moral rights, these disclaimers are both legal assertions and symbolic acknowledgements of an author's and publisher's good intentions. A third category of disclaimer applies to statements renouncing responsibility for consequences resulting from financial, medical, or legal advice offered in books. This type of disclaimer is not represented above, but is probably the most familiar to most readers, and has proven the most effective in protecting authors and publishers from lawsuits.

With the advent of general access to copiers, printers, and digital networks, and the concomitant increase in the amount of material made public but not published through traditional channels, writers sought to claim certain rights without some of the restrictions embedded in copyright law. Scholarly publishing simultaneously began to question the business model of creating and donating work to journals that their institutional libraries then had to purchase from publishers. As one significant step in the Open Access movement, a United States non-profit corporation, Creative Commons, was established in 2001. Creative Commons administers and revises the licences it designs, with anyone free to apply any or all of the rights that are available. None of these rights override copyright law, though they do permit an author to waive certain provisions. The current version of the Creative Commons licence, 4.0, addresses four concerns. The first is that the original author must be acknowledged if a piece is reproduced or incorporated into a derivate work (attribution). The second is that if a work is reused in a derivative work, the subsequent licence for the new work cannot be more restrictive than the original licence (share-alike). The third restricts reuse and reproduction to non-commercial use, and the fourth restricts reproductions from altering the original work (no derivates). Such licences offer an intriguing blend of some of the legal, business, and ethical concerns reflected in both

[12] Natalie Zemon Davis, '"Any Resemblance to Persons Living or Dead": Film and the Challenge of Authenticity', *Yale Review* 86 (1986–7): 457–82.

❧ **Fig. 5.3** *Another representative copyright page from Priya Parmar's 'Vanessa and Her Sister'*

copyright and moral rights. Creative Commons licences are usually displayed as part
of the copyright statement on the copyright page.

EDITION STATEMENTS

While publishers find it useful to keep track of printings of works that go through
multiple editions, they are also reluctant to signal to readers how often (or how
infrequently) they actually alter a text. They usually wish to highlight the release of a

'new and improved' edition, and welcome the opportunity to release an established work with a more recent date on the title page, thereby breathing new life into it for the bookstore shelf. On the other hand, they regard the number of copies printed and even the number of reprints as commercially sensitive. As a consequence, the amount and accuracy of information recorded on the copyright page about an edition's history is extremely variable.

Although the term 'edition statement' can apply to any book with a notice regarding a new or revised edition, it possesses particular complexity in relation to books published in the past century, when a bestseller might mean tens of thousands of copies sold. The inability of consumers to distinguish reissues due to stereotyping or photographic reproduction encouraged publishers to include such statements.[13] However, wording was never prescribed, resulting in a wide variety of phrasing that can confuse as much as clarify. This situation led John Carter to dedicate a whole section of his *ABC for Book Collectors* to the word 'First', in an effort to pin down terms like 'First English edition', 'First published edition', and 'First separate edition'.[14] Library cataloguers record such statements when cataloguing, but they do so by exact quotation to avoid the risk of misinterpreting the phrases in any particular case. Of all the information on the copyright page, the edition statement is the piece that ought to be most helpful to the book historian, yet is likely to be the element requiring the most thorough investigation to establish the precise bibliographical status of a particular edition.

QUALITY AND STANDARDS STATEMENTS

From the late eighteenth century the constant expansion of the demand for paper led to widespread experimentation with different fibres and methods of breaking down those fibres into a fineness suitable for paper production. While some methods appeared practical at the time, they have since proven problematic, because the chemical residues have reacted with air over time to create the huge problem that we now refer to as brittle paper or acidification. While no inexpensive methods to reverse the deterioration of existing books have emerged, producers moved quickly to develop standards to reassure consumers that their paper would withstand the test of time. Most often found in cloth-bound books aimed particularly at the scholarly and library markets, these standards have continued to evolve in response to environmental concerns about sustainable production of the raw materials and are increasingly found in a wide range of titles. The first International Organization for

---

[13] See Alexandra Franklin's discussion of woodcuts in Chapter 16 for stereotyping.

[14] John Carter and Nicolas Barker, *ABC for Book Collectors*, 8th edn (London: British Library; New Castle, DE: Oak Knoll, 2006), pp. 103–4.

Standardization guidelines for paper durability were publicized in 1993, and rely on ensuring that producers buffer the paper sufficiently to counteract acidification over time. That same year the Forest Stewardship Council began to include symbols or wording to indicate that the wood pulp paper used in a book came from sustainably grown forests. Similar concerns had arisen with respect to the petroleum-based inks and solvents used in printing. Alternatives were developed from the 1970s, and soy-based inks are now a common, and often highlighted, feature of modern printing. When these details are provided, they are almost always recorded on the verso of the title page.

One particular genre of print, political party publications, has also tended to highlight the local, unionized printers used to publish the material. The 'Union Label' movement was especially strong in the United States, and union logos were common on many sorts of printed materials in the mid-twentieth century. Now they have become rare outside the political arena, in part because so much commercial book printing is done offshore, particularly in Asia.

There are also other, less regulatory indicators of quality that find expression on copyright pages. These may include statements about the typeface and point size of the type, recognition of the designer, credits for illustrations and cover art, and, most often in scholarly and literary titles, acknowledgements of financial support from government or research institutions.

CATALOGUING INFORMATION

No single technological change has had as much impact on the copyright page as computerization. While libraries could cope with a slowly enlarging book stock through card catalogues, the emergence of chain bookstores with large and constantly changing inventories encouraged the development of the Standard Book Number (SBN) in Britain from 1965. The SBN went international in 1967 to become the 10-digit ISBN and, in response to the needs of digital barcodes, to move to a 13-digit system from 2005. The final digit of the ISBN is a check digit, providing a match to the last digit of the sum resulting from a mathematical calculation using the other numbers in the ISBN. The check digit is easily checked by computers and reduces the likelihood of transposition or errors in copying. ISBNs now serve as the basis for both electronic library cataloguing and online retailing.

Prior to standardized book numbers, each publisher had its own way of tracking the different editions and formats it produced. One technique, always found on the copyright page if present, was the printer's key or number line, found in many books published during the second half of the twentieth century. In the representative copyright page reproduced in Fig. 5.2, from the fourteenth edition of the *Chicago Manual of Style* (1993), the array of digits in the eighth line indicate that the copy from which this image is taken is part of the fourth printing of the fourteenth edition, published in 1998.[15] These lines enabled publishers to strike off the relevant indicators as the number of printings increased over time. The term 'strike off' applied literally for books printed from metal type, because the digits would have been part of a stereotype plate of the page that could easily be removed with a chisel. By the time the University of Chicago Press published the fourteenth edition, the printer would have moved to photographic reproductions of the text, but it was still a simple task to remove the image of the number. The requirement that each new edition or different format (audiobook, epub) obtain a new ISBN has negated the need for the number line, but it is a feature to which book dealers and collectors attach significance for determining the priority and value of editions.[16]

The crucial information required for cataloguing that cannot be conveyed through numerical identifiers is subject headings. So from the late 1990s in books printed in English-speaking jurisdictions publishers began to include CIP—Cataloguing in Publication—data and most countries with national libraries now provide a CIP service to publishers. In the *Chicago Manual of Style* example (Fig. 5.2), the subject headings indicate the elaborate subheadings created and managed by the Library of Congress, as well as providing suggested Library of Congress and Dewey Decimal call numbers. If the title were part of a series, the series title and number in the series would also ordinarily be recorded as part of the cataloguing information.

As if technology sought to provide a fitting coda to this brief history, electronic books have once again moved the copyright statement in English-language publications to the back of the book, simply to obtain more space to record the more complex ownership and distribution arrangements of digital media. As this logical, though seemingly backward-looking, move demonstrates, the multi-layered efforts to control a book's status will continue to evolve in response to changes in technologies, legislation, and user needs, and those users will be the managers of book production and knowledge organization rather than typical readers. But wherever it is located and however much the content varies by historical period or national boundaries, the essential functions of the copyright page will remain—to record a book's business details: the rights of its creator, its production history, its marketing, and its distribution. And those details will remain essential to the book as it makes its meaning in the world.

---

[15] 'What Is a Numberline?', *Bibliology Blog*, https://www.biblio.com/blog/2010/12/what-is-a-numberline/.

[16] See the set of four ISBNs listed on the verso of the title page of James Raven's *What Is the History of the Book?* (Cambridge: Polity, 2018), which lists distinct numbers for Mobi, epub, hardback, and paperback formats. Book history will truly have arrived when the title acquires an audiobook ISBN.

CHAPTER 6

Tables of contents
Joseph A. Howley

Where do you begin a book? Quite possibly, you began this book by—after skimming the introduction—turning to the table of contents, and selecting a chapter to read. Perhaps it was this one. Perhaps it was another. Perhaps you used the table of contents to find a chapter, then continued reading the chapter after that, and the one after that; or perhaps one of those chapters made reference to another, and you used the table of contents to find *that* new chapter, and turned there. Perhaps, in all that back-and-forth, you will read the entire book, not cover-to-cover but on a path of your own choosing. Or perhaps, when you are done with the book, there will be a chapter you never made it to. Perhaps it will be this one.[1]

The anonymous medieval text we call the *Chronicle of 754* describes the crossing of the Arab general Musa bin Nusayr from North Africa to Spain, via the port of Algeciras, with a strikingly bookish image:

> Musa himself, approaching this wretched land across the straits of Cádiz and pressing on to the pillars of Hercules—which point out the entrance to the port like an *indicio* to a book (*quasi tomi indicio porti aditum demonstrantes*), or like keys in his hand revealing and unlocking the passage—entered as a destroyer into the long plundered and godlessly invaded Spain.[2]

'*Indicio*' denotes a navigational paratext first encountered when opening a book (*tomus*), a first port of call that both *comes first* and also *points the way*—moreover, that *unlocks*, 'like keys in the hand', the reader's journey through the book. These two notions, of announcing what follows and of guiding interpretation, are essential to our story.

A 'table of contents', for our purposes, is a summary or abbreviated account of the contents of a book, *in the order of their appearance within the book* (while an 'index'—discussed in Chapter 20 of this volume—lists contents ordered by some other principle).[3] Its placement at the front or back of the book has varied throughout its history and thus cannot be a determining criterion; anyway, either front or back

---

[1] This chapter was completed before I was able to access the newly published but obviously essential Georges Mathieu (ed.), *La Table des Matières. Son histoire, ses règles, ses fonctions son esthétique* (Paris: Classiques Garnier, 2017).

[2] *Cont. Hisp.* 70. For the Latin, T. Mommsen, *Chronica minora saec. IV. V. VI. VII* (Munich: Monumenta Germaniae Historica, 1894), p. 353. My translation follows that of K. M. Wolf, *Conquerors and Chroniclers of Medieval Spain* (Liverpool: University of Liverpool Press, 1990). I am grateful to Dr Rachel Stein for directing me to this passage, and to Professor Wolf for discussing his translation with me.

[3] A. Riggsby, 'Guides to the Wor(l)d', in *Ordering Knowledge in the Roman Empire*, ed. J. König and T. Whitmarsh (Cambridge: Cambridge University Press, 2007), pp. 88–107. Note that Riggsby ascribes to 'table of contents' the segmentation of text, a feature which, in the present volume, is strictly speaking the purview of 'chapter headings'.

provides equally quick access.[4] We are concerned here, then, with the list whose defining feature is that it reflects the sequence of the text itself.

'Sequence' is the textual property most implicated by tables of contents: they both represent the sequence of the text to come, and insert themselves at the head of that sequence, doubly mediating the text. The prolepsis they offer invites the reader to jump ahead, facilitating a non-linear sequence of reading that defies the sequence of the book. For this reason, tables of contents appear differently in different genres of book: they occur most frequently and earliest in books that are subject to 'reference'-style reading (before alphabetic or other ordering principles come to obviate them), but come to feature sometimes even in novels, where their history is tied up with that of the chapter heading (see Chapter 12 of the present volume).

More importantly, as book parts, tables of contents occupy an uncertain zone between the physical book and the metaphysical text. We know them today as distinct material elements of a volume, something added by a publisher or editor (so it is that editions of the same text from different dates may have different tables, or no tables at all). But our earliest tables of contents are transmitted from antiquity, parts of *text* with no ancient editions to attest to their presentation or use. Below, I follow these ancient tables of Latin classics as they emerge from centuries of manuscript transmission into the age of print, to see how it is that they become parts of books.[5] The peculiar liminality of the table of contents as book part provides a case study in the various tools and methods that the book historian—or book-historically-minded student of literature—needs at her disposal.[6]

🪬📖🪬

Like so many stories that begin in antiquity, this one's origins are shrouded in loss. Pliny the Elder, introducing the table of contents to his *Natural History* (sometime before 79 CE), cites as his authority to do so one Soranus, a writer of the second century BCE whose work (with its table) is lost to us.[7] Pliny's is one of four surviving Latin tables of contents we can speak of with certainty as 'original';[8] all four occupy

---

[4] When and how different regional printing cultures of Europe settled on the placement of tables of contents would be the topic of a much larger study.

[5] Chief among my omissions is the tradition of biblical *capitula*, a rich and distinct tradition worthy of its own study, on which see principally D. De Bruyne, *Sommaires, divisions et rubriques de la Bible latine* (Namur: Godenne, 1914), trans. P.-M. Bogaert, *Summaries, Divisions and Rubrics of the Latin Bible* (Turnhout: Brepols, 2015).

[6] I refer to several editions held at the Morgan Library, but with the exception of one manuscript, this is a story that can largely be told with editions present in any special collections library.

[7] Pliny *NH* Pr. 33. Riggsby, 'Guides', p. 90. Essential reading on Pliny's table and its afterlife through the age of print is A. Doody, *Pliny's Encyclopedia: The Reception of the Natural History* (Cambridge: Cambridge University Press, 2010).

[8] Others surely existed in both Latin and Greek; see Nicholas Dames's chapter in this volume for discussion of Epictetus's *Discourses*, whose chapter headings functioned like those of Gellius discussed below.

a generic range we might think of as technical or quasi-technical, characterized by 'miscellaneous' structures that seem to demand something like a table of contents. The pharmacological *Compositiones* of Scribonius Largus, the agricultural *de Re Rustica* of Columella, and Pliny's comprehensive *Natural History* all date to the first century CE, while the *Attic Nights* of Aulus Gellius, a collection of antiquarian essays from the later second century CE, is our latest classical example.[9] To this we should add in Greek the *Discourses* of Epictetus (d. 135 CE), edited by Arrian. Though the tables of contents originally came at the beginning of each work, after the Preface (with the exception of Columella, whose table comes in his eleventh book), by the middle ages it was not uncommon for them to be distributed to the beginning of each volume.[10] This process may have coincided with the transition, sometime around the third century, from scrolls to codices, but need not have; such redistribution is as much of a boon to convenience in one format as in the other (the codex user need only flip back a handful of pages to find the table for the present volume, while the scroll user need not reach for a second 'table' scroll).

What unites these classical tables is not just their presence in the text but their accompaniment by authorial instructions for the table's use, all of which use a language of seeking and finding.[11] But some of these texts, particularly Gellius and Epictetus, seem to play a more philosophical game with the chapter headings that make up their tables, using them to engage the reader in reflection on, or focus their attention within, the chapter they refer to.[12] In this way, in antiquity, tables of contents are already not only the first port of call but 'keys in the hand', guiding not just access but interpretation.

How did a table of contents 'work' in antiquity as a navigational device? Some indication may be given by a fragment, held in the Morgan Library, of a manuscript of

---

[9] There are many interesting and peculiar cases of ancient Latin texts transmitted with titles and intertitles; see the definitive study B. Schröder, *Titel und Text: zur Entwicklung lateinischer Gedichtüberschriften* (Berlin: De Gruyter, 1999).

[10] As the term 'volume' reminds us, ancient Greek and Roman books that occupied several scrolls would become one codex, complicating the journeys of ancient tables. On Columella see J. Henderson, 'Columella's Living Hedge: The Roman Gardening Book', *Journal of Roman Studies* 92 (2002): 110–33, 111–13. This placement at the head of each book is also the situation of the biblical *capitula*, which served as much to summarize the content of a book of the Bible as they did to facilitate navigation (if not more so): L. Light, 'French Bibles c. 1200–30 and the origin of the Paris Bible', in *The History of the Book in the West: 400 AD–1455*, ed. J. Roberts and P. Robinson (Farnham: Ashgate, 2010), pp. 262–5. Originally published in R. Gameson (ed.), *The Early Medieval Bible: Its Production, Decoration and Use* (Cambridge: Cambridge University Press, 1994), pp. 168–73.

[11] Riggsby, 'Guides', p. 91. Note that Epictetus's table, though thought to be ancient, does not fit this category because the text's preface makes no mention of it. Tables transmitted in classical texts that do not make explicit reference to the table's presence may invite identification as scribal interpolation.

[12] See further discussion in chapter 1 of J. A. Howley, *Aulus Gellius and Roman Reading Culture: Text, Presence and Imperial Knowledge in the Noctes Atticae* (Cambridge: Cambridge University Press, 2018).

Pliny the Younger's *Letters* made around 500 CE.[13] The fragment, six bifolia of a larger codex, is the end of Book 2 and the beginning of Book 3 of the *Letters*, including a table of contents for Book 3 following the explicit/incipit that marks the book division. The table is distributed over a verso and recto, and care has been taken with its disposition: four ruled lines have been left unused at the bottom of each page to create a symmetric block across the opening, and small red dots have been added adjacent to the lowermost and outermost pricking on each page as if to finish squaring off the area.[14] Like the scrollwork around the explicit/incipit, the table alternates between red ink for each letter's addressee and black ink for its incipit in the following format (I use boldface to indicate the rubricated text):

AD CALVISIVM RVFVM	TO CALVISIUS RUFUS
NESCIOANVLLVM	'I don't know whether any...'
AD VIBIUM• MAXIMUM	TO VIBIUS MAXIMUS
QUOD•IPSE AMICISTVIS	'Something I myself, for your friends...'
AD CAERELLIAE HISPVLLAE	TO CAERELLIA HISPULLA
CVMPATREMTVVM	'Since your father...'
[etc.]	

The *Letters* collects correspondence from Pliny's private life, artfully arranged out of chronological order for literary effect. One could read them in the given order, and draw inferences and connections between subsequent letters; or one could try to work against the arranged order so as to trace Pliny's relationships with different individuals who appear throughout the correspondence. This table seems to encourage the latter mode: each rubricated line announces the letter's addressee ('To Calvisius Rufus') as a sort of title.

In fact, the table provides a number of pieces of information about each letter: first, its sequential position on the book; second, its addressee; and third, its incipit. Together, this information makes it possible to flip quickly to a desired epistle, because of how the scribe marks the beginning of a new epistle. A new epistle is offset into the left margin, often rubricated and dotted, making both addressee and

---

[13] For dating, codicology, and images of this MS, see E. A. Lowe and E. K. Rand, *A Sixth-Century Fragment of the Letters of Pliny the Younger: A Study of Six Leaves of an Uncial Manuscript Preserved in the Pierpont Morgan Library New York* (Washington, DC: Carnegie Institution of Washington, 1922). On this fragment's table of contents (or 'index') and its implications for reading Pliny's letters, see R. Gibson, 'Starting with the Index in Pliny', in *The Roman Paratext*, ed. L. Jansen (Cambridge: Cambridge University Press, 2014), pp. 33–55 (with clearer images) and J. Bodel, 'The Publication of Pliny's Letters', in *Pliny the Book-Maker*, ed. I. Marchesi (Oxford: Oxford University Press, 2015), pp. 13–104.

[14] The placement of this dot has been adjusted by erasure on f48v. Perhaps attracted by the symmetric project, the scribe omitted one entry in the table, which has been added minutely in the appropriate position.

incipit visually distinctive, a common feature for breaking out sections of a text dating back to antiquity.[15]

This is a table of contents because of the sequential order of the list and because of the way in which each entry provides a descriptive title for each epistle. Rather than reproduce the salutation, where the addressee is always in the dative (e.g., *C. Plinius Calvisio suo salutem*, 'Gaius Pliny [sends] greetings to his friend Calvisius'), the rubricated heading places the addressee in the accusative: *ad Calvisium Rufum*, 'To Calvisius Rufus'. The inclusion of full names in the table, which are omitted from the epistles themselves, suggests the table has its origins with the author himself.[16]

There is no way to be sure how common such devices were in antiquity; we are at the mercy of our transmitted evidence, and the extent to which we believe that post-classical manuscripts can represent classical paratext. When we find tables of contents in medieval manuscripts, we must consider whether they have been transmitted from an authorial original, copied from an earlier scribe's addition, or added for this copy; indeed, nearly every medieval manuscript table is unique in some way.

Two factors are important to the rise of tables in medieval books. First, when scribes or readers encountered prose texts already visibly or notionally divided into smaller units, like essays, they might have been inclined to add (or supplement existing) tables to such texts; such divisions may have been emphasized by the transmission of chapter headings (often called *capita*—'heads', singular *caput*—in antiquity, but later often *capitula*; in Greek, κεφάλλια), or may have been latent in the text and invited the addition of such headings. But the increasing appearance of tables of contents should also be understood as part of developments in reading practices. Changes in monastic reading cultures around the twelfth century have been identified with the appearance of various devices for facilitating faster, non-linear 'reference' reading, of which tables are just one; these trends affected scripture, classical text, and new contemporary writing.[17] Medieval makers and users of books experimented with ways of describing, distilling, and outlining the contents of books, and with ways of presenting those experiments to themselves and their fellow readers. Tables of contents continued to be transmitted from antiquity with some Latin classics even as they were born again in the studious scriptoria of

[15] S. Butler, 'Cicero's capita', in *The Roman Paratext*, ed. L. Jansen (Cambridge: Cambridge University Press, 2014), pp. 73–111.

[16] Gibson, 'Starting with the Index in Pliny', p. 45.

[17] Olga Weijers, *Dictionnaires et répertoires au moyen âge. Une étude du vocabulaire* (Turnhout: Brepols, 1991), pp. 94–9 distinguishes between 'tables des matières', which I have called tables of contents, and 'tables alphabétiques', which I would call indexes: see Chapter 20 of the present volume for more on this distinction, and for the complexity of naming these devices. Weijers offers a fuller account of the medieval table, which is tied up with these various other devices and strategies; see also Christopher de Hamel, 'The European Medieval Book', in *The Book: A Global History*, ed. Michael F. Suarez and H. R. Woudhuysen (Oxford: Oxford University Press, 2013), pp. 59–79.

the final centuries before print came to Europe. But when we speak of tables of contents today, we generally mean parts of a printed book, and it is to print that now I move on.

🦌📖🦌

The tables of contents that appear in fifteenth-century editions of Latin classics are those that appeared in the manuscripts that found their way to those print shops; the earliest printed tables are more characteristic of the late medieval or early modern book than they are of the printed book per se. The early decades of print see book makers and users continuing to consider the question of what tables were and should be, even as they found how amenable print was to a more modern rival of the table: the index (see Chapter 20 of the present volume).

For any classical text that reached the age of print with its table of contents, we find the printer of every incunabular edition making slightly different decisions about what to do with the ancient table. But copies of the same edition were not even always bound in the same way. Before the advent in the 1490s of foliation and subsequently pagination, only the signing of gatherings indicated to the binder in what sequence the quires of a book should be bound. It was not uncommon to print tables of contents on gatherings signed independently from the main text (e.g., a-n for the main text, A-B for the table). In the absence of page numbers, a register of signatures, or a title page, binders had no indication from the printer of whether a table of contents belonged at the front of the book or the back.[18] So surviving copies of the same book might attest two binding orders (e.g., a-nA-B vs. A-Ba-n), neither of which has any claim to 'correctness'. In the process of being printed, the table moved from the virtual to the material realm.

The 1469 *editio princeps* of Aulus Gellius' *Noctes Atticae* features the free-floating gatherings for the ancient table; a copy in the Morgan Library with its table bound in the front is foliated in red manuscript, and those folio numbers added to the ancient table. Furthermore, while this edition, like most incunables, reprints each chapter's *caput* as the title of its corresponding essay, it omits that instance of the *caput* for the first essay of each book; the same MS hand has restored these (perhaps in obedience to the printer's preface, which exhorts the reader to read 'all the *Noctes*, and their headings').[19] That is to say, after this copy left the print shop, someone decided to not only amplify the table's navigational function, but also to restore the damage done to its interpretive function.

---

[18] Nonetheless, tables of contents are sometimes referred to as 'front matter' or 'preliminaries'. This separation of text and paratext into differently signed gatherings puts a fine and material point on to what extent a table of contents is or is not 'part' of a given book. NB: it has been suggested to me that printers may have indicated binding order if they shipped or sold sheets prefolded.

[19] Johannes Andreas, prefatory epistle to the 1469 *Noctes Atticae* of Sweynheyn and Pannartz, f5r.

Some texts had acquired tables in their transmission. Manuscripts and editions of Isidore's *Etymologies*, for example, vary in whether and how they present (a) the topics of each book and (b) the *capitula* within individual books.[20] Fragments of a tenth-century manuscript at the Morgan show both the listing of numbered *capitula* at the beginning of *Etymologies* Book 3 and those numbers reproduced in the margins of each column.[21] Isidore's monumental work also reminds us that tables of contents can sometimes emerge from prefatory or introductory material (rather as modern academic monographs ritually include a section of the introduction that describes each chapter's argument in turn; although not in our present volume). The prefatory material transmitted with *Etymologies* concludes thus: 'In order that you may quickly find what you seek in this book, o reader, what is written below reveals to you what matters the author of this book has discussed in each volume: in the first book, on Grammar and its Parts; in the second book,... [etc]'. The 1472 Augsburg edition prints the ensuing table of contents as a continuous paragraph of text; a copy in the Morgan Library has been numbered by hand in the margins (*Liber primus, 2us, 3us &c*) running alongside this paragraph, and identified in the margin as a table of contents (*tabula generalis*). Meanwhile, this edition also prints a full list of *capitula* as a separate unsigned gathering (bound at the end of the book in the Morgan's copy). To this we can compare the 1473 Strasburg edition, which breaks the book-level table out into individual lines of text, but also distributes the sub-book *capitula* listings to the head of each book, making for less flipping back and forth to the separate gatherings, but also no ability to survey the entire table at once. These *capitula* are printed in a tabular format for the first book, as if attracted into that form by the book-level table that has just appeared, though for subsequent books they are printed as a continuous paragraph. In early incunabula, there is as much variation in the locations and presentation of tables as can be found in manuscripts; in different incunable editions of the geographer Solinus, we find the same *capitula* printed as a table with numbers and again as headings in the text (1473 Venice), as a table but *not* as headings in the text (1474–5 Rome), or as a numbered table and then as headings without numbers (1480 Parma).[22]

We might be tempted to suppose that once they began appearing in editions of some Latin classics, the evident value of tables of contents would lead to their addition to other works, especially in the competitive environment of early print,

---

[20] Some form of the tables in Isidore dates back to the text's revision by the Bishop Braulio: S. A. Barney, W. J. Lewis, J. A. Beach, and O. Berghof, *The Etymologies of Isidore of Seville* (Cambridge: Cambridge University Press, 2006), 34. For their messy transmission, Schröder, *Titel und Text*, pp. 146–50.

[21] Morgan MS G.28, two partial and disbound leaves. The *capitula* divisions seem to agree with the modern edited text, but the numbering (as often) does not.

[22] The variation in aftermarket alterations or supplements to tables is as wide as that in printing; for example, the Princeton copy of the 1480 Parma edition has had Roman numerals added to the intertitles in manuscript. This is a reminder that as many copies of an early modern book should be consulted as possible.

where printers sought any edge to make their editions more attractive. But an initial survey of Latin incunabula between their first editions and the end of the incunabular period shows little sign of this: having compared editions from the 1460s to the 1970s with those from the 1490s of Pliny the Younger, Cicero's *Letters*, Suetonius, Catullus, and Martial, I do not find any indication that tables are added to these texts by incunabular printers. We might conclude from this that in these early decades, the table of contents was still understood to be *part of the transmitted text*, rather than something *added by printers*.

The definitive new feature printers would be hastening to add by the beginning of the sixteenth century was the alphabetic index. Gellius's *Noctes*, so richly admitting of humanist mining for interesting words and facts from antiquity, acquires printed alphabetic indexes in earliest forms, echoing the manuscript indexes that had already circulated among both print and manuscript copies in the fifteenth century.

The Aldine Gellius (1515) opens with a topical alphabetic index at the front of the book, and prints Gellius's table of contents at the end of the text. But where the alphabetic index is keyed to the volume's pagination, the ancient Gellian table still refers only to book and chapter—no attempt is made to integrate the volume's pagination into the ancient table. The ultimate triumph of modern index over ancient table finds its final form in the various mid-sixteenth-century post-Aldine editions of Gellius that copy both Aldine text and paratext, such as the 1550 Lyons.[23] At the end of the text, these editions jump straight to the Greek glosses, omitting the ancient table entirely. In its place, like the ransom note for a purloined treasure, they print a sort of apology for its absence: 'The table of contents which Gellius's *Noctes* has in this location I have omitted, noble reader, both because the headings are appended to each essay individually, and because a most bountiful *Index* has been added in which may be found anything that is worth taking note of.'

The presence in Isidore of tables for the whole work, and for individual volumes, raises the question of scales of table making. In addition to chapter tables, we also find tables listing sequentially the *multiple works within a single volume*, whether a manuscript miscellany (i.e., a codex containing several texts), a *sammelband* (multiple printed works bound together), or an omnibus printed edition. The 1493 edition of Gellius's *Noctes* at the Harry Ransom Center in Texas is bound in *sammelband* with several other works, including Boccacio, and an owner has provided a listing of the volume's disparate works, in order, in the white space on the Boccacio's title page—a reader-supplied table of contents to a unique collection (Fig. 6.1).

A 1500 Venice edition of Pliny the Younger, with other works included, opens with a modest list, arranged in a triangle (but certainly not a table), of 'What things are included in this humble little effort' (*Quae in isto continentur opusculo*).[24] Aldus

---

[23] In 1503 Aldus had published a screed against the pirates of Lyons, to no apparent effect.

[24] The 1500 edition of Albertinus Vercellensis, f1r.

❧ **Fig. 6.1** *A sammelband with a manuscript table of contents on the title page of the first bound work. The second entry indicates another of the works bound in this volume: a 1493 edition of Gellius' 'Noctes Atticae' (with its own printed ancient table of contents). HRC Incunable 1494 B63g. Image courtesy of the Harry Ransom Center, Texas*

would sometimes list a volume's contents in its preface.[25] But he also printed title tables: the 1497 Aldine Iamblichus et al. opens with a sequential list of works, titled 'Index of those things which are contained in this book'. The 1498 Aristophanes opens with a sequential list of the plays, and the 1502 Herodotus lists the volumes of the *Histories* with their corresponding muses (instead of numbers). The first leaf in the 1513 Caesar features not only a list of the included works and paratexts (maps! glossaries!) but also a dolphin-and-anchor device, prominently filling the rest of the page; table of contents and advertisement are one (Fig. 6.2).

The 1508 Pliny the Younger (nine books, plus a tenth of correspondence with Trajan) also includes his *Panegyricus*, Suetonius's *Lives of Grammarians and Rhetoricians*, and the enigmatic portent-chronicler Julius Obsequens. The volume opens with an alphabetic index of addressees in the first nine books of letters, then a sequential list of the Trajanic letters by topic, then sequential lists of the contents of the remaining works. Ten years later the press would add an alphabetic word index for the entire volume; in the Aldine press we see how, as modern paratext supersedes ancient paratext and becomes more sophisticated, it tends away from the sequential and towards the alphabetical.[26]

Before the widespread and consistent provision of foliation or pagination, sequential representation of a book's contents was the most functional way of guiding navigation through the text. The sequentiality of the table of contents is thus, in part, a simple reflection of the basic physical structure of the premodern book, whether scroll or codex: tables are sequential because books are sequential. As page numbers become ubiquitous, books can more aggressively deny their sequentiality, more aggressively invite non-sequential reading, and so seem to require non-sequential paratext in the form of the index; early modern miscellany becomes more miscellaneous and more densely augmented with navigational paratext, like the 1508 Aldine edition of Erasmus's thousands of *Adages* that proudly boasts a duplex index.[27]

Even as the table remains the first port of call, it is the index that seems, like keys in the hand, to unlock so much more. Although the table of contents becomes a conventional element of Western books, its role shifts: supplanted as a navigational

---

[25] For Aldine prefaces see the *I Tatti* editions of Manutius's Prefaces to the Greek and Latin Classics: N. G. Wilson, *The Greek Classics* (Cambridge, MA: Harvard University Press, 2016) and J. N. Grant, *Humanism and the Latin Classics* (Cambridge, MA: Harvard University Press, 2017).

[26] In the preface to his 1502 edition of Pollux's *Onomasticon*, Aldus specifically explains that each book is prefaced not with an alphabetical index but a sequential table, which he calls *capita rerum*, borrowing (intentionally or not) the term Gellius had used for his own table twelve centuries earlier (see Nicholas Dames's chapter in this volume).

[27] The second of these indexes was so enticing to one frustrated reader that they added a third manuscript index *to that index* in the copy now at the Houghton: A. Blair, 'Corrections Manuscrites et Listes d'*Errata* a la Renaissance', in *Esculape et Dionysos: Mélanges en l'honneur de Jean Céard*, ed. J. Dupèbe, F. Giacone, E. Naya, and A.-P. Pouey-Mounou (Paris: Droz, 2008), pp. 269–86.

Fig. 6.2 *The first leaf of the 1513 Aldine Caesar, listing both texts and paratexts in the volume, accompanied by the Aldine device. Image courtesy of Scott Clemons*

device, it now functions also as an advertisement, not only of the book's content, but of the hierarchies, structure, and intent of the author's project.

Is the tension between the book maker's order and the book user's desire to read freely a power struggle? Pliny the Elder's great imperial 'encyclopaedia' has attracted this sort of reading, which associates knowledge gathering with imperial expansion and acquisition, and so the imposition of textual order (through a table of contents) with the imposition of imperial order (at the point of a sword). Gathered literature, like a conquered empire, requires structure imposed from above.

A favourite scholarly touchstone on this concept has long been Borges's thought experiment *The Celestial Emporium of Benevolent Knowledge*, a supposed Chinese encyclopaedia (made famous by Foucault in *The Order of Things*),[28] whose categories for kinds of animal ('Those that belong to the emperor', 'Those that are trained', 'Fabulous ones', 'Stray dogs', 'Those included in the present classification') illustrate how the categories into which knowledge is written reveal culturally specific—even alien—ideology.[29] But encyclopaedic writing is not the only, perhaps even the most popular, form of gathered writing. Other genres, such as the epistolary or essay collection, are defined not by universality or comprehensiveness but by idiosyncrasy, the individuality of life and thought and reading. Where tables encode classification, they impose order; but where they invite the reader to chart her own path, they bestow asequentiality.

Perhaps the better Borgesian point of reference for all this, then, is his story 'The Garden of Forking Paths'.[30] Here China also serves as an exotic space for philological fantasy: the protagonist learns of his ancestor's labyrinthine novel, which explored every permutation of every decision or chance outcome in its plot, yielding a riotous superfluity of possible paths through the same narrative world. The impossibility of the reading experience represents both experientially and metaphorically a vision of a multiverse:

> Unlike Newton and Schopenhauer, your ancestor did not believe in a uniform and absolute time; he believed in an infinite series of times, a growing, dizzying web of divergent, convergent, and parallel times. That fabric of times that approach one another, fork, are snipped off, or are simply unknown for centuries, contains *all* possibilities.[31]

---

[28] M. Foucault, *The Order of Things: An Archaeology of the Human Sciences* (New York: Vintage, 1973).

[29] The *Emporium* is described in Borges's essay 'John Wilkins' Analytical Language': J. L. Borges, *Collected Nonfictions*, ed. Eliot Weinberger (London: Penguin, 1999), p. 231.

[30] J. L. Borges, *Collected Fictions*, trans. A. Hurley (London: Penguin, 1998), pp. 119–28.

[31] Borges, *Collected Fictions*, p. 127.

This multiverse is also the experience of reading—the sheer impossibility of reconstructing with certainty any one specific reader's path through a text, not least a text (such as the very volume you are reading now) whose structure and paratext seem to not only facilitate but also to encourage non-linear reading. The *Garden* is, one character explains, a riddle whose answer is 'time', and tables of contents, by invoking sequentiality, remind us that books are objects that unfold in time, and unfold differently to every reader in her own time. Each route through the forking paths of reading is unique not just to every reader, but to every act of reading. This is always true—text may be fixed, while meaning is recreated by readers—but the table of contents makes it acutely and self-evidently true, reminding us that the devices with which books facilitate their own reading undermine the fixity of the text they contain, and their makers' control over how their users experience it.

CHAPTER 7

Addresses to the reader,

Written by,
Meaghan J. Brown

While intimately familiar to us, the printed book entered Western culture like other technologies: first through a process of analogy, and subsequently a process of differentiation. In the early years of printing in English, printers, authors, and translators felt the need to explain to a relatively new type of anonymous audience what made these books different from manuscripts. As audiences became familiar with the technology of print, what needed to be explained changed. Textual producers used direct addresses to track the shifting concerns of readers, as both audience expectations and the cultural norms surrounding print evolved. Closely tied to older discursive traditions about the making of books, such as those found in manuscript colophons and compilers' statements, printed addresses 'To the Reader' explain the acquisition or creation of the text, changes made to it during the printing process, and its ability to meet readers' needs. Borrowing language and in some cases epistolary formatting from dedications to named patrons, these texts addressed groups of anonymous potential readers, anticipating criticism and attempting to guide reader response. Unlike many manufactured objects, books provide an opportunity for their creators to describe what they are, how they came to be, and why their audience should buy them.

In the first book printed in English, William Caxton frames his translation of Raoul Le Fèvre's *Recueil des histoires de Troyes* with an autobiographical explanation of his choices as both translator and printer. He presents himself as an industrious translator, albeit one who was 'born & lerned myn englissh in kente in the weeld' and who should thus be excused for his 'brode and rude englissh'.[1] In the final epilogue, Caxton justifies the 'grete charge and dispense' at which he 'practysed & lerned…to ordeyne this said book in prynte' on account of demand for the work in England: 'be cause I haue promysid to dyuerce gentilmen and to my frendes to adresse to hem as hastely as I myght this sayd book'.[2] These books were 'not wreton with penne and ynke as other bokes ben' and he feels the need to explain several key features of the new technology: the look of the text in 'the maner & forme as ye may here see', the speed and quantity of production, and that 'euery man may haue them attones'.[3] Although writing from Bruges, Caxton sketches a theoretical audience united by their possession of 'oure englissh tonge', residence in 'the royame of Englond', and—he hopes—the purchase of this book.

The sixteenth century saw a number of such direct addresses to general readers. The vast majority of these are short prose works, typically one page, although later

[1] William Caxton, *Recuyell of the Historyes of Troye* (Bruges, 1473?), EEBO image 2a.

[2] Ibid., EEBO image 351b.

[3] Ibid.

epistles can run much longer. A few appear in verse, indebted to 'go little book' poems made famous in English by authors including Chaucer or to the tradition of encomia, poems in praise of either the author or the work. Prose addresses were often packaged with epistolary elements borrowed from dedications to named patrons (see Chapter 8 of this collection). These features often included a header identifying the group addressee, a salutation, a closer, and more rarely a signature. Prior to 1700, headers reading 'To the Reader' are by far the most common way of delineating these direct addresses, although they might carry other labels, such as 'prologue' or 'advertisement'. Headers vary more widely after 1700, from the generic 'Preface' to the succinct 'Why'.[4] As Mary Astell notes in 1721, what distinguishes these paratexts from others is their direct address to a generalized readership and their function in describing the text that follows: 'According...to ancient and laudable Custom, I have thought fit to let you know by way of Preface, or Advertisement, (call it which you please) that here are many fine Figures within to be seen'.[5]

The majority of direct addresses to readers come from the author, translator, printer, or others who had a direct hand in creating the work. Either the header or the signature could indicate the author of the epistle, by given name or title. The Coverdale Bible, for example, includes an epistle headed 'A prologue. Myles Couerdale Vnto the Christen reader', which directly follows Coverdale's dedicatory epistle to the king—a typical arrangement that prioritized the formal dedication.[6] Some epistles from 'The Translator' and 'The Printer' emphasize the collaborative nature of printing, as William Seres did: 'Now at the length (gentle reader) through the diligence of Maister Hoby in penninge, and mine in printing, thou has here set forth vnto thee, the booke of the Courter'.[7] Other writers may contribute direct addresses that praise the author or the work at hand; these typically follow the formal dedication and the authorial (or printerly) 'to the Reader'. William Shakespeare's First Folio has several in this vein by Ben Jonson, from a poem titled 'To the Reader' in praise of the Droeshout engraving and the work it illustrates, to the famous poem 'To the memory of my beloued, the Author Mr. VVilliam Shakespeare: and what he hath left vs'.[8] Printers' epistles are less likely to be signed with a proper name than translators' or authors' addresses. The use of a singular generic trade persona has the ability to

[4] James Henry Ferguson, 'Preface', in *The Philosophy of things* (Denver, CO, 1922), pp. i–xiv; David Graham Phillips, 'Why', in *The Husband's Story: A Novel* (New York: D. Appleton, 1911), p. 1.

[5] [Mary Astell], 'The Preface', *An Essay in defence of the female sex, in a letter to a lady. Written by a lady* (London: for S. Butler, 1721), p. i.

[6] Miles Coverdale, 'A prologe. Myles Couerdale Vnto the Christen reader', *Biblia the Byble, that is, the holy Scrypture of the Olde and New Testament, faithfully translated in to Englyshe* (Southwark?: J. Nycolson, [1535]), ✠4ᵛ.

[7] William Seres, 'The Printer to the reader, greetyng', in Baldassarre Castiglione, *The courtyer of Count Baldessar Castilio*, trans. Thomas Hoby (London: William Seres, 1561), A2r.

[8] Ben Jonson, 'To the memory of my beloued, the Author Mr. VVilliam Shakespeare: And what he hath left vs', in *Mr VVilliam Shakespeares comedies, histories, & tragedies: published according to the true originall copies* (London: Isaac Iaggard and Edward Blount, 1623), ᵖA4ʳ.

smooth over some of the complexities of print production, hiding printing shared among several printing houses, or work stopped and restarted by a new printer.

While printers' epistles are common throughout the early modern period, by the early seventeenth century there is evidence that readers expected to be addressed by the author of the work. In 1619, the publisher Thomas Snodham notes that because the publication 'is *prest* for public view' without authorial consent, the author

> will not greet the *Reader* so much as with a letter of Commendations; yet considering that in these days...it is quite beside the custome to put forth a *Poem*, with out a *Dedicatorie preamble*, let mee...salute the courteous *Reader* with a few words of complement.[9]

Snodham's claim that the author has refused to provide such an epistle is undermined by his next statement, 'Who the *Author* is I know not, & therefore on his behalfe I will be silent'.

By 1700, there are likewise indications that the inclusion of epistles at all was considered a bit mercenary: Sir Thomas Browne's publisher termed authorial addresses 'the Equipage of a flaunting *Dedication* or a Prefatory *Epistle*' appearing 'like a painted young Whore in the Frontispiece of a Nanny-House, to inveagle Customers'—although he did so in an epistle 'The Bookseller to the Reader'.[10] Printers' addresses dwindle in number as authorial control over texts increases, so that by the twentieth century the presence of sincere epistles from publishers are largely limited to fine press productions, reprints of historical documents, and essay and story collections—in other words, productions that need to explain the sources of their text. The 1902 Doves Press edition of Milton's *Paradise Lost* takes advantage of the nostalgic quality of the address, including 'The Printers to the Reader' along with an errata list and other paratexts that had, by that time, fallen out of favour.[11] Readers' expectations about authorship and authorial modesty matter when it comes to which types of these addresses remain in use. The foreword, a short prose address by a named writer other than the author or printer, retains elements of the early addresses: it focuses on praising the author or the work's contents and often bears epistolary elements such as date lines and a signature. In a form familiar to modern scholars at the opening of a *festschrift*, Grant Showerman's introduction to Adeline Belle Hawes' *Citizens of Long Ago: Essays on Life and Letters in the Roman Empire*

---

[9] Thomas Snodham, 'The Printer to the Reader', in Pasquil [pseud.], *Pasquils palinodia, and his progresse to the tauern where the suruey of the sellar, you are presented with a pleasant pynt of poeticall sherry* (London: Thomas Snodham, 1619), A2ʳ.

[10] J. S. [J. Nutt?], 'The Bookseller to the Reader', in Thomas Brown, *A Collection of Miscellany Poems, Letters, &c.* 2nd ed (London: J. Nutt, 1700), π2ʳ.

[11] T. J. Cobden-Sanderson and Emery Walker, 'The Printers to the Reader', in John Milton, *Paradise Lost: A Poem in XII Books* (Hammersmith: Doves Press, 1902), p. 14.

praises the author and describes her writing's value to specific kinds of readers, concluding with a signature line dated from Madison, Wisconsin.[12] Nearly always signed, these epistles take advantage of the named authority of a third party to bolster the appeal of the work. For the even shorter direct addresses that cropped up on book jackets and wrappers, which often serve the same function, see Chapter 22 of this present volume, on blurbs.

As authorial control over book production grew, authors' prefaces gained prominence as writings that 'give the reader a glimpse of the writer's mind'.[13] An early review of Henry James's New York Edition in 1908 notes that the 'feature of highest value that the new editions presents' is a 'series of prefaces in which is presented the germ of the story, the process of its growth and the environment that offered favoring aids to its furtherance'.[14] James's prefaces are unusual enough in 1908 to warrant specific notice: 'It is a high privilege to be admitted into the workshop of the novelist and be shown how the work of fabrication was accomplished'.[15] Linda Simon notes that 'Criticism has ranged from praise to exasperation, from critics taking the prefaces as invitations into James's creative world to those seeing the prefaces as distancing and exclusionary, characterised by unintended irony, overt duplicity, and lack of self-knowledge'.[16] Addresses to readers attempted to guide responses to a text by describing its origins, goals, and excusing its faults; readers did not always read them compliantly.

Early modern readers are often, if perhaps hopefully, characterized as 'courteous' or 'kind' towards the texts that follow. Encouraging book buying as a form of identity expression, some 'To the Reader' epistles mention pre-print demand for a specific title as a motivating factor for bringing it to press: good Christians want to buy this book, 'true harted' Englishmen have asked for it, every learned doctor needs it. When Richard Watkins addresses his edition of George Pettie's *A Petite Pallace* 'To the Gentle Gentlewomen Readers', however, he acknowledges that his restriction on his audience could, at best, be taken for a wish: 'Readers, whom by my will I woulde haue onely Gentlewomen, and therefore to you I direct my woords'.[17] Pettie's address shows that although addresses to men are far more common, women were also

---

[12] Grant Showerman, 'Introduction', in Adeline Belle Hawes, *Citizens of Long Ago: Essays on Life and Letters in the Roman Empire* (New York: Oxford University Press, 1934), p. vii.

[13] Herbert J. C. Grierson and Sandys Wason, 'An Introduction on Introductions Being a Preface to Prefaces', in *The Personal Note: Or First and Last Words from Prefaces, Introductions, Dedications, Epilogues* (London: Chatto and Windus, 1946), p. 1.

[14] 'Review of *The Novels and Tales of Henry James*', *Literary Digest* (21 March 1908): 418.

[15] Ibid.

[16] Linda Simon, 'Instructions to the Reader: James's Prefaces to the New York Edition', in *The Critical Reception of Henry James* (London: Boydell and Brewer, 2007), p. 30.

[17] Richard Watkins, 'To the Gentle Gentlewomen Readers', in *A Petite Pallace of Pettie his pleasure contaynyng many pretie hystories by him set foorth in comely colours, and most delightfully discoursed* (London: By R. W[atkins], [1576]), A.ii.ʳ.

targeted as a distinct group of book buyers. By the early seventeenth century, these selective addresses had become familiar enough to draw the attention of satirists. Ben Jonson prefaces the first quarto of *Catiline his Conspiracy* with a pair of epistles, 'To The Reader in Ordinarie' and 'To the Reader Extraordinary'; the former he tolerates, since the 'Muses forbid, that I should restrayne your medling', but he prefers the latter: 'You I would vnderstand to be the better Man…to you I submit myselfe, and work'.[18] As John Kerrigan notes, 'in the addresses "To the Reader" printed with early modern literary texts there is a recurrent stress on division', one that lends itself to gestures like Jonson's that provide readers with multiple options for classifying themselves.[19] Conveniently, disliking the play classifies you as an 'Ordinarie' reader, and wouldn't we all like to be extraordinary?

Shaping readers' expectations meant pre-emptively dealing with the bad as well as promoting the good in one's publications. Authors and printers take the opportunity to highlight elements of the publication they feel might cause concern among their readers, whether it be the accuracy of the text, a complicated apparatus, or issues of authority. In the early years, addresses 'to the reader' attempted to anticipate readers' objections to typographical and substantive errors, such as those caused by copytext that is 'combrouse what for enterlinyng and yll writyng' or the author's absence 'at the printing of this book, whereby I might haue vsed his aduise in the correction of the same'.[20] Printers' epistles blamed authors for being negligent or absent, just as authors' epistles blamed printers for being inattentive. Books printed abroad by non-native English speakers were particularly prone to error, a fact exploited by the printer of a pro-Catholic piece in 1580, who requested that readers correct faults found 'for although I haue had great care and bene very diligent in the correcting thereof, yet because my Compositor was a straunger and ignorant in our Englishe tongue and Orthographie, some faultes are passed vnamended of me'.[21] Actually printed in East Ham, the epistle bolsters the fiction of publication on the Continent told by the title page. These discussions of error eventually become relegated to a separate, often terminal paratext, the errata list (see chapter 19 in this volume).

---

[18] Ben Jonson, 'To the Reader in Ordinarie' and 'To the Reader extraordinary', in *Catiline his Conspiracy* (London: [William Stansby?] for Walter Burre, 1611), A3ʳ.

[19] John Kerrigan, 'The Editor as Reader: Constructing Renaissance Texts', in *The Practice and Representation of Reading in England*, ed. James Raven, Helen Small, and Naomi Tadmor (Cambridge: Cambridge University Press, 1996), p. 112.

[20] Thomas Berthelet, 'The Printer to the Reader', in Plutarch, *The table of Cebes the philosopher* (London: by Thomas Berthelet, [1545?]), A1ᵛ; Henry Denham, 'The Printer to the Reader', in Reginald Scot, *A perfite platforme of a hoppe garden* (London: Henry Denham, 1574), B3ʳ.

[21] John Lion [pseud, Greenstreet House Press], 'To the Reader' in Anonymous, *A reply to Fulke, In defense of M. D. Allens scroll of articles, and booke of purgatorie. By Richard Bristo Doctor of Diuinitie* (Louaine [i.e. East Ham]: Iohn Lion [i.e. Greenstreet House Press], 1580), 3E4ᵛ.

Although early addresses to the reader appear throughout printed works, over the first 150 years of printing, epistles slowly became standardized as prefatory matter. This placement was ideal for discussing the acquisition or creation of texts and the author or printer's reason for publishing it. Textual producers regularly attribute the acquisition of copy to friends, eager readers, and other invested parties who wish it to be better known. When William Caxton published Thomas Malory's *Le Morte Darthur* in Westminster in 1485, he portrayed himself as responsive to readers, the 'noble lordes and gentylmen' who 'enprysed [him] to enprynte a book of the noble hystoryes of the sayd kynge Arthur... after a copye vnto me delyuerd'.[22] Caxton uses his address not only to establish how he acquired his copytext, but to describe a demand for the Arthurian legends defined by class: if this is a story noblemen want, buying it has aspirational class appeal. William Ponsonby similarly, but more generically, ties Edmund Spenser's *Complaints* to the commercial response to his previous efforts in publishing *The Faerie Queene*: 'Since my late setting foorth of the *Faerie Queene*, finding that it hath found a fauourable passage amongst you; I haue sithence endeuoured by all good meanes (for the better encrease and accomplishment of your delights,) to get into my handes such smale Poemes of the same Authors' (Fig. 7.1).[23] Ponsonby presents himself as the agent to bring Spenser's text to print in service of readers who have demonstrated their interest through purchasing the *Faerie Queene*.

Describing additions or changes made to the text in the printing process allows authors, editors, and printers to distinguish the current work from other available copies of a text, or to link multiple related items that they had assembled. In 1532, the printer Thomas Berthelet prefaced John Gower's *De Confessione Amantis* with a description of his role in verifying and correcting the text. Berthelet 'thought it good to warne the reder, that the writen copies do not agre with the prynted' and supplies the missing prologue from available manuscripts in his new edition.[24] Despite the fact that prefatory materials were often printed last, and gatherings could be assembled at the end of the printing process in whatever order needed, printers and authors employed medial or terminal addresses to stress the timeliness of additions. Christopher Barker, printer to the Queen, connects *A true and plaine declaration of the horrible treasons, practised by William Parry* with an epistle describing an eyewitness account, claiming that it came to him 'When I had taken in hande, and beganne the printing of this treatise'.[25] Acquisition narratives make up the largest

[22] William Caxton in Thomas Malory, *Le Morte Darthur* (Westminster: William Caxton, 1485), f. iii'.

[23] William Ponsonby, 'The Printer to the Gentle Reader', in Edmund Spenser, *Complaints Containing sundrie small poemes of the worlds vanitie.* (London: for William Ponsonby, 1591), A2'.

[24] Thomas Berthelet, 'To the Reder', in John Gower, *De Confessione Amantis* (London: Thomas Berthelet, 1532), aa3'.

[25] Christopher Barker, 'The Printer to the Reader', in William Parry, *A true and plaine declaration of the horrible treasons, practised by William Parry the traitor, against the Queenes Maiestie* (London: Christopher Barker, [1585]), F4'.

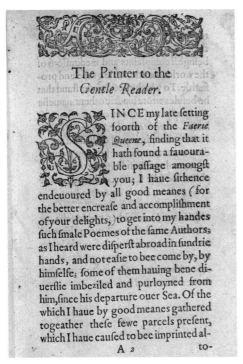

The Printer to the
Gentle Reader.

SINCE my late setting
foorth of the *Faerie
Queene*, finding that it
hath found a fauoura-
ble paßage amongst
you; I haue sithence
endeuoured by all good meanes (for
the better encrease and accomplishment
of your delights,) to get into my handes
such smale Poemes of the same Authors;
as I heard were disperst abroad in sundrie
hands, and not easie to bee come by, by
himselfe; some of them hauing bene di-
uerslie imbeziled and purloyned from
him, since his departure ouer Sea. Of the
which I haue by good meanes gathered
togeather these fewe parcels present,
which I haue caused to bee imprinted al-
to-
A 2

❧ **Fig. 7.1** *William Ponsonby, 'The Printer to the Gentle Reader', in Edmund Spenser, 'Complaints Containing sundrie small poemes of the worlds vanitie' (London: for William Ponsonby, 1591), sig. A2r. Folger STC 23078 copy 2. By permission of the Folger Shakespeare Library*

portion of addresses to readers, as they provide an opportunity to justify publication and commend the text in hand.

Another significant category of epistles are those which identify the author, whether by name or quality. In his 1550 epistle to *The vision of Pierce Plowman*, Robert Crowley describes William Langland's biography—and his own efforts to verify it: 'Beynge desyerous to knowe the name of the Autoure of this most worthy worke, (gentle reader)', he gathered 'aunciente copies' and consulted 'such men as I knew to be more exercised in the studie of antiquities, then I my selfe haue ben'.[26] In the 1770s, Phillis Wheatley's publisher similarly relies on experts, describing sworn affidavits from 'the best Judges' that this 'young Negro Girl' was 'thought qualified to write' the poetry published in her name.[27] Anticipating scepticism, Wheatley's

[26] Robert Crowley, 'The Printer to the Reader', in William Langland, *The vision of Pierce Plowman* (London: [Richard Grafton] for Robert Crowley, 1550), *2ʳ.

[27] Archibald Bell, 'To the Publick', in Phillis Wheatley, *Poems on Various Subjects, Religious and Moral* (London: printed for A. Bell, and sold by Messrs. Cox and Berry, King-Street, Boston 1773), π4ʳ.

To the PUBLICK.

AS it has been repeatedly fuggefted to the Publisher, by Per-
fons, who have feen the Manufcript, that Numbers
would be ready to fufpect they were not really the Writings of
PHILLIS, he has procured the following Atteftation, from
the moft refpectable Characters in *Bofton*, that none might have
the leaft Ground for difputing their *Original.*

WE whofe Names are under-written, do affure the World,
that the POEMS fpecified in the following Page, * were (as we
verily believe) written by PHILLIS, a young Negro Girl, who
was but a few Years fince, brought an uncultivated Barbarian
from *Africa,* and has ever fince been, and now is, under the
Difadvantage of ferving as a Slave in a Family in this Town.
She has been examined by fome of the beft Judges, and is
thought qualified to write them.

His Excellency THOMAS HUTCINSON, *Governor,*

The Hon. ANDREW OLIVER, *Lieutenant-Governor.*

The Hon. Thomas Hubbard,	*The Rev.* Charles Cheuney, D. D.
The Hon. John Erving,	*The Rev.* Mather Byles, D. D.
The Hon. James Pitts,	*The Rev.* Ed. Pemberton, D.D.
The Hon. Harrifon Gray,	*The Rev.* Andrew Elliot, D.D.
The Hon. James Bowdoin,	*The Rev.* Samuel Cooper, D.D.
John Hancock, *Efq;*	*The Rev.* Mr. Samuel Mather,
Jofeph Green, *Efq;*	*The Rev.* Mr. Joon Moorhead,
Richard Carey, *Efq;*	*Mr.* John Wheatley, *her Mafter.*

N. B. The original Atteftation, figned by the above Gentlemen, may be feen by applying to *Archibald Bell,* Bookfeller,
No. 8, *Aldgate-Street.*

* The Words " *following Page,* " allude to the Contents of
the Manufcript Copy, which are wrote at the Back of the
above Atteftation.

❦ **Fig. 7.2** *Archibald Bell, 'To the Publick', in Phillis Wheatley, 'Poems on Various Subjects,*
Religious and Moral' (London: printed for A. Bell and sold by Messrs. Cox and Berry, King-Street,
Boston, 1773), π4r. Irvin Department of Rare Books and Special Collections, University of South
Carolina Libraries, Columbia, SC, PS866 W5 1773

publisher advertises that 'The original attestation, signed by the above Gentlemen, may be seen by applying to *Archibald Bell*, Bookseller' (Fig. 7.2).[28]

Bell's affidavits were offered to readers who had good reason to doubt the narratives of literary composition and print publication that framed their texts. The practice of employing addresses to readers as literary framing devices emphasized the importance of such texts in guiding reader interpretations. As Michael Saenger puts it, at times 'front matter can be quite literary, in the sense that it is imaginative and stylistically developed'.[29] Imaginative addresses range from frame narratives of poets at work, such as the one that contextualizes the mid-Tudor *Mirror for Magistrates*, to outright lies intended to increase sales of the published work or disguise illegal printing. John Awdelay, the publisher and author of the coney-catching pamphlet *The fraternitye of vacabondes*, used a verse 'Printer to the Reader' to claim that his (fictional) author's anonymity was part of a plea deal designed to protect him from fellow criminals.[30] George Gascoigne's *Hundreth Sundrie Flowres* includes an address by an unnamed printer who casts doubt on its tale of stolen letters, noting that the multiple letter writers 'have therefore (each of them) politiquely preuented the daunger of misreport, and suffered me the poore Printer to runne avvay vvith the palme of so perilous a victorie'.[31] This address is notably inconsistent with the actions ascribed to the fictional printer 'A. B.' in the letters themselves. The self-reflexive quality of 'To the Reader' addresses encouraged authors to treat them as an opportunity for playing with readers' expectations. Mark Twain employed the form in *Puddin'head Wilson* to humorously deflect legal responsibility for the 'law chapters in this book' onto a 'William Hicks'.[32] Although sincere addresses to readers largely fell out of use in the nineteenth century, fictional 'To the Reader' frame narratives found fertile ground.[33]

Reprints offer some of the best opportunities to examine the differing ways addresses to readers can function, including the interplay between earnest and fictionalized addresses, as a text is reinterpreted and recontextualized for new audiences. The first edition of the *Mirror for Magistrates* was conceived, the printer John Wayland tells his readers in 1554, as 'some necessary & profitable worke' to keep his presses

---

[28] Ibid.

[29] Michael Saenger, *The Commodification of Textual Engagements in the English Renaissance* (Aldershot: Ashgate, 2006), p. 18.

[30] John Awdelay, 'The Printer to the Reader', in *The fraternitye of uacabondes As wel of ruflyng vacabondes, as of beggerly, of women as of men, of gyrles, as of boyes, with their proper names and qualities* (London: John Awdelay, 1575), A1ʳ.

[31] Anonymous, 'The Printer to the Reader', in George Gascoigne, *A hundreth sundrie flowres* (London: Henry Bennyman [and Henry Middleton] for Richard Smith), A2ʳ.

[32] Mark Twain, 'A Whisper to the Reader', in *Pudd'nhead Wilson and those extraordinary twins* (New York: Harper, 1899), pp. vii–ix.

[33] David Seed, 'Framing the Reader in Early Science Fiction', *Style* 47, no. 2 (2013): 137–67.

busy while awaiting the text of the Marian Primer.[34] The outline of the project sketched in Wayland's formal 'Prynter to the Reader' epistle, including the starting point for the ghostly histories and its purpose, reappears as the poets-at-work frame narrative of 1559. The frame narrative keeps 'the printer' as the project's instigator, despite a change in publisher.[35] Fifty years and twelve instalments later, Richard Niccols, the editor of the 1609/10 *Mirror for Magistrates* once again employs a practical 'To the Reader' epistle 'To acquaint you in briefe with what is done in this impression'.[36] Nearly 900 pages long, Niccols's edition of the *Mirror* contains multiple epistles, including an 'Epistle Dedicatorie' by a previous editor that first appeared in 1574 and separate epistles for some of his lengthier additions, such as *England's Eliza*, a 'hymn' to Queen Elizabeth.

While some printers took the opportunity offered by reprints to put their own stamp on a work, in other cases, 'To the reader' texts prove to be remarkably sticky paratexts. Although many describe specific circumstances of production, new editions included them long after these circumstances are no longer applicable. When Valentine Simmes and Thomas Creede reprinted Caxton's *Recuyell* in 1596/7, they appended a new 'The Printers to the curteous Reader' that borrows some of Caxton's language while disparaging his translation. The epistle concludes with a lament that 'if leisure had serued, we would haue had the same in better refined phrases, and certaine names that bee amisse, conferred with Authours, and made right'.[37] These pains, the printers explain, will be taken with the next edition: 'if wee finde your fauourable accepting heereof to be such, as wee may shortly haue a second impression, we will haue all amended'.[38] This claim is repeated through the sixth edition; in the seventh, published in 1663, the printer (now Samuel Speed) realizes he probably should have corrected those faults by now. His epistle notes that they 'are in this [edition] corrected and amended'.[39] The same epistle survives, roughly unchanged, through the eighteenth edition, published in Dublin in 1738. It is difficult to know

---

[34] John Wayland, 'Prynter to the Reader', in John Lydgate, *The Fall of prynces. Gathered by John Bochas, fro[m] the begynnyng of the world vntyll his time, translated into English by John Lidgate monke of Burye Wherunto is added the fall of al such as since that time were notable in Englande: diligently collected out of the chronicles* (Londini: in aedibus Johannis Waylandi, [1554]), †1v.

[35] William Baldwin, 'William Baldwin to the Reader', in *A myrroure for magistrates* (Londini: In aedibus Thomae Marshe, [1559]), A1r.

[36] Richard Niccols, 'To the Reader', in *A mirour for magistrates being a true chronicle historie of the vntimely falles of such vnfortunate princes and men of note, as haue happened since the first entrance of Brute into this iland, vntill this our latter age* (London: Felix Kingston, 1610), A4v.

[37] [Thomas Creede and Valentine Simmes], 'The Printers to the curteous reader, health and happinesse', in Raoul Le Fèvre, *The auncient historie, of the destruction of Troy... Translated out of French into English, by W. Caxton*, ed. William Fiston (London: Thomas Creede [and Valentine Simmes], 1596/7), (æ).4r.

[38] Ibid.

[39] 'The Printer to the Courteous Reader, wisheth Health and Happiness', in Raoul Le Fèvre, *The destruction of Troy in three books*, 7th edition (London: R. I. for S[amuel] S[peed], to be sold by F[rancis] Coles... and C. Tyus, 1663), A2v.

whether later publishers retained Creede and Simmes's framework for the text—and by extrapolation, their redeployment of Caxton's rhetoric—because they saw it as integral to the text as a whole, or because it simplified typesetting to follow an exemplar closely. The subtle changes to this address over its many reprintings, however, illustrate the tension later printers encountered between plausibly depicting the circumstances of textual production and recreating a known and effective framework for a popular text.

Addresses to readers create moments of intentional disruption to the immersive experience of reading, reminding their audience that they are consuming texts which were consciously constructed. Throughout their history, these addresses highlight the elements of printed books that their creators expect to be contentious, from the early form of printed letters to the choices made in re-editing short stories for an anthology. While these epistles can tell us a great deal about the position of printed books in society, it is important to remember that one of their primary functions was to make the text they were attached to appeal to readers with the power to purchase it. As John Heminges and Henry Condell said in Shakespeare's First Folio, readers 'wil stand for your priuiledges wee know: to read, and censure. Do so, but buy it first. That doth best commend a Booke, the Stationer saies.'[40]

---

[40] John Heminges and Henry Condell, 'To the great Variety of Readers', *VVilliam Shakespeares comedies, histories, & tragedies*, ᴮA3ʳ.

Chapter 8
Acknowledgements and Dedications
Helen Smith

To the ~~kindly gentle understanding idle captious cavilling loathed~~ reader

This chapter could not have been written without the support of friends and colleagues. With more support, it might have been written on time. Thanks to the editors for their patience. My work has been informed by conversations with or near the most influential scholars in my field; I am grateful for their discrimination in recognizing my talents, and would like to remind them that 'acknowledgements…bring together metamessages about the value of the ties binding author and acknowledged and about commitment to these ties in times to come'.[1] Obligations work both ways; print endures.

I would like to thank my precursors in the field: [*insert list here*], as well as anyone who has ever dedicated a book/building/boat/poem/plot of ground to anyone. I would add 'and family', but it has been a long time since my parents were willing to read my work, and the dog was little or no help. The most relevant research, especially that which renders my own redundant, was published too late for inclusion in this chapter. Other scholarly debts are relegated to the footnotes, particularly if the writer is wittier or more insightful than I am.[2] My greatest debt is to the internet.[3]

Perhaps I should not admit that in writing like this, I am making myself self-conscious. I would like you to think that I am well connected, clever, funny, or, preferably, all of the above. Judge this work kindly; better yet, recognize that you are not qualified to judge it at all. If paratexts are zones designed to mediate the reader's engagement with the text—to lay down aspects of the laws by which it may be received—dedications and acknowledgements are sites that prickle with the expectation of being misread, and the knowledge that attempts to corral the reader will always fall short.

Dear reader, consider yourself part of an august tradition. Roman authors pledged their works to patrons, some named within the body of the text: Memmius Gemellus in Lucretius's *De rerum natura*; Maecenas, whose name became a metonym for

[1] Eyal Ben-Ari, 'On Acknowledgements in Ethnographies', *Journal of Anthropological Research* 43 (1987): 63–84, 68.

[2] On the uneasy connections between dedications and patronage, see Dustin Griffin, *Literary Patronage in England, 1650–1800* (Cambridge: Cambridge University Press, 1996); Richard McCabe, *'Ungainefull Arte': Poetry, Patronage, and Print in the Early Modern Era* (Oxford: Oxford University Press, 2016); Valerie Schutte, *Mary I and the Art of Book Dedications: Royal Women, Power, and Persuasion* (New York: Palgrave Macmillan, 2015); and Franklin B. Williams, *Index of Dedications and Commendatory Verses in English Books before 1641* (London: Bibliographical Society, 1961).

[3] https://www.buzzfeed.com/jzebarrow/the-27-greatest-book-dedications-you-will-ever-rea-mvjw?utm_term=.guAVJJ2gm#.qa6rRR2vd.

generous patronage, in Virgil's *Georgics*. In medieval manuscripts, authors and scribes presented their works to influential readers and commissioners, developing the tradition of the dedicatory epistle which acknowledged, or attempted to call into being, a relationship of favour and exchange (see Chapter 7 of this volume). Printed dedications made more overt the tension between a private address and a wider readership, not least as they began to supplement the dedication proper with a subsequent letter 'To the reader', attempting to cover multiple bases. According to its title page, the first monolingual English dictionary, published in 1604, was intended for 'the benefit & helpe of Ladies, Gentlewomen, or any other vnskilfull persons'.[4] Its author, Robert Cawdry, dedicated the book to five noble sisters: both the dedication, which emphasizes the text's utility to 'strangers' (foreigners) and children, and Cawdry's letter 'To the reader', which dwells on the practicalities of the book and how to navigate it, work hard to distinguish the five named female dedicatees from the 'vnskilfull', feminized crowd of the title page.

Writers across the centuries have faced the tricky question of how to sound sincere when your editor has reminded you that a dedication is *de rigeur*. The great Elizabethan naturalist, William Turner, failed spectacularly: he noted that his book had been about to go to press when his printer reminded him of the need for 'some both mighty and learned Patron to defend my laboures against spitefull and envious enemies... and declare my good minde to him that I am bound unto by dedicating and geveng these labours unto him'.[5] Turner's peculiarly honest account offers an insight into the collaborative nature of all aspects of book production; the 'great man' to whom he addressed his last-minute dedication was none other than Queen Elizabeth. This example raises questions too about the relationship between patronage and permission (prospective or retrospective).

Early dedications frequently used the terms of 'acknowledgement', a tradition that endured through several centuries of print. In 1667, for example, Nicholas Billingsley addressed the last of three jangling and awkwardly constructed acrostic dedicatory verses to 'The Right Worshipfull Sr Trevir Williames Knigt and Barronet [*sic.*]', admitting that 'Great love your WoRship shew'd to me I do / Here send a mEan acknowledGement to you' (Fig. 8.1).[6]

It was not until considerably later that acknowledgements established themselves as a separate genre. In 1960, a guide to compiling a high school yearbook notes: 'Some yearbook staffs like to devote the last page... to "a last word," acknowledgements or a "thank you" to the people who have helped in the production of the book',

---

[4] Robert Cawdry, *A table alphabeticall conteyning and teaching the true writing, and vnderstanding of hard vsuall English wordes* (London, 1604), A1r.

[5] William Turner, *The first and seconde partes of the herbal of William Turner* (Cologne: [Heirs of] Arnold Birckman, 1568), *2r.

[6] Nicholas Billingsley, *A Treasury of Divine Raptures Consisting of Serious Observations, Pious Ejaculations, Select Epigrams...* (London: T. J. for Thomas Parkhurst, 1667), A3v–A4r.

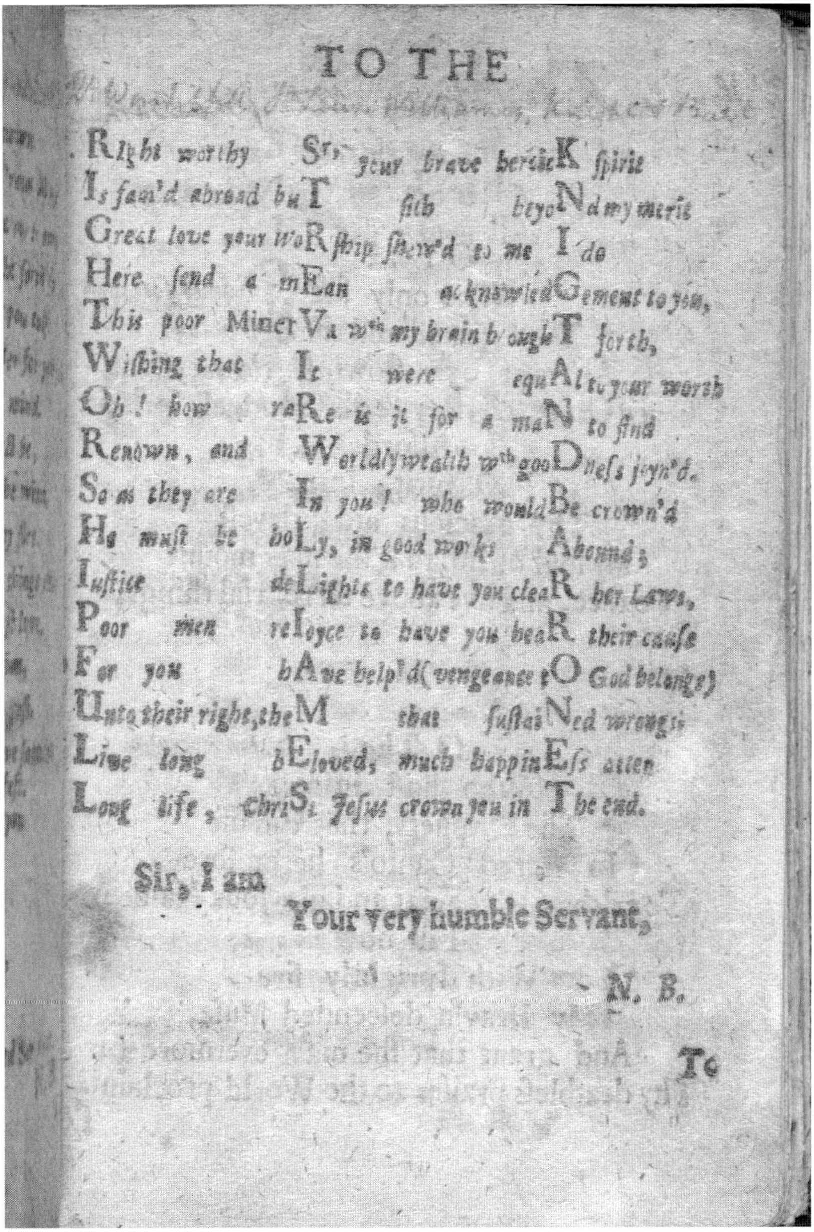

TO THE

Right worthy Sr your brave heroicK spirit
Is fam'd abroad buT filh beyoNd my merit
Great love your woRship shew'd to me I do
Here send a mEan acknowledGement to you,
This poor MinerVa wth my brain brought forth,
Wishing that It were equAl to your worth
Oh! how raRe is it for a maN to find
Renown, and Worldly wealth wth goodNess joyn'd.
So as they are In you! who would Be crown'd
He must be hoLy, in good works Abound;
Iustice deLights to have you cleaR her Laws,
Poor men reIoyce to have you beaR their cause
For you hAve help'd (vengeance tO God belongs)
Unto their right, theM that sustaiNed wrongs
Live long bEloved, much happinEss atten
Long life, chriSt Jesus crown you in The end.

Sir, I am

Your very humble Servant,

N. B.

Fig. 8.1 *A triple acrostic in the dedication to Nicholas Billingsley, 'A Treasury of Divine Raptures Consisting of Serious Observations, Pious Ejaculations, Select Epigrams…' (London: T. J. for Thomas Parkhurst, 1667), A3v–A4r. By permission of the British Library Board*

in other words, an 'acknowledgements page'. 'If you decide to do this,' the guide continues sternly, 'plan the layout and typography of this message so it will harmonize with the style of the rest of the annual'.[7] This concern for typography (if not necessarily for consistency) has marked dedications across the ages: modern dedications are centred in fragmentary shapes akin to verse; older books often use a different font for the dedication, or taper its final lines into a concluding triangle.[8] Christopher Ricks heaped scorn on *The Bloomsbury Dictionary of Dedications* (1990) not only for its unoriginal choices but for printing them 'in a mangled form as run-on sequences and not as what they truly are, a form of inscription'.[9] Dedications of buildings, in the ancient world, were carved onto their pillars or frontispieces (an architectural form before it was architextural, as Luisa Calè notes in Chapter 3 of this volume).

Alongside nostalgia for a more sincere dedicatory age came the meta-dedication, the anti-dedication, and the dedication whimsical. Charles Bukowski was not as original as he may have thought when he fronted *Post Office* (1971) with the words 'This is presented as a work of fiction and dedicated to nobody'. In 1622, John Taylor, the water poet, who frequently engaged in paratextual play, dedicated *Sir Gregory Nonsence his newes from no place* first of all 'To the (Sir Reuerence) Rich Worshipped, Master Trim Tram Senceles, great Image of Authority and Hedgborough of the famous City of Goteham' and then, in a second short address that made clear the identity of this peculiar hybrid, 'To nobody'.[10]

In *The Advancement of Learning* (1605), Sir Francis Bacon railed against the practice of dedication, insisting that

> Bookes (such as are worthy the name of Bookes) ought to haue no Patrons, but Truth and Reason: And the ancient custome was, to dedicate them only to priuate and equall friendes, or to intitle the Bookes with their Names, or if to Kings and great persons, it was to some such as the argument of the Booke was fit and proper for.[11]

Bacon's own dedicatee, King James I, if he read as far as the middle of Bacon's first book to find this passage, was presumably invited to recognize himself in the select

---

[7] Calvin J. Medlin, *Yearbook Layout* (Ames, IA: Iowa State University Press, 1960), p. 129.

[8] See, for example, George Baker's elegantly printed *The composition of making of the moste excellent and pretious oil called oleum* (1574), which features an italic dedication with concluding triangle and rotated pilcrow, followed by black letter text in the address 'To the reader' and throughout; the Roman, and ostentatiously verbose, dedication of John Lyly's *Euphues and his England* (1588), which tapers off before a black letter address 'To the Ladies and Gentlewomen of England'; and Shakespeare's much-discussed italic dedication to Southampton in *Venus and Adonis* (1595).

[9] Christopher Ricks, 'Umpteens', *London Review of Books* 12, no. 22 (22 November 1990): 16–17, 17.

[10] John Taylor, *Sir Gregory Nonsence his newes from no place* (London, 1622), A3r–A4v.

[11] Francis Bacon, *The Oxford Francis Bacon IV: The Advancement of Learning*, ed. Michael Kiernan (Oxford: Clarendon Press, 2000), p. 20.

category of 'fit' reader, an appropriate recipient for a book which aimed to build the foundations of the state through a restructuring of philosophical inquiry.

A century and a half later, Samuel Johnson published an essay in *The Rambler*. Prefaced with an epigram from Homer, in untranslated Greek, the essay is determinedly highbrow, inviting its readers either to understand its opening lines and enter a community of the learned, or pass over the inscrutable letters, duly oppressed by Johnson's weighty learning.[12] Dedications, 'the work on which all the power of modern wit has been exhausted', are, Johnson complains, a 'species of prostitution...which destroys the force of praise, by shewing that it may be acquired without deserving it'.[13] I have avoided this danger by dedicating this chapter only to the reader who is sufficiently sophisticated to approve, and sufficiently learned to deserve praise without reservation.

The question underpinning Johnson's blast is simple: what is the market rate of a dedication? ('To my creditors,' announces Michael Moorcock's *The Steel Tsar* (1981), 'who remain a permanent source of inspiration'.) In 1612, the playwright Nathan Field dedicated his *A Woman is a Weathercock* (1612) to 'Any woman that hath been no weather-cock' (i.e. fickle) and concluded

> I Did determine, not to haue Dedicated my Play to any Body, because forty shillings I care not for...And now I looke vp, and finde to whom my Dedication is, I feare I am as good as my determination: notwithstanding I leave a libertie to any Lady or woman, that dares say she hath been no weather-Cocke, to assume the Title of Patronesse to this my Booke.[14]

It is tempting to read Field's waspish statement of non-dedication as revealing a predictable market in dedications in the early seventeenth century, but forty shillings was a proverbial sum to indicate poverty in this period, suggesting the notorious stinginess of patrons, rather than the specific reward offered to any author.

In 1718, an anonymous writer, later identified as Thomas Gordon, penned *A dedication to a great man, concerning dedications*. The letter bemoans the hard reward of 'a Sort of Coin, call'd *Promises*, stamp'd with his Honour, but never current amonst Shop-keepers and Victuallers'.[15] To guard against this unwelcome outcome Gordon suggests a standard contract and bill of articles, including such merchandise as 'For Praising your Ancestors, unknown', and 'For admiring your Lady's Beauty, unsight, unseen' (A4v). Book 8, chapter 9 of Lawrence Sterne's *Tristram Shandy*, first published in 1765, offers up a dedication, lacking only the crucial details of 'matter,

---

[12] Echthrus gar moi keimos, omos aidao pulusin, / Os ch eteron men keuthei eni phresin, allo de bazei (*The Iliad*, Book 9, line 412 translated by Pope as 'Who dares think one thing, and another tell, My soul detests him as the gates of Hell').

[13] Samuel Johnson, 'Dedication', *Rambler* 136 (6 July 1751): 32, 31.

[14] Nathan Field, *A woman is a weather-cocke* (London, 1612), A3r.

[15] Thomas Gordon, *A dedication to a great man, concerning dedications* (London, 1718), A3v.

form, and place', for purchase at the eye-watering sum of fifty guineas. Such ironic commentaries expose the relationship between art and commerce: the intimate connection between writing for a reader and writing for reward. The words you are currently reading are, rest assured, written in expectation of no greater remuneration than a contributor copy of this handsome volume, and the gloss of association with a congerie of learned contributors (contents page as CV).

Think pieces abound on the art of acknowledgements. For some, they offer 'an all-too-rare view of the writer as actual human being... the only true thing amid a pack of lies'.[16] Such a trusting approach not only ignores the long tradition of the faux-dedication, where paratext translates into meta-fiction (perhaps most famously in Walter Scott's *Ivanhoe*, where 'Laurence Templeton' sets out in praise of 'Dr Dryasdust'); it also sets the acknowledgements page beyond the reach of rhetoric, suggesting that its purpose of recording debts is transparent. Others are more cynical: Sam Sacks bemoans the vogue for acknowledgements as a symptom of 'commercial rot', a version of 'the online pop-up ad... garrulously narcissistic and strewn with clichés'.[17]

For Terry Caesar, the acknowledgements page is a relentless leveller: 'Everything is all of a piece and everyone fits. Acknowledgements, in sum, constitute the consolingly *democratic* gesture whereby the book, no matter how scholarly, demonstrates its accountability as a social product.'[18] A particular effect is achieved through sarcasm or irony, modes in which acknowledgements and dedications 'serve both as releases and concealments', inviting the reader to look beyond the bare facts of the dedication to the vexed histories beneath.[19] That tradition is satirized to darkly comic effect in Paul Theroux's 'Acknowledgements' to his 1980 collection *World's End*, in which what seems at first a conventional record of obligations gradually reveals itself as a confession of murder. As Jan B. Gordon notes, the inclusion of biographical detail in acknowledgements, and the insistence on multiple debts, may be read, finally, less as an admission of collectivity and more as an assertion of authorial selfhood: 'used to bond coercively an identity between ownership and authenticity that had become severed'.[20]

It is tempting to use the dedication not to articulate debts but to repay grievances. Thanks to the University of York, my present employer, for giving me a job; no thanks for rejecting my undergraduate application all those years ago (it worked out

[16] Anna North, 'On Acknowledgements', *Paris Review*, 6 July 2011: https://www.theparisreview.org/blog/2011/07/06/on-acknowledgements/.

[17] Sam Sacks, 'Against Acknowledgements', *New Yorker*, 24 August 2012: https://www.newyorker.com/books/page-turner/against-acknowledgments.

[18] Terry Caesar, *Conspiring with Forms: Life in Academic Texts* (Athens, GA: University of Georgia Press, 2010), p. 34.

[19] Ben-Ari, 'On Acknowledgements in Ethnographies', p. 71.

[20] Jan B. Gordon, *Gossip and Subversion in Nineteenth-Century British Fiction: Echo's Economies* (Basingstoke: Macmillan, 1996), p. xii.

fine). In 1935, E. E. Cummings borrowed $300 from his mother, and arranged with the printer Samuel Jacobs to publish a book of poetry. Though his initial plan had been to title his book *70 Poems*, in the end he called it *No Thanks*: a two-word distillation of the response he had received from fourteen different publishers. Cummings' 'dedication' took the form of a concrete poem: the names of each publisher stacked to form the shape of a funeral urn.

NO

THANKS

TO

Farrar & Rinehart

Simon & Schuster

Coward-McCann

Limited Editions

Harcourt, Brace

Random House

Equinox Press

Smith & Haas

Viking Press

Knopf

Dutton

Harper's

Scribner's

Covici-Friede

Cummings' joke is a complex one: the publishing houses, gatekeepers of culture, become the cultural artefact, both poem and memorializing object.

Dedications and acknowledgements make the private public. My daughter Anna is two and has hindered the writing of this chapter in inventive, delightful, sleep-depriving style (back shortly). Few go as far as the palaeontologist who used the acknowledgements to an article in *Current Biology* to ask his girlfriend, 'Lorna, will you marry me?'[21] But late in life T. S. Eliot wrote a nakedly affectionate 'A dedication to my wife', a poem, rather than a dedication per se, which celebrates 'the rhythm that governs the repose of our sleeping / the breathing in unison'. Eliot ended the poem with an uneasy acknowledgement: 'But this dedication is for others to read: / These are private words addressed to you in public'. Does its conclusion undercut the intimacy of the poem's domestic reading? Or does it, unexpectedly, intensify it, offering Valerie Eliot the frisson of knowing herself the one, singular addressee amid a sea of readers (as special to the aging writer as you, kind reader, are to me)?

---

[21] Caleb M. Brown and Donald M. Henderson, 'A New Horned Dinosaur Reveals Convergent Evolution in Cranial Ornamentation in Ceratopsidae', *Current Biology* 25, no. 12 (2015): 1641–8. She appears to have accepted.

Perhaps it is more that dedications perform intimacy in private, over and again, initiating a series of book-bound exchanges, which cannot be fully imagined or delimited by the writer. (Mum, I really didn't think you'd read this.) How do authors negotiate the gap between the implied reader of the dedication—the dedicatee themselves, whether named in full, by first name only, by inside joke, or by teasing initials—and its 'real' readers: those who pick up the book and make it their own? Mark Danielewski's *House of Leaves* (2000) makes the problem explicit: its dedication reads 'This is not for you'. J. K. Rowling was more generous, offering a seventh portion of the dedication prefacing *Harry Potter and the Deathly Hallows* (2007) 'to you, if you have stuck with Harry to the very end'.[22]

The truly intimate dedication is the hand-written addition: of the *c.* thirty first editions of Arnold Bennett's works held at Keele University Library, nearly all carry a manuscript inscription from Bennett to his sister, Tertia. In 2012, the novelist Ann Patchett revealed her discomfort with acknowledgements as a genre, insisting that she prefers to give individual, signed copies to those who have supported her, not least in case a printed dedication becomes a haunting record of a failed friendship.[23] But in its modern form, a product of the post-Dickensian book signing, the author's signature becomes not a mark of special affection but a record of an encounter with literary celebrity; the text is authenticated by contact with its author. Some readers add further, bespoke dedications, repurposing books as gifts to forge or influence friendships, love affairs, and family dramas, and attempting to add a record of their discrimination, taste, affection, or influence permanently to the book.[24] The online catalogue description of one copy of Italo Calvino's postmodern romp, *If on a Winter's Night a Traveller*, notes as its 'only blemish' a 'penned dedication on front endpaper'.[25]

This record of my debts, mingled with a survey of others', is out of place. In a scholarly monograph, acknowledgements should (usually) be at the front; in a work of fiction they are tidied away at the back. Dedications have (nearly) always gone at the front. The placement is politic: in academic books, acknowledgements offer a means to publish the author's CV and boast of influential friends. Ben-Ari, a social anthropologist, reflects upon the practices of ethnographers who fulsomely thank the peoples they study, safe in the knowledge that those subjects will read neither their gesture nor their research. '[T]he formulation of acknowledgements,' he suggests, 'is related to strategic choices in careering, the management of relations in

[22] Both cited in David Barnett, 'Stories Told by Book Dedications', *Guardian*, 20 July 2011: https://www.theguardian.com/books/2011/jul/20/book-dedications.

[23] Henriette Lazaridis, 'The Story behind the Story: An Appreciation of Authors' Acknowledgements', *Millions*, 9 January 2012: https://themillions.com/2012/01/the-story-behind-the-story-an-appreciation-of-authors-acknowledgments.html.

[24] W. B. Gooderham has published a collection of dedications found in second-hand books as *Dedicated to...the Forgotten Friendships, Hidden Stories and Lost Loves Found in Second-Hand Books* (Ealing: Bantam Press, 2013).

[25] https://www.abebooks.co.uk/Winters-Night-Traveller-Calvino-Italo-Minerva/1834413177/bd.

the anthropological community, the construction of ethnographic credibility and authenticity, and the creation of images of anthropologists as social persons.'[26]

Acknowledgements and dedications are multidirectional, speaking inwards by illuminating questions of influence and construction, and outwards to readers real and imagined, as well as to the social world in which the text has been nourished (or malnourished) and brought forth. In fiction, in contrast, the relegation of debts to the closing pages forms part of the post-Romantic tradition of celebrating solitary genius: who, in a work of imagination, wants the illusion of mastery punctured by the gritty textures of scholarly research?[27]

Ben-Ari categorizes acknowledgements as 'lists or inventories...fixing or ordering devices for enumerating certain categories and subcategories'.[28] Such a definition occludes the narrative and persuasive functions of the dedication or acknowledgements, but is a fitting recognition of the prevalence of particular conventions or tropes: in modern books, the inclusion of particular groups, ranked, as Terry Caesar puts it, 'from general to personal'.[29] The modern acknowledgements page must include thanks to friends, family, and, for the fortunate, funders; in early modern England, key metaphors made frequent appearances, from the meagre gift to the foundling in need of protection, and the debilitating awareness of a debt too great to be repaid.

Perhaps the most peculiar convention is the claiming of errors as the author's own: a practice which, Caesar suggests, reacts against the collective ethos of the acknowledgements page.[30] It si only in solecism that the author can assert responsibility for the txet. This stands in contrast to the conventions of early print, in which errata lists point to the incompletion of the text, and authors and printers cheerfully and insistently blame one another for the mistakes of the book. John Taylor satirized this tradition in *Sir Gregory Nonsence*, insisting that 'if the Printer hath placed any line, letter or sillable, whereby this large volume may bee made guilty to bee vnderstood by any man, I would haue the Reader not to impute the fault to the Author, for it was farre from his purpose to write to any purpose' (A4v).

In the twentieth and twenty-first centuries, the vogue has been for dedications that imply sentiment (Banban, I love you more than anything); in the sixteenth and seventeenth, the fashion was primarily for dedications that conveyed prestige. Dedications, often lengthy and conventional, functioned, Arthur Marotti suggests, as '(misleading) signs of celebrity-endorsement', attempting to write into being a relationship between dedicator and dedicatee.[31] Some early modern writers were

---

[26] Ben-Ari, 'On Acknowledgements in Ethnographies', p. 63.

[27] See Jack Stillinger, *Multiple Authorship and the Myth of Scholarly Genius* (Oxford: Oxford University Press, 1991); for an egregious example see the author's note and acknowledgements to Hilary Mantel's *Wolf Hall* (2009).

[28] Ben-Ari, 'On Acknowledgements in Ethnographies', p. 65.

[29] Caesar, *Conspiring with Forms*, pp. 30–1.

[30] Caesar, *Conspiring with Forms*, p. 39.

[31] Arthur Marotti, 'Poetry, Patronage, and Print', *Yearbook of English Studies* 21 (1991): 2.

Marotti's equals in scepticism. Michael Drayton, addressing part of the 1599 edition of his *Englands heroicall epistles* 'to his worthy and dearly esteemed friend, Master James Huish', complained: 'I thinke some…put the names of great men in theyr bookes, for that men should say there was some thing good; onely because indeede theyr names stoode there'.[32] Gordon's *A Dedication to a Great Man* cheerfully acknowledges the artificiality of the enterprise: 'Your Lordship and I are not at all acquainted, I therefore take Leave to be very familiar with you' (A2r). He goes on:

> I have known an Author praise an Earl for twenty Pages together, tho' he knew nothing of him, but that he had Money to spare… This Practice being general, it is a very easy Matter to guess, by the Size of the Panegyrick, how wealthy the Patron may be, or how hungry the Author; if it exceeds three Pages, you may pawn all the Blood in your Body upon it, the Writer has fasted three Days; and that his Lordship, among all his other good Parts, has at least ten thousand Pounds a Year. (A2v)

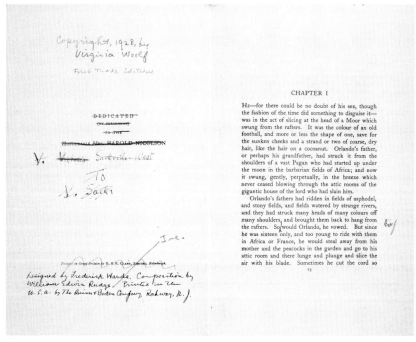

Fig. 8.2 *Virginia Woolf, 'Orlando': corrected page proofs, 9 June–22 July 1928. © The Society of Authors as the Literary Representative of the Estate of Virginia Woolf. Courtesy of the Mortimer Rare Book Collection, Smith College Special Collections*

[32] Michael Drayton, *Englands Heroicall Epistles* (London: J. Roberts for N. Ling, 1599), H3r.

It is hard to pinpoint the moment when the dedication shrank: Gérard Genette suggests it was a victim of its own expansion, becoming subsumed in the new genre of the introduction around the end of the nineteenth century.[33] Reduced in size, the dedication's function threatens to elide with that of the title page epigraph, a tag which signals the learning of the author (or perhaps the publisher), and claims an intellectual and creative debt. Perhaps it is a modernist phenomenon. 'To Ezra Pound,' wrote T. S. Eliot, at the beginning of *The Waste Land*, 'Il miglior fabbro' (the better craftsman). Virginia Woolf agonized over the wording of her dedication of the gender-swapping, period-hopping *Orlando*, before finally settling on, simply, 'V. Sackville West' (Fig. 8.2).

I could write much more on the subject of brevity, but I have already gone on too long. It remains only to apologize to those colleagues, friends, and slight acquaintances I have not mentioned, to attribute my mistakes to previous scholars and meddling editors, and to hope that under the wing of your protection this little chapter may find a home safe from the winds of criticism and accurate interpretation.

I typed it myself.[34]

---

[33] Gérard Genette, *Paratexts: Thresholds of Interpretation*, trans. Jane E. Lewin (Cambridge: Cambridge University Press, 1997), pp. 123–4.

[34] See the twitter hashtag, #ThanksForTyping.

CHAPTER 9

PRINTERS' ORNAMENTS AND FLOWERS

Hazel Wilkinson

The invention of moveable type made texts mechanically reproducible, but printing did not represent a clean break from scribal conventions: the elaborate borders, flourishes, and initial letters of illuminated manuscripts were transposed into print almost from its inception, as printers' ornaments. Ornamental designs were cut in relief into wood or metal, and inked to produce large head and tailpieces, while smaller blocks were used for initial letters, or to provide flourishes between sections. Alternatively, decorations could be achieved with ornamental type, known as printers' flowers, or fleurons. Set by the compositor like alphabetical type, but featuring abstract or simple figurative images instead of letters, fleurons could be used individually or worked up into complex patterns.

Before 1500, woodblock ornaments were more common in continental Europe than in Britain, though Theodoric Rood was producing print embellishments in Oxford from the beginning of the 1480s, and William Caxton began using woodcut borders in London in the 1490s.[1] The first decades of printing in Britain represent a transitional phase between manuscript and print, in which ornaments were read as the printed stand-ins for manual illuminations. Incunabula made for wealthy customers were often hybrids in which a printed text was sent to an illuminator to be hand coloured. The Morton Missal, printed in London by Richard Pynson in 1500, is regularly cited as 'the first artistic [printed] book produced in this country'.[2] It was an elaborate production, featuring extensive ornamentation, printed music, and rubrication throughout. Still, in some copies the printed initials and borders were taken as guides and painstakingly painted over in colour.[3] The following decades witnessed a surge in the use of ornaments in Britain, which Plomer attributes to the Reformation, since an unprecedented number of bibles and books of common prayer were printed, and embellishment was often deemed essential for sacred texts: to beautify the page was to pay homage to its contents.[4] With increased usage, ornaments developed a visual language of their own that distinguished them from their illuminated forebears. The ornaments used by Caxton's successor, Wynkyn de Worde (d. ca. 1534) are a good example. David Scott Kastan reports that only twenty of Caxton's books were decorated or illustrated in some way, compared to 500 of de

---

[1] Henry R. Plomer, *English Printers' Ornaments* (London: Grafton, 1924), p. 20.

[2] Plomer, *English Printers' Ornaments*, p. 20. On the Missal see Katja Airaksinen, 'The Morton Missal: The Finest Incunable Made in England', *Transactions of the Cambridge Bibliographical Society* 14 (2009): 147–79.

[3] The copy in Trinity College, Cambridge features such overpainting. See Airaksinen, 'The Morton Missal', pp. 163–4.

[4] Plomer, *English Printers' Ornaments*, pp. 22–3.

Worde's.[5] The latter's growing preference for ornaments is evident in the evolution of his printer's device, which he used to brand his publications. Early examples of de Worde's device, used ca. 1499, feature his name and Caxton's initials with some simple vines.[6] De Worde's devices went through various utilitarian iterations until around 1520, when he began using a device featuring a vaulted and frescoed arcade, with a view of a cityscape, and a night sky, along with cherubs and soldiers; de Worde's name was crammed into a small plinth (see Fig. 9.1).[7] The block's job as a device (to identify the printer) is all but eclipsed by its elegance and interest as an ornament. The change in his device corresponded with a more extensive use of ornament throughout de Worde's books: decoration had become part of his visual vocabulary.

Several of de Worde's blocks began life as illustrations cut for a specific text, only to be repurposed elsewhere with no particular relationship to content.[8] As with other types of images (see Chapter 16 of this volume), the recycling of custom-made ornaments continued into the Elizabethan period. In 1593, William Ponsonby had a border cut for the title page of Philip Sidney's *Arcadia*, featuring Sidney's heraldry and Arcadian characters. The border was later recruited for editions of Machiavelli (1595) and Spenser (1611), its specific allusions functioning more loosely as decoration. Evidently, printers were happy both to use blocks that stood out from the text, and to look for new parallels between contents and ornament stock. Perhaps inspired by the freedom with which ornaments were repurposed by early printers, seventeenth- and eighteenth-century blocks depicted all manner of things (Figs 9.2 and 9.3). Certain conventional images appear regularly (cherubs and angels, lions, birds, fruit), but the early eighteenth-century printer John Watts (fl. 1684–1755), for example, owned headpieces depicting such subjects as an artist sketching classical ruins, a fleet advancing on a harbour, an astronomer gazing through a telescope, a goatherd playing a pipe to his flock, and the birth of Venus. Elaborate and unconventional ornaments draw the eye away from the text and direct it to the very different imaginative world of the image, a world created by the engraver and compositor, not the author. The craftspeople who produced block ornaments in the handpress period are largely anonymous. Block ornaments were not normally included in printed type specimens, suggesting that their producers were probably independent craftspeople, rather than employees of foundries. Very precise copies were made of some popular designs,

[5] David Scott Kastan, 'Print, Literary Culture and the Book Trade', in *The Cambridge History of Early Modern English Literature*, ed. David Loewenstein and Janel Mueller (Cambridge: Cambridge University Press, 1999), pp. 81–116, 88.

[6] R. B. McKerrow, *Printers' and Publishers' Devices in England and Scotland 1485–1640* (London: Bibliographical Society, 1913), no. 11.

[7] McKerrow, *Printers' and Publishers' Devices*, no. 46a.

[8] Joseph A. Dane, *What Is a Book? The Study of Early Printed Books* (Notre Dame, IN: University of Notre Dame Press, 2012), p. 128.

❧ **Fig. 9.1** *Wynkyn de Worde's device, from 'The Cronycles of Englonde' (1528), by permission of the Special Collections and Archives, Cardiff University*

presumably by more than one hand, and these were used by multiple printers. Occasionally, artists incorporated their initials into ornamental blocks, potentially allowing them to be identified. John Watts used blocks featuring the initials of the engraver Elisha Kirkall (1682?–1742). The wealthy Watts could afford large sets of ornaments made by a reputable artist, and Kirkall evidently sold him ornaments in different sizes corresponding to various page formats, each in a coherent style. A less affluent printer, or one who was setting up shop might well have cut their own ornaments in house. The young Benjamin Franklin taught himself to cut type and engrave ornaments to make up for a lack of materials in Philadelphia in the 1720s, when type was still almost exclusively imported from Europe.[9] For woodcuts, strong and durable wood, such as box, pear, and apple, were favoured. Designs could also be cut into a type metal surface. Rather than use a thick metal block, the design could be engraved into a metal sheet and nailed to a woodblock to raise it to the same height as the type.

Fleurons were cast in type metal by the type founder and sold to the printer along with founts of alphabetical type, to which they corresponded in size. A foundry might produce specimen sheets suggesting possible arrangements of fleurons, but otherwise their design was left to the compositor. Unlike block ornaments, fleurons could be set within a line of text, and early printers sometimes used them to fill up a line at the end of a paragraph, mimicking the scribal practice of justifying short lines with flourishes.[10] Fleurons could be used individually, or arranged into complex head and tailpieces, borders, and embellishments around initial letters, consisting of upwards of scores of individual pieces of type. Since many popular designs were asymmetrical, their assembly required both care and creativity. From

❧ **Fig. 9.2** *An example of a headpiece from 'The Works of Beaumont and Fletcher' (London: J. and R. Tonson and S. Draper, 1750). Photographs from author's own copy*

[9] Benjamin Franklin, *Autobiography and Other Writings*, ed. Ormond Seavey (Oxford: Oxford University Press, 2008), p. 55. Franklin's ornaments can be consulted in C. William Miller, *Benjamin Franklin's Philadelphia Printing 1728–1766* (Philadelphia, PA: American Philosophical Society, 1974).

[10] This practice is employed in de Worde's 1507[?] edition of Nicholas Love's translation of St Bonaventure, *Meditationes Vitæ Christi* (ESTC S109702).

🌿 **Fig. 9.3** *An example of a tailpiece, from 'The Works of Beaumont and Fletcher' (London: J. and R. Tonson and S. Draper, 1750). Photographs from author's own copy*

their beginning, fleurons used a visual code that was already well established in a variety of media, from drawings to sculpture, architecture, lacework, and book bindings. Islamic geometric forms were familiar from the pattern sheets that circulated in late fifteenth-century Europe for use by scribes, embroiderers, and lace workers.[11] Gothic, Romanesque, and classical architectural details made their way first into illuminated manuscripts and later into books, via their bindings. Bookbinders cut arabesques, flowers, birds, and animals into brass stamps, which were heated and applied to the damp leather of the binding in elaborate arrangements, and left blind or filled with gold leaf. The fifteenth-century Venetian, Aldus Manutius (ca. 1452–1515), produced a vine-leaf design for his bindings, still known as the Aldine leaf, and the arabesques designed by the French printer Robert Granjon (1513–89) became particularly popular in Britain. Although abstract fleurons were generally preferred to figurative designs, a number of printers experimented with new images in later years. William Caslon produced skulls and hourglasses for use on elegiac literature in the eighteenth century; the Glaswegian typefounder Alexander Wilson

---

[11] For a fifteenth-century illuminator's manual see the facsimile of *The Göttingen Model Book*, ed. Hellmut Lehmann-Haupt (Columbia, MO: University of Missouri Press, 1972). A notable printed British example is Thomas Geminus, *Morysse and Damashin Renewed and Encreased* (London, 1548).

created typographical wasps, exhibited in a 1789 specimen of his type; and miniature soldiers were cut in Madrid in 1799.[12]

Juliet Fleming has investigated the ways in which fleurons signify care, labour, and skill beyond what is 'necessary' for the transmission of the text.[13] Fleming uses the example of early English prayer books, in which every page was surrounded by a frame of elaborate type ornaments:

> These frames were so commonly used for prayer books as to function almost as a generic marker for them—to own such a book is already to move towards prayer; you might say that the ornament marks an intention to pray, or even (what might be much the same thing), that it is a prayer itself.[14]

John Conway's *Meditations and Praiers* (1569) is one book in which fleurons 'so dominate the text as to raise the question, not easily answered, as to whether they are part of the work or extraneous to it'.[15] The skilled labour behind the print process is easily forgotten when reading becomes immersive. Like the unconventional blocks discussed above, fleurons refocus the reader's attention on the *mise-en-page*, on the creative use of ink and white space. Sixteenth- and early seventeenth-century printers used fleurons exuberantly, but by the 1680s Joseph Moxon was declaring them 'now accounted old-fashion, and therefore much out of use' in his printing manual.[16] If their usage had somewhat declined during the seventeenth century, it may have been symptomatic of the state of English typography: the Star Chamber decree of 1637 and the Licensing Order of 1643 limited the number of English type foundries to four, so most type used by London presses was imported from the Netherlands, or cast in London in Dutch matrices. However, the lapse of the Licensing Order in 1694 breathed new life into English typefounding, and notably Caslon cut new fleurons, modelled on continental styles, which grew steadily in popularity. Caslon's early specimen sheets in the 1720s featured only a few rows of flowers, but his 1764 specimen featured four pages of ornamental type. By the mid-century, Samuel Richardson was making memorable use of Caslon's fleurons in *Clarissa* (1748; Fig. 9.4), where they mark narrative time and space.[17] He not only

[12] William Caslon, *A Specimen of Printing Types* (London: Dryden Leach, 1764); Alexander Wilson, *A Specimen of Printing Types* (Glasgow, 1789); *Muestras de los punzones y matrices de la letra que se funde en el obrador de la Imprenta Real* (Madrid, 1799).

[13] Ornaments occasionally have a practical purpose: a tailpiece could physically support a large blank area of paper in the press, or a border might (Fleming points out) 'protect the text as the edges of [a] tiny book get worn away in use'. *Cultural Graphology: Writing after Derrida* (Chicago, IL: University of Chicago Press, 2016), p. 75.

[14] Fleming, *Cultural Graphology*, p. 75.

[15] Fleming, *Cultural Graphology*, p. 75.

[16] Joseph Moxon, *Mechanick Exercises on the Whole Art of Printing (1683–84)*, ed. Herbert Davis and Harry Carter (Oxford: Oxford University Press, 1958), p. 24.

[17] On Richardson's creative use of fleurons see Anne C. Henry, 'The Re-mark-able Rise of '…': Reading Ellipsis Marks in Literary Texts', in *Ma(r)king the Text: The Presentation of Meaning on the Literary Page*, ed. Joe

Let. 58.   Clariſſa Harlowe.   363

When I parted with my Charmer (which I did, with infinite reluctance, half an hour ago) it was up-on her promiſe, that ſhe would not ſit up to write or read. For ſo engaging was the converſation to me (and indeed my behaviour throughout the whole of it was confeſſedly agreeable to her) that I inſiſted, if ſhe did not directly retire to reſt, that ſhe ſhould add another happy hour to the former.

To have ſat up writing or reading half the night, as ſhe ſometimes does, would have fruſtrated my view, as thou wilt obſerve, when my little plot un-ravels.

* * * *

WHAT—What—What now !—Bounding villain ! wouldſt thou choak me !—

I was ſpeaking to my heart, Jack !—It was then at my throat.—And what is all this for ?—Theſe ſhy women, how, when a man thinks himſelf near the mark, do they *tempeſt* him !

* * * *

Is all ready, Dorcas ? Has my Beloved kept her word with me ?—Whether are theſe billowy heavings owing more to Love or to Fear ? I cannot tell for the ſoul of me, of which I have moſt. If I can but take her before her apprehenſion, before her elo-quence, is awake—

Limbs, why thus convulſed ?—Knees, till now ſo firmly knit, why thus relaxed ? Why beat ye thus together ? Will not theſe trembling fingers, which twice have refuſed to direct the pen, fail me in the arduous moment ?

Once again, Why and for what all theſe convul-ſions ? This project is not to end in *Matrimony,* ſurely !

But the conſequences muſt be greater than I had thought of till this moment—My Beloved's deſtiny or my own may depend upon the iſſue of the two next hours !

R 2   I will

❧ **Fig. 9.4** *Fleurons in Richardson's 'Clarissa', 3rd edn (London: for S. Richardson, 1751), vol. 4, p. 363. Reproduced by kind permission of the Syndics of Cambridge University Library. Shelfmark: S727.d.75.25*

used them to signal interruptions and breaks in the narrative, he assigned characters their own particular fleurons, allowing the decorative marks to take on personalities; disturbingly, Lovelace's fleurons invade Clarissa's letters as he gains control over her.[18] As a printer-author, Richardson was uniquely placed to exploit the creative opportunities of fleurons. In most printed texts, fleurons and ornaments are non-authorial, though this is not always the case: Alexander Pope, for example, issued instructions to his printer on the placement of ornaments.[19]

For all the narrative work that Richardson's fleurons do, Janine Barchas points out that they ultimately exist outside the epistolary fiction (we are not supposed to imagine that they were made by the letter writer): 'the printer's ornament remains an articulation of the printing press, a conventional feature of book production which designates the text in which it appears as a public novel, not a private letter'.[20] Ornaments no longer functioned as printed stand-ins for manuscript illuminations, but had instead become 'an articulation of the printing press' which conferred 'public' status on a text. As if in confirmation of this, several eighteenth-century printers used ornaments that explicitly celebrated the art of printing. A favourite tailpiece of Samuel Palmer's depicted the interior of a printing office; William Bowyer had a tailpiece designed to commemorate the fire that destroyed his premises in 1712; and numerous printers used ornaments celebrating Gutenberg and Caxton. A common image in seventeenth- and eighteenth-century block ornaments is the printed book, either closed with a decorative binding, or open with miniature ornaments on its pages. A clear change is evident between the fifteenth and the mid-eighteenth centuries: whereas in the earlier period ornaments were conceived as a way of imitating manuscript, two centuries later they were conceptualized as part of the particular visual identity of the printed book, inside and out.

As evidence of work and craftsmanship, both fleurons and block ornaments are useful to the bibliographer in determining the provenance of printed material. In the printing office, fleurons were not stored in the compositors' type cases along with alphabetical type. Fleurons would typically have been kept in a draw below the imposing stone, where the components of the page were assembled before inking. Because complex designs in fleurons took time to arrange, compositors sometimes kept an arrangement standing when the other components of the page were taken apart to be reset. Hence a single arrangement might appear multiple times in a book, particularly if (as was often the case) more than one work was being printed

---

Bray, Miriam Handley, and Anne C. Henry (Aldershot: Ashgate, 2000), pp. 120–43, 131; Janine Barchas, *Graphic Design, Print Culture, and the Eighteenth-Century Novel* (Cambridge: Cambridge University Press, 2003), p. 257; Anne Toner, *Ellipsis in English Literature: Signs of Omission* (Cambridge: Cambridge University Press, 2015), pp. 67–76.

[18] Toner, *Ellipsis*, p. 76.

[19] See James McLaverty, *Pope, Print, and Meaning* (Oxford: Oxford University Press, 2001), p. 61.

[20] Barchas, *Graphic Design*, p. 133.

simultaneously. If an identifiable arrangement of fleurons appears in two books, and one has a known printer (because they are identified on the title page, or in other documentary evidence), we can be certain that the same printer was responsible for both books.[21]

Whereas an arrangement of fleurons had a short lifespan, block ornaments were durable and could remain in a printer's possession for decades. A unique hand-cut ornament, or a uniquely damaged or worn cast, can also allow us to identify the printer of a book. Since printers are known to have lent each other blocks, a single appearance in an unattributed book of an ornament owned by a known printer is not entirely solid ground for an identification, but where several examples can be found a persuasive portfolio of evidence can be built.[22] Wear and tear to the block can make the impression more distinctive, and more useful as evidence. With repeated use both wood and metal wore down, and wood was liable to warp and crack. When the raised surface of a metalcut wore down, the nails used to fix it to the supporting woodblock could become visible in the printed impression. This reveals that the block was metal, and the appearance of nails can help to distinguish between copies or casts. A sign that an impression was made from a woodblock is the presence of wormholes (actually made by burrowing beetles). Successive appearances of new wormholes in ornaments can be used to determine in which order undated items were printed. In a neat encounter between bibliography and biology, it has been shown that wormholes can also be used to determine whether a book was printed in northern or southern Europe, thanks to the different sizes of southern and northern European beetles.[23]

The printer Philip Luckombe declared in 1770 that ornamental type had reached an apogee, thanks to recent innovative designs, which enabled printers 'to make flower-pieces of oval, circularly, and angularly turns, instead of having hitherto been confined either to square or to circular flowers'.[24] But Luckombe 'feared, that head-pieces, fac[totum]s, and tailpieces of flowers will not long continue…considering that the contriving and making them up, is attended with considerable trouble and loss of time'.[25] This was a prescient warning: changes to copyright law in 1774 ended the London booksellers' longstanding monopoly on reprints of British classics, which led to a sharp increase in printing activity within and outside London. On the newly competitive market cheap books became available to new audiences, but rapid production schedules, coupled with a drive to capitalize on resources by using small

[21] Hazel Wilkinson, 'Printers' Flowers as Evidence in the Identification of Unknown Printers: Two Examples from 1715', *The Library* 7, no. 14 (2013): 70–9.

[22] On this method of identification see the works of Keith Maslen, particularly *Samuel Richardson of London, Printer* (Otago: University of Otago Press, 2001).

[23] S. Blair Hedges, 'Wormholes Record Species History in Space and Time', *Biology Letters* 9 (2013).

[24] Philip Luckombe, *History of the Origin and Progress of Printing* (London, 1770), p. 289.

[25] Luckombe, *History*, p. 289.

type and narrow margins, meant there was little time or space for ornaments in books in the new style. Furthermore, while upmarket illustrated books retained a place in the industry, advances in the engraving arts, famously led by John Bewick (1753–1828), caused traditional ornaments to appear crude by comparison.

In books produced on machine presses from the nineteenth century, ornaments did not retain the cross-genre popularity which they had enjoyed in the hand-press period. An ever increasing number of books were produced with little or no orna-mentation, and although initial letters and borders survived and flourished in certain Regency and Victorian publications, reduced costs of production meant it was now practical to commission custom-made illustrative vignettes, which no longer had to be recycled as ornaments in order to prove cost-effective, as they had been in the Renaissance.[26] This was epitomized in the 1835 Paris edition of Alain-René Lesage's *Gil Blas*, for which the illustrator Jean Gigoux designed 850 vignettes inspired by the text, which were engraved by an army of low-paid workers. The vignettes were printed alongside the text, often in the positions traditionally occupied by ornaments. The result is an impressive and 'almost continuous combination of text and image'.[27] Some non-illustrative initial letters and head and tailpieces were used, but the pref-erence was clearly for a more specific relationship between image and text than ornaments traditionally allowed. Fleurons continued to be cast and used, even if they were no longer employed as extensively in the mainstream book trade as they had been a century earlier. New methods of casting and making matrices resulted in finer and more intricate details.[28] This allowed more delicate figurative designs to be pro-duced, setting nineteenth-century fleurons apart from their more predominantly abstract forebears. Novel designs reflected changing technologies by depicting ships and trains, and advances in the study of the natural world showed their influence in fleurons depicting fish, birds, and animals.[29]

From the nineteenth century to the present, block and type ornaments have continued to be a staple of small or private handpresses. Letterpress printers were invited to submit specimens of their type compositions for the *Printers' International Specimen Exchange*, published annually between 1880 and 1898. The specimens encouraged a new interest in historical fleurons and ornaments, which was fuelled by the establishment of the Monotype Corporation Philadelphia in 1887; a branch was opened in London in 1897, followed by a factory in Surrey in 1899.

---

[26] For samples of Victorian frames and initials see Carol Belanger Grafton (ed.), *Pictorial Archive of Printer's Ornaments from the Renaissance to the 20th Century* (New York: Dover, 1980). For more samples of Victorian ornaments see Zeese and Company's *Specimens of Electrotypes* (1885), and H. H. Green's *Specimens of Printing Types* (1852).

[27] John Buchanan-Brown, *Early Victorian Illustrated Books* (London: British Library; New Castle, DE: Oak Knoll, 2005), p. 17.

[28] Mark Arman, *Fleurons: Their Place in History and in Print* (Thaxted: Workshop, 1988), p. 23.

[29] John Ryder, *Flowers and Flourishes* (London: Bodley Head, 1976), p. 10.

The Monotype Corporation pioneered a method of producing fine books using hot-metal typesetting, for which they commissioned new typefaces which would characterize twentieth-century printing. In the 1920s Stanley Morison was appointed typographical advisor to the corporation. Morison was the editor of *Fleuron* a journal of historical typography, and under his influence the Monotype Corporation recast an array of early modern typefaces.[30] Another champion of the fleuron in the early twentieth century was the Curwen Press. Originally founded in 1863 as a music printer in Plaistow, east London, by the 1920s the Curwen Press was printing a huge variety of material, and advocating the creative use of new, rather than historically inspired, fleurons and ornaments. They employed artists such as Lovat Fraser, Albert Rutherston, Percy Smith, and Randolph Schwabe to cut ornaments in art deco and art nouveau styles, for the press's exclusive use. Curwen's distinctive three-colour borders of fleurons were seen publicly as well as in limited-edition books: a contract with British Rail, for example, led to the production of elaborately ornamented menus for station restaurants across Britain. Beyond Curwen, the typographer David Bethel produced the first new post-war fleurons in 1957, as part of his typeface called Glint (Plate 5). This became popular enough to inspire the foundation of a Glint Club in Antwerp, members of which played the 'Glint Game' by competing to find new arrangements of the typeface's fleurons. Beatrice Ward, historian of typography and an employee of the Monotype Corporation, was an enthusiastic advocate of Glint, and she produced at least seventy-five unique monochrome arrangements with Bethel's fleurons before moving on to two colours.[31] Ward wrote of the Glint fleurons that 'they coalesce under your eyes into much larger and more spectacular ornaments', and for the art of arranging them she used the phrase 'the grammar of ornament'.[32] The Glint fleurons are still in use; the reader interested in contemporary ornament usage might consult the collection of Shakespeare's sonnets produced in 2016 for the Bodleian Library on 154 small presses worldwide, many of which are beautifully decorated in traditional and contemporary styles.[33]

There is still much to learn about the grammar of ornament. New interest in the social history of reading and the materiality of the text has led a slowly increasing number of editors to wonder, with Juliet Fleming, whether ornaments 'are part of the work or extraneous to it'. Henry Woudhuysen and Katherine Duncan-Jones provide a rare discussion of their copytexts' fleurons in their edition of Shakespeare's poems, and more recently Christopher Ricks and Jim McCue have reproduced images of

[30] Frederic Warde, *A Book of Monotype Ornaments* (London: Lanston Monotype Corporation, 1928).

[31] See David Bethel, 'Creating Printers' Flowers', in *Type and Typography: Highlights from Matrix* (West New York, NJ: Mark Batty, 2003), pp. 256–67, 216.

[32] Beatrice Ward, quoted in Bethel, 'Creating Printers' Flowers', p. 261.

[33] Bodleian Library, shelf mark Rec. a.36.

ornaments used in an occasional poem by T. S. Eliot.[34] Many canonical texts were elaborately ornamented in their early incarnations, and if modern critical editions can thoughtfully account for this fact, we may find that the grammar of ornament articulates itself in new ways, and leads us to a heightened understanding of texts, and their early reception.

[34] *Shakespeare's Poems*, ed. Katherine Duncan-Jones and H. R. Woudhuysen (London: Arden, 2007), p. 502; *The Poems of T. S. Eliot*, ed. Christopher Ricks and Jim McCue (London: Faber, 2015), p. 313.

CHAPTER 10
CHARACTER LISTS

Tamara Atkin *the author of this chapter*

Since the publication of her first romantic novel, *Riders* back in 1985, each of Jilly Cooper's Rutshire novels has been prefaced with a list of characters. With each new offering, these lists have grown longer and more complicated, so that her most recent—*Mount!* (2016)—occupies a full eleven pages and includes not only the main human characters but also all of their well-loved pets. It is here that we first meet 'Paris Alvaston Dora Belvdon's boyfriend. Ice-cool Adonis simultaneously reading Classics at Cambridge and forging a highly successful acting career', 'Marketa A gorgeous, voluble, volatile, voluptuous Penscombe stable lass from the Czech Republic who adores horses and the opposite sex', and 'Mr Wang (Zixin) A Corrupt Chinese mafia warlord who is cruelly colonizing Africa. Also sexual predator known as "The Great Willy of China"'. In the words of one affectionate reviewer, 'No other writer could get away' with such an extensive cast list.[1] But in a novel of some 650 pages, it serves a very real function. By acting as a gateway to Cooper's fantasy landscape of over-sexed horse-riding toffs, it helps the reader keep tabs on a seemingly endless cast of characters. At the same time, it performs another, subtler function: to make the text legible as belonging to Cooper's Rutshire Chronicles series. Like the title (a single, exclamative word), title page design (created using a restricted but symbolic palette of gold, red, black, and white), and illustration (all tight jodhpurs and whips; what might best be characterized as 'equestrian sexy'), the character list in *Mount!* self-consciously echoes the layout and tone of Cooper's earlier novels. For Simon and Schuster, her English publishers, these iterable elements offer a way to market the book, reassuring a loyal readership that this is a novel like all her others: populated with its cast of bed-hopping horse whisperers, peppered with cringe-worthy puns, *Mount!* is designed—in all senses of the word—to attract readers susceptible to the charms of Cooper's particular brand of nostalgic wish fulfilment.

Character lists are not indigenous to novels, and their primary association—even today—remains with the category of text for which they were invented: drama. The purpose of this chapter is to explore their origins as a print innovation for the articulation English vernacular of drama at the beginning of the sixteenth century, and then to trace their subsequent use in prefacing other kinds of texts, both in the early modern period and beyond. To date no fewer than three separate articles have attempted quantitative overviews of the history and development of the dramatic character list in the early modern period.[2] Suggesting that the changing form of such lists

---

[1] Jenny Colgan, '*Mount!* by Jilly Cooper review—daft, boozy joy', *Guardian*, 15 September 2016: https://www.theguardian.com/books/2016/sep/15/mount-by-jilly-cooper-review.

[2] See Gary Taylor; 'The Order of Persons', in *Thomas Middleton and Early Modern Textual Culture: A Companion to the Collected Works*, ed. Gary Taylor and John Lavagnino (Oxford: Oxford University Press, 2007), pp. 31–79;

illustrates the transformation of playbooks from practical manuals for players to valued objects designed for private study, these essays contribute to bigger arguments about British drama's achievement of literary status at some point in the late sixteenth or early seventeenth century. This chapter does not attempt anything similar, but is nonetheless concentrated on early printed dramatic character lists. The reasons for this focus are two-fold. First, character lists are, by and large, a print innovation. Though there are some anomalous manuscript examples that predate their appearance in print, their regular appearance in early printed English playbooks is a testament to the invention of stationers in developing strategies for making drama legible as a distinct category of text. Comparing pre-print examples with those developed by early printers, I seek to problematize the view that early printed character lists functioned to facilitate performance, and instead suggest their primary function was to help articulate the form of drama as a print commodity. In this regard, it is helpful to acknowledge that while character lists would eventually develop in ways that made them useful to authors—and here Cooper is a prime example—for much of their early history they were editorial in design and function. While the attribution of unsigned paratextual material remains notoriously tricky, where there is evidence of authorial involvement—as there is for the three 1547/8 editions of John Bale's plays—it tends to suggest investment (in all senses of the word) in the success of the play as book.[3] Early printed character lists should therefore be understood as contributing to the conventions adopted for marketing drama for leisure-time reading and other uses. Second, though character lists began as a dramatic paratext, they very quickly had an impact on the print expression of other categories of text: first dialogues, but eventually novels and other fictional writing. This chapter therefore moves from a consideration of the origins of early character lists in script and print, to demonstrate their subsequent impact on the presentation of other texts of all kinds.

DRAMATIC CHARACTER LISTS BEFORE PRINT

English vernacular plays first appeared in print in the 1510s and 1520s, and by the middle of the century the inclusion of a prefatory character list had become the norm. Following the opening of London's commercial theatres in the 1570s the practice fell out of favour for a time, but by 1630 the inclusion of a list of characters was

Tamara Atkin and Emma Smith, 'The Form and Function of Character Lists in Plays Printed before the Closing of the Theatres', *Review of English Studies* 65 (2014): 647–72; and Matteo Pangallo, '"I will keep and character that name": Dramatis Personae Lists in Early Modern Manuscript Plays', *Early Theatre* 18 (2015): 87–118.

[3] On Bale's involvement in the publication of his plays and other works, see the third chapter of my book *Reading Drama in Tudor England* (London: Routledge, 2018), pp. 101–44.

once again standard.[4] In the earliest decades of their appearance in print, the title page was the preferred location; a presentational decision explained by the fact that early printed books were sold uncut (making most 'openings' unavailable to browsers of quarto and smaller-format books) that in turn suggests such information may have been regarded as part of a playbook's vendibility. In time, however, character lists were supplanted from the title page by other kinds of information—about acting companies and the theatres with which they were associated—and moved to alternative prefatory positions, typically the verso of the title page. So while Randall McLeod has tasked modern editors, especially those of Shakespeare's plays, with insinuating 'the dramatis-personae list...between the title page and the opening of Act 1, Scene 1', this was already the preferred position in most early modern editions printed after 1576.[5] In short, if you bought a printed playbook in 1550, you would almost always find a title page character list; if you bought one after 1630 you would more likely than not find one among its first pages.

The adoption of a prefatory character list as a customary dramatic paratext was swift by any standards, but is all the more striking in the context of earlier manuscript conventions for the presentation of both vernacular and classical plays. Only two medieval English dramatic manuscripts contain character lists—the Macro manuscript copies of *Wisdom* (copied late fifteenth century) and *The Castle of Perseverance* (copied mid-fifteenth century)—and these are presentationally distinct from those associated with printed drama.[6] For instance, the list of 'xxxvj ludentium' that accompanies the sole witness to the morality play *The Castle of Perseverance* occurs after the text of the play (on f. 191r), and lists each of the characters continuously rather than as separate entries. Modern editors of the play have tended to obscure these features, presenting the character list in ways that conform with conventions in fact invented by early printers of vernacular drama: in David Klausner's 2010 TEAMS edition the list has been moved to the front of the volume and divided into separate entries. In its original manuscript context, the list for *The Castle of Perseverance* shares more with contemporary conventions for the presentation of stage directions than those that dictated the subsequent arrangement of printed character lists (Fig. 10.1).

Given in Latin as a series of imperative phrases ('Hec sunt nomina ludentium / In primus ij vexillators. Mundus et cum eo voluptas stulticia et garcio' ('Here are the names of the players/First, two flagbearers. The World, and with him Pleasure, Folly,

---

[4] The link between the displacement of character lists from playbooks and the rise of commercial acting companies with fixed London theatres is considered in Taylor, 'Order', pp. 58–60.

[5] Random Cloud, '"The very names of the Persons": Editing and the Invention of Dramatick Character', in *Staging the Renaissance: Reinterpretations of Elizabethan and Jacobean Drama*, ed. David Scott Kastan and Peter Stallybrass (New York: Routledge, 1991), pp. 88–96, 95.

[6] *Wisdom* (Washington, DC, Folger, MS V.a.354, ff. 98r–121v), f. 121r; *The Castle of Perseverance* (Washington, DC, Folger MS V.a.354, ff. 154r–191v), f. 191r. There is no character list in the surviving Digby fragment of *Wisdom* (Oxford, Bodleian Library, MS Digby 133, ff. 158r–169v). I exclude from this count medieval plays that survive in post-medieval manuscripts.

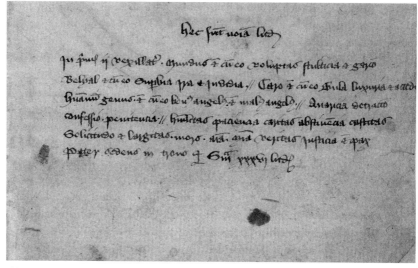

❧ **Fig. 10.1** *Character list on the final recto of 'The Castle of Perseverance' (Washington, DC, Folger MS V.a.354, ff. 154r–191v), f. 191r. Reproduced with the kind permission of the Folger Shakespeare Library, Washington, DC*

and a Servant, etc.'), it is quite unlike anything to occur in print.[7] And, as Pamela King has noted, with its cast of characters listed 'not purely by precedence but also by allegiance', it is clearly designed to function in tandem with the famous set diagram that occurs on the verso of the same folio, 'giving the reader further assistance with the play's essentially schematic meaning, where spatial relationships . . . are given clear moral value'.[8] Neither quite a record of past performance nor an aid for future performance, *The Castle*'s manuscript is indicative of the kinds of transformations all plays undertake when remediated as material books made of paper and ink. Its character list, while different to later print examples, represents a compelling early experiment in the articulation of drama as a textual form.

Like medieval vernacular dramatic manuscripts, character lists do not seem to have been a regular feature of manuscript or incunable witnesses to classical drama. And their inclusion in later print editions of classical plays may have been prompted by their earlier use for translations of Senecan drama rather than vice versa. The character list on sig. A3[v] of a 1589 London edition of Seneca in Latin (STC 22217), for instance, clearly follows the form and layout of those adopted for earlier editions of Seneca in translation, including both the stand-alone editions of

[7] In the early 1530s the printer John Rastell experimented with a back position in two playbooks, but in all other early modern playbooks printed before, during, and after the playhouse era (1576–1642), a front position is favoured. Latin is used only infrequently, and typically only for translations of classical plays; one notable exception is the character list on the verso of the title page of John Bale's *Three Laws* ([1548?], STC 1287). These features are therefore rarely adopted and never converge in print.

[8] Pamela M. King, 'Morality Plays', in *The Cambridge Companion to Medieval English Theatre*, ed. Richard Beadle (Cambridge: Cambridge University Press, 1994), pp. 240–64, 247.

the 1560s and the subsequent 1581 collected edition (STC 22228). What some early classical manuscripts *do* have, however, are illuminated *aediculae* (tabernacle frames) of masks. The three earliest illuminated manuscripts of Terence, for instance, all adopt this structural framing device and include an initial *aedicula* ostensibly depicting the characters in order of appearance.[9] It is even possible that this manuscript convention influenced the early print articulation of English vernacular drama, since the use of woodcut figures on some early printed dramatic title pages seem to have served a very similar function. In *Jack Juggler*, an anonymous mid-century interlude often attributed to the schoolmaster Nicholas Udall, a more conventional printed list of 'The Players names' is accompanied by woodcut images of three of the characters, each of which is identified by name on an adjacent banderole (a ribbon like scroll): 'Iak iugler', 'M. boūgrace', and 'Dame coye' (Fig. 10.2). All three of these woodcuts are factotums, generic stock images that had long lives prior to their appearance on the title page to *Jack Juggler*. And in the case of the woodcut used to represent 'M. boūgrace', a lineage can be traced going back as far as Antoine Vérard's 1503 edition of *Therence en françois*, in which a version of the same cut is used to represent both Pamphile in *Andria* and Cherea in *Eunnuchus*.[10] Its deployment on the title page to this mid-Tudor interlude therefore creates a visual analogy for the debt the play owes to classical drama; *Jack Juggler* is based on Plautus's *Amphitryon*.

DRAMATIC CHARACTER LISTS AND THE PRINT ARTICULATION OF DRAMA

As I suggested at the opening of this chapter, printed character lists have often been taken as an indicator of a play's receptive horizons, and are frequently adduced to further arguments about the emergence of drama as a literary genre around the turn of the seventeenth century. As far as the earliest playbooks are concerned, the coincidence of title page character lists with instructions for the division of roles ('Foure men may well and easelye playe thys Interlude') has tended to support the view that mid-Tudor drama was only rarely intended for leisure-time reading.[11] 'Every buyer,' Matteo Pangallo has argued, 'was a potential amateur player, and the potential amateur players were most likely the primary targets of early London play publishers.'[12] In contrast, he has suggested that with the rise of the professional theatres character lists were inflected to attract different kinds of users, silent readers who imagined a fictionalized performance or memorialized one that had already taken place.

---

[9] J. R. Green, *Theatre in Ancient Greek Society* (London: Routledge, 1994), p. 163.

[10] The use of this particular woodcut in English books of all kinds is discussed extensively (though not exhaustively) in Martha Driver, *The Image in Print: Book Illustration in Late Medieval England and Its Sources* (London: British Library, 2004), pp. 55–67.

[11] This example is taken from *Impatient Poverty* (1560, STC 14112.5), title page.

[12] Pangallo, 'Dramatis Personae', p. 95.

❧ **Fig. 10.2** *Title page to 'Jack Juggler' ([1562?], STC 14837). Rosenbach Museum and Library, El1. Aja. Reproduced courtesy of the Rosenbach Museum and Library, Philadelphia, PA*

The history of the development of the character list, from a document aimed at creating a performance to a document aimed at imagining either a fiction or a past performance, is therefore the history of the transformation of the play-reading public itself, from one of potential amateur producers to one of almost entirely consumers.[13]

But precisely how useful were early printed character lists to the players construed as their primary users? While some early lists do provide information useful for the mounting of productions—for example, the costuming notes that are given in both editions of *Three Laws* ([1548?]; 1562, STC 1288) and on the title page to *Jacob and Esau* (1568, STC 14327)—more often the advice is generic, unlikely to be of any real use to a group of would-be actors. Take for instance the title page to *Lusty Juventus* ([*c.* 1565], STC 25149; [*c.* 1565], STC 25159.5), which announces 'Foure may play it easely, takyng such par/ tes as they thinke best: so that any one tak / of those partes that be not in place at once'. More than one critic has read this account of theatrical exigencies as evidence that amateur actors were the intended market; presumably, professional actors would not have required an explanation of the mechanics of doubling.[14] But lacking specific instructions for the division of roles, this note—which reoccurs on the title pages to the two subsequent editions ([*c.* 1565], STC 25149, [*c.* 1565, STC 25149.5)—posits the conditions for any putative future production in rather vague terms; nine roles, four actors, but who plays whom and when?[15] Such questions are still more pertinent when asked of plays like *Wealth and Health* ([1565?], STC 14110) and *Common Conditions* (1576, STC 5592), which provide unworkable doubling schemes; both plays require more actors than the number specified in their character lists. When drama first began to be printed—and here it is worth remembering that playbooks made up a tiny percentage of a book trade that was small by European standards—printers experimented with ways of articulating its forms, rendering it distinct from but similar to other, related categories of text. Indeed, the proximity of plays to other types of text could often afford certain opportunities; labelling *Everyman* (printed four times between 1518 and 1534) as 'a treatyse ... in maner of a morall playe' was presumably a way of extending markets to include readers of treatises as well as those of plays *and* to suggest that the ways of reading the former might also extend to the latter. But the inclusion of doubling instructions marks a tendency in the opposite direction: rather than reading by way of analogy with other related genres, the co-incidence of character lists with doubling instructions suggests that printers had begun to develop ways of making

[13] Pangallo, 'Dramatis Personae', p. 98.

[14] Jane Griffiths, 'Lusty Juventus', in *The Oxford Handbook of Tudor Drama*, ed. Thomas Betteridge and Greg Walker (Oxford: Oxford University Press, 2012), pp. 262–75, 270; Pangallo, 'Dramatis Personae', p. 95.

[15] Other, roughly contemporary lists provide more detailed instructions for the division of roles. I discuss these in my article '"The Personages that Speake": Playing with Parts in Early Printed Drama', *Medieval English Theatre* 36 (2014): 48–69, esp. 51–4.

drama readily and distinctly identifiable as a printed form. It is this, rather than their intended use as performance aids, that perhaps explains the prevalence of character lists on the title pages of England's earliest printed plays.

In time, as conventions for the use of character lists in making drama and the dramatic legible crystalized, character lists could be used not only to signal the play qua play, but also to distinguish between different dramatic genres. A good example is the list prepended to the second edition of *The Knight of the Burning Pestle* (1635, STC 1675). Since the list is absent in the first edition, Gary Taylor has speculated that it must have originated with the printer (Nicholas Okes) or publisher (John Spencer), a conclusion that seems justified given that the play's authors, Francis Beaumont and John Fletcher had been dead some years when the edition was published.[16] The list is presented on sig. [A]4v under the sober heading 'The Speakers Names'. No fewer than fifty-eight dramatic character lists printed through 1642 adopt similar titles, but overwhelmingly the heading is associated with a specific cluster of related play-types as identified by *The Annals of English Drama*: closet translation, Inns of Court, occasional, and university. In other words, it tends to be used for character lists associated with plays that were not intended for performance on London's public stages. *The Knight of the Burning Pestle*, which is described on its title page 'Acted by Her Majesties Servants / at the Private house in *Drury lane*', is not therefore the kind of play typically associated with headings of this kind. By using a title more typically associated with closet drama, the play's stationers have clearly inflected their character list in ways that allow it to partake in the kind of generic travesty that is a defining feature of Beaumont and Fletcher's play. Paradoxically then, it is the inappropriateness of 'Speakers' as a title for this list that makes it especially well suited to the play.

The Knight of the Burning Pestle's list is idiosyncratic in other ways too. It begins by listing characters in order of appearance:

> The Prologue
> Then a Cittizen
> The Cittizens wife, and
> *Raph* her man, sitting be-
> low amidst the Specta-
> tors.

The list's temporal sequencing is made explicit by the conjunctive adverb 'then' so that the Citizen's entry onto the list is construed as a textual and typographic analogy for his entry onto the stage. But the list spatializes relations too; Raph is not given a separate entry and is instead listed after the Citizen's Wife, on a separate line, as 'her man'. 'Below' her both on the list and in the opening positions it invokes, his

---

[16] Taylor, 'Order', 61.

entry doubly confirms his status as her social inferior. In this respect, the list is surprisingly similar to the one appended to *The Castle of Perseverance*, which, as we have seen, also spatializes meaning in this way; the entry for Rafe is not unlike the one given in the manuscript of *The Castle* for 'Pater sedens in trono' ('God sitting on his throne'). And as with the list's heading, such choices may have been deliberate on the part of *The Knight*'s publishers. Though any direct influence is far from likely, the archaic feel of *The Knight*'s list is certainly in keeping with the play's lampooning of chivalric romance.

CHARACTER LISTS BEYOND DRAMA

All lists do more than enumerate a set of items. Giving literal priority to one entry over another, they always and inevitably hierarchize meaning.[17] *The Knight*'s list, for instance, names characters in order of appearance, a structural principle that may be a consequence of its publishers working from a copy-text with no comparable list; entries may simply have been added with the introduction of each new character. But character lists afford numerous other ways of ordering information—size and importance of dramatic role; social rank; gender; family or plot grouping—thereby shaping the text's interpretive possibilities.[18] And this point is crucial since it highlights the role character lists play in making drama legible. For in making drama intelligible and readable, such lists embody the distance all plays inevitably travel from any historical or even putative moment of performance when they are reconstituted as material text. Moreover, it is this two-fold principle of legibility—the making of something that is both recognizable and decipherable—that also explains the inclusion of character lists in non-dramatic settings.

Shortly after dramatic character lists appeared in print, they began to be used for the print publication of dialogues. Plays and dialogues have long been recognized as contiguous, so the appearance of character lists in early editions of printed dialogues offers a neat typographical illustration of the proximity of these two categories of text. In William Turner's dialogue *The Examination of the Mass* [1548?], both the debt to and independence from contemporary dramatic character lists is immediately apparent (Fig. 10.3). The list offers no instructions for the doubling of parts, or indeed any other aspect of performance or staged reading. Moreover, the heading identifies the 'names' explicitly as 'the speakers in thys *Dialogue*' (my emphasis). But the fact that a list is included at all highlights the quasi-dramatic nature of all dialogues and illustrates one way that printers sometimes used paratexts to register the generic proximity of different categories of text.

---

[17] See Taylor, 'Order', 66.

[18] For examples of lists arranged according to each of these guiding principles see Atkin and Smith, 'Form and Function', pp. 658–66.

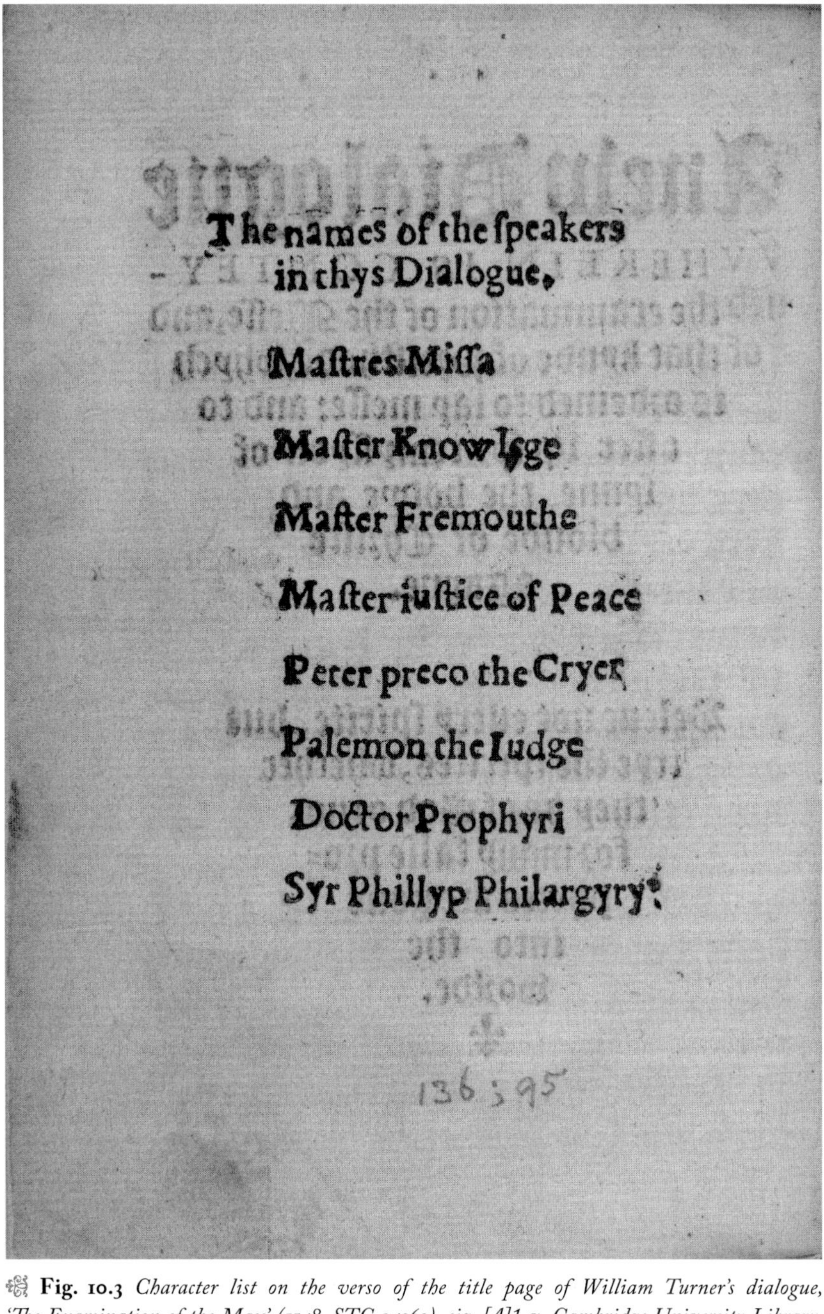

The names of the fpeakers
in thys Dialogue,

Maftres Miffa

Mafter Knowlṣge

Mafter Fremouthe

Mafter iuftice of Peace

Peter preco the Cryer

Palemon the Iudge

Doctor Prophyri

Syr Phillyp Philargyry:

136 ; 95

❦ **Fig. 10.3** *Character list on the verso of the title page of William Turner's dialogue, 'The Examination of the Mass' (1548, STC 24363), sig. [A]1 v. Cambridge University Library, Syn. 8.54.90. Reproduced by kind permission of the Syndics of Cambridge University Library.*

NAMES of the Principal PERSONS.

MEN.

George Selby, *Efq*;
John Greville, *Efq*;
Richard Fenwick, *Efq*;
Robert Orme, *Efq*;
Archibald Reeves, *Efq*;
Sir Rowland Meredith, *Knt.*
James Fowler, *Efq*;
Sir Hargrave Pollexfen, *Bart.*
The Earl of L. *a Scotiſh Nobleman.*
Thomas Deane, *Efq*;
Sir CHARLES GRANDISON, *Bart.*
James Bagenhall, *Efq*;
Solomon Merceda, *Efq*;
John Jordan, *Efq*;
Sir Harry Beauchamp, *Bart.*
Edward Beauchamp, *Efq*; *his Son.*
Everard Grandiſon, *Efq*;
The Rev. Dr. Bartlett.
Lord W. *Uncle to Sir* Charles Grandiſon.
Lord G. *Son of the Earl of* G.

WOMEN.

Miſs HARRIET BYRON.
Mrs. Shirley, *her Grandmother by the Mother's Side.*
Mrs. Selby, *Siſter to Miſs* Byron's *Father, and Wife of Mr.* Selby.
Miſs Lucy, } Selby, *Nieces to*
Miſs Nancy, } *Mr.* Selby.
Miſs Orme, *Siſter of Mr.* Orme.
Mrs. Reeves, *Wife of Mr.* Reeves, *Couſin of Miſs* Byron.
Lady Betty Williams.
The Counteſs of L. *Wife of Lord* L. *elder Siſter of Sir* Charles Grandiſon.
Miſs Grandiſon, *younger Siſter of Sir* Charles.
Mrs. Eleanor Grandiſon, *Aunt to Sir* Charles.
Miſs Emily Jervois, *his Ward.*
Lady Mansfield.
Lady Beauchamp.
The Counteſs Dowager of D.
Mrs. Hortenſia Beaumont.

ITALIANS.

Marcheſe della Porretta, *the Father.*
Marcheſe della Porretta, *his eldeſt Son.*
The Biſhop of Nocera, *his ſecond Son.*
Signor Jeronymo *della* Porretta, *third Son.*
Conte della Porretta, *their Uncle.*
Count of Belvedere.
Father Mareſcotti.

Marcheſa della Porretta.
Signora Clementina, *her Daughter.*
Signora Juliana Sforza, *Siſter to the Marcheſe della* Porretta.
Signora Laurana, *her Daughter.*
Signora Olivia.
Camilla, *Lady* Clementina's *Governeſs.*
Laura, *her Maid.*

THE

By the eighteenth century, character lists were being used for other kinds of fictional writing. The list in Samuel Richardson's *Sir Charles Grandison* (1753) is one of the earliest to occur in a novel, making the novelistic character list almost as old as the novel as a textual category (Fig. 10.4). Listed under the main heading 'Names of the Principal Persons', and divided into various subheadings, 'Men', 'Women', and 'Italians', the list clearly follows the organizational logic of contemporary dramatic character lists, including those prepended to plays printed in Richardson's own workshop. In doing so, the list not only reflects Richardson's familiarity with conventions for the articulation of drama, it suggests he used that awareness to reflect 'the epistolary novel's larger theatricality'.[19] And, by externalizing stage techniques used elsewhere in the novel, the list functions to revise the reader's expectations of the epistolary genre, asking them to imagine themselves not as a snoop (reading other people's letters), but as a member of an audience of the theatre-going public. Although a very different kind of novel, the list for Cooper's *Mount!* similarly functions to mould its readers. Organized alphabetically, some of the book's smaller, subordinate characters are described in terms of their relationship to characters not yet listed. 'EDWARD ALDERTON' is listed among the other As, but his description as 'Rupert Campbell-Black's nineteen-year-old American grandson' makes little sense unless the reader already knows who Rupert Campbell-Black is; *his* entry does not appear for a further two pages.[20] The result is a list that functions by assuming familiarity with Cooper's more popular characters, casting all readers—irrespective of their knowledge of her oeuvre—as long-time fans and intimates of her work.

❧ ▢ ❧

In his seminal work on paratexts, Genette leaves out character lists, describing them 'as little more than announcements'.[21] But character lists are, in fact, far more than announcements, and quite as much as other paratexts like title pages, dedicatory epistles, and addresses to the reader, they enable a 'text to become a book', making it legible as such to its readers.[22] Like the other kinds of lists encountered within the pages of a book—tables of contents, errata lists, indexes—they order meaning, delineating terms of precedence and relationship, and in making sense of texts as books, they help define horizons of reception.

---

[19] Janine Barchas, *Graphic Design, Print Culture, and the Eighteenth-Century Novel* (Cambridge: Cambridge University Press, 2003), pp. 188–9, 193.

[20] For dramatic examples in the same vein, see Atkin and Smith, 'Form and Function', 663.

[21] Gérard Genette, *Paratexts: Thresholds of Interpretation*, trans. Jane E. Lewin (Cambridge: Cambridge University Press, 1997), p. 399.

[22] Genette, *Paratexts*, p. 2.

CHAPTER 11

Daniel Sawyer

'This lessoun ye schulen fynde writen al out tofore in the xxv leef of these leefes,' says an explanatory note in bright red ink in an early fifteenth-century manuscript. Apparently the leaves 'ben markid…on the right side of the leef, in the higher part of the margyn'.[1] They are indeed numbered, just as described, so that the top-right corner of the very page bearing this note says 'xxvi folium' ('the twenty-sixth leaf') in the hand of the scribe who copied the main text. The 'lessoun' is a Bible reading, and the note occurs within a lectionary, a collection of readings arranged for the liturgical year. The thought of a reader six centuries ago navigating via numbers might seem familiar, for today we still use numbering to find our way when reading. But there are stranger elements here too: the numbers mark leaves, rather than pages; no one today would feel compelled to highlight, in such explicit terms, the exact positioning of numbering on the page; and the numbering does not even apply to the whole book, as the 'xxvi folium' is in fact folio 282 in the manuscript as a whole. This particular outbreak of leaf numbering—foliation—is a boutique navigational aid designed for this specific lectionary, and the lectionary only takes up one section within the manuscript. The note anticipates readers who are unfamiliar with the idea of foliation, and is at pains to explain the system in detail. So, then, this note reminds us that there were in the past multiple systems for identifying books' parts, and that the one we take for granted today—page numbering, or pagination—is not a natural feature of the codex format itself. In fact, the best approach to the various book parts discussed below is a consideration of just what *is* essential to the codex.

Pairs of leaves folded into gatherings or quires make the codex a codex.[2] The physical separation of each leaf from the others permits movement within the text with a speed and precision impossible on scroll or roll. This is a boon both to readers, who can cross-reference and wander, and to producers, who can rearrange or replace books' component parts. However, the codex of leaves grouped into gatherings only permits precise navigation; it does not actively encourage it. Producers and readers therefore desire systems which track codices' physical structures explicitly. Identifying leaves and the gatherings into which they are grouped makes production easier, and identifying leaves and pages makes reading easier. The codex therefore sometimes

[1] Oxford, Bodleian Library, MS Laud Misc. 388, f. 282ra; orthography, punctuation, and word division silently modernized. I am grateful to Cosima Gillhammer for bringing this example to my attention.

[2] The word for several pairs of leaves—several bifolia—folded together into one binding unit varies across different subfields within codicology and bibliography: crudely speaking, these units tend to be called 'quires' in manuscripts and 'gatherings' or 'signatures' in printed books. I use 'gathering' here throughout to mean a unit of folded leaves regardless of the nature of the book in which it survives. The confusing multiple meanings of 'signature' are briefly discussed below.

manifests systems which mark its constituent parts: catchwords, gathering and leaf signatures, foliation, and pagination. All of these features can serve as evidence in book history, but they resist rapid incorporation into literary-critical arguments. Rarely is a scholar able to argue from one of these that, say, a particular audience was expected, or a particular effect invited. Moreover, catchwords, signatures, and numbers are also small markings, and so offer limited material for the detailed study of scribes' hands or printers' metal (Fig. 11.1). Nevertheless, these parts identify the book's most fundamental structures, and so demand attention. We can best understand them by separating out their purposes and audiences. For gatherings, leaves, and pages are distinct entities, and the systems which track them are aimed at different uses and users. To perceive the book through each of these systems in turn is, therefore, to cycle through varying understandings of the codex. Summarized together, their histories show how the book moved gradually and unevenly towards increasing predictability and uniformity. Not all parts of this movement were inevitable, and some of these systems were rejected at points along the way: this is a process of decline and disappearance as well as one of development.

SIGNATURES

Signatures and catchwords are the systems discussed here which might be least familiar today. 'Signature' has several meanings (see below), and here I mean specifically written or printed signs indicating leaves' places within gatherings, or gatherings' places within books, or both pieces of information at once. Signatures are usually letters or numbers, and occasionally other punctuation marks, added most often to the bottom margins of recto pages. In manuscripts which feature leaf signatures, the signatures most often number every leaf of each gathering's first half; so in a gathering of eight leaves the first four leaves might be marked *i–iv*. Gathering signatures, meanwhile, most commonly take the form of a letter or number on the recto of each gathering's first leaf, or on the verso of the gathering's last leaf—that is, on one of the exterior sides of the outermost bifolium, where they can be easily found. Signatures allow producers to keep leaves and gatherings in order, and they appear early in the codex's history, in late antiquity.[3] Surviving early medieval examples are limited in number but well spread across time and space: gathering signatures appear in, for instance, the sole surviving copy of Books XL–XLV of Livy, copied in fifth-century Italy, and in the 'Vercelli Book' of Old English homilies and poems, copied in tenth-century England.[4] However, although signatures were known in early medieval European book production, they were not a default option. They proliferated in the thirteenth century and became standardized in the

---

[3] Eric G. Turner, *The Typology of the Early Codex* (Philadelphia, PA: University of Pennsylvania Press, 1977), pp. 77–8.

[4] Vienna, Österreichische Nationalbibliothek, MS Lat. 15; Vercelli, Biblioteca e Archivio Capitolare, MS 117.

Page number

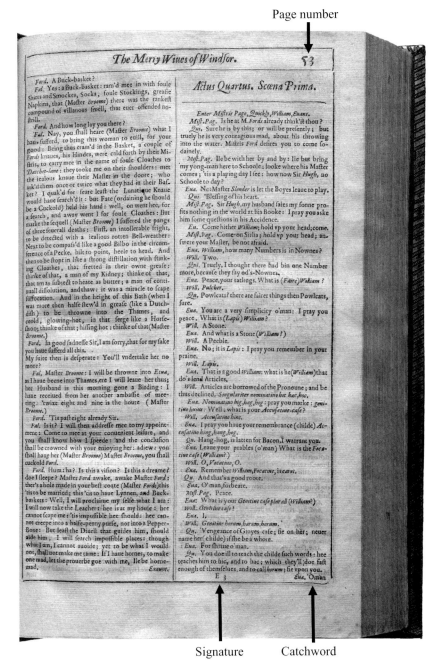

Signature   Catchword

Fig. 11.1 *'Mr William Shakespeares Comedies, Histories, & Tragedies, &c' ('First Folio'), STC 22273 (London, 1623), p. 53, E3r; Washington, DC, Folger Shakespeare Library, STC 22273 Fo. 1 no. 5. Used by permission of the Folger Shakespeare Library under a Creative Commons Attribution-ShareAlike 4.0 International License*

fifteenth century. In practice later medieval book producers often combined leaf and gathering signatures, so that—again assuming a manuscript of consistent eight-leaf, four-bifolium gatherings—the first gathering's first four leaves might be marked *A.i, A.ii, A.iii,* and *A.iv,* the second gathering's first four leaves *B.i, B.ii, B.iii, B.iv,* and so on. This conveniently combined form was rapidly adopted in print in the incunable period.[5] In early print, signatures are so ubiquitous that the word has come by synecdoche also to be used to mean 'gathering' or 'quire'.

Signatures can be used as evidence of an intended binding order and the loss of material, but they are not always consistent throughout the book and can also be mined for other production information: one copy of the Middle English poem *Piers Plowman,* for instance, was copied by two scribes and displays multiple overlapping signature systems.[6] At minimum, anyone examining or describing a book should check that the signatures match the physical order of leaves and gatherings. In special cases they also have direct literary-critical applications.[7] Seen from the perspective of the history of the book as a whole, signatures are creatures of the period—the very long period, encompassing the entire manuscript age, and much of the history of print—in which books were usually bound some time after their production. Their disappearance is a marker of increasing predictability in the book and of the shift of the responsibility for binding from owners to producers.

CATCHWORDS

'Catchwords' can refer to two different book features. First, a word or phrase usually written or printed in the bottom margin on the verso of the gathering's final leaf, matching the first word or phrase of the recto of the subsequent gathering's first leaf, and primarily added to facilitate the correct arrangement of the gatherings during binding. Catchwords of this sort were adopted into early medieval Latin books in Spain and southern France, perhaps around the turn of the eleventh century, possibly from Arabic manuscripts.[8] Although they were deployed in early print, catchwords'

---

[5] Margaret M. Smith, 'Printed Foliation: Forerunner to Printed Page Numbers?', *Gutenberg-Jahrbuch* 63 (1988): 58 (fig. 1).

[6] Oxford, Bodleian Library, MS Bodley 814; see for example f. 90 (the second leaf of gathering IX⁶), which is marked 'b' in one hand—a pure leaf signature—and, more faintly, 'I ij' in another the other—a signature indicating gathering and leaf.

[7] Rebecca Bullard, 'Signs of the Times? Reading Signatures in Two Late Seventeenth-Century Secret Histories', in *The Perils of Print Culture: Book, Print and Publishing History in Theory and Practice,* ed. Jason McElligott and Eve Patten (Basingstoke: Palgrave, 2014), pp. 118–33.

[8] Michelle P. Brown, *A Guide to Western Historical Scripts from Antiquity to 1600* (Toronto: University of Toronto Press, 1990), p. 4. Ayman Fu'ād Sayyid, *Al-Kitāb al-'Arabī al-makhṭūṭ wa-'ilm al-makhṭūṭāt,* 2 vols (Cairo: al-Dār al-Miṣrīyah al-Lubnānīyah, 1997), 1, pp. 45–6, dates the earliest catchwords in Arabic manuscripts to the early ninth century (referenced in Adam Gacek, *Arabic Manuscripts: A Vademecum for Readers* (Leiden: Brill, 2009), p. 50).

utility declined as book production became more mechanically reliable and as the responsibility for binding shifted to book producers and so, like signatures, they have disappeared in modern print. Catchwords differ from signatures, pagination, and foliation in their gestural, linking quality: they point to the start of a gathering which they do not themselves occupy. They are also unusual since they make use of the book's main text, yet are not necessarily read themselves—indeed, someone need not be literate to use catchwords when ordering gatherings. They could, then, sometimes be treated as writing reduced to shapes, and they might be one of the most unread types of writing found in books. In early print a second type of catchword developed: a word or word fragment printed in the bottom margin of any or potentially all pages in an early printed book, matching the next page's first word. During imposition, when individual pages were assigned their places on the larger sheets of paper which would be folded into gatherings after printing, these catchwords could be used to keep the pages in the correct order. During book production, then, page-by-page catchwords helped producers track the interaction between the book's text and its physical structure before that physical structure had even been created. Such catchwords can therefore sometimes grant insights into printers' practices, usually through moments of inaccuracy.[9] Once the book was finished, meanwhile, this type of catchword could smooth the reader's transition from page to page, perhaps particularly if the book was read aloud. Page-by-page catchwords became standardized in Western European printing in the middle of the sixteenth century, although printers in Paris persisted in including only gathering catchwords of the older kind, on the gathering's final verso.[10] Once footnotes became a standardized feature in some printed books, they received their own, separate page-by-page catchwords. Footnotes create a second possible flow of reading across page transitions, underneath the main text, and footnote catchwords explicitly indicated this flow's existence.

Catchwords of either the older type or the newer page-by-page type were not normally the objects of active thought on the part of producers or readers. Manuscripts, however, occasionally contain examples executed with conscious whimsy by scribes who clearly did read them. In one later medieval English collection of verse and prose most of the catchwords inhabit simple text-ink scrolls, but a few carry drawings related to the text at hand. For example, at a gathering transition in the manuscript's copy of Hoccleve's *Regiment of Princes* the catchword reads 'Gold sylver', and here the scribe wrote the two words in separate circles; someone, perhaps still the scribe, then painted the 'Gold' circle yellow.[11] This is an actively representational catchword. The choice to leave a circle without pigmentation to

---

[9] See for example Carl D. Atkins, 'The Application of Bibliographical Principles to the Editing of Punctuation in Shakespeare's "Sonnets"', *Studies in Philology* 100, no. 4 (Autumn 2003): 500–1.

[10] Philip Gaskell, *A New Introduction to Bibliography* (Oxford: Oxford University Press, 1972), p. 53.

[11] Oxford, Bodleian Library, MS Digby 185, f. 87ᵛ.

represent 'sylver' also suggests a willingness to see the brown parchment surface as shining white: navigational features sometimes offer insights into book producers' perceptions if each example is checked carefully. Later in the book a drawing of a man's head is positioned so that the catchword 'Senec sayth' ('Seneca says') grows from his lips; the earlier representational catchword makes it likely that this is an image of Seneca and not, as many other marginal drawings in medieval manuscripts are, an unidentifiable and perhaps generic figure (Fig. 11.2).[12] The visual reinforcement of the words arbitrarily highlighted by the catchword system was a thinkable choice for at least one scribe. However, this scribe's actions also emphasize the pragmatic nature of most other catchwords: he chose to draw meaning, while almost all other scribes chose not to.

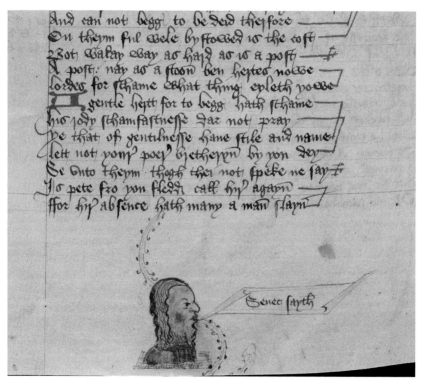

Fig. 11.2 *Oxford, Bodleian Library, MS Digby 185, ff. 135v–136r. A rare example of a catchword with representational decoration probably depicting the catchword's text (here, Seneca speaking). The text, 'Senec sayth', matches the opening words of the next page, which is the start of a new gathering. By permission of the Bodleian Libraries, University of Oxford*

[12] MS Digby 185, f. 135ᵛ.

Catchwords and signatures are ways of seeing the codex as a collection of gatherings, with little or no reference to the book's main text. These markings are writing, but they are writing aimed primarily at a readership of book producers, not at readers. They track physical structure, but since binding did not always follow their instructions they represent an aspiration towards a particular arrangement, an aspiration which was not always matched by binders' actions.[13] Once a book had been bound, catchwords and signatures might have had an ornamental function: they were sometimes lightly decorated, and there might also have been a pleasure to be found in their orderly succession. Readers might, nevertheless, react to them with distaste or just indifference. In books without defined, explicit borders surrounding each page, catchwords and, especially, signatures could be trimmed away during binding. Indeed, the book producers who added such systems in the first place might sometimes have expected that readers would remove them in due course: there are manuscripts in medieval bindings which were certainly trimmed by medieval owners.[14] Catchwords and signatures therefore challenge us to think about book parts which were sometimes temporary. Conventionally we think of material evidence in books as something which accumulates in layers; that is, we have a *stratigraphical* model for books' histories. Losses along the road of a book's life are usually felt to be the result of outside interference, interference which is implicitly unwelcome: we might maintain a non-judgemental, quasi-anthropological stance towards past owners who trimmed marginal notes and cut out beautiful initials for their scrap-books, but we still regard their actions as unforeseen interventions. Sometimes, however, the binder's blade trimming signatures away from a medieval manuscript might have been doing just what the original scribe expected: removing structural notes which had reached their point of planned obsolescence. Producers' marks departed, leaving the stage to other marks aimed at an audience of later readers.

FOLIATION AND PAGINATION

Foliation and pagination are marks primarily aimed at later readers. They are also more straightforward to describe, and more straightforward in their function. Either every leaf or every side of every leaf—that is, every page—is assigned a number. Readers can then identify relatively precise locations within the book, or precise stretches from one numbered part to another, and they can pass these identifications on to other readers. Foliation and pagination have probably both been known since the codex first proliferated: both systems appear in fragments from late-antique Greek codices.[15] Neither system was ever widespread in Western

---

[13] Consider for example the entertaining mess described in O. S. Pickering, 'Brotherton Collection MS 501: A Middle English Anthology Reconsidered', *Leeds Studies in English* n.s., no. 21 (1990): 144.

[14] Such as Oxford, Bodleian Library, MSS Laud Lat. 8 and Laud Misc. 488.

[15] Turner, *Early Codex*, 74–6.

European manuscripts, however: as my opening example shows, even in the fifteenth century foliation could be regarded as a specialized practice. Some medieval foliation was probably added during production, as in at least one copy of the first full English translation of the Bible.[16] However, not all *medieval* foliation is *scribal*: a fifteenth-century reader could foliate a twelfth-century manuscript. To further complicate matters, some medieval finding systems referred to numbered openings rather than leaves—in other words, each double-page, verso-and-recto spread in the book was a single numbered entity—and so when leaves are not explicitly specified, what reads as foliation might in fact be the numbering of openings.[17] Most manuscript codices which survive today are foliated, and most related scholarship uses folio numbers for reference, but the foliation involved is normally the work of modern owners or librarians.[18]

Why did foliation and pagination become standardized quite late, after being used by at least some producers early in the codex's history? The spatial and mental inefficiency of Roman numerals might be one factor. But Arabic numerals were known to some in Western Europe from at least the twelfth century, while Roman numerals were deployed for foliation and pagination in early print—and, in any case, readers could create their own non-numerical foliation systems if they wished.[19] Another, more important, factor is spatial variation between different manuscripts. Because handwriting by different scribes and in different styles varied in size, the distribution of the same text across leaves varied from copy to copy.[20] Scribes only rarely reproduced texts' exact divisions into pages and such precisely reproductive copying was slow work.[21] Since the distribution of text across leaves varied, neither pagination nor foliation could enable consistent referencing across multiple copies. Texts therefore accrued bespoke navigational tools tied to their content rather than

---

[16] Oxford, Bodleian Library, MS Bodley 296: rectos of ff. 1–176 foliated in Roman numerals in both red ink and black ink.

[17] The scribe's index in London, Lambeth Palace, MS 260 (ff. 138ʳ–139ᵛ) is keyed to numbered openings. See also Richard H. Rouse and Mary A. Rouse, *Preachers, Florilegia and Sermons: Studies on the 'Manipulus florum' of Thomas of Ireland*, Studies and Texts 47 (Toronto: Pontifical Institute of Mediaeval Studies, 1979), p. 33; and Paul Saenger, 'The Impact of the Early Printed Page on the History of Reading', *Bulletin du bibliophile* (1996): 237–301.

[18] Note that the references given in manuscript studies often use pre-existing *foliation* to refer to *pages*: 'f. 70r' is a page, the recto side of a leaf.

[19] A foliation system using dots and letters rather than numbers is discussed in Richard Rouse, 'Cistercian Aids to Study in the Thirteenth Century', in *Studies in Medieval Cistercian History II*, ed. J. R. Sommerfeldt, Cistercian Studies 24 (Kalamazoo, MI: Cistercian Publications, 1976), pp. 123–34, 129–30.

[20] This very lack of consistency created a medieval copy-identification device, the *secundo folio* record: as—in prose texts, at least—copies by different scribes would reliably have different words at the start of the recto page of their second leaf, it was possible to record those opening words of the second leaf in catalogues as a unique identifier for a specific copy. See James Willoughby, 'The *Secundo folio* and Its Uses, Medieval and Modern', *The Library* 12, no. 3 (2011).

[21] London, British Library, MSS Harley 4196 and Cotton Galba E.ix, for example, were copied from the same exemplar and reproduce that exemplar's pagination and lineation.

to the codex's own arbitrary structure: numbered divisions into parts and chapters which enabled relatively granular reference. At least one text-neutral navigational system did exist, in which a chapter in any given text could be divided into rough sevenths lettered *a* to *g*. This system was developed for reference to the Bible in the first half of the thirteenth century, probably by Dominican friars in Paris.[22] It was also applied to other texts, sometimes in a modified form (division into sixths, for instance, or division into elevenths), and some medieval manuscripts carry marginal letterings which interface with it.[23] However, and unlike foliation and pagination, this system too was tied to content, not codicological structure.

Printing, when it functioned as intended, guaranteed that the same content would appear on the same pages in every codex of an edition, and so facilitated the adoption of leaf and page numbering. However, the system which benefitted first was not pagination, but foliation, and even foliation was not adopted as fast as signatures were. Rather, foliation was adopted tentatively and experimentally during the incunable period, and more enthusiastically in the early sixteenth century.[24] For example, the books of hours produced in the first half of the sixteenth century by a prolific Parisian printer of books for English use, François Regnault, were foliated.[25] Foliation in Regnault's practice appears in the form 'Fo.xv.' at the top right-hand corner of the page: his foliations thus explicitly refer to leaves, but do so using abbreviation, rather than the full word *folium* seen in my opening example. Books of hours were organized tools for regular prayer; they anticipated cross-referential reading, but readers might have been expected to be, or quickly to become, quite familiar with their structure and function. Yet foliation was included anyway, together with a table of contents linked to folio numbers at these books' ends. So, foliation in Regnault's practice seems an entirely conventional component of conventional books. For a time, for many readers, foliation was probably a dominant navigation system. However, around the start of the sixteenth century pagination began to be adopted, and it spread rapidly: in Smith's sample, it appears in more than half of books being printed in the 1550s.[26] By the century's end pagination had supplanted foliation and become a standardized practice. At roughly the same rate,

[22] R. H. Rouse and M. A. Rouse, 'The Verbal Concordance to the Scriptures', *Archivum fratrum praedicatorum* 44 (1974): 8–10.

[23] Charles F. Briggs, 'Late Medieval Texts and Tabulae: The Case of Giles of Rome, *De regimine principum*', *Manuscripta* 37 (November 1993): 258.

[24] Smith, 'Foliation', pp. 56–9, 67–9. See also Saenger, 'Impact', pp. 263–75.

[25] See, for example, *Hore beatissime virginis Marie ad legitimum Sarisburiensis ecclesie ritum, cum quindecim orationibus beate Brigitte, ac multis alijs orationibus pulcherrimis, et indulgentijs, cum tabula aptissima iam vltimo adiectis*, STC 15945 (Paris: François Regnault, 1526; copy consulted: Oxford, Bodleian Library, Douce BB 185); or *Hore beatissime virginis marie ad legitimum Sarisburiensis ecclesie ritum cum quindecim orationibus beate Brigitte, ac multis aliis orationibus pulcherrimis, et indulgentiis, cum tabula, aptissima iam vltimo adiectis. M.D.xxxiiii*, STC 15984 (Paris: François Regnault, 1534; copy consulted: Oxford, Bodleian Library, Gough Missals 177).

[26] Smith, 'Foliation', p. 69 (fig. 2).

though beginning a few decades earlier in the 1470s, Arabic numerals displaced Roman numerals in print for both numbering practices. One possible explanation for pagination's spread is that its greater granularity attracted humanist printers and readers, who found that precision useful when handling texts in the more challenging language of Greek.[27] Pagination has changed little since its stand-ardization, and is now a universal expectation in books, where it can usually be found 'on the right side of the leef, in the higher part of the margyn'.

AFTER THE CODEX? AFTER THE BOOK?

Today the idea of 'the book' includes texts presented on the internet and through e-readers. Web pages are continuous electronic rolls, without foliation or pagination, while e-readers present texts page by page, varying the amount of text displayed to readers' specifications. On e-readers, then, the divisions between pages do not necessarily match from copy to copy—a little like the situation before print, when variation between different scribes' hands gave each manuscript copy its own unique foliation.[28] Wikipedia, the world's standard encyclopaedia, uses internal links to numbered headings with six possible stages of hierarchy, not unlike the divisions into numbered and titled sections used in later-medieval reading. However, social media sites, rather than e-books and simple web pages, dominate reading time for many, and these might escape the idea of the book altogether. 'Pages' on Facebook, Instagram, or Twitter provide a changing flow of individual posts, ordered and in part selected by algorithms. These services provide few navigational aids. Although it is possible to retrieve information from them precisely, the necessary knowledge can be specialized: Facebook posts, for example, do have unique individual web addresses, but many Facebook users do not know this. Furthermore, many of us now primarily read these services through mobile phone screens, in bespoke apps which offer only limited navigational tools. The dominant metaphors in these systems are those of the feed and the timeline, not the book.

All four of the systems discussed here, by contrast, are tied to the codex. Unlike some other book parts, these various systems are points of contact between books' textual content and their physical construction. They might be quiet and ostensibly unexciting types of evidence, but they can help scholars as indications of particular uses, and as signs of consistency or disruption in production. As topics in and of themselves, meanwhile, these systems invite further investigation. A more fine-grained history of the early medieval catchword across different manuscript traditions, for example, might not only add to the history of the book, but also track channels of

[27] Saenger, 'Impact', pp. 275–8.

[28] For a working evaluation of the e-book see Naomi S. Baron, *Words Onscreen: The Fate of Reading in a Digital World* (Oxford: Oxford University Press, 2015), especially pp. 209–14.

contact and codicological influence across and beyond Europe. Considering these systems together, as I have here, also reveals the variation in their purposes and audiences. They all mark intersections between textual content and physical object, but they differ in how explicitly they relate to physical structures: signatures and gathering catchwords are more closely tied to books' physicality than foliation and especially pagination. Their histories show how, over time, books became less and less explicitly physical, as printing became more standardized and reliable. Yet these marks also remind us that the history of the book is neither a story of 'natural' progress, nor a wholly technologically determined process: scribes could turn practical tools into whimsical engagements with their text, while foliation had a brief spell of success in which it might have seemed to be the future of book design. These systems have been the understated machinery which keeps the codex running.

CHAPTER HEADS

Nicholas Dames

Headings of the kind that start this very chapter are older than print, older even than the codex. One of the earliest manifestations of the chapter heading in the West can be located in a collection of bronze fragments, conventionally called by classical epigraphists the *tabula Bembina* after their sixteenth-century owner Cardinal Pietro Bembo. These fragments, inscribed on both sides, seem to have once been on display in a forum in the region of Urbino; their subject is a series of legal statutes dating to the later second century BCE. One fragment of particular interest lays out a *lex repetundarum*, or 'recovery law', which set up a court, with a jury of equestrians without senatorial connections, to establish compensation for extortionate senatorial confiscation of money or property abroad.[1] As an aspect of the Gracchan reforms, the fragment is a subject of fascination for historians of Roman law. But we might pause at one of its less frequently discussed peculiarities: the presence of chapter heads.

Each heading is set off from the end of a previous section by a small intervening space the size of a few characters.[2] Some examples include:

de nomine deferundo iudicibusque legundeis [Concerning prosecution and the choosing of jurors]
de reo apsoluendo [Concerning the acquittal of the defendant]
de reo condemnando [Concerning the condemnation of the defendant]
de leitibus aestumandis [Concerning the assessment of damages]
de praevaricatione [Concerning collusion][3]

These rubrics are unusually early; one source attests that no other such headings exist in an inscribed Roman statute until the Flavian period, roughly 200 years later.[4] Despite their antiquity, however, they are uncannily familiar in form. They are both summaries (of the passage they introduce) and graphic features (segmenting the text for legibility as well as analytic clarity). Even more remarkably, their syntactical form—a noun phrase introduced by the ablative *de*—prefigures two millennia of the look and function of chapter heads in a multitude of languages.

---

[1] For a description of the fragments and their historical context, see Andrew Lintott, *Judicial Reform and Land Reform in the Roman Republic: A New Edition, with Translation and Commentary, of the Laws from Urbino* (Cambridge: Cambridge University Press, 1992).

[2] See Shane Butler, 'Cicero's *Capita*', in *The Roman Paratext: Frame, Texts, Readers*, ed. Laura Jansen (Cambridge: Cambridge University Press, 2014), pp. 73–111, p. 83.

[3] Transcriptions and translations are from *Roman Statutes*, ed. M. H. Crawford, vol. 1 (London: Institute for Classical Studies, 1996), pp. 67–73, 87–93.

[4] Ibid., p. 49.

By the time that the codex was dominant in Western culture, a host of textual genres display such headings: histories, autobiographies, scientific and grammatical treatises, sacred texts. Take a further example, from a genre where the chapter head became a site of aesthetic play: the novel. A not untypical example from the mid-eighteenth century, the fifth chapter of the fifth book of Charlotte Lennox's 1752 *The Female Quixote* is titled as follows: 'In which will be found one of the former Mistakes pursued, and another cleared up, to the great satisfaction of Two Persons; among whom, the Reader, we expect, will make a Third' (Fig. 12.1). Compared to the relative concision of the early Roman heading, Lennox's is playfully elongated and acutely self-conscious. It refers to a 'Reader', establishing itself as a mode of direct address. It alludes to other textual moments ('one of the former Mistakes'), establishing itself as an interruption in an ongoing series of events. Its summary is opaque—it does not encapsulate the contents of the unit it announces so much as instigate a kind of curiosity about them.

Yet it bears nonetheless a basic formal resemblance to its Roman legal ancestor. It too is a syntactical fragment, a prepositional phrase only, if elaborated by a succession of qualifications. Although set off from the main text that follows by italic type, it does not receive much in the way of visual distinction; what separates it from its numerical tabulation and the text it introduces is empty space the size of one line of regular type. The form of the Roman rubric has been bent toward new tonal registers but not unrecognizably altered, despite the vast difference between the texts in which they are found.

To ask what a chapter head *is* means to ask what it *does*, and how that function holds onto a certain linguistic form and visual appearance despite countless other technological or aesthetic changes. A good starting point is the long persistence of the head's conventional grammar. The characteristic prepositional phrase of Western chapter heads (of, on, in which, about, concerning) and later gerund phrases (containing, involving) all suggest a direction or a movement, to where something resides or into where something is located. It is a segmenting and labelling gesture that spatializes the text into a series of discrete loci, but in which the label itself stands partially aloof from the space it labels.

That half-aloofness is one of the key aspects of the chapter head's longevity. As Ego Dionne has noted, chapter divisions are one of the more durable and persistent forms that paratexts take, because they are neither purely paratextual nor purely textual; they can be ascribed to authors, editors, or even, in a trick of voice common to the classical novel, narrators.[5] As such they tend to survive intact any remediation, unlike the other navigational aids—pagination, running heads—that develop with the codex. They may belong to the world of the indexical, the world that permits or encourages nonlinear or discontinuous access to the text, but they also are part of the

[5] See Ego Dionne, *La Voie aux chapitres: Poétique de la disposition romanesque* (Paris: Seuil, 2008), p. 214.

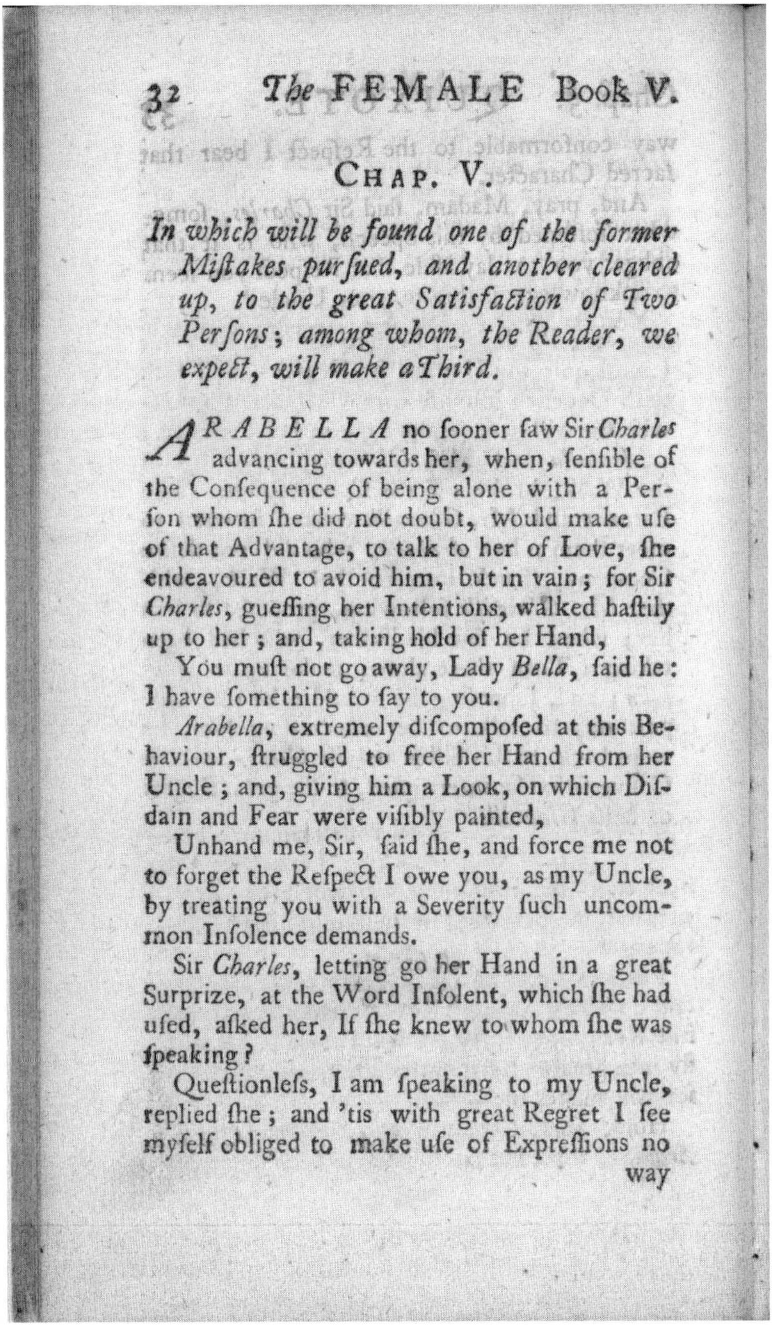

32   *The* FEMALE Book V.

CHAP. V.

*In which will be found one of the former
Miſtakes purſued, and another cleared
up, to the great Satisfaction of Two
Perſons; among whom, the Reader, we
expeẞ, will make a Third.*

*A*RABELLA no ſooner ſaw Sir *Charles*
advancing towards her, when, ſenſible of
the Conſequence of being alone with a Per-
ſon whom ſhe did not doubt, would make uſe
of that Advantage, to talk to her of Love, ſhe
endeavoured to avoid him, but in vain; for Sir
Charles, gueſſing her Intentions, walked haſtily
up to her ; and, taking hold of her Hand,

You muſt not go away, Lady *Bella*, ſaid he:
I have ſomething to ſay to you.

Arabella, extremely diſcompoſed at this Behaviour, ſtruggled to free her Hand from her
Uncle ; and, giving him a Look, on which Diſ-
dain and Fear were viſibly painted,

Unhand me, Sir, ſaid ſhe, and force me not
to forget the Reſpeẞ I owe you, as my Uncle,
by treating you with a Severity ſuch uncommon Inſolence demands.

Sir *Charles*, letting go her Hand in a great
Surprize, at the Word Inſolent, which ſhe had
uſed, aſked her, If ſhe knew to whom ſhe was
ſpeaking ?

Queſtionleſs, I am ſpeaking to my Uncle,
replied ſhe ; and 'tis with great Regret I ſee
myſelf obliged to make uſe of Expreſſions no
way

Fig. 12.1 *The parodic eighteenth-century head. Charlotte Lennox, 'The Female Quixote', vol. 2
(London, 1752), p. 32. Courtesy of the Rare Book and Manuscript Library, Columbia University*

discursive, referential aspect of the text, both a tool and the object constructed by the tool. As the primary lingering trace of informational or consultative reading within literary genres otherwise devoted to producing immersive, continuous reading, chapter heads always implicitly allude to an indexical function that they might nonetheless (as in Lennox) be discarding or even parodying. This is in fact the central path the history of the chapter head takes.

The genres first accompanied by heads—technical works; florilegia; directions for spiritual or ethical edification; holy scripture—were more informational than literary.[6] Equally notably, the chapter head clearly pre-exists the codex, despite what would seem to be the clumsiness attached to the indexical use of heads in the scroll; as the *tabula Bembina* suggests, the chapter head may in fact come to the scroll from the 'topography' of legal texts and inscriptions.[7] This genealogy has escaped the notice of some of the form's pre-eminent theorists, such as Gérard Genette, who attributes the syntactical formula of the chapter head to the medieval period.[8] However practically useful the chapter head in a scroll might have been, the fact remains that the impulse to use them arises in the context of an intellectual culture given to encyclopaedism and within texts that, in the words of the philologist Hermann Mutschmann, are meant less to be read than consulted or looked up.[9]

Yet however much chapter heads have a fairly consistent original purpose, and a style of considerable longevity, confusions abound. Three confusions in particular: where they belong in a given text; to whom they should be ascribed; and what they should even be called—or placement, origin, and terminology.

The placement of chapter heads is by no means a settled question in antiquity, and while a rough consensus is reached by the time of the early modern codex, variations still abound. The essential issue relates to the indexical function of the head: should it be present within the text, at the start of the unit it announces, or should it also be present in a separate table? Should it be sequentially numbered—demonstrating its place in a series, its subordination to a finding scheme—or stand alone? How much prominence, typographically, does it deserve? All of these design questions centre on the balance between the two imperatives of the chapter head: its indexical or finding function and its segmenting function.

---

[6] See Pierre Petitmengin, '*Capitula* païens et chrétiens', in *Titres et articulation du texte dans les ouvrages antiques*, ed. J.-C. Fredouille, Marie-Odile Goulet-Cazé, Philippe Hoffmann, and Pierre Petitmengin (Paris: Institut d'Études Augustiniennes, 1997), pp. 491–507, p. 500.

[7] I borrow the term 'topography' from Matthijs Wibier, 'The Topography of the Law Book: Common Structures and Modes of Reading', in *The Roman Paratext: Frame, Texts, Readers*, ed. Laura Jansen (Cambridge: Cambridge University Press, 2014), pp. 56–72.

[8] See Gérard Genette, *Paratexts: Thresholds of Interpretation*, trans. Jane E. Lewin (Cambridge: Cambridge University Press, 1997), p. 300.

[9] See Hermann Mutschmann, 'Inhaltsangabe und Kapitelüberschrift im Antiken Buch', *Hermes* 46, no. 1 (1911): 93–107, 95.

The evidence from the earliest lists of heads that are produced along with the texts they divide is scattered, but what they do demonstrate is a constant reciprocal influence between tables of contents and the head per se.[10] On the one hand there is the example of Pliny's *Natural History*, where the extant manuscript witnesses include three different treatments of heads: gathered in a separate Book 1, a *summarium*, separate from the text of the *History* itself; a dispersal of the *summarium*, in which the heads of each separate book of the *History* are placed at the start of the respective books; and a combination of the previous two methods. To add to the confusion, at an early stage of the text's transmission editors placed heads—some borrowed from the *summarium*, some invented for the occasion—at the start of their particular sections.[11] Here a trajectory seems dimly evident, in which a table becomes *chapterized*, finding its way into the text itself and thus becoming a kind of segmentation rather than an index. Columella's *On Agriculture* (*De re rustica*) has a table situated near the end of the work, but most of its heads appear in the main text as well, seemingly from the beginning of its textual lifespan; such is not the case, however, with Aulus Gellius's *Noctes Atticae*.[12] By the third and fourth centuries CE, however, the relationship between tables and intertitles has become tighter. An excellent example of this symbiosis is the fifth-century biblical pandect Codex Alexandrinus, where a numbered list of heads prefaces each Gospel book, while chapter breaks are indicated by marginal numbers and running heads at the top of each page, integrating the indexical and segmenting functions more tightly than in the tradition of Latin florilegia. Contemporary codices, where chapter heads normally start at the top of the page, cosseted by white space, veer toward segmentation: a graphic emphasis of the chapter unit as a unit, and a corresponding de-emphasis of the head's indexical function.

Ascription is another dilemma of the chapter head. Well into the era of the codex, heads are as likely to be editorial in origin as authorial. As Joseph Howley shows in Chapter 6 in the present volume, Gellius seems to have been responsible for his heads, and later writers—as in the ecclesiastical histories of Eusebius and Bede—drafted their own; but the editorial work of providing chapter heads was a significant aspect of the intellectual labour of late antiquity. Often the chapter head was a student's contribution to the work of a master, as with Porphyry's edition of Plotinus's

[10] A mutual relation charted by Bianca-Jeanette Schröder, *Titel und Text: zur Entwicklung lateintscher Gedichtüberschriften, mit Untersuchungen zu Lateinischen Buchtiteln, Inhaltsverzeichnissen und anderen Gliederungsmitteln* (Berlin: de Gruyter, 1999), pp. 153–4.

[11] See Aude Doody, *Pliny's Encyclopedia: The Reception of the* Natural History (Cambridge: Cambridge University Press, 2010), pp. 98–106. See also A. Riggsby, 'Guides to the Wor(l)d', in *Ordering Knowledge in the Roman Empire*, ed. Jason Kong and Tim Whitmarsh (Cambridge: Cambridge University Press, 2007), pp. 88–107, 93–8.

[12] Riggsby, 'Guides', pp. 98–101. For a thorough account of Gellius's heads, see Joseph Howley, 'How To Read the *Noctes Atticae*', in *Aulus Gellius and Roman Reading Culture: Text, Presence and Imperial Knowledge in the Noctes Atticae* (Cambridge: Cambridge University Press, 2018).

Enneads or (as we will see in more detail) Arrian's compilation of Epictetus's *Discourses*.[13] Editorial control over heads continued, however, even within genres where the head might be construed as a creative form; we have evidence that the Victorian novelist Elizabeth Gaskell left the composition of heads, and even occasionally the location of chapter divisions to be so headed, to the discretion of her publishers.[14]

Finally, the very name 'chapter head' is an anachronism within a tradition where the terminology is bewilderingly varied, and often constitutively blurred between the head itself and the location of the head or their collection into a unit (a table or list). Columella called them *argumenta*, although that could refer to the collection of his book's lists rather than the individual heads; Gellius used *capita rerum*, or 'main topics', although again the referent could easily be the list itself rather than its contents.[15] A slightly more specific term, *titulos* or *tituli*, was employed by Jerome, Cassiodorus, and Priscian; but Jerome also employed *argumenta*, while generally using *capitulum*—the closest to the modern 'chapter head', cognate to the Greek κεφάλαια—to refer to passages or units of text rather than their titles.[16] *Breviculus*, as used by Augustine and others, referred to summaries that may or may not have functioned as chapter heads, and may or may not have referred to the list rather than the items of the list.[17] In Porphyry's preface to the *Enneads*, he claims to have written both κεφάλαια and ἐπιχειρήματα: the first ('heads') indicating a brief title, the second ('arguments') likely a slightly longer synopsis, the latter a usage that persisted into early printed bibles like the 1560 Geneva Bible.[18] What is evident here is a constant semantic oscillation between three possible referents: the individual head itself, wherever it might be; the list of heads as a collection; and the unit of text marked off by the head. The confusion is constitutive: as the mediation point between a text's segmentation (its appearance to a continuous reading) and its navigability (its appearance to a discontinuous reading), the head encompasses both index and unit.

Lurking in these ambiguities—of physical placement, ascription, and even terminology—is an opportunity. However rote and conventional the chapter head could be, it remained flexible as well, capable of ironic homage to norms or pointed use to address intellectual questions raised by the threshold expectations of a title's

[13] On Eusebius, see Gustave Bardy's introduction to the *Ecclesiastical History* in *Sources chrétiennes 31* (Paris: Cerf, 1952), p. vii.

[14] See Josie Billington, 'On Not Concluding: Realist Prose as Practical Reason in Gaskell's *Wives and Daughters*', *Gaskell Journal* 30 (2016): 23–40.

[15] Riggsby, 'Guides', p. 91.

[16] For these usages and others, see Schröder, *Titel und Text*, pp. 323–6; Petitmengin, 'Capitula', pp. 492–5.

[17] Cyril Lambot, 'Lettre inedité de S. Augustin relative au "De Civitate Dei"', *Revue Bénédictine* 51 (1939): 109–21.

[18] See Anthony Grafton and Megan Williams, *Christianity and the Transformation of the Book: Origen, Eusebius, and the Library of Caesarea* (Cambridge, MA: Harvard University Press, 2008), p. 39.

relation to its unit. Two very different examples, from different genres and vastly different historical situations, can help illustrate the range of intentional purposes to which the chapter head could be put beyond indexical or segmenting functions; both could be summarized as the use of the chapter head as a mode of inquiry.

The first is a second-century text, the *Discourses* of Epictetus, as transcribed and, most likely, arranged into units with heads, by his disciple Arrian.[19] While often hewing to the familiar 'about' clauses of late-classical heads (here the Greek περὶ), Arrian's heads demonstrate a noteworthy flexibility of form and purpose. His περὶ-clauses promise terminological discussions ('On steadfastness', 'On friendship'), but others take interrogatory forms ('What does philosophy promise?', 'What is the law of life?'); some address an interlocutor ('To those who have set their hearts on advancement in Rome'); and yet others take the form of propositions ('That logic is indispensable').[20] The variety of forms suggests the equally wide variety of rhetorical situations that a teacher like Epictetus might employ on a daily basis, and Arrian's refusal to squeeze these interactions into a conceptual straightjacket. It also suggests that the heads are not merely indexical. They seem in fact to be a series of experiments on the relation between title or unit, or initial perception and later understanding.

Understanding Arrian's heads in this way helps situate what have often been taken as their errors or sloppiness.[21] Some of the heads seem to overspecify what is, in the body of the text, a more capacious discussion; heading 1.5 ('Against the Academics') leads to a discussion of mental 'petrifaction' of which the Academics of the heading are only an instance. Others seem to play with readerly presuppositions: 2.2 ('On calmness of mind') and 2.22 ('On friendship') both lead to discussions of their opposites, while the head for 1.17 ('That logic is indispensable') seems to refer only to the opening of the unit, most of which is taken up by a discussion of self-sufficiency.[22]

Presuppositions are, in fact, the overriding interest we could ascribe to Arrian's practice of heading. In Epictetus's terminology, 'preconceptions' (προλήψεις) are the set of concepts derived from perceptions that define for us the general force and meaning of the things we perceive. These 'preconceptions' are derived naturally or spontaneously, by induction, from our perceptions, and as such may be only partially

---

[19] See the commentary of Robert Dobbin in *Epictetus: Discourses Book 1* (Oxford: Clarendon, 1998), p. 65; or Jackson Hershbell, 'The Stoicism of Epictetus: Twentieth Century Perspectives', *Aufstieg und Niedergang der Römischen Welt II* 36, no. 3 (1989): 2148–63.

[20] Translation of the heads by Robin Hard from *Epictetus: Discourses, Fragments, Handbook* (Oxford: Oxford University Press, 2014).

[21] See Dobbin, *Epictetus*, p. 128.

[22] See Dobbin, *Epictetus*, p. 161, where he in fact proposes 'On Self-Sufficiency' as a superior title for the section.

developed or rationalized, although they nonetheless embody general truths.[23] We might think of a preconception as a kind of naturally indexical kind of knowledge: useful, just as the chapter head, for organizing and tagging our perceptions. The problem, as Epictetus is at pains to explain, is that not every preconception is a perfect fit with the particular instance it tags. The first sentences of 1.22, 'On preconceptions', explain:

> Preconceptions are common to all people, and one preconception doesn't contradict another. For who among us doesn't assume that the good is beneficial and desirable, and that we should seek to pursue it in every circumstance? And who among us doesn't assume that what is just is honourable and appropriate? When does contradiction arise, then? It comes about when we apply our preconceptions to particular cases.[24]

The problem is not that preconceptions can be in themselves mistaken, it is that they can be a mismatch with the experience they preface, thereby failing at their indexical task. On this score Epictetus recommends a constant process of double checking that the general judgement of preconceptions matches the particular quality of experiences, so that they may shift from 'natural' to 'systematically examined preconceptions' (διηρθρωμέναις ταῖς προλήψεσι).[25]

The relation of general to particular is at once the structure of Epictetus's epistemology and the challenge of Arrian's practice of heading. Employing the language of textual arrangement, Epictetus argues that 'it is impossible for us to adapt these preconceptions to the corresponding realities unless we have subjected them to systematic examination, to determine which reality should be ranged under (ὑποτακτέον) which preconception'. The act of subjoining heads, of course, is also the act of 'determining which reality should be ranged under which preconception'—which label is appropriate to which experience. As Epictetus warns, that match is often not what one initially expects. Arrian's seemingly inapposite heads could be thought of as provoking a constant testing or evaluation: can I trust this label standing on the threshold of this experience?

Arrian's heads are therefore reflections upon their own indexicality, by virtue of how they mirror the mind's habit of seeking to match particulars to generalities. As an intellectual challenge this aspect of the chapter head has remarkable longevity; it can be found in Hugh of St Victor's early twelfth-century Didascalicon, which offers an explanation that would have been recognizable to Arrian:

---

[23] Useful studies of Epictetus' 'preconceptions' include Henry Dyson, *Prolepsis and Ennoia in the Early Stoa* (Berlin: de Gruyter, 2009); A. A. Long, *Stoic Studies* (Cambridge: Cambridge University Press, 1996); F. H. Sandbach, 'Ennoia and Prolepsis in the Stoic Theory of Knowledge', *Problems in Stoicism*, ed. A. A. Long (London: Athlone, 1971).

[24] Hard, *Epictetus: Discourses*, p. 48.

[25] Ibid., pp. 49, 94–5.

The ancients called such an outline an 'epilogue', that is, a short restatement, by headings, of things already said (*brevis recapitulatio supradictorum appellata est*). Now every exposition has some principle upon which the entire truth of the matter and the force of its thought rest, and to this principle everything else is traced back.[26]

'Preconception' has become *principium*, but the intellectual task of finding a suitable generality for a given particular is for Hugh as much as for Arrian the meaning of the chapter head.

Other genres and historical periods will seek to pose other questions through the chapter head. In the history of European fiction, heads persisted even though they had lost their indexical function, and in the process they acquired new effects: signalling the opportunity for a break from sequential reading; teasingly referring to plot revelations or 'cliffhangers'; echoing earlier moments to indicate a plot's architectonics. The loss of indexicality was initially, and for a long while, signalled by parody; from the self-conscious anti-summaries in novels like *The Female Quixote* to the extravagantly self-cancelling heads of early Dickens—as in chapter 16 of *The Pickwick Papers* (1836–7), 'Too full of adventure to be briefly described'—novelistic chapter heads mimicked the syntax of informational labels in order to signal the mismatch between such labels and the continuous, immersive reading that novels implicitly sought. Their uselessness was their comedic point. Indeed, starting in the late eighteenth century, the chapter head increasingly vanishes from European novels; neither Austen nor Tolstoy, to mention two prominent examples, employed them.[27] But by the mid-nineteenth century, a new use emerged, palpable at first simply on the basis of a new brevity.

A few instances of the vanishing of the head's traditional prepositional syntax, from the 1830s and 1840s, makes the shift clear:

'Ceci Tuera Cela' (Victor Hugo, *Notre Dame de Paris*, book 5, chapter 2)
'L'ennui' (Stendhal, *Le Rouge et le noir*, chapter 6)
'Mediation' (Harriet Martineau, *Deerbrook*, chapter 11)
'Contrasts' (Dickens, *Dombey and Son*, chapter 33)
'Progression' (Anne Bronte, *The Tenant of Wildfell Hall*, chapter 6)

These are deliberately opaque labels, with only a vestigial relation to any kind of finding aid, and their earnestness seems to derive from the essay rather than the romance. While they do present the same intellectual challenge as Arrian's

---

[26] *The Didascalicon of Hugh of St Victor: A Medieval Guide to the Arts*, trans. Jerome Taylor (New York: Columbia University Press, 1991), p. 93. Latin original from C. H. Buttimer, ed., *Hugonis de Sancto Victore Didascalicon de studio legendi* (Washington, DC: Catholic University Press, 1939), p. 60.

[27] Although, famously, Tolstoy did head one chapter of *Anna Karenina* (1873–7)—the chapter 'Смерть' [Death], on the death of Nikolai Levin—reaching for a threshold effect when narrating the most profound of thresholds.

heads—determining the relation between a head's generality and its particular instantiation in the action of the chapter—they are also, peculiarly, narratorial speech acts. They exist, that is, both outside of and within the diegesis; they raise a question of voice (who speaks this chapter head?) that is also a question of ontology (from what world, or time, does this head come?).

This is true of first-person narratives, which situate chapter heads as retrospective assessments of the events narrated; but it is equally true of third-person narratives, where heads can produce a strange suturing effect, tying characters' voices to a narratorial voice in the peculiarly unlocatable, extra-diegetic space of the chapter head. Often this effect is achieved by *quotation*: Hugo's head, for instance, is taken from the despairing words of Claude Frollo, Notre-Dame's archdeacon. More commonly it is by *implication*, as the boredom in Stendhal's chapter is that of the provincial wife and mother Madame de Rênal, who can scarcely dare to articulate to herself what the chapter head announces to the reader. In some hands the chapter head can achieve highly complex effects as it negotiates between those two positions. In Anthony Trollope's *Framley Parsonage* (1860–1), a chapter head such as 'Is She Not Insignificant?' picks up and transforms a bit of character speech (Fig. 12.2). The proud and inflexible Lady Lufton, faced with the prospect of her son marrying the commoner Lucy Robarts, is driven to tell him: 'She is—insignificant.'[28] It is a pronouncement, both hesitant and defiant, that is interrogated within the chapter:

> That she was a good girl, in the usual acceptation of the word good, Lady Lufton had never doubted...It was quite possible for her also to love Lucy Robarts; Lady Lufton admitted that to herself; but then who could bow the knee before her and serve her as a queen? Was it not a pity that she should be so insignificant?[29]

The assertion of his heroine's 'insignificance' is chromatically shifted between three different registers: direct quotation ('She is'); free indirect discourse ('Was it not a pity that...?'); and the double negative of the chapter head's interrogatory form ('Is She Not...?'), which derives from, but cannot any longer be wholly located within, Lady Lufton's speech. What the chapter head stages in Trollope is the contagion of speech itself, spilling beyond the confines of the novel's action, as if to refuse the distinction between paratext and text, narrated world and our world; his heads pay homage to the refusal of our words to remain our own.[30]

This play with the ontology of fiction is not as far from the epistemological tests of Arrian's heads as it might seem. While adapted to the different demands of their respective genres, both push indexicality into reference; rather than labelling a unit,

[28] Anthony Trollope, *Framley Parsonage*, ed. P. D. Edwards (Oxford: Oxford University Press, 1980), p. 517.

[29] Ibid., p. 520.

[30] I discuss Trollope's titling practices at greater length in 'Trollope's Chapters', *Literature Compass* 7, no. 9 (2010): 855–60.

213

CHAPTER XII.

IS SHE NOT INSIGNIFICANT?

AND now a month went by at Framley without any increase of comfort to our friends there, and also without any absolute deve'opment of the ruin which had been daily expected at the parsonage. Sundry letters had reached Mr. Robarts from various personages acting in the Tozer interest, all of which he referred to Mr. Curling, of Barchester. Some of these letters contained prayers for the money, pointing out how an innocent widow lady had been induced to invest her all on the faith of Mr. Robarts' name, and was now starving in a garret, with her three children, because Mr. Robarts would not make good his own undertakings. But the majority of them were filled with threats;—only two days longer would be allowed and then the sheriff's officers would be enjoined to do their work; then one day of grace would be added, at the expiration of which the

❦ **Fig. 12.2** *The suturing of nineteenth-century heads. Trollope, 'Framley Parsonage', vol. 2 (London: Smith, Elder, 1861), 213. Courtesy of the Rare Book and Manuscript Library, Columbia University*

they establish a temporal relation between head and unit, in which the head will look differently before and after the unit has been read. It is perhaps the temporality the chapter head indicates—despite the fact the head would seem to have no temporality itself—that lurks behind these historically disparate uses. Exploring his own idiosyncratic recourse to chapter heads, the narrator of Thomas Mann's *Doktor Faustus* (1947) pauses to wonder what chapter heads do:

> As with earlier sections, I would do better not to give this one its own number, but to identify it as properly belonging to the previous chapter, as its continuation. The right thing would be to forge ahead without any deep caesura, for this is still the chapter entitled 'The World,' the chapter about my late friend's relationship or lack of relationship with the world.[31]

How deep, how easily or arduously forded, is the caesura a chapter head presents? In asking this question, so often posed by the head in its various guises since antiquity, we acknowledge how far it has come from its indexical origins.

---

[31] Thomas Mann, *Doctor Faustus: The Life of the German Composer Adrian Leverkuhn as Told by a Friend*, trans. John Woods (New York: Vintage, 1999), p. 417.

CHAPTER 13

Epigraphs

—Rachel Sagner Buurma

Epigraphs never have anything to do with the book.

Fran Ross, *Oreo*

The first epigraphs belong to buildings, not to books. Or at least, the first uses of the word refer to permanent inscriptions on buildings, monuments, pillars, and metal plaques rather than the quotations that appear on title pages and head book chapters. In the mid-eighteenth century, Johnson's *Dictionary* defined 'epigraph' merely as 'an inscription'; not until the nineteenth century did the word regularly refer to an excerpt or quotation printed at the beginning of a literary text as a kind of reference point, interpretive guide, example, or counterexample designed to orient the reader to the text.[1] As a word, 'epigraph' thus carries with it the sense of priority, of inscription in many media, and a sense of a being written-on, written-before, or written-above denoted by the word's Greek roots.

The origins of the modern, literary epigraph are murky; the armorial motto is one possible precursor. In early modern texts, the epigraph or motto commonly found on the title page of a volume or beneath the title of an individual poem in a collection more often referred to the author of the work than to the work itself. First found on coats of arms, the motto migrated into the book to become 'useful to a poet as a coded signature added at the end of a poem printed anonymously, where it served as an actual or pretended way of disguising his identity from the uninitiated'.[2] Milton's *Poems* (1645), for example, features a title page epigraph drawn from Virgil's seventh *Eclogue* that commands the shepherds of Arcady, as Louis Martz notes, to '[b]ring ivy-leaves to decorate your rising poet'; it both makes a claim about the author and his future and at the same time 'prepares the way for the many Vergilian characters and scenes to be encountered in the English poems here'.[3] The epigraph begins to refer more regularly to the text rather than to the author in the mid-seventeenth century, though the older usage persists through the nineteenth century.[4]

---

[1] The first edition of Johnson's *Dictionary* defines 'epigraphe' as 'An inscription on a statue', which becomes merely 'An inscription' in later editions. (The *Dictionary* itself sported an epigraph from Horace's *Epistles*.)

[2] Ann Ferry, *The Title to the Poem* (Stanford, CA: Stanford University Press, 1996), p. 232. Gérard Genette suggests, like Ferry, that the author's coat of arms—specifically, the quotations that sometimes appear upon coats of arms—might be considered the epigraph's forerunner. See Gerard Genette, *Paratexts*, trans. Jane E. Lewin (Cambridge: Cambridge University Press, 1997), p. 144.

[3] Louis Lohr Martz, *Poet of Exile: A Study of Milton's Poetry* (New Haven, CT: Yale University Press, 1980), p. 36.

[4] Ferry, *The Title to the Poem*, p. 233.

It is difficult to mark the moment when epigraphs become popular in European literature. Gérard Genette notes that he finds no trace of an epigraph in French literature before the seventeenth century, and in English books printed before 1700, epigraph-like texts appear primarily in sermons to introduce biblical texts for explication. What is clear is that the eighteenth century saw the wide proliferation of epigraphs drawn from all kinds of sources and introducing all kinds of texts. Periodicals, printed play-texts, travelogues, treatises, biographies, religious works, and all manner of other forms and genres drew on past texts, particularly those from the well-known classical authors, though Shakespeare and a wide array of less known and more contemporary authors rapidly gained ground over the course of the century. Fiction in English offers an especially dramatic example of this change. Early eighteenth-century works of fiction seldom have epigraphs; when they do they almost always draw on classical sources. Later in the century novels become more likely to have epigraphs, and these increasingly draw from more recent works.[5]

FUNCTIONS

The modern epigraph is most likely to comment in some way on the work it begins. It opens up questions about what meaning the reader is intended to draw from the epigraph and apply to the text. The epigraph's very existence raises questions of tradition, authority, and intentionality; we might even say that it creates a structurally literary situation. The nature of *what* an epigraph says about a text ranges from the relatively clear through the very ambiguous to the nearly opaque. Genette notes that 'one can suspect some authors of positioning some epigraphs hit-and-miss, believing—rightly—that every joining creates meaning and that even the absence of meaning is an impression of meaning'.[6] In her 1974 novel *Oreo*, Fran Ross takes an even stronger position, warning the reader with tongue in cheek after offering a series of four epigraphs of her own that 'Epigraphs never have anything to do with the book'.[7] Some epigraphs seem to seek to evade the form's playful and expansive literariness by narrowly defining their domain; epigraphs that proffer expanded versions of literary references made in titles, for example, seem to be longing for the (superficially) simpler life of the footnote (for which, see Chapter 18 of this volume).[8] In his four-category taxonomy of the epigraph's functions, Genette divides two

---

[5] For more detail, see the Early Novels Database project: https://github.com/earlynovels/end-dataset, for epigraph-related subsets including 18c-epigraphs.tsv.

[6] Genette, *Paratexts*, pp. 157–8. For Genette's taxonomy of epigraph functions see pp. 156–60.

[7] Fran Ross, *Oreo* (New York: New Directions, 2015 [1974]), p. vi. Beginning her page of epigraphs to *Oreo* with 'Oreo defined: someone who is black on the outside and white on the inside', the next three of Ross's epigraphs are equivocally fictional utterances ascribed to the historical figures: the author ('Oreo, ce n'est pas moi'), Flaubert ('A likely story'), and Wittgenstein ('Burp!').

[8] Genette implies that the epigraph as commentary on the title is a twentieth-century phenomenon, but other scholars have found this function earlier on; see Ferry, *The Title to the Poem*.

straightforward functions of commenting on the text or the author from what he describes as two 'more oblique' uses.[9] The first of these associates the text with another author, literary tradition, or genre; in this the epigraph might join or compete with similar work done by the dedication and preface.[10] The other more oblique use is 'the epigraph-effect', the effect of signalling the 'culture' or 'intellectuality' that the mere presence of an epigraph conveys.[11]

In practice, of course, most literarily interesting epigraphs cannot be fully accounted for in any taxonomy or description of epigraphic functions. The famous double epigraphs appearing at the head of each chapter of W. E. B. Dubois's *The Souls of Black Folk* (1903) offer an especially good example; in each pair, each epigraph points the reader to some aspect of the chapter, while the contrast between each pair invokes the book's concept of double consciousness and helps uphold the book's overall double structure. In each chapter opening, Dubois pairs a piece of poetry (drawn primarily from works by white European or American writers) with excerpts of the music (but not the lyrics) of spirituals (or 'Sorrow Songs', as Dubois called them) which are drawn from collections of spirituals sung by Fisk University's Jubilee Singers and others.[12] The epigraph pairs gesture to the chapter themes. In the chapter 'Of Mr. Booker T. Washington and Others', on debates about the social and economic future of African American people, the poetic epigraph from Canto 2 of Byron's *Childe Harold's Pilgrimage* (1812) urges its reader 'Hereditary bondsmen! Know ye not / Who would be free themselves must strike the blow?', while the lyrics to the quoted spiritual 'A Great Camp Meeting in the Promised Land' encourage its auditor 'O, Walk together children / Don't you get weary'.[13] Yet on the page, the musical notation of the spiritual only, not the lyrics, appear; as Brent Edwards explains, it is important to notice that Dubois 'chooses not to include the lyrics to the spirituals', possibly in order to 'mark another barrier for the [white] reader, in another form—to suggest, again, the inner life "within the Veil", a mode of knowledge and "striving" that remains difficult to reach, if not inaccessible, using the imperfect and limited means of white culture'.[14] And more broadly, Edwards shows, the epigraphs are part of the 'interwoven pattern of thesis and antithesis, "forethought" and "afterthought" that

[9] Genette, *Paratexts*, p. 158.

[10] Genette specifies association with a relatively 'prestigious' author, literary tradition, or genre and implies that the goal is to raise the text's status, but one can easily find and imagine examples in which the connection to another author, tradition, or genre has other aims.

[11] Genette, *Paratexts*, p. 158.

[12] On the meanings and sources of the epigraphs see Brent Edwards, 'Introduction' to W. E. B Dubois, *The Souls of Black Folk*, ed. Brent Hayes Edwards (Oxford: Oxford University Press, 2007), p. xxii. On Dubois' sources for the spirituals, Edwards cites Ronald M. Radano, 'Soul Texts and the Blackness of Folk', *Modernism/Modernity* 2, no. 1 (January 1995): 85–7 and Eric J. Sundquist, *To Wake the Nations: Race in the Making of American Literature* (Cambridge, MA: Harvard University Press, 1993), pp. 490–525.

[13] Dubois, *The Souls of Black Folk*, p. 33.

[14] Edwards, 'Introduction', p. xxi.

characterises *The Souls of Black Folk*.[15] Pointing to the chapters' themes and at the same time withholding them from some readers, connecting the work to particular poetic and musical traditions and making meaning out of the comparison between those traditions, the example of *Souls* suggests some of the complex literary possibilities of the epigraph.[16]

Epigraphs do informational as well as literary work. Just as tables of contents or indexes (Chapters 6 and 20 of this volume) point a reader to a particular page containing a certain word or treating a specific topic, epigraphs teach readers by alerting them to what kinds of overarching themes they might expect to find developed in the following pages. Especially as changes in print technology, paper making, copyright, and transportation allowed the world of print to grow and circulate along with an expanding reading audience, epigraphs came to function as another paratextual technology of information management. Epigraphs can also act as a kind of more visible and cited literary reference legible to a wider array of readers than the unmarked literary references that occur within texts. This function is consonant with the way that the use of epigraphs expands with the growth of the new middle-class reading public in the eighteenth and nineteenth centuries. New readers, beneficiaries of a widening education and growing paths to literacy, knew English but not necessarily the classical or modern literary traditions well enough to be able to track implicit and unmarked references embedded within texts. Epigraphs offered a clearer type of allusion; their positioning at the opening of a work or chapter, and the author attribution they usually included, clearly identified them for readers. The epigraphs characteristic of English Gothic novels of the later eighteenth century, for example, could have filled a commonplace book with selections from Shakespeare, James Thomson, James Beattie, and William Collins. And the Greek and Latin epigraphs drawn from classical sources popular earlier in the eighteenth century were increasingly translated into English for widening audiences.

EPIGRAPHS IN NOVELS (AND CHARACTERS)

The novel was a latecomer to the eighteenth century's enthusiasm for epigraphs, but, as the proliferation of epigraphs in Gothic novels suggested, it eventually embraced them wholeheartedly. As Janine Barchas argues, Genette's claim that the use of epigraphs in the eighteenth century was a widespread practice is an understatement, since the print matter of the century is awash in epigraphic text—from 'the panoply

---

[15] Edwards, 'Introduction', p. xxii.

[16] For readings of the meaning of the epigraphs, see (among many others) Sundquist, as well as Ross Posnock, *Culture and Color: Black Writers and the Making of the Modern Intellectual* (Cambridge, MA: Harvard University Press, 1998), pp. 263–4. For a detailed sense of the epigraphs' particular meanings, especially the ways in which some of the poems relate to histories of abolition and anti-slavery, see Daniel Hack, *Reaping Something New: African American Transformations of Victorian Literature* (Princeton, NJ: Princeton University Press, 2016), pp. 176–206.

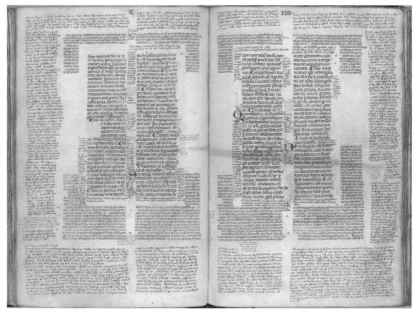

🦋 **Plate 1** *Late thirteenth-/early fourteenth-century Italian manuscript, with central text flanked by multiple layers of peripheral paratextual commentary. Decretales Gregorii IX, Berkeley, Robbins MS 5, ff. 193v–194r. The Robbins Collection: University of California, Berkeley, School of Law, www.digtial-scriptorium.org*

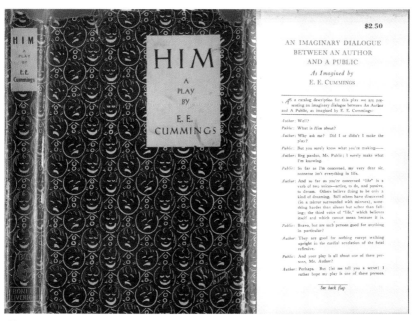

🦋 **Plate 2** *E. E. Cummings' 'Him' (1927), featuring a dialogue between author and public on the inner flap. By kind permission of W. W. Norton on behalf of the E. E. Cummings estate. Image courtesy of the Beinecke Rare Book and Manuscript Library, Yale University*

AGATHA CHRISTIE

The Secret of Chimneys

Plate 3 *The dust jacket of Agatha Christie's 'The Secret of Chimneys,' as treated by Joe Orton and Kenneth Halliwell. Reproduced with the permission of Islington Local History Centre/Joe Orton Estate*

Plate 4 *Aristotle [Opera] (Venice, 1483), PML 21194–5 vol. 1, f. 2r. By permission of The Pierpont Morgan Library and Museum, New York*

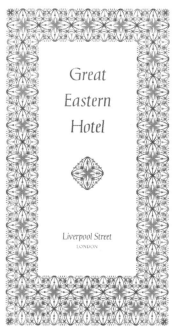

Plate 5 *Glint fleurons on menu card, Great Eastern Hotel, 1967. Photographed by Mike Ashworth*

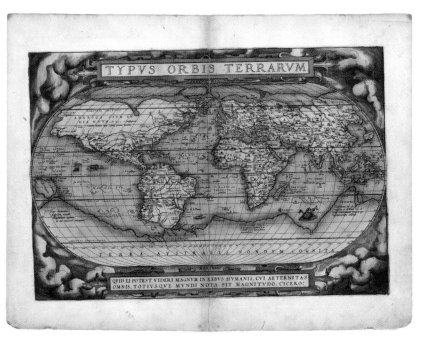

Plate 6 *World map. Hand-coloured copperplate engraving from Abraham Ortelius, 'Theatrum Orbis Terrarum' (Antwerp, 1570). Washington, DC: Library of Congress*

Plate 7 *World map. Hand-coloured engraving from Joan (Johannes) Blaeu, 'Atlas Maior' (Amsterdam, 1662). Reproduced by permission of the National Library of Scotland*

🪷 **Plate 8** *From Jos Ramo Zeschan Noamira, 'Memoria instructiva sobre el maguey o agave mexicano' (Mexico: I. Julian, 1837). Courtesy Special Collections, The Rivera Library, University of California, Riverside*

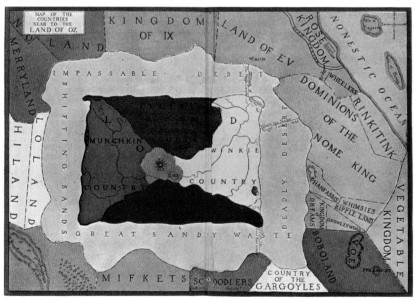

🪷 **Plate 9** *The endpapers of 'The Wizard of Oz' (Chicago, IL: Reilly and Lee, 1908)*

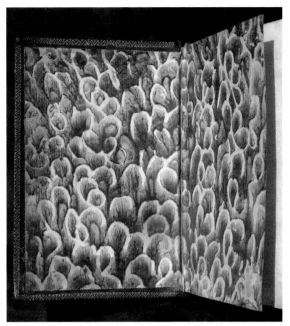

Plate 10 *Paste paper endpapers on a volume with gilt dentelles. Image courtesy of Lawrence A. Miller, http://www.virtual-bookbindings.org*

Plate 11 *One two-page spread from a massive Aschaffenburg catalogue, showing a selection of about 2,000 samples in the catalogue. The company produced dozens of catalogues. The number of papers in them used for endleaves is gargantuan. (Collection of the author; photograph by the author)*

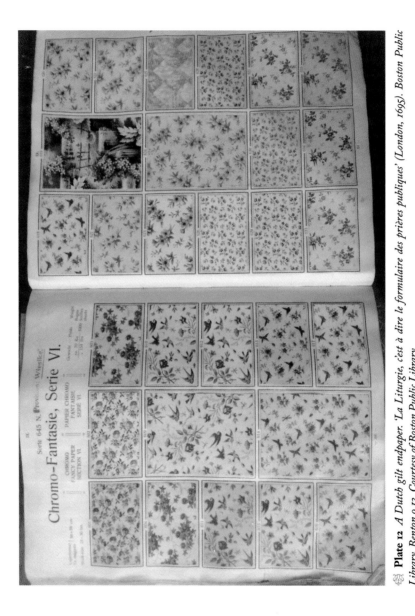

Plate 12 *A Dutch gilt endpaper. 'La Liturgie, c'est à dire le formulaire des prières publiques' (London, 1695). Boston Public Library, Benton 9.12. Courtesy of Boston Public Library*

of epigraphs printed at the tops of periodicals' to apposite epigraphs to the century's major poems, essays, and even reference works (such as Johnson's *Dictionary*). Barchas argues that fiction's abstinence from this eighteenth-century trend is noteworthy; the exception for novels was in the 1750s, when writers like Fielding and Smollett briefly experimented with title page epigraphs from classical writers in untranslated Greek and Latin in order, she argues, to signal 'the *gravitas* of the novel's heritage' by connecting it with the classical tradition of the satire and epic.[17] By the last third of the eighteenth century, epigraphs had become widespread; Leah Price notes that '[b]y the turn of the century, chapter mottos were already ubiquitous enough to lend a polemical edge' to novels, like Austen's, that did not contain them.[18] Gothic novels such as Ann Radcliffe's were especially known for the many epigraphs that appeared not just on their prefatory pages, but at the head of each chapter. The works of Shakespeare, Virgil, Horace, Pope, and Dryden were especially popular sources, but the literary well from which eighteenth-century novels drew epigraphs was surprisingly wide and deep. Some even turned to slightly earlier writers of prose fiction—Elizabeth Boyd's *The Happy-Unfortunate, or, the Female-Page: A Novel* draws its epigraph from Delarivier Manley's *The New Atlantis*, while Herbert Croft's *Love and Madness* opens with a passage from Aphra Behn's *Oronooko*.

Epigraphs in the novel raise all of the familiar questions about the paratext's function, but also introduce a new one: its fictionalization. For when epigraphs begin to appear in fiction, they quickly become a part of the novel's signature function of representing the imaginings of other minds. Though Austen's novels were epigraph-less themselves, they offer an important clue to how this worked. As readers have noticed, the poetry read by Austen's middle-class heroines like Catherine Morland and Fanny Price is familiar not just from anthologies and single-author collections of poems, but also from the epigraphic world of the Gothic novel.[19] In the beginning of the self-reflexive, Gothic-satirizing *Northanger Abbey*, we learn that Catherine reads poetry by Pope, Thomson, Gray, and Shakespeare as part of, as the narrator puts it, her 'training' to become the heroine of a novel. Finished in 1803 (though not published until 1817), *Northanger Abbey* collects the kinds of poetic epigraphs found heading the chapters of contemporary Gothic (and other) novels and introduces them to Catherine *before* the point in the plot when she travels to Bath and first encounters the Gothic novels—including Ann Radcliffe's *The Mysteries of Udolpho* and *The Italian*—whose influence colours her experience for the middle section of the novel.

[17] Janine Barchas, *Graphic Design, Print Culture, and the Eighteenth-Century Novel* (Cambridge: Cambridge University Press, 2003), p. 88.

[18] Leah Price, *The Anthology and the Rise of the Novel from Richardson to George Eliot* (Cambridge, MA: Harvard University Press, 2000), p. 91.

[19] Price, *The Anthology and the Rise of the Novel*, p. 91. Price points out that it is 'the presence of quotation—rather than the context of the narrative—[that] gives us the earliest clue to the gothic intertext of *Northanger Abbey*', p. 92.

Northanger Abbey makes of Catherine, that is, the kind of Gothic heroine out of whose mouth the epigraphs found in Ann Radcliffe novels might appear. *The Mysteries of Udolpho*, after its autographic general epigraph, begins its first chapter with a quotation from 'Autumn' in James Thomson's 'The Seasons': 'home is the resort / Of love, of joy, of peace and plenty, where, / Supporting and supported, polish'd friends / And dear relations mingle into bliss.'[20] Catherine Morland, long before reading *Udolpho*, learns from Thomson's 'Spring' section of 'The Seasons' that 'It is a delightful task / To teach the young idea how to shoot.'

Through imagining such quotations as part of the furniture of a novel heroine's mind, Austen makes a retrospective claim about the status of the epigraph in Radcliffe's novels. Austen reminds us that in Radcliffe's novels, the epigraph is not limited to being an authorial gesture towards a thematic element or a signal of literary or generic affiliation, but may be something quite different: evidence of the possible expression of a heroine's thoughts.[21] By populating novel heroine Catherine Morland's mind with just the range of reference Radcliffe's epigraphs manifest, Austen suggests that the epigraphs of *Udolpho* and *The Italian* are manifestations of those novels' characters' minds. This suggestion of Austen's gives more point to the famous wish expressed in *Northanger* for the heroines of novels to be in solidarity with one another.[22] And in this way, Austen assists in the retrospection fictionalization of the epigraph even as she avoided epigraphs herself.

The novel therefore initiated a transformation of the epigraph's function from a text deployed by an author, editor, or publisher to comment on the title or work, or to make a claim about the work's literary tradition or prestige, into a text that might rather be an expression of a character's mind. And the late eighteenth-century proliferation of epigraphs in novels developed concurrently with the increasing use of free indirect discourse, the technique through which (usually third-person) narration preserves its tense and person while taking on the language and perspective of a particular character. Together, these two formal innovations raised the possibility that epigraphs might belong to or be the thoughts of characters, and allowed the epigraph to join the novel's existing well-developed affordances for imagining other paratextual elements like prefaces and introductions as part of fiction rather than belonging to a firmly separate ontological realm. George Eliot's *Middlemarch* (1871)—a novel

---

[20] I use Genette's term 'autographic epigraph', as he does, to mean 'an epigraph written by the author' themselves (p. 145).

[21] Kate Rumbold suggests this fictionalization of the Gothic epigraphs when she notes that Shakespearean epigraphs in Radcliffe 'might appear to be the province of the detached, authoritative narrator, but they often articulate the way that characters see the world, and themselves'. *Shakespeare and the Eighteenth-Century Novel: Cultures of Quotation from Samuel Richardson to Jane Austen* (Cambridge: Cambridge University Press, 2016), p. 134.

[22] In *Paratexts* Genette speculates generally on the possibility that the 'epigrapher' (epigraph selector) may be in some cases a character, and cites Rousseau's *Julie* as one work that raises the question of whether the epigraph is selected by the author or part of the 'found manuscript' and therefore part of the fiction (p. 154).

whose epigraphs have been much discussed—exercises this new power when it opens with an epigraph from Beaumont and Fletcher's early modern play *The Maid's Tragedy*: 'Since I can do no good because a woman, / Reach constantly at something that is near it.' The epigraph's place at the beginning of the first chapter raises the possibility that it might belong to either the chapter, to the paperbound Book I (as the unit of this chapter's first publication), or to the novel to come as a whole. And its placement—both initially after the prelude's ironic reference to the 'blundering lives' of women and the diffusiveness of their effect on the world—also opens the possibility of ascribing the epigraph's first-person sentiment to Dorothea herself or (more ironically, given Eliot's achievements by that time) to 'George Eliot'. Further evidence that at least some of *Middlemarch*'s epigraphs belong to characters rather than narrator or author comes in those uncanny 'moments in Middlemarch when characters seem to quote from a chapter's epigraph, an unsettling trick'.[23]

Middlemarch's first epigraph seems to fit nearly all of the possibilities of how an epigraph might have functioned over time, from its possible origins as an authorial motto migrating onto the first pages of the book to represent the author to commenting on the work's text to hooking the work into a literary—or other—tradition. And *Middlemarch*'s epigraphs also seem to encompass almost the entire world of where an epigraph might come from: classical sources and modern sources; self-authored 'excerpts'; poetry, drama, and fiction. Earlier in her career, however, Eliot offers an example of an epigraph whose genre works to narrow rather than proliferate meanings. First published anonymously in *Blackwood's Magazine* in July 1859, *The Lifted Veil* is a long first-person short story in which Latimer, a sensitive soul who can both see into the future and into the minds of others, narrates the story of his life in the moments before he knows he is going to die. Epigraphless in its original magazine publication, when *The Lifted Veil* was republished as part of the Cabinet Edition of Eliot's collected works it appeared with an allographic poetic epigraph: 'Give me no light, great Heaven, but such as turns / To energy of human fellowship; / No powers beyond the growing heritage / That makes completer manhood.' Looking back on her career in her complete works, Eliot reclaims for her oeuvre an originally uncollected and anonymous text, giving it an epigraph that explicitly could not be assigned to the poetry-challenged first-person narrator: a poem that begs for only that illumination that—unlike Latimer's sympathy-destroying clairvoyance—aids 'fellowship'. Yet in composing for that purpose a first-person poem that asks for 'powers' that will make 'completer manhood', Eliot also continues to insist that this author-claimed epigraphic space identifies her creative power as masculine. If in the early nineteenth century Austen claimed the epigraphs of Ann Radcliffe for the minds of characters, by the late nineteenth century Eliot drew on the novel's by then entrenched tradition

---

[23] John Plotz, *Semi-Detached: The Aesthetics of Virtual Experience since Dickens* (Princeton, NJ: Princeton University Press, 2017), p. 410.

of thinking about epigraphs as potentially belonging to characters when she wrote an epigraph designed specifically to put some distance between narrator and author.

THE FATE OF THE EPIGRAPH
IN THE DIGITAL AGE

What is happening to the epigraph in the digital age? Low-quality mass digitization has been unkind to the epigraph, as it has been unkind to many other paratextual forms—prefaces, indexes, footnotes—designed for the printing press, the paper page, and the bound book rather than the scrolling screen and the distributed, platform-bound e-book. Such paratexts often fare badly when originally printed books are digitized and served up on screens and e-readers. Their unfamiliar layout and place-ment, separate from the main blocks of text, often confuse the optical character recognition software that works to translate photographs of printed books into machine-readable text, rendering them illegible. And epigraphs containing elements that don't easily translate into alpha-numeric text often disappear entirely. The sorrow songs in *The Souls of Black Folk*, for example, vanish completely in the (widely used) Project Gutenberg edition because they are represented by images of musical notation; their omission erases the epigraphs' core meanings, leaving the impression that this ground-breaking book on African American life and culture relies entirely on single epigraphs drawn from works primarily by white Anglo American authors.

But even when an epigraph survives a text's digital reproduction, it is more likely than ever to remain unread. Some readers have, of course, always skipped or skimmed epigraphs; as Peter Stallybrass points out, the history of discontinuous reading is long, and Ann Blair and Leah Price note that skipping and skimming are perhaps more time-honoured than cover-to-cover reading.[24] We can see epigraphs themselves as related to the long history of excerpting and commonplacing original texts so that readers can peruse only the best bits, so it seems only fair that, in turn, epigraphs them-selves sometimes stood out as a part of the book that readers may easily skate over. But while epigraphs might have been something that *some* readers *might* skip, more recently epigraph-skipping has been hard-coded into some e-book devices, which often vault over paratexts to open directly to the first page of the main text. As Ellen McCracken notes in 2016,

> [u]pon opening an Amazon digital book on a portable device, readers imme-diately see the first page of the main text, because the device is programmed to

---

[24] Peter Stallybrass, 'Book and Scrolls: Navigating the Bible', in *Books and Readers in Early Modern England*, ed. Jennifer Andersen and Elizabeth Sauer (Philadelphia, PA: University of Pennsylvania Press, 2002), pp. 42–79, p. 42.

skip the cover and copyright page, and other important material the author has included as front matter such as the table of contents, dedication and epigraph.[25]

It is almost as though new digitization protocols and text-serving platforms sense that in these earlier paratexts they have competitors whom they must vanquish; optical character recognition mangles the index and the footnote with the goal of holding out the search of a newly machine-readable text as a replacement; epigraphs are rendered illegible but suggestion engines, Amazon reviews, and GoodReads offer alternative opportunities for intertext as education.

Yet in many forms and genres of born-digital texts, the epigraph persists, with new mark-up standards and other forms of encoding that enable both machine and human reading. TEI has a form for encoding epigraphs, as does Wikibooks; the APA Style includes standards for formatting epigraphs in publications, and the LaTeX digital typesetting program includes more than one package designed to render epigraphs in different styles.[26] And new forms remediate the functions of the print epigraph into digital media and platforms. Websites—particularly those that hosted the early blogosphere—often have epigraphs; email signature quotations reconfigure the history through which mottos associated with authors became epigraphs associated with texts, since they are quotations attributed to others but which stand in some relation to the author of the email. While the digital representation of the printed text seems to deform the epigraph, then, the epigraph appears to have made the transition to born-digital formats surprisingly smoothly; given the internet's emphasis on intertextuality, excerpting, and textual recirculation, perhaps this should not be a surprise.

[25] Ellen McCracken, *Paratexts and Performance in the Novels of Junot Díaz and Sandra Cisneros* (Basingstoke: Palgrave Macmillan, 2016), p. 40. It is worth noting that many e-readers have a tab that can take the reader back to these other elements, though they are sometimes deformed by the translation into digital forms.

[26] LaTeX package: https://ctan.org/pkg/epigraph?lang=en; APA Style blog: http://blog.apastyle.org/apastyle/2013/10/how-to-format-an-epigraph.html; Wikibooks: http://en.wikibooks.org/wiki/Template:Epigraph; TEI epigraph markup standard: http://www.tei-c.org/release/doc/tei-p5-doc/en/html/ref-epigraph.html.

CHAPTER 14

(*Stage Directions* TIFFANY STERN)

This chapter tells the history of what have come to be called 'stage directions': short, practical performance or reader-oriented instructions,
often in pigeon Latin, of unclear authorship, that typically start, end, and
intersperse a printed play. It is in three parts, beginning in the eighteenth
century when the phrase 'stage direction' was co-invented by Alexander Pope and
Lewis Theobald as a term for non-authorial directives in Shakespeare. It then turns
to medieval and early modern plays, asking what a 'stage direction' was before it had
a title, where it was situated on the page, what language it employed, who may have
written it and for whom, and whether indeed it was 'it' before two words defined it
as one entity. Finally, the chapter considers the 'stage direction' after the term became
established, asking how the rise of the theatre's 'stage director' affected what 'stage
directions' were on page and stage. Throughout, then, the chapter tells two different
and only partially connected stories: one is the story of the term 'stage direction', and
the other the story of the thing(s) 'stage direction'.

THE INVENTION OF 'STAGE DIRECTIONS'

The phrase 'stage direction' was created by the editor and poet Alexander Pope, and
the editor and playwright Lewis Theobald, in the course of a disagreement over a
line in Shakespeare's *Henry V*. There is, famously, in the 1623 folio text of that play,
a passage in which Mistress Quickly says of the dying Falstaff that 'his nose was a
sharpe as a Pen, and a Table of greene fields' (TLN 838–9).[1] As the observation does
not make immediate sense, Pope, in his 1725 edition of the works of Shakespeare,
emended it. He argued that the end of the line was a 'direction crept into the text
from the margin'; that there must have been a 'Property man' at that time called
'Greenfield'; and that the original direction, which he extracted from the speech, will
have been 'A Table of Greenfield's'.[2]

Theobald was incensed not just by Pope's solution—when he published his own
edition of Shakespeare's *Works*, he introduced the emendation of the line commonly
accepted now, 'and a' babbled of green fields'[3]—but also by the ignorance of staging
it betrayed. The 'Stage-Direction', he explained, enlarging on Pope's 'direction' to
underline the performance nature of the directive, would never be placed in the text
at the moment of need; rather, it would be 'mark'd . . . at about a Page in Quantity

---

[1] *First Folio* quotations are taken throughout from the facsimile prepared by Charlton Hinman, *Mr William Shakespeares Comedies, Histories, & Tragedies* [*The Norton Facsimile*] (New York: Norton, 1968), using the through-line numbers (TLN) of that edition.

[2] William Shakespeare, *The Works*, ed. Alexander Pope, 6 vols (1725), 1, p. xviii.

[3] William Shakespeare, *The Works*, ed. Lewis Theobald, 7 vols (1733), 4, p. 30.

before the Actors quoted are to enter, or the Properties be carried on'.[4] Thus 'stage direction' was born: it originally indicated an advanced note to a props man that had (Pope) or had not (Theobald) been rammed mistakenly into Shakespeare's text.

Theobald did, however, adopt 'stage direction' as his term for non-authorial paratext. In his 1733 edition of Shakespeare's *Works*, he used 'stage directions' for dumb shows, writing a scathing gloss to the first words of the dumb show for *The Murder of Gonzago* in Shakespeare's *Hamlet*, 'Enter a King and Queen very lovingly'. Pointing out that the stars of the ensuing play are not a king and a queen but a duke and a duchess, he expostulated: 'Thus have the blundering and inadvertent Editors...given us this Stage-Direction'.[5] The blame for the discrepancy, Theobald believed, belonged to John Heminges and Henry Condell, the actors in Shakespeare's company who, as 'editors', had brought the first folio to the press: 'Royal Coronets being at first order'd by the Poet [Shakespeare] for the Duke and Dutchess, the succeeding Players...mistook 'em for a King and Queen'. In this instance, 'stage direction' is not a text written by a prompter for a property man, but a text written by actors for readers.[6] 'Stage directions', then, were from the first understood to be by and for a range of people; what they shared was that they were non-authorial and marred the process of reading Shakespeare's plays.

'Stage direction', and the opprobrium that came with the term, was accepted wholesale by later eighteenth-century editors. Of '*Re-enter fighting, and Macbeth is slain*', the editor George Steevens wrote, in 1773, that 'This stage-direction...proves, that the players were not even skilful enough to prevent impropriety'. His irritation, again levelled at Heminges and Condell, arises from the confusion between this direction and the one immediately afterwards: 'Macbeth is here killed on the stage, and a moment after Macduff enters, as from another place, with his head on a spear'.[7] These illogical directions, Steevens insisted, were 'unShakespearean'. His fellow editor Edmond Malone agreed, maintaining, in 1790, that 'many of the stage-directions' in Shakespeare's works 'appear to have been inserted by the players; and they are often very injudicious'.[8]

Intriguingly, countries across the continent also started inventing terminology for what we now call 'stage directions' in the eighteenth century. Several, borrowing from one another, adopted versions of the ancient Roman word 'didascaliae', which dates from around the first century BC: 'didascalie' (France); 'didascalia' (Italy); 'didascalia' (Spain). But the Latin (via Greek) word chosen had ramifications of its own. Originally

---

[4] Lewis Theobald, *Shakespeare Restored* (1726), p. 138.

[5] Shakespeare, *Works*, ed. Theobald, 7, p. 295.

[6] In fact dumb shows often had a different heritage from dialogue, and this kind of discrepancy is not unusual. See Tiffany Stern, 'Inventing Stage Directions; Demoting Dumb Shows', *Stage Directions and Shakespearean Theatre*, ed. Sarah Dustagheer and Gillian Woods for Arden Shakespeare (London: Methuen, 2018), pp. 19–43.

[7] William Shakespeare, *The Plays*, ed. Samuel Johnson and George Steevens, 10 vols (1773), 4, p. 530.

[8] William Shakespeare, *The Plays and Poems* ed. Edmond Malone, 10 vols in 11 parts (1790), 4, p. 435.

it had meant the notices about production supplied with Roman plays—when the first performance had taken place; the names of the play's prompters, composers, and actors; who the Roman consul was that year, and so forth: the term did not literally mean 'stage directions' as there were none on the Roman texts. So continental 'didascaliae' were and are every bit of text that is not the play's dialogue, including the list of dramatis personae, the title, act and scene divisions, as well as 'stage directions'. European critics referring to 'didascaliae' recognize the diversity of paratext generated by a play as a result, and tend not to be concerned with its authorship. But in Anglophone countries, the narrowness of the phrase 'stage direction' has isolated a subset of paratext, and unified it as though it has a fixed meaning and author— despite the fact that in its earliest usages, 'stage direction' had several meanings, and was thought of as non-authorial.

'STAGE DIRECTIONS' BEFORE THE PHRASE

What came to be grouped under the term 'stage direction' was a series of passages in early modern plays that resembled one another in terms of page layout and, sometimes, language, but not authorship or readership. Indeed, it was the shared features of 'stage directions' that often hid the divergent origins of printed playbooks altogether, which might have, behind them, an authorial text, a text marked up for performance, a text marked up for readers, or a combination of all three. What needs exploration, then, is why and how a series of separate play interventions came to look visually similar and share a common(ish) language.

Practices developed for medieval mystery and morality plays explain the placement and language of early modern 'stage directions'. These plays, handwritten, and not for publication but annual performance, were authored by priests; 'stage directions' tended to be added to them later by practitioners, either when mounting a performance, or when recording performance advice for succeeding generations. As 'stage directions' were not usually written when the play was, they were likely to be in a different hand from the rest of the play, and placed around the dialogue; they were, further, often 'boxed', rubricated (written in red ink), or highlighted with slashes, brackets, or dashes so they were not confusable visually with the actual 'play' in performance. This layout, separating the poetry to be spoken from the practical advice that was not— though, as Butterworth points out, with 'considerable inconsistency as to the positions that stage directions occupy on the page'[9]—aided the running of productions so much that when scribes rewrote plays afresh, they would inscribe dialogue first, and stage directions second, in the margins and 'separated' by hand or placement.

---

[9] Philip Butterworth, *Staging Conventions in Medieval English Theatre* (Cambridge: Cambridge University Press, 2014), p. 4.

Stage directions, by their very appearance, were relegated: page layout stated that they were less important than the dialogue they accompanied.

Early modern plays inherited layout from medieval manuscript practice, and tended to place the words to be spoken in the central space of a printed page with the speech prefixes and words for action around the outside, though where on the outside took time to determine.[10] The first secular play ever to be printed in English, Henry Medwall's *Fulgens and Lucrece* (1512–16), has its directions in the margin and heralded, as is the start of each speech, by pilcrows (Fig. 14.1a); Ulpian Fulwell's *Like Will to Like* (1568) has some stage directions centred and indented and some on the right and boxed or bracketed (Fig. 14.1b); Robert Wilson's *Three Ladies of London* (1584) has stage directions centred, or ranged right, and in roman type while the dialogue is in blackletter (Fig. 14.1c); George Peele's *Edward I* (1593) has stage directions in italics when the play is in roman type (Fig. 14.1d). As these examples show, a shared grammar for stage directions was only slowly being developed: past, present, and future tense were all experimented with ('And gaue him a good blow on the buttocke'; 'he kysseth Diccons breeche'; 'Here they shall syng)',[11] as were hortative, imperative, and participle forms ('Here let Lucar open the boxe and dip her finger in it'; 'smite him in the neck with a swoord'; 'pointing to one standing by').[12] Why a simple present tense was ultimately adopted may have been to save words, though it had the invigorating effect of making stage directions happen in real time rather than recall a past performance or predict a future one.

As the above also shows, a shared system for the appearance and placement of stage directions also took a while to come into being. Only by the 1590s was the marginal and italic form somewhat settled on. Why that choice was made cannot be traced to a single printer, so may relate to general printing house needs. The words that make up stage directions put pressure on certain letters, particularly capital E for 'Enter' and 'Exit': extracting these from separate 'italic' boxes preserved the full range of roman letters for the play's dialogue. Since then, directions have tended to be italic, marginal, and present tense, though variants of each remain possible.

The page layout finally settled upon, which presents the dialogue as though it is a poem, and the directions as though they are its gloss, has had interpretative implications. Stage directions seem to be a 'comment' on the play they flank, rather than part of it, and are often treated with less respect than the dialogue. And, as directions are in a secondary space—a space, moreover, characterized by its emptiness—they seem easy to add to. Plays of the early modern period in second and third editions

---

[10] For more, see Linda McJannet, *The Voice of Elizabethan Stage Directions* (Newark, DE: University of Delaware Press, 1999).

[11] William Stevenson, *Gammer gurtons nedle* (1575), C4r, B2r; John Bale, *Kynge Johan* (1538) ed. J. Payne Collier (1838), p. 41.

[12] Robert Wilson, *Three Ladies of London* (1584), E1v; Thomas Preston, *Cambises* (1570), c2v; Ulpian Fulwell, *Like Will to Like* (1587), A3r.

Fig. 14.1 *(a) Henry Medwall, 'Fulgens and Lucres' (facsimile) (New York: G. D. Smith, 1920 [London: John Rastell, 1512?]), sig. e4r; (b) Ulpian Fulwell, 'Like Will to Like' (London: John Allde, 1568?), sig. Bɪr; (c) Robert Wilson, 'Three Ladies of London' (London: John Danter, 1592), sig. Bɪr; (d) George Peele, 'King Edward the First' (London: Abel Jeffes, 1593), sig. I2r. All images by permission of the Folger Shakespeare Library*

often contain changes to stage directions though the words of the dialogue are unchanged—Shakespeare's *Richard III* in its third quarto (1603), for instance, has additional 'explanatory' or necessary (but previously absent) printed stage directions, while the Folger Shakespeare Library's printed copy of *The Two Merry Milkmaids* (1620) has early modern manuscript stage directions added onto the text in two different hands.[13] The marginal nature of stage directions made them not simply open to multiple or collaborative authorship: they positively invited it.

The patchy Latin of early modern stage directions, too, suggests they can be added to by others—in that 'stage directions' across plays sound more like one another than like their plays' 'author(s)'. 'Stage-direction language' indeed has 'multiple authorship' in its origin as it descends, again, from medieval manuscript tradition (not, as might be suspected, from printed classical plays, which did not have stage directions in their earliest versions). While medieval plays, originally in Latin, were slowly translated into the vernacular for audiences, stage directions, which were by and for practitioners only, retained their original language.[14] Over time, English crept in but Latin didn't

---

[13] Leslie Thomson, 'A Quarto "Marked for Performance": Evidence of What?', *Medieval and Renaissance Drama in England* 8 (1996): 176–210.

[14] For more, see T. H. Howard-Hill, 'The Evolution of the Form of Plays in English during the Renaissance', *Renaissance Quarterly* 43 (1990): 112–45.

entirely creep out, the result being the English/Latin medley that typifies a lot of early modern plays—'*Exit the Watch. Manet Captain*' reads Marston's *Insatiate Countesse*; '*Exeunt omnes, præter Consta.* and *Gage*' reads Massinger's *City-Madam*.[15] This 'stage-direction language' had rules of its own. Some verbs conjugated and hence remained 'Latin', like 'exit'/'exeunt' and 'manet'/'manent', and others, like 'enter', already at a remove from the Latin 'intrat'/'intrant', did not conjugate and behaved in 'English' fashion. The word order of both entrances and exits, however, was firmly Latinate, irrespective of language, with the verb first and the proper noun second ('*exit Bosola*', for instance, rather than '*Bosola goes out*'). This language, which ensured stage directions resembled one another, but were distinct from all other text, added to the notion that these were unstable passages, open for anyone to write, moderate, or change and not tightly linked to an author.

It is only the specific functions of (some) 'stage directions' of the early modern period that reveal who they were written for, and so hint at who may have written them. For instance, there is a subset of so-called 'stage directions' that aren't about staging at all. These are directions for the theatre's scribe; they might therefore logically be called 'scribe directions'.[16] Scribe directions include the note in Thomas Kyd's *The Spanish Tragedy* against a letter beginning 'For want of incke receive this bloudie writ'. It reads, 'Red incke'.[17] This direction is for the writer of the stage letter, who is being instructed to use red ink in order to create a property letter that looks 'bloody' to the audience. Usually such directions are placed around 'stage scrolls' (papers to be read on stage); indeed, the titles that often herald such scrolls—'the letter', 'the riddle', 'the proclamation'—are probably directions telling the scribe to create those particular documents.[18]

Other paratexts are apparently for 'stage keepers' and/or 'prompters'. Examples include the direction in L. S.'s *Noble Stranger*: '*Enter* Plod *with a Boxe, in which are little pieces of paper rold up: A Table set forth*'.[19] This may instruct a stage keeper to create and fill such a box; it certainly tells a stage functionary, probably a prompter, to make sure that a box is supplied to the actor and a table is brought onstage. It bears a similarity to the directions which, as Theobald had pointed out, are for props or people to be made ready for a future stage moment. The printed Quarto of Shakespeare and Fletcher's *Two Noble Kinsmen* has such 'advanced' directions, asking for '2. Hearses' to be 'ready with Palamon; and Arcite: the 3. Queenes. Theseus:

---

[15] John Marston, *The Insatiate Countesse* (1613), E1v. Thomas Heywood, *If you knovv not me, you know no bodie* (1605), D1r.

[16] For more on scribe directions, see Tiffany Stern, *Documents of Performance* (Cambridge: Cambridge University Press, 2009), pp. 154, 181–4.

[17] Thomas Kyd, *Spanish Tragedy* (1592), E1v.

[18] See Stern, 'Scrolls', in *Documents of Performance*, pp. 174–200.

[19] L. S., *Noble Stranger* (1640), G3r.

and his Lordes ready'.[20] These directions tell a backstage person, again, probably the prompter, which people and things are to be gathered and made 'ready' at the correct doors for a forthcoming entrance.

None of the directions described so far are for an actor. Probably, indeed, actors were never the direct recipients of early modern stage directions, as they learned plays from individual 'parts', not the full play text. Though actors' parts did contain stage directions, and though these might have been extracted from the full play—rendering them, on the full play, further 'scribe directions'—parts may equally have contained different, actor-specific directions. With only one English professional actor's part surviving from the period, for 'Orlando' in Greene's *Orlando Furioso*, there is not much information to go on: nevertheless, the part's directions are brief and Latinate against the full play's explanatory English. Thus the 'Orlando' part has the one-word Latin direction 'Inchaunt',[21] where the *Orlando* printed playbook (admittedly of the play in a different version) has 'Hee drinkes, and she charmes him with her wand, and [he] lies downe to sleepe'.[22] It is worth recalling that playbook directions for entrances and exits are of most immediate use to the prompter, who needs to direct stage traffic, as are action directions like 'whispers' or 'dies'—as the prompter needs to know when *not* to prompt because staged silence is required. Printed playbooks, at one remove from actors' texts, are similar to, and are sometimes copied from, the text that was in the prompter's hands.[23] It is likely that many of their directions are for, and sometimes by, the prompter.

Then there are directions that would never work in performance. They include the 'massed entrances' found in several early modern plays including some by Jonson, Shakespeare, and Middleton—in which every person who is to speak is apparently made to 'enter' at the start of the scene—which have been attributed to the habits of Ralph Crane, the scribe, as he tried to give plays on the page a classical aspect. They also include the directions that eighteenth-century editors noticed with such condemnation, like the instruction in Macbeth for '*A shew of eight Kings, and Banquo last, with a glasse in his hand*' (*Macbeth*, TLN 1657–8). As, in the speech to come, the *first* king is said to resemble Banquo, while the *last* is said to carry a looking glass, Theobald protested that 'The Editors' (Heminges and Condell, again) 'could not help blundering even in this Stage-Direction', which, indeed, does contradict the dialogue.[24] Such directions seem to be (wrong) attempts to help the reader visualize the staging; as they are non-performable, the word 'stage' sits oddly on them. They are 'reader directions'.

[20] John Fletcher and William Shakespeare, *The Two Noble Kinsmen* (1634), C3v.

[21] The 'Part' of Orlando, Dulwich MSS 1: http://www.henslowe-alleyn.org.uk/images/MSS-1/Article-138/08r. html.

[22] Robert Greene, *Orlando Furioso* (1594), G1r.

[23] Warren Smith, 'New Light on Stage Directions in Shakespeare', *Studies in Philology* 47 (1950): 173–81, p. 178.

[24] Shakespeare, *Works*, ed. Theobald, 5, p. 443.

Harder to sort out is who wrote these varied paratexts. The 'reader directions' have been said to be by 'editors' preparing texts for the page, but could in fact be by anyone from playwright to compositor in the printing house; other, scribal and more 'stagey' directions may be by playwrights, prompters, or other stage functionaries, or a stage-focused compositor. Playwrights will probably have written some of the directions, though surviving manuscripts suggest they did so haphazardly; other professionals seem often to have added to what was there.[25] Only a particular kind of direction is certainly authorial: the 'implied' stage direction, embedded in the language (like 'weepe / Not, gentle boy'), which does not take stage direction form at all.[26] The other type of stage direction sometimes thought to bear the hallmark of a play-wright's authorship is more questionable. 'Fiction' directions like *Witches vanish* (*Macbeth*, TLN 179)—'vanish' here meaning, in staging terms, 'exit'—are often said to originate in a playwright, because they come from someone deeply involved in the story's narrative. But such directions may equally, of course, be particularly intense 'reader directions' or, alternatively, may have been theatrically explicable. It is easier to say who directions are for than who they are by.

With 'scribe directions', 'stage keeper directions', 'prompter directions', and 'reader directions', as well as 'implied directions', however, what is clear is that there is no single type of text that is a 'stage direction'—indeed, as shown, not all surviving such directions are even about staging. Perhaps that is why, in the period, there was no collective terminology for these paratexts. Only 'entrances and exits' are spoken of as a staging unit—famously, in Shakespeare's *As You Like It*, men and women on the stage of the world 'have their *Exits* and their *Entrances*' (TLN 1120)—and only entrances and, sometimes, exits were on occasion further extracted onto special documents, 'backstage plots'.[27] The lack of a broader terminology for 'stage direction' underlies the notion that instructions and recollections, imaginings and fact, texts for scribes, texts for prompters, texts for readers are not one thing, even if made to share layout and language. What is ironic is that the phrase used to categorize them has hidden the range of what they actually are.

'STAGE DIRECTIONS' AFTER THE PHRASE

A change in the theatres of the late nineteenth century altered stage directions for-ever. The prompter, whose job had been to facilitate performance of the play as received, was relegated; a new role was created, that of the actor manager, later called the 'director'. It was the job of the director to give a unique, creative, personal inter-

---

[25] W. B. Long, "'A bed / for Woodstock": A Warning for the Unwary', *Medieval and Renaissance Drama in England* 2 (1985): 91–118.

[26] Francis Beaumont, *Phylaster* (1620), C4r.

[27] For more on backstage plots see Tiffany Stern, 'Backstage-Plots', in *Documents of Performance*, pp. 201–31; for more on entrances see Mariko Ichikawa, *Shakespearean Entrances* (Basingstoke: Palgrave, 2002), *passim*.

pretation to the plays he or she was overseeing—which often contradicted, or left little space for, the playwright's own artistic stage vision. The battle for creative ownership of the play, between playwrights and directors, was born. It took place in stage directions.

Nineteenth-century playwrights, usually denied access to rehearsals, began to use stage directions to dictate what they wanted from performance in an attempt to lead, rival, or stymy 'stage directors'. Directors then and ever since have largely ignored these intrusions. Modernist theatre practitioner and theorist Edward Gordon Craig, who expressed his ideas in 'theatrical' dialogue form, declared as early as 1905 that authorial stage directions were 'an offence to the men of the theatre':

> STAGE DIRECTOR: If to gag or cut the poet's lines is an offence, so is it an offence to temper with the art of the stage-director.
> PLAYGOER: Then is all the stage direction of the world's plays worthless?
> STAGE DIRECTOR: Not to the reader, but to the stage-director, and to the actor—yes.[28]

Almost one hundred years later, in 2003, director Jean Schiffman explained how she had been taught to 'cross out stage directions on the first reading'; acting and teaching director Amy Glazer was instructed likewise, being told 'it's a sign of a bad actor to even look at stage directions'.[29] Against this, a few possessive play-wrights fought a counterbattle. Samuel Beckett, author of two plays that consist only of stage directions, *Act without Words I* and *Act without Words 2*, wrote detailed and prescriptive directions for all his performances, his *Endgame* instructing the actor of Hamm phrase by phrase what to do:

> My...dog?
> *(Pause.)*
> Oh I am willing to believe they suffer as much as such creatures can suffer. But does that mean their sufferings equal mine? No doubt.
> *(Pause.)*
> No, all is a—
> *(he yawns)*
> —bsolute,
> *(proudly)*
> the bigger a man is the fuller he is.
> *(Pause. Gloomily.)*
> And the emptier.
> *(He sniffs.)*[30]

---

[28] Gordon Craig, *The Art of the Theatre* (Edinburgh: T. N. Foulis, 1905), pp. 29–30.

[29] Jean Schiffman, 'Taking Directions', *Backstage*, 5 March 2003: https://www.backstage.com/news/taking-directions/.

[30] Samuel Beckett, *Endgame* (New York: Grove Press, 1958), p. 2.

Performers given permission to put on Samuel Beckett's plays are contractually obliged to follow his stage directions by his estate. But even Beckett was not able to prevent the American Repertory Theatre's 1983 director-led production of *Endgame*; instead, he had a bitter note inserted, by legal demand, into the programme: '[This] production which dismisses my directions is a complete parody of the play as conceived by me'.[31]

As, with the rise of the director, stage directions became ever less significant in production terms, so they became correspondingly more powerful on the printed page. New copyright laws—an international law of 1887 in Europe, an 1891 law in the United States—partly brought this about. Before the laws, playwrights had relied on performance for payment, and often avoided publication, as theatre companies could legally perform any play once it was in print. But the new laws protected plays in print from unsanctioned performance. Now playwrights started to conceive of two lives for their dramas, one on the stage, one on the page. The result was the stage direction written with the page specifically in mind: the 'literary' stage direction—or, rather, the 'literary direction' as there is often little stagy about them. Bernard Shaw's plays feature almost exclusively 'literary directions'. His *Man and Superman* (1905), for instance, has directions that are sometimes four pages long; they are generally unactable:

> *Hector Malone is an Eastern American; but he is not at all ashamed of his nationality. This makes English people of fashion think well of him, as of a young fellow who is manly enough to confess to an obvious disadvantage without any attempt to conceal or extenuate it.*[32]

This background information, written with Dickensian aplomb, gives the character of Malone a rich pre-history, allowing the play on the page to rival, or be seen as a version of, a novel.

A consequence of playwrights' new focus on stage directions is that the term once again changed meaning. 'Stage directions' came to be thought of as texts by playwrights for actors (that they are often for readers has not made it into conventional definitions). A 1929 dictionary describes stage direction as 'a direction printed or written with a play, as to the manner in which it is to be acted', and similar such definitions have been supplied ever since.[33] Even the *Oxford English Dictionary*, which traces the term 'stage direction' only back to the 1790s, calls it 'a direction inserted in a written or printed play where it is thought necessary to indicate the appropriate action, etc.'[34]

---

[31] Legal insertion in American Repertory Theater's programme for *Endgame* (1984).

[32] Bernard Shaw, *Man and Superman* (New York: Brentano's, 1905), p. 61.

[33] Funk and Wagnall's *New Standard Dictionary of the English Language* (1929), 4, p. 2361.

[34] 'Stage, n.', *OED Online*, Oxford University Press, June 2016.

In fact, stage directions remain as mixed in authorship and intention as before, depending on the version of the text published. 'Acting editions' of plays, like those published for Samuel French, largely concern particular performances, and are likely to be taken from production prompt books including theatrical 'stage directions'; 'literary' versions are likely to preserve an authorial text with authorial stage directions, though, if also post-production, may well include performance notes too.

What hasn't changed is the appearance and placement of stage directions: they keep, by and large, the format developed for them in the medieval and early modern period, and are often marginal, italic, and, in terms of 'enter' and 'exit', in Latinate word order. As a result, stage directions are still made to broadcast their nature as secondary texts, open to revision and change; they tend to be treated as such. This can be seen in modern editorial practice: editors of historic plays, reverent to dialogue, often add to or modify stage directions, while also excluding them from line numbering. They render these tiny texts authorially suspect and hard to quote as a result.

Stage directions have always been in every respect—placement on the page, look, phraseology, authorship (and hence moment of creation and intended reader), necessity, and treatment—awkwardly different from the dialogue they surround. It is the term used to define them that has enforced, and latterly brought about, notions of their authoriality and purpose. Only when we realize that a stage direction is not always for the stage, is not necessarily a direction, and does not have the consistency over time that its appearance suggests, will we come nearer to decoding this—or, rather, these—fascinating and variable souvenirs of stage and page.

CHAPTER 15 RUNNING TITLES   CLAIRE M. L. BOURNE

The pages of books have many kinds of heads—from the capitula (¶) once used by medieval scribes to signal the start (*caput*, or head) of each new unit of text to chapter headings that still divide longer works into smaller sections. They also have headlines—a line of text at the top of each page that normally consists of a page number, some blank space, and a few words that specify the title of the book, describe the content of the section or page, and/or announce the name of the author. Running titles, as the lexical components of page headlines are often called, have been an integral feature of book design for more than 2000 years. Visibly situated at the head of the page, they have long provided 'intelligence' for readers seeking to navigate and interpret the contents of all kinds of books. Why, then, do we—and by 'we' I mean both everyday readers *and* historians of reading—pay so little attention to them? They are, after all, staring us right in the face.

For one, running titles are ubiquitous. The *fact* they exist on the pages of most books is taken for granted, and by extension, their *content* is hardly seen as remarkable. Insofar as running titles have been studied, it has been for their typographic errors and what those errors can reveal about the logistics and contingencies (read: contaminations) of early book production.[1] The goal of such scholarship has been to isolate and strip away features of the text made outside the author's control in order to illuminate what the author (almost always Shakespeare) wrote.[2] But by insisting on the status of running titles as vagaries of publication and limiting our interest to what running titles can tell about how books were made, these practices have effectively glossed over the dynamic ways that running titles—in all their messiness—are and have been designed for use. In particular, they anticipate the readerly practices of biblio-customization: both gathering texts together and pulling them apart. In other words, running titles make or break the book.

I have elected to use 'running title' to describe this page-design feature, but it has also been called various forms of 'headline', 'running head', 'running headline', and 'page head'.[3] (Technically, a *headline* is the whole line of text at the top of the page, including

---

[1] In particular, see Fredson Bowers, 'Notes on Running-Titles as Bibliographical Evidence', *The Library*, 4th series, 19, no. 3 (1938): 315–38.

[2] Charlton Hinman, *The Printing and Proofreading of the First Folio of Shakespeare* (Oxford: Clarendon Press, 1963), esp. pp. 171–5.

[3] R. B. McKerrow, *An Introduction to Bibliography for Literary Students* (Oxford: Clarendon, 1928), p. 26; and *John Carter's ABC for Book Collectors*, 9th edn, rev. Nicolas Barker and Simran Thadani (New Castle DE: Oak Knoll, 2016), p. 141.

page numbers.) Sometimes, distinctions are made among 'running' titles (the title of the book); 'section' titles (names of the book's subdivisions); and 'page' titles (summaries of the page's contents).[4] The difficulty of articulating what this 'book part' actually *is* has surely made it difficult to study what it *does*, or *is designed to do*.

As late as the seventeenth century, there was no prescription for what information should be included in running titles or what function they should serve for readers. Instructions for what kind of text—content or design—to set at the top of the page are conspicuously absent from Joseph Moxon's otherwise detailed printing manual from 1683.[5] But Guy Miège's *The English Grammar* (1688) delivered: '[T]here is commonly at the head of every Page a Title expressed in a few Words, called the *Running Title*. And, if the Book consists of several distinct Matters, the Title runs accordingly.'[6] According to Miège, a book's 'Running Title' was usually short and often modified to reflect, with varying levels of specificity, the contents of the page (or opening) it headed. In the early days of print, what it meant for the title to 'run accordingly' with the 'distinct Matters' of a book was quite literally debatable. Equally contentious was which 'few Words' would best describe a book's 'Matters' (and by whom). At stake in these decisions was the power to circumscribe readers' encounters with and interpretations of the book's contents. Running titles *ran* insofar as they extended through the space of the book ('at the head of every Page') *and* in time (as aids to memory). They simultaneously allowed readers to run *with* or *away from* the makers' designs for reading—to submit to it or resist it. After all, books with running titles made it easier for readers to jump around.

By the late seventeenth century, running titles had been, in one form or another, a feature of book design for more than a millennium. Closely associated with the rise of the codex, they are present in the top margins of many of the earliest extant Latin manuscripts.[7] Running titles fell out of regular use in the early Middle Ages, possibly because they provided little material support for *lectio*, a monastic reading practice that stressed the slow, deliberate, and linear digestion of a single text.[8] As early as the twelfth century and in step with the rise of scholastic reading practices, running titles began to appear once more in the top margins of manuscript codices. They were suddenly useful again: the twelfth century was when 'to think became a craft',

[4] Seán Jennett, *The Making of Books*, 4th edn (New York: Frederick A. Praeger, 1967), pp. 293–6.

[5] Joseph Moxon, *Mechanick Exercises: Or the Doctrine of Handy-works. Applied to the Art of Printing*, vol. 2 (London: Joseph Moxon, 1683).

[6] Guy Miège, *The English grammar, or, The grounds and genius of the English tongue* (London: Guy Miège, 1688), sig. K1v.

[7] E. A. Lowe, 'Some Facts about Our Oldest Latin Manuscripts', in *Paleographical Papers, 1907–1965*, ed. Ludwig Bieler (Oxford: Clarendon, 1972), I, pp. 199–201.

[8] Malcolm Parkes, 'The Influence of the Concepts of *Ordinatio* and *Compilatio* on the Development of the Book', in *Scribes Scripts and Readers. Studies in the Communication, Presentation and Dissemination of Medieval Texts* (London: Hambledon, 1991), pp. 35–70, pp. 53–4.

one that required 'closer scrutiny of the arguments' and, by extension, a set of textual apparatuses that could enable a variety of readerly itineraries through increasingly complex multi-text and subdivided volumes.[9]

The reappearance and perceived utility of running titles was somewhat sporadic to begin with, but by the beginning of the thirteenth century, *ordinatio*—the structure of reasoning within a given work—was being clearly articulated via a system of textual organization that made use of running titles. As a result, they became more and more noticeable through the use of colour and decorative flourishes.[10] In terms of content, running titles often alerted readers to which section of the text they were reading (i.e., which number book, chapter, part, psalm, etc.). They also supplied concise descriptions that framed the text in more qualitative ways. Running titles became even more crucial under the auspices of *compilatio*—the practice of gathering distinct writings, usually of a single author, into large, bound volumes. In these cases, running titles not only helped readers distinguish and navigate discrete parts of complex arguments in stand-alone texts, but they also made it easier to differentiate one work from another in books made up of many. They became a salient component of a 'concomitant apparatus' that made pre-modern 'knowledge systems' readily available to contemporary scholars for digestion and critique.[11]

The utility of running titles was not lost on the earliest European printers looking to ease readers' transitions to a new mode of textual publication. The advent of print was by no means 'revolutionary' for book design, which was (and continues to be) notoriously conservative.[12] Printers appropriated textual arrangements that readers would have already recognized from scribal *mise-en-page*, including that familiar line of text at the top of every page. Despite this continuity, though, running titles in early modern printed books were neither conventional in their typographic design nor consistent in the kind of information they supplied to readers. Even so, both the makers and readers of early printed books remained alert to their functional and hermeneutic potential. Sometimes, running titles guided readers towards a particular way of understanding the text; and sometimes, they helped readers track their progress through or around the volume. Sometimes, they reinforced an aspect of the text by repeating or digesting information introduced on the title page; and sometimes,

[9] Parkes, '*Ordinatio*', p. 37.

[10] Mary A. Rouse and Richard H. Rouse, *Authentic Witnesses: Approaches to Medieval Texts and Manuscripts* (Notre Dame, IN: University of Notre Dame Press, 1991), pp. 198 and 200; and Parkes '*Ordinatio*', p. 53.

[11] Parkes, '*Ordinatio*', p. 64.

[12] Goran Proot, 'Converging Design Paradigms: Long-Term Evolutions in the Layout of Title Pages of Latin and Vernacular Editions Published in the Southern Netherlands, 1541–1660', *Papers of the Bibliographical Society of America* 108, no. 3 (2014): 269–305, 302.

they just identified the title of the book over and over again. In much rarer cases, running titles obscured questionable content on a page or an opening in order to deflect detractors.[13] 'Learned' readers were presumed to be able to intuit the utility of running titles, as well as detect and correct mistakes in them. Less practised readers were assumed to actually need the cognitive assistance that running titles provided.

Early modern books rarely supplied explicit instructions about *how* particular features of *mise-en-page* worked, but running titles were put to such a wide variety of practical and polemic ends that they often necessitated such mediation from authors and stationers alike. For example, Catholic theologian Thomas Stapleton's anti-Protestant polemic *A Counterblast of M. Hornes Vayne Blast* (1567)—an exceptionally long rejoinder to the Bishop of Winchester Robert Horne's own attempt to neutralize concerns about English royal supremacy—offered advice about what the book's running titles were designed to do: because Stapleton was bound to 'the same order and course' of the book to which he was responding, he kept readers oriented by 'not[ing] at the toppe of eache page, in one side the yeare of the Lorde, on the other side, the...Principal matter in that place debated' (sig. ****2v) (see Fig. 15.1). Printing the year against the inner margin and describing the 'Principal matter' discussed on the two-page spread in the outer margin made it possible for readers 'at the first sight euen by turning of a leafe' to 'knowe, both where thou arte, and what is a doing'. Stapleton claimed that the running titles provided 'clere Intelligence' for readers wishing to find specific content or their way around the book.

The importance of running titles to writers of intricate religious polemics persisted into the seventeenth century. In 1604, the Bishop of Winchester Thomas Bilson published, at the request of the by then deceased Queen Elizabeth I, a riposte

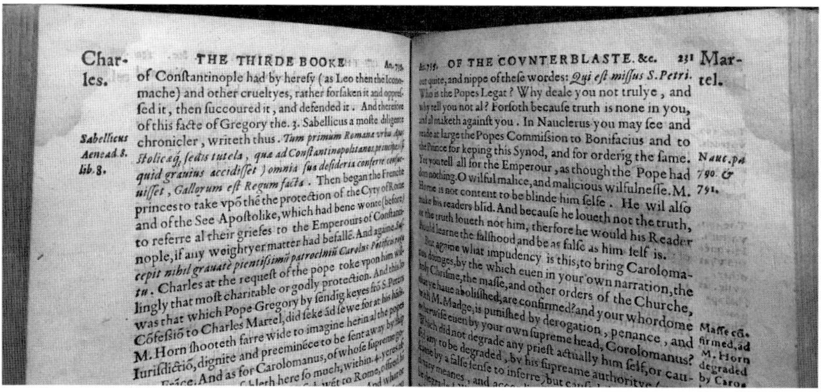

Fig. 15.1 *Thomas Stapleton, 'A counterblast to M. Hornes Vayne Blast' [1567], sigs m2v–m3r. Folger Shakespeare Library*

---

[13] See Matthew Day, '"Intended to Offenders": The Running Titles of Early Modern Books', in *Renaissance Paratexts*, ed. Helen Smith and Louise Wilson (Cambridge: Cambridge University Press, 2011), pp. 32–48, p. 47.

to those who criticized his public effort to uphold the belief (officially endorsed by the Church of England twice) that Christ descended bodily into hell.[14] But readers did not need to read the whole *Survey of Christs Sufferings*, topping out at a whopping 600 folio pages, to grasp the shape and content of Bilson's argument. As the title page announced, they could simply skim 'the titles ouer the pages', which are closely tailored to the content of each page (sig. ¶1r) (see Fig. 15.2). If the book itself seemed TL;DR, the running titles supplied a bona fide version of Bilson's argument.

As in Stapleton and Bilson's books, running titles were particularly useful in books containing texts that 'answered' the claims of previously published material. As such, they continued to articulate *ordinatio*—the order and arrangement of particularly complex texts. A special 'Advertisement to the Reader' at the beginning of George Ridpath's anti-theatrical treatise *The Stage Condemn'd* (1698) aims to clear up any confusion about the order and logic of his argument:

> THE Heads treated on in this Book don't follow the same order as they are set down in the Title Page, because the Author was obliged to take them as they occur'd in the Books, that he answers; but all of them may easily be found out by the Running Titles.[15]

For Ridpath, the running titles offered a more accurate reflection of the stages of the argument as published than the order of contents advertised on the title page.

Given their capacity to guide readers around intricate arguments, the accuracy of running titles was of some importance to certain writers. Some noted but excused errors. Clergyman John Tombes informed readers of his octavo treatise *Christs Commination against Scandalizers* (1641) that there were 'sundry faults escaped…in the running titles', but he also expressed confidence that 'learned' readers would 'easily amend' them and that, if they did not, the running titles were 'not likely either to hinder or pervert the understanding of the rest'.[16] George Swinnock complained about 'the unsuitableness of some of the page titles' in his *Heaven and Hell Epitomized* (1659) and blamed the printer for failing to provide 'a running Title according to the several heads which were handled' (i.e., that corresponded to titles of each subsection). Swinnock directed readers to the table of contents, promising it would 'make full satisfaction' for the 'error' in the running titles.[17] Likewise, Richard Blome blamed the printer of his illustrated account of British territories in America for having 'neglected to fix the Running-Title on the top of every Page'.[18] If the erroneous

---

[14] Thomas Bilson, *The suruey of Christs sufferings for mans redemption* (London: John Bill, [1604]).

[15] George Ridpath, *The stage condemn'd* (London: John Salusbury, 1698), sig. A4r.

[16] John Tombes, *Christs commination against scandalizers* (London: Edward Forest, 1641), sig. *6r.

[17] George Swinnock, *HEAVEN and HELL EPITOMIZED* (London: Thomas Parkhurst, 1659), sig. C8r.

[18] Richard Blome, *The present state of His Majesties isles and territories in America* (London: Dorman Newman, 1687), sig. A3v.

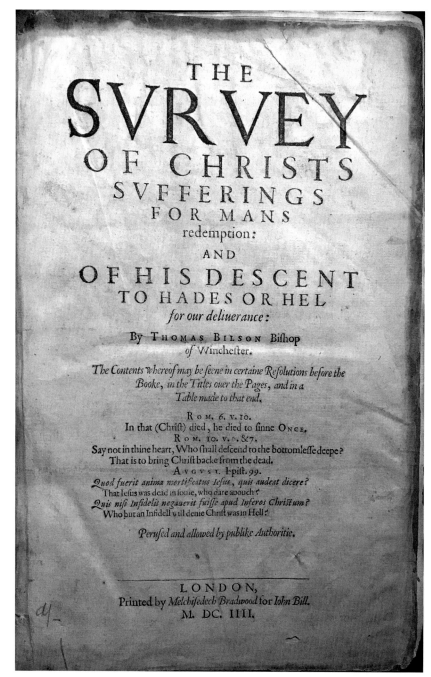

Fig. 15.2 *Title page of Thomas Bilson, 'The suruey of Christs sufferings' (1604). Folger Shakespeare Library*

running titles could not orient readers towards a geographical place Blome discussed (i.e., also a place in the book), the information in the table on the facing page would.

Other writers were far less accommodating. The errata list in William Allen's 1683 treatise on Catholicism states that the 'Running Titles of the Book [are] mistaken' with no further details.[19] Similarly, Samuel Clark blamed the printer for inserting an 'improper' running title in part of his 1698 treatise on good works without specifying the exact offense.[20] And the translators of Jean Claude's *Defence of the Reformation* (1683) complained that 'the word *Historical*, in the Running-Title'—which reads across page openings throughout the book as 'An Historical DEFENCE | of the REFORMATION'—'was inserted' without their 'Consent'.[21] Implicit here is that readers simply ignore the adjective—an impossible ask given that it appears at the top of just about *every* page. The epistle to the reader of John Cameron's defence of the reformed church apologizes for using the word 'Preiudice', which appears 'in many passages of this book beside the *running title*', in the French sense of the term. Readers are instructed not to interpret the word as 'an ill preconceit, as wee commonly take it' but rather as 'a probable ground for any preconceit of a thing, either good or bad' (sig. π2r).[22] Running titles could therefore both pre-empt *and* create confusion.

In many other cases like these ones, readers are supplied with information to properly interpret running titles and correct noted errors, which could occur because printers failed to change the text at the top of the page to correspond to a new section of the book, or because of localized misprints or misspellings. Taken together, these instances of 'mistaken' and 'improper' running titles expose a persistent tension between the logistics of book production and the desires of writers for intelligible texts. Attempts to address these errors also suggest that readers paid attention to running titles and used that information—sometimes in conjunction with and sometimes in lieu of other finding aids—to inform their reading.

Sometimes running titles were exactly right, but not in the way the book's makers intended. For instance, the English poet Luke Milbourne used running titles to eviscerate John Dryden's 1697 translation of Virgil by claiming that the text would be wholly unrecognizable 'if the *Name of Virgil* had not been bestow'd…in *large Characters*…in the *Running Title*' (see Fig. 15.3).[23] The book's 'Running Title'— '*VIRGIL's | PASTORALS*', '*VIRGIL's | ECLOGUES*', etc.—reminded readers that they were still reading Virgil each time they turned the page, no matter how much

[19] William Allen, *Catholicism, or, Several enquiries* (London: Walter Kettilby, 1683), sig. c8v.

[20] Samuel Clark, *Scripture-justification* (London: Thomas Parkhurst, 1698), sig. [A]4v.

[21] Jean Claude, *An historical defence of the Reformation* (London: John Hancock, 1683), sig. C2v.

[22] John Cameron, *An examination of those plausible appearances which seeme most to commend the Romish Church, and to preiudice the reformed* (Oxford: Edward Forest, 1626). STC 4531

[23] Luke Milbourne, *Notes on Dryden's Virgil* (London: R. Clavill, 1698), sig. A2v.

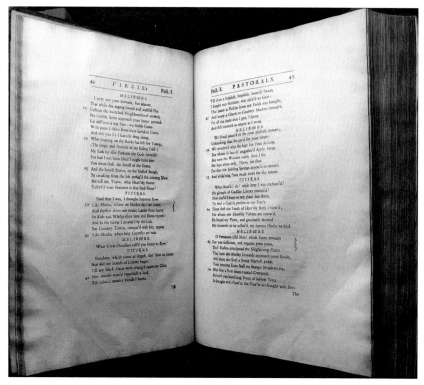

Fig. 15.3 *John Dryden, 'The works of Virgil containing his Pastorals, Georgics and Aeneis' (1697), sigs B1v–B2r. Folger Shakespeare Library*

Dryden had mangled the text. Milbourne also insisted that the translated text would be immediately recognizable to readers as Virgil 'without the *Advertisement of the Running Title*' if Abraham Cowley, rather than Dryden, had translated it (sig. C7r). Even if the publisher Jacob Tonson had designed the running titles to make the book read as an authoritative translation, Milbourne encouraged readers to misread them as a corrective to Dryden's 'impertinent' translation. Whether interpreted correctly or not, running titles represent bids by writers and stationers to referee readers' interactions with their books.

In the first century of print, running titles became part of a design agenda that implicated readers in the process of defining what books were—or could be. More specifically, running titles helped enable the readerly practice of gathering single-text books together into bespoke collections—just as, more recently, they have supported the widespread practice of breaking texts apart via new technologies of

RUNNING TITLES 🌿 201

textual reproduction. Far from being skeuomorphs (that is, familiar but ultimately vestigial and therefore useless design features), running titles in volumes containing just one text anticipate how books as objects might be manipulated and used. I will use early printed plays as an example.

In the 1490s, Richard Pynson printed Terence's comedies with a consistent schema of running titles that differentiated one part of the book from another—the title of the relevant play appears on rectos and the act number on versos.[24] However, none of the two-part vernacular plays published in the early sixteenth century—1 & 2 *Fulgens and Lucres* (1512–16?), 1 & 2 *Gentleness & Nobility* (c. 1525), and 1 & 2 *Nature* (1530–4?)—featured running titles, or finding aids of any kind. These relatively slim playbooks encouraged linear reading. The earliest extant English vernacular playbooks to be printed with running titles were John Bale's *The Temptation of Christ* (1547?), *The Chief Promises of God unto Man* (1547?), and *The Three Laws* (1548?), all printed on the continent by Derek van der Straten. The first of these, which survives in only one copy, announces 'Comœdia Ioannis Balei | De Christi tentatione' across the top of each page opening. It seems pretty likely that this playtext once belonged to a three-part collection of plays.[25] (The texts of the other two plays are now lost.) Here, then, running titles were mobilized to articulate *compilatio*. The other two playbooks were not published in collection. But, still, they feature running titles—ones that break down the playtext as a whole into smaller parts, that is, *acts*. In particular, Bale's *Three Laws* octavo reads like some of the religious polemics I discuss above. The running titles provide an abstract of the whole play: the successive the corruption of Natural Law (Act 2), Mosaic Law (Act 3), and Christian Law (Act 4), and, eventually, the restoration of all three in Act 5: 'Restauratio legum diuinarum. | Actus quintus' (see Fig. 15.4).

After showing up on the pages of the Bale–van der Straten playbooks, running titles start appearing with notable regularity in editions of single-play playbooks that were marketed to readers as belonging to a larger corpus—in particular, the seven single-play editions of 'Englished' Seneca plays published between 1559 and 1566. All seven playbooks attributed the plays to Seneca; all seven were published in octavo format; and all seven bore titles with ordinal numbers to suggest their place in a stable ten-play sequence (Seneca's entire dramatic oeuvre). Because the books all *looked* the same, readers could imagine gathering, if not actually collecting and binding, them together sequentially in *sammelband*, a phenomenon that Tara L. Lyons calls the 'ideation of a complete and ordered collection'.[26] These books' running titles are implicated in this design strategy in that they also anticipate collection.

---

[24] Terence, *Comœdiæ sex* (London: Richard Pynson, 1497).

[25] Aaron T. Pratt, 'The Status of Printed Playbooks in Early Modern England', PhD diss. (2016), chapter 2, n7.

[26] Tara L. Lyons, 'Genealogies of the Collection: Seneca in Print' [unpublished], p. 5.

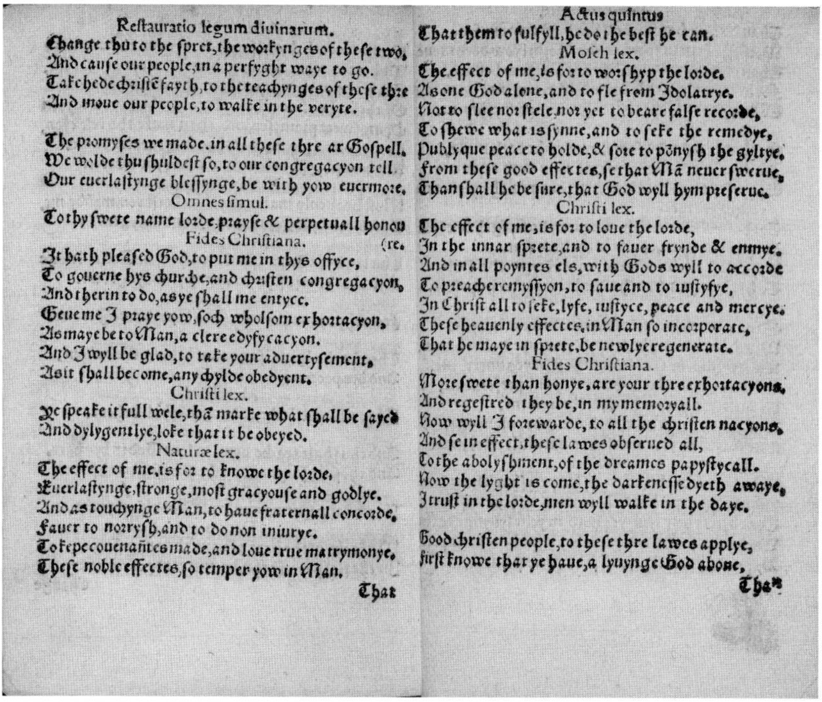
Restauratio legum diuinarum.
Change thu to the spret, the workynges of these two,
And cause our people, in a perfyght waye to go.
Take hede christẽ fayth, to the teachynges of these thre
And moue our people, to walke in the veryte.

The promyses we made, in all these thre ar Gospell.
We wolde thu shuldest so, to our congregacyon tell
Our euerlastynge blessynge, be with yow euermore.
Omnes simul.
To thy swete name lorde, prayse & perpetuall honou (re.
Fides Christiana.
It hath pleased God, to put me in thys offyce,
To gouerne hys churche, and christen congregacyon,
And therin to do, as ye shall me entyce.
Geue me I praye yow, soch wholsom exhortacyon,
As maye be to Man, a clere edyfycacyon.
And I wyll be glad, to take your aduertysement,
As it shall become, any chylde obedyent.
Christi lex.
Ye speake it full wele, thã marke what shall be sayed
And dylygentlye, loke that it be obeyed.
Naturæ lex.
The effect of me, is for to knowe the lorde,
Euerlastynge, stronge, most gracyouse and godlye.
And as touchynge Man, to haue fraternall concorde,
Fauer to norrysh, and to do non iniurye.
To kepe couenañtes made, and loue true matrymonye.
These noble effectes, so temper yow in Man.
That

Actus quintus
That them to fulfyll, he do the best he can.
Mosch lex.
The effect of me, is for to worshyp the lorde.
As one God alone, and to fle from Idolatrye.
Not to slee nor stele, nor yet to beare false recorde,
To shewe what is synne, and to seke the remedye,
Publyque peace to holde, & sore to põnysh the gyltye.
From these good effectes, se that Mã neuer swerue,
Than shall he be sure, that God wyll hym preserue.
Christi lex.
The effect of me, is for to loue the lorde,
In the innar sprete, and to fauer frynde & enmye.
And in all poyntes els, with Gods wyll to accorde
To preache remyssyon, to saue and to iustyfye,
In Christ all to seke, lyfe, iustyce, peace and mercye.
These heauenly effectes, in Man so incorporate,
That he maye in sprete, be newlye regenerate.
Fides Christiana.
More swete than honye, are your thre exhortacyons,
And regestred they be, in my memoryall.
Now wyll I forewarde, to all the christen nacyons,
And se in effect, these lawes obserued all,
To the abolyshment, of the dreames papystycall.
Now the lyght is come, the darkenesse dyeth awaye,
I trust in the lorde, men wyll walke in the daye.

Good christen people, to these thre lawes applye,
First knowe that ye haue, a lyuynge God aboue,
That

Fig. 15.4 *John Bale, 'The Three Laws' (1548?), Mal. 502, sigs F7v–F8r, by permission of the Bodleian Libraries, University of Oxford*

Announcing only the title of the play (and, in some cases, Seneca's name), they did nothing to help readers navigate the content of each individual octavo (see Fig. 15.5). But they suddenly became functional when readers chose to bind some or all of the editions together by helping those readers navigate the new, larger whole. And, indeed, copies of three of these octavos in the Pforzheimer Collection at the Harry Ransom Center show compelling evidence of having once been bound together.[27]

In the wake of the individual Seneca playbooks, more and more single-play volumes started coming to press with running titles. By the 1580s, it was on trend to see running titles at the top of page openings in single-play playbooks. In most cases, the running title text replicated the title of the play as it appeared on the title page, frequently pared down due to space constraints. Playbook running titles often drew attention to plays' generic affiliations, sometimes with a bit of evaluation ('A pleasant conceited Comedie'; 'The most excellent Tragedie'; 'THE TRVE TRAGEDIE'; etc.). Just as references to genre invited readers to encounter plays through the lens of known conventions (especially how a play would likely end), modifiers that assessed quality or the kind of reaction a play was supposed to elicit reminded readers

[27] *Herucles Furens* [Pforz 860], *Thyestes* [Pforz 865 copy 1], and *Troas* [Pforz 866].

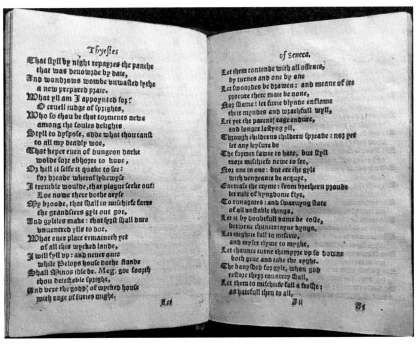

Fig. 15.5 'THE SECONDE TRAGEDIE…entituled Thyestes' (1560), sigs C4v–C5r, Folger Shakespeare Library

that play reading could be both a critical *and* an affective activity. 'Lamentable' appears in running titles for *Locrine* (1595) and *Romeo & Juliet* (1599), for example (see Fig. 15.6).

Running titles in single-play playbooks thus had hermeneutic potential—whether purposeful or incidental—even when they did little else to manage readers' encounters with the books as physical objects. It is easy to assume, then, that the practical function of running titles had faded by the time professional plays gained traction in the London book trade—the 1590s—and to dismiss running titles in playbooks-sold-separately as residue of an outdated textual navigation system. While single-play quartos, like many other kinds of single-text volumes, *were* typically printed and sold individually (in a material sense), they were designed to encourage readers to collect and bind them in *sammelbände* with other quartos, especially other plays.[28] The running titles in standalone playbooks were complicit in this strategy. As such, the standardization of format (most plays were published in quarto) was not the only factor that facilitated the collecting of loosely stitched pamphlet books into customized bound volumes. Running titles anticipated this practice, too. They provided

---

[28] Aaron T. Pratt, 'Stab-Stitching and the Status of Early English Playbooks as Literature', *The Library*, 7th series, 16, no. 3 (2015): 304–28.

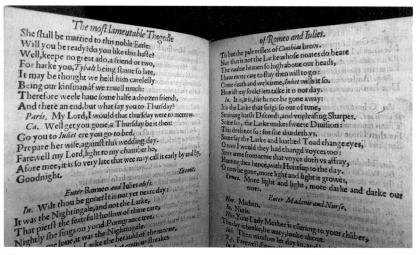

Fig. 15.6 'THE MOST EXcellent and lamentable Tragedie, of Romeo and Iuliet' (1599), sigs B4v–C1r, STC 22323 (Copy 2), Folger Shakespeare Library

tailor-made collections with the beginnings of a finding aid that readers could supplement with scribal tables of contents, or not.

The remains of an early playbook *sammelband* now at the Folger Shakespeare Library suggests that one of the book's readers actually attended to the running titles of the quartos that comprised the volume. (The collection was subsequently broken apart and its contents individually rebound.) According to a manuscript list of titles still bound in with *The Blind Beggar of Alexandria* (1598), the first play in the collection, the volume consisted of another twelve quartos (see Fig. 15.7).[29] Published between 1568 and 1628, all but the two earliest quartos feature running titles, which in most cases replicate the title of the play that appears on the title page.[30] In two cases where the title-page title and running titles are substantively different, however, the person who wrote the manuscript catalogue followed the text of the running title instead. William Warner's translation of Plautus' *Menaechmi*, which came to press as *MENAECMI. A pleasant and fine Conceited Comædie*, appeared as '*A pleasant Comedie called | Menechmus*' in its running titles and 'Menechmus' in the catalogue. Similarly, Robert Wilson's *Three Lords and Three Ladies of London* was recorded in the catalogue as '3 Lords of London' (without mention of the ladies), following the running titles ('*The stately Morall of | the three Lords of London*') instead of the title page (*The Pleasant and Stately Morall, of the three Lordes and three Ladies of London*). The creator of the hand-written list (whether or not he or she was the compiler) heeded the running

---

[29] STC 4965, Folger Shakespeare Library.

[30] In one case (*Hans Beer-pot*), the title in the catalogue matches only the title page title.

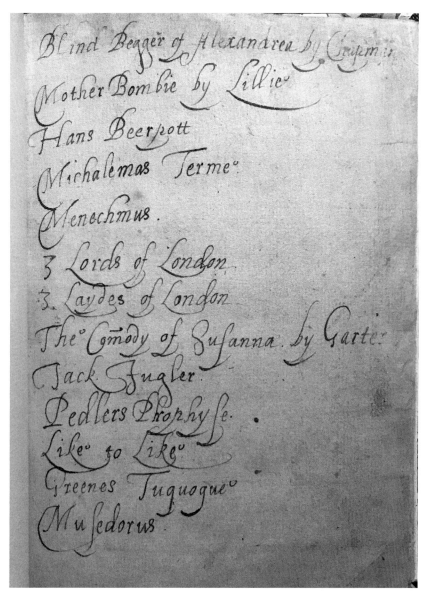

Blind Begger of Alexandrea by Chapm:

Mother Bombie by Lillie

Hans Beerpott

Michalemas Terme°

Menechmus .

3 Lords of London.

3. Laydes of London.

The° Comody of Sufanna . by Garter

Jack Jugler

Pedlers Prophyse.

Like° to Like°

Greenes Tuquoque°

Mufedorus .

🎴 **Fig. 15.7** *Sammelband catalogue, bound with STC 4965, Folger Shakespeare Library*

titles when setting about to record the contents of the *sammelband*. In conjunction with the customized catalogue, the running titles gave this reader and others who may have gotten their hands on the book a system of visual scaffolding by which they could easily view the book's contents at a glance and flip to a certain play in the collection without the need for page numbers. This *sammelband* shows how running titles in single-text quartos were designed proleptically to accommodate the practice and art of collection.

In *The Elements of Typographic Style*, Robert Bringhurst suggests that running titles (he calls them 'running heads') 'are useless if the reader has to hunt for them'. From as early as the sixth century, scribes used different scripts and sizes of lettering to make running titles more visible. In print, typographic differentiation (the use of roman for running titles when the main text was printed in blackletter; or italic when the main text was printed in roman) was common. For Bringhurst and other modern typographers, the payoff of making running titles visible is to 'remind readers which intellectual neighbourhood they happen to be visiting'. Indeed, Milbourne called attention to the effectiveness of the 'large Characters' Tonson used for the running titles in Dryden's translation of Virgil to ensure that, in spite of Dryden, readers remembered they were still in Virgil's neighbourhood. Whichever way you read the book, though, that neighbourhood was hell.

Given the practical origins of running titles, they are, for the designer Bringhurst, most useful today in 'anthologies and works of reference' and all but 'pointless' in books 'with a strong authorial voice or a unified subject'. (And, indeed, when early modern *sammelbände* were broken apart in the nineteenth century to make neat, individually bound books, running titles lost the utility they once had in collection.) Bringhurst insists, however, that the primary function of running titles in the interim has been to provide 'insurance against photocopying pirates'. Technologies of textual reproduction—obviously no longer limited only to the 'photocopying machines' that Bringhurst cites—threaten both textual integrity and intellectual property. But this is a threat mitigated by the presence of running titles that advertise the name of the book and/or author across every opening. Even if photocopying 'easily separate[s] ... a chapter or page' from the book, running titles endure as a record of the book to which the chapter or page belongs. (Ironically, Bringhurst's manual includes running chapter and section titles, but no indication of the book's title or author's name.)

Running titles in modern printed books anticipate the frequent fragmentation of unified volumes, an inverse of the way the running titles in the single-text quartos of the sixteenth and seventeenth centuries anticipated the widespread readerly interest in gathering, compiling, and assembling. However, even the fracturing of a book through photocopying—or scanning or photographing or other forms of digital imaging—looks forward to new, bespoke readerly configurations of the copied texts (in folders, for example, both tangible and digital). As such, running titles continue to function as the head and chief intelligence of the page. Even on the popular Amazon Kindle, running titles announcing the title of the book (not chapter titles or author name) are available at the top of the screen—only if readers want to see them. But they are not redundant on these devices that boast a number of different finding aids. After all, these handheld machines store hundreds, even thousands, of books (i.e., 'titles') and are, as such, a twenty-first-century version of medieval *compilatio*. Running titles persist in such electronic formats as reminders of the particular book to which the text—sometimes unpaginated and scrollable; sometimes adjustable in size and brightness; and often otherwise non-descript— belongs. Here, as before, running titles are the book's way of asserting through space and through time its identities, origins, contexts, and/or matters and of inciting readers to navigate, remake, or break it according to their own needs and desires.

CHAPTER 16

WOODCUTS

Alexandra Franklin

In 1603, the Court of the Stationers' Company, the body regulating the printing and bookselling trade in Great Britain, heard the rival claims of two printers to the woodcuts of coins that were bound with annual 'Calendars', the almanac and writing tables.[1] The conflict was over literally, and also figuratively, the right to print money. For over a century, woodcuts had illustrated books of literature (like the *Hypnerotomachia Poliphili*) and science (Vesalius's book of anatomy); in the 1530s Martin Luther was anxious to ensure that new wood-cuts for the German Bible reflected Protestant theology,[2] and in that same decade woodcuts designed by Hans Holbein of the 'Dance of Death' began a long career, accompanying translations of Corrozet's text into several languages. Woodcut pic-tures disseminated the Tudor monarchy's self-projection to the English nation.[3] Yet it was indicative of both the reach and the status of woodcuts by 1603 that the case in front of the Stationers' Company Court concerned that very prosaic publication, a pocket diary.[4]

In the hand-press period, woodcuts as parts of books appeared most often as designs printed on a page with the text. Woodcut did not immediately replace, but derived from and supported, the hand decoration of books in the fifteenth century.[5] As well as illustration and decoration within the book, woodcut images were used to make patterned book covers, and when title pages began to feature as parts of the printed book these could be fully xylographic (the text carved from a woodblock), or might include a woodcut image or ornament with metal type, or *passepartout* wood-cut borders, into which the necessary type for every new title was set.[6] The union of woodblock and type, two relief printing surfaces, was the most straightforward way to incorporate illustration or decoration into printed books. This, together with the

---

[1] William Jackson (ed.), *Records of the Court of the Stationers' Company 1602–1640* (London: Bibliographical Society, 1957), p. 4.

[2] Bridget Heal, *A Magnificent Faith: Art and Identity in Lutheran Germany* (Oxford: Oxford University Press, 2017), pp. 25–6.

[3] James Knapp, *Illustrating the Past in Early Modern England: The Representation of History in Printed Books* (Aldershot: Ashgate, 2003), pp. 154–5.

[4] Antony Griffiths, *The Print before Photography: An Introduction to European Printmaking, 1550–1820* (London: British Museum, 2016), p. 486; Adam Smyth, 'Almanacs and Ideas of Popularity', in *The Elizabethan Top Ten: Defining Print Popularity in Early Modern England*, ed. Andy Kesson and Emma Smith (Farnham: Ashgate, 2013), pp. 125–33; Peter Stallybrass, 'Hamlet's Tables and the Technologies of Writing in Renaissance England', *Shakespeare Quarterly* 5, no. 4 (Winter, 2004): 396.

[5] Lilian Armstrong, 'The Impact of Printing on Miniaturists in Venice after 1469', in *Printing the Written Word: The Social History of Books, circa 1450–1520*, ed. Sandra Hindman (London: Cornell University Press, 1991), pp. 174–202, pp. 192–6.

[6] Margaret M. Smith, *The Title Page; Its Early Development* (London: British Library, 2000), p. 76.

durability of the woodblock, was the practical consideration that largely influenced the place of woodcuts in the anatomy of the book. Yet the result of these physical facts was a history in which woodcut assumed many roles and characters.

A design is carved into a plank of wood (pear, apple, or other hard fruit wood), leaving raised all the areas intended to be printed. The raised lines of the design receive a coating of ink, from which the impression may be taken simply by rubbing the back of paper placed over the inked block, or the woodblock and metal type can be printed together in a press (see Fig. 16.1). The impression is a mirror image of the design on the block. Wood engraving is another technique for producing a relief printing surface (in which the raised portions receive the ink); it is distinguished from woodcut by the closer-grained type of wood used (usually box) and by cutting on the end grain rather than on the plank (along the grain); correspondingly sharper tools are used. A relief printing surface could be made by cutting or punching designs in other materials, such as metal.[7] Much of what follows on the subject of woodcuts is true of impressions from any relief printing surface that could be printed in a press alongside type in a single operation.

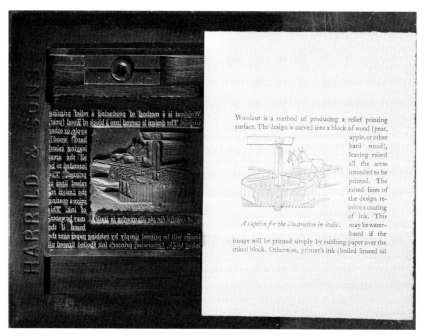

✻ **Fig. 16.1** *A printing surface formed from individual metal type letters and a relief block. Photograph by David Stumpp*

---

[7] Antony Griffiths, *Prints and Printmaking: An Introduction to the History and Techniques*, 2nd edn (London: British Museum, 1996), pp. 29–30; 60.

The art of printing pictures from carved woodblocks preceded the invention of movable type in Europe.[8] Woodblocks were used to stamp multiple images on sheets of paper or cloth, and some of these early woodcut images were introduced into books by readers, pasted, pinned, or sewn to the pages.[9] However small the picture, and however simple the design, these might add a key point of readerly attention to the book. In the margins of a sixteenth-century manuscript prayer book from Lower Saxony are pasted three printed images, a young woman and two lions. Each of these flimsy paper cut-outs is hardly bigger than a fingernail, but in their new context they give visible form to important devotional concepts of the soul as the 'bride of God' and of Christ as a lion, resurrected to defeat Death.

In the earliest precisely dated European book containing woodcut images and movable type—*Der Edelstein* (1461), published by Albrecht Pfister in Bamberg—the woodcuts were printed separately into spaces left on the page, an indication, perhaps, that the workshops for producing woodcuts and text were not yet integrated.[10] Later, both Pfister and Gunther Zainer in Augsburg began issuing books with woodblocks and type printed together in the same forme. The first printed book illustrations produced in England came from William Caxton's press in 1481, with *Mirrour of the World*; here again there was some lack either in skill or in organization, as the labels for diagrams of the cosmos are written in by hand. In other circumstances, woodcut images could appear in close association with lettering and metal type: skilled woodcutters could carve letters into the block, or a gap could be cut into the woodblock to allow metal type to be inserted (see Fig. 16.2). Spaces for inserting type in speech bubbles within early modern woodcuts suggest that a woodblock could serve multiple publications.[11]

An elegant way to combine text and image was to cut both by hand into one plank of wood.[12] The earliest surviving examples of European blockbooks date from the 1460s and 1470s, from the same period as typographic books.[13] Rather than necessarily a precursor of typography, xylography could be seen as an early form of stereotyping, useful for printing schoolbooks and devotional texts whose contents changed little

---

[8] Peter Parshall and Rainer Schoch et al., *Origins of European Printmaking: Fifteenth-Century Woodcuts and Their Public* (New Haven, CT: Yale University Press, 2006), pp. 21–3.

[9] Nigel F. Palmer, with binding descriptions by Andrew Honey, 'Blockbooks, Woodcut and Metalcut Single Sheets', in *A Catalogue of Books Printed in the Fifteenth Century Now in the Bodleian Library, Oxford*, ed. Alan Coates et al. (Oxford: Oxford University Press, 2005), pp. 1–50.

[10] See also Claire Bolton, *The Fifteenth-Century Printing Practices of Johann Zainer, Ulm, 1473–1478* (Oxford: Oxford Bibliographical Society, 2016), pp. 51–2.

[11] Seth Lerer, 'The Wiles of a Woodcut: Wynkyn de Worde and the Early Tudor Reader', *Huntington Library Quarterly* 59, no. 4 (1996): 381–403, 386–7.

[12] Woodblocks were used to print text in China before the ninth century CE; a copy now in the British Library is the earliest known dated complete book of woodblock printing on paper, made in 868.

[13] Bettina Wagner (ed.), *Blockbücher Des 15. Jahrhunderts: eine Experimentierphase im frühen Buchdruck: Beiträge der Fachtagung in der Bayerischen Staatsbibliothek München am 16. und 17. Februar 2012* (Wiesbaden: Harrassowitz, 2013).

✣ **Fig. 16.2** *A nineteenth-century wood-engraved diagram, showing hand-cut letters (d and f) and a metal type letter (e) inserted after the block was cut. Collection of Richard Lawrence*

from decade to decade, without the need for expensive metal type or even a press, as the pages could be printed by rubbing paper over the inked surface. The fully wood-cut book also enabled an intricate integration of text and image. Each page of the blockbook *Biblia Pauperum* is a typological lesson framed in architectural borders, juxtaposing scenes from the Old and New Testaments, with Bible quotations unfurling on banderoles around the scenes.[14] By comparison, in a typographic edition from 1462 the woodcuts and type, and thus the visual and textual components, are rather rigidly separated into rectangular zones.

The Aldine masterpiece *Hypnerotomachia Poliphili*, published in 1498, reveals the potential of woodcut as an integral part of the typographic book. The design as a whole plays with the balance between text and image, and the typography itself is richly visual. Illustrations are worked into the design as woodcut figures inset into the areas of text, but words are also worked into the illustrations. Images of tombs and monuments bearing inscriptions are formed with woodcuts incorporating xylography or type, and sometimes both.

---

[14] Tobin Nellhaus, 'Mementos of Things to Come: Orality, Literacy, and Typology in the *Bibila Pauperum*', in *Printing the Written Word: The Social History of Books, c. 1450–1520*, ed. Sandra Hindman (London: Cornell University Press, 1991), pp. 292–321.

Within a few decades of Gutenberg's invention, acquiring sets of woodcuts for religious texts, or popular texts by medieval or classical authors, became the business of book printers or publishers, who commissioned cuts from specialist craftsmen.[15] Caxton's edition of Aesop's *Fables* in 1484 used copies of the woodcuts from a Lyons edition of 1480 which were copies of those used by Johannes Zainer in Ulm in 1476.[16] In the illustration of science books, discussed below, authors might be closely involved in the commissioning of woodcuts, but many cases of publisher- or printer-selected illustration can be found in the early centuries of print.[17] Catalogues of woodcuts from European books of the fifteenth and sixteenth centuries reveal the extent to which printers copied and reused woodblocks.[18] A printer could hope to achieve tens of thousands of impressions from the matrix; more than the print run of a single edition.[19] The durability of woodblocks had the paradoxical effect that, while the image on the printing surface might remain unchanged, the impressions from a single woodblock could multiply promiscuously between the pages of other works, in combination with other images.

From an early period, printers devised ways of reusing woodblocks. Ingeniously, in the printing of Terence's *Comedies* (1496), the printer Johannes Reinhardi used assemblages of woodblocks, one for each character and one for the background, to print the character groupings for each scene. The Nuremberg *Chronicle* (1493) was an elaborately illustrated book, with some openings showing genealogies arranged across two-page spreads, the separate woodcuts designed to align pictorially depicted 'branches' of the family tree. Yet the printer made the 650 woodblocks do their work by repeating some cityscapes and portraits. A similar effect was achieved in two important English illustrated books of the 1560s; in Holinshed's *Chronicle* 212 woodcuts produce 1,026 images, and Foxe's *Actes and Monuments* used a repeated image of a martyr in flames.[20] Woodcuts recurring within a single edition lay open an important history of the physical production of the book; their appearance in more

[15] Karen L. Bowen and Dirk Imhof, 'Reputation and Wage: The Case of Engravers Who Worked for the Plantin-Moretus Press', *Simiolus: Netherlands Quarterly for the History of Art* 30, no. 3/4 (2003): 161–95.

[16] Daniel De Simone (ed.), *A Heavenly Craft: The Woodcut in Early Printed Books: Illustrated Books Purchased by Lessing J. Rosenwald at the Sale of the Library of C. W. Dyson Perrins* (New York: G. Braziller, in association with the Library of Congress, Washington, DC: 2004), pp. 50–1.

[17] Lerer, 'Wiles of a Woodcut', p. 389.

[18] See especially Edward Hodnett, *English Woodcuts, 1480–1535* (Oxford: Oxford University Press, 1973); Ruth Samson Luborsky and Elizabeth Morley Ingram, *A Guide to English Illustrated Books, 1536–1603* (Tempe, AZ: Medieval and Renaissance Texts and Studies, 1998); *Harvard College Library, Department of Printing and Graphic Arts: Catalogue of Books and Manuscripts*, compiled by Ruth Mortimer, under the supervision of Philip Hofer and William A. Jackson (Cambridge, MA: Belknap Press of Harvard University Press, 1964–); Ina Kok, *Woodcuts in Incunabula Printed in the Low Countries* (Houten: HES and De Graaf, 2013).

[19] Griffiths, *The Print before Photography*, pp. 60–1.

[20] James Knapp, *Illustrating the Past in Early Modern England: The Representation of History in Printed Books* (Aldershot: Ashgate, 2003), pp. 188–91, 248.

than one place in the finished volume draws attention to the temporal process of printing, as the various components, including type and woodblocks, were joined together for each quire or gathering, separated, and recombined for the next.

When a woodblock appears with an entirely different text, we can assume that the printer found it expedient to use his or her existing stock, but this does not mean that the use was careless, or that the image was meaningless.[21] What does an image illustrate—or *how* does it illustrate—if it is used in different contexts? Composition, as well as content, could suggest meaning. Small square woodcuts of emblematic figures from a fortune-telling book published in 1610 (Fig. 16.3) reappeared in a broadside in 1652.[22] The broadside printer formed the woodblocks into a rectangular enclosure for a text entitled the 'Mirror of Drunkenness'. In this new configuration they frame a moral looking glass, the trope for any document that helps Christians to examine their souls.[23]

In the context of a widely recognized religious and secular iconography, images can often be understood as emblematic, rather than simply generic. On the front and back of the wrapper of an 1816 French alphabet book are two woodcut images of birds.[24] These are the raven and dove, sent out from the Ark by Noah, enclosing the schoolbook in an appropriate symbolism of hope. The contexts of reuse could be disparate, but not necessarily incompatible: woodcuts of men's heads appeared in both 1556 and 1613 editions of a guide to physiognomy; between these dates, they were used on a ballad celebrating the execution of conspirators in the Babington plot (1586).[25] Were these 'physiognomic' heads or the heads of executed traitors, helpfully revealed, by their physiognomy, to be cruel, wanton, and deceitful (Fig. 16.4)?

The example of physiognomy is a reminder that woodcuts were important in the production of science books.[26] In practical terms, there were advantages to the use of relief-printed diagrams (whether in wood or cast metal), because these enabled early printers to place images close to explanatory text on the page, as in Erhard Ratdolt's publications of Euclid in Venice in the 1490s. Leonhart Fuchs praised the woodcutters responsible for illustrations of his herbal (1542) but also

---

[21] Ruth S. Luborsky, 'Connections and Disconnections between Images and Texts: The Case of Secular Tudor Book Illustration', *Word and Image* 3 (1987): 74–83; Knapp, *Illustrating the Past*, pp. 162–206.

[22] Alexandra Franklin, 'Making Sense of Broadside Ballad Illustrations in the Seventeenth and Eighteenth Centuries', in *Studies in Ephemera: Text and Image in Eighteenth-Century Print*, ed. Kevin D. Murphy and Sally O'Driscoll (Lewisburg, PA: Bucknell University Press, 2013), pp. 172–5.

[23] Matthew Brown, *The Pilgrim and the Bee: Reading Rituals and Book Culture in Early New England* (Philadelphia, PA: University of Pennsylvania Press, 2007), pp. 71–2.

[24] *Alphabet du premier age, où les prières, les sept Pseaumes, et les Litanies des Saintes sont au-long* (Narbonne: Caillard fils, 1816) (Morgan Library, New York, PML 86152).

[25] Ruth S. Luborsky, 'Woodcuts in Tudor Books: Clarifying Their Documentation', *Papers of the Bibliographical Society of America* 86, no. 1 (1992): 67–81, 80.

[26] Sachiko Kusukawa, *Picturing the Book of Nature: Image, Text, and Argument in Sixteenth-Century Human Anatomy and Medical Botany* (Chicago, IL: University of Chicago Press, 2011), pp. 64–9.

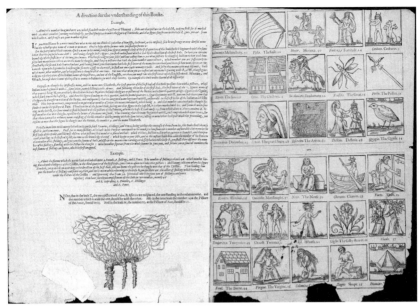

🌿 **Fig. 16.3** *An opening from Andrea Ghisi, 'Wits laberynth, or, The exercise of idlenesse. Englished and augmented' (London, 1610). Printed by Thomas Purfoot, to be sold by John Budge. The preface ends with a woodcut ornament in a 'cul de lampe' shape, as an elegant terminus to the page; here, the shape is formed by a botanical illustration printed upside-down. To the right, square woodcuts serve the prognostication game. Some of these formed the borders of a 1652 broadside, the 'Mirror of Drunkenness'. By permission of the Bodleian Libraries, University of Oxford; Bodleian G 2.9 Jur*

noted that the quality of his work rested on having a *different* woodblock for each plant, while other authors had allowed the reuse of blocks.[27] Woodcuts of the highest quality were an important part of the outstanding sixteenth-century work on anatomy, Andreas Vesalius's *De Humani Corporis Fabrica*.[28] Even so, the copies of these pirated for a London publication were made as engravings, signifying the growing reputation of the intaglio medium.[29] Apart from the fine detail that was possible in a metal engraving, it may be that there was developing by this time what Antony Griffiths identifies as a psychological aversion to woodcut: the cheapness of the medium, and the reputation of woodcuts as sometimes repeated, or recycled from other works, instilled a feeling of distrust and a perception of low quality.[30]

[27] Sachiko Kusukawa, 'Leonhart Fuchs on the Importance of Pictures', *Journal of the History of Ideas* 58, no. 3 (July 1997): 403–27, 406.

[28] J. B. de C. M. Saunders, and Charles D. O'Malley, *The Illustrations from the Works of Andreas Vesalius of Brussels* (New York: Dover, 1950, repr. 1973), pp. 47–8. See Sean Roberts's discussion of this point in Chapter 17.

[29] Thomas Geminus, *Compendiosa totius anatomie delineatio* (London, 1545).

[30] Griffiths, *The Print before Photography*, pp. 21, 181, 486.

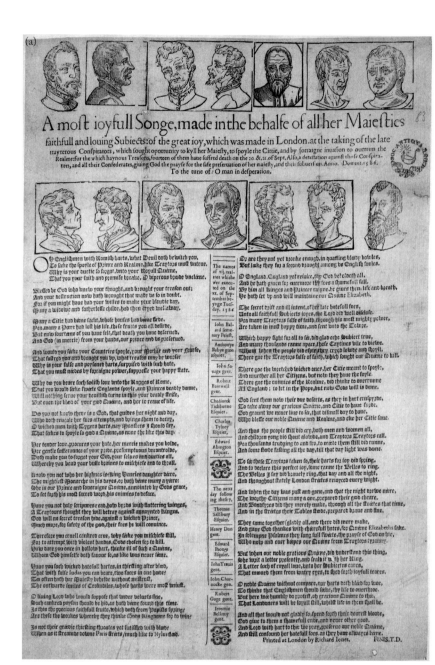

Fig. 16.4 *The reuse of woodcuts with different texts. The images of heads were used in Bartolommeo della Rocca Cocles, 'A brief and most pleasau[n]t epitomye of the whole art of phisiognomie' (London: By Iohn Waylande [1556]). Later uses are shown here: (a) A most ioyfull Songe, made in the behalfe of all her Maiesties faithfull and louing Subiects: of the great ioy… at the taking of the late trayterous Conspirators… for the which haynous Treasons, fourteen of them haue suffred death on the 20. &. 21. of Sept.…Anno. Domini. 1586. Society of Antiquaries, ref. Lemon 83; By permission of the Society of Antiquaries*

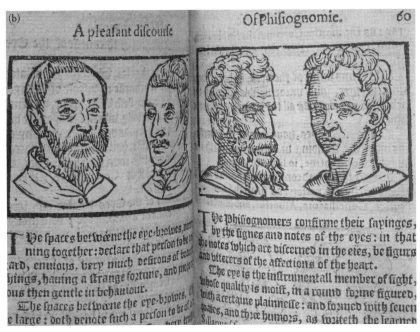

A pleafant difcourfe

Of Phifiognomie. 60

The fpaces betwéene the eye-bzoives, meaning together: declare that perfon to be aard, enuious, very much defirous of things, hauing a ftrange fortune, and moft ous then gentle in behauiour.

The fpaces betwéene the eye-bzoives, if large: doth denote fuch a perfon to be of

The Phifiognomers confirme their fayinges, by the fignes and notes of the eyes: in that the notes which are difcerned in the eies, be figurs and btterers of the affections of the heart.

The eye is the inftrumentall member of fight, whofe quality is moift, in a round forme figured, with a certaine plainneffe: and formed with feuen coates, and thrée humors, as writeth the learned

Fig. 16.4 *(b) Thomas Hill, 'A pleasant history: declaring the whole art of physiognomy' (London: W. Jaggard, 1613): ff. 59v–60r. By permission of the Bodleian Libraries, University of Oxford, Bodleian Douce H 66*

Some woodcut impressions did show damage to the blocks from cracks and worm holes, proving that woodblocks were used for decades beyond their original creation. It was also possible to extend the life of a block by modification: a portion could be removed and a new 'plug' recarved in its place. Excision of some element of the design might be done to suit a new subject, or because the image had become unacceptable for religious or ideological reasons.[31] Woodblocks used in the first edition of the English Bishops' Bible in 1568 were imported from Cologne, but the image of God was replaced with the tetragrammaton.[32] New woodblocks were made for the second folio edition in 1572 and these were later used on broadside ballads during the 1620s.[33]

We may understand why woodcuts were used in certain contexts by understanding styles of visual representation, habits of reading, and the audience for

[31] David Davis, '"The vayle of Eternall memorie": Contesting Representations of Queen Elizabeth in English Woodcuts', *Word and Image* 27, no. 1 (2011): 65–76; an example of revisions to the woodblock because of an error in printing is given in Charles Gérard, 'Un exemplaire exceptionnel du Dante di Brescia de 1487', *La Bibliofilia* 4 (1903): 402. I am grateful to Matilde Malaspina for drawing this to my attention.

[32] Colin Clair, 'The Bishops' Bible 1568', *Gutenberg Jahrbuch* (1962): 287–90; Margaret Aston, 'The Bishops' Bible Illustrations', *Studies in Church History* 28 (1992): 267–85.

[33] Margaret Aston, 'Bibles to Ballads: Some Pictorial Migrations', in *Christianity and Community in the West: Essays for John Bossy* (Aldershot: Ashgate, 2001), pp. 106–36.

woodcut-illustrated publications. From the middle of the sixteenth century, when intaglio began to replace woodcut as the favoured medium for illustrations of higher-priced books, woodcuts started their association with cheaper illustrated books and older texts, and they gained a nostalgic value, associated with childhood reading. The woodcuts on broadside ballads from the middle of the seventeenth century became so representative of popular literature in England that several were copied again in the eighteenth century.[34] The recognizable figure of a man was hand copied more than eight times in two centuries (one woodblock survives in the British Museum), suggesting that this familiar image was intended to attract readers to each new text.[35]

If readers were seeing impressions from woodblocks made half a century earlier, or copied from earlier models, it is important to consider the aesthetic effect of these antique pictures, and the habits of reading they enabled. Roger Chartier's argument is that popular reading culture emphasized 'repetition more than invention: each new text was a variation on already known themes and motifs'.[36] This was not a habit entirely confined to poorer readers. Typology was an established mode of reading which enabled an image to represent both the present and the past.[37] The endlessly under-construction cathedral of Cologne was projected back to Old Testament times in a woodcut illustration of 1 Esdras in the 1478–9 Cologne Bible. Conversely, if an old Bible woodcut of King Solomon was used in a cheap ballad, an early seventeenth-century reader might easily recognize the reference to King James, especially because the latter assiduously encouraged this comparison.[38] Furthermore, repetition was also a fact of real life: the theatre of state was designed to display a continuity of power, so that a *passepartout* woodcut of a scaffold with removable bodies enabled an accurate, if not very artistic, depiction of public executions in London, well into the nineteenth century.[39]

Woodcuts were used to illustrate textbooks, and works at the cheaper end of the book market, in the eighteenth century.[40] An unusual case that nevertheless sums up the status of woodcut in eighteenth-century literary publications is Laurence

---

[34] *Specimens of Early Wood Engraving: Impressions of Wood-Cuts from the Collection of Mr Charnley* (Newcastle, 1858).

[35] Giles Bergel et al., 'Content-Based Image Recognition on Printed Broadside Ballads. The Bodleian Libraries' ImageMatch Tool', *IFLA Library* e-print, http://library.ifla.org/id/eprint/209 (2013): 5–6.

[36] Roger Chartier, 'Reading Matter and "Popular" Reading: From the Renaissance to the 17th Century', in *A History of Reading in the West*, ed. Guglielmo Cavallo and Roger Chartier; trans. Lydia G. Cochrane (Oxford: Polity, 1999), p. 278.

[37] Tessa Watt, *Cheap Print and Popular Piety, 1550–1640* (Cambridge: Cambridge University Press, 1991); Paul Korshin, *Typologies in England, 1640–1820* (Princeton, NJ: Princeton University Press, 1982), p. 31.

[38] Aston, 'Bibles to Ballads', note 28.

[39] Griffiths, *The Print before Photography*, p. 405.

[40] Martyn Ould, 'The Workplace: Places, Procedures, and Personnel 1668–1780', in *The History of Oxford University Press; Volume I. Beginnings to 1780*, ed. Ian Gadd (Oxford: Oxford University Press, 2013), p. 231.

Sterne's *Tristram Shandy*. Both the famous black page in Volume I—'Alas, poor Yorick!'—and the crazily curving 'line of the story' in Volume VI are relief prints. These two abstract images—the uncut block of black, Sterne alleges, hiding 'many opinions, transactions, and truths', the other design tracing the whole narrative arc of the novel up to that moment—represent unspoken or summarized text, while the pictorial frontispieces designed by Hogarth for the second edition are printed from metal engravings.

Between 1788 and 1800 two English artists, both trained in metal engraving, took relief printing in almost opposite directions, each with significant consequences. William Blake's process of 'relief etchings' was revealed to him by a vision of the spirit of his brother Robert with the suggestive words, 'this will give the whole, both poetry and figures, in the manner of stereotype'.[41] The metal plates, meticulously printed in small numbers, incorporated text and image in the same way as fifteenth-century blockbooks. The other artist, Thomas Bewick, developed a compelling style of illustration in wood engraving for works of natural history, and also for editions of Aesop. Many of the blocks were stereotyped and thus appeared in other printed works such as chapbooks, posters, and ballads.[42]

Bewick's success is credited with improving the reputation of wood engraving, which became an important medium for the creation of illustrations for novels, magazines, and newspapers until the end of the nineteenth century. As well as some mechanization of carving, wood-engraved blocks were becoming increasingly easy to reproduce, an effort which had a long history.[43] But this mass production of imagery could seem mechanical compared to the work of early masters such as Albrecht Dürer. An aim to recapture the grandeur of woodcut in its incunable phase inspired William Morris, in the 1890s, to commission woodcut illustration and decoration for printed books and, like Blake, to attend to the look of the whole page, indeed of the whole opening; yet his comment that the decorations and illustrations of the Kelmscott publications were 'inimitable'[44] conceals the fact that some were printed from electrotypes.[45]

---

[41] Allan Cunningham, *Great English Painters, Selected Biographies from 'Lives of Eminent British Painters'*, ed. W. Sharp (London, 1886), p. 285.

[42] Peter C. G. Isaac, *William Davison's New Specimen of Cast-Metal Ornaments and Wood Types: Introduced with an Account of His Activities as Pharmacist and Printer in Alnwick, 1780–1858* (London: Printing Historical Society, 1990).

[43] James Mosley, 'Dabbing, *abklatschen, clichage …*', *Journal of the Printing Historical Society* 23 (Autumn 2015): 73–5. John Jackson and W. A. Chatto, *A Treatise on Wood Engraving, Historical and Practical* (London: Chatto and Windus, 1881), pp. 647–8, 722.

[44] *A note by William Morris on his aims in founding the Kelmscott press, together with a short description of the press by S.C. Cockerell & An annotated list of the books printed thereat* (London: Hammersmith Kelmscott Press, 1898).

[45] Paul Needham, John Dreyfus, and Joseph R. Dunlap, *William Morris and the Art of the Book* (London: Oxford University Press, 1976), p. 87.

In the anatomy of the book, images printed from woodblocks might form the whole body (as in blockbooks) or might constitute some, or all, of the visual content of the edition. The repetition and reappearance of the images in different publications is a reminder to readers, then and now, that each edition existed not only as an organic whole leaping fully formed from the press but also, from another point of view, as the temporary alignment of constituent parts, each lending its weight and associations.[46]

---

[46] Luborsky, 'Woodcuts in Tudor Books'; Knapp, *Illustrating the Past*, pp. 49–50.

CHAPTER 17

ENGRAVINGS

Sean Roberts

Wrought from copper plates by artisans drawing upon the tools and techniques of the goldsmith and armourer, engravings were, for much of the fifteenth century, incorporated only awkwardly and sporadically into the printed book. Professional affinity between woodcutters and early book printers, craft secrecy, and above all the inconvenience and expense arising from the need to print engravings and books on separate presses mitigated against their initial success as illustrations. Yet if intaglio prints—so-named from the Italian verb for *to cut*—were slow off the mark, they proved in succeeding generations to be late bloomers. Engravings provided readers and viewers with a level of subtlety, precision, and graphic density only rarely matched by their woodcut cousins.[1] World maps, astronomical charts, anatomical demonstrations, and records of flora and fauna came to rely on and traffic in the dazzling surface effects achieved by engravers. Engraving became, by the seventeenth century, a vital part of an illustrated book culture which relied upon the bravura naturalism of printmaking to catalogue, promote, and profit from colonization, exploration, and adventurism within an ever expanding early modern world.

Printing, and especially that of images, we are often told, is simple.[2] Yet if the concept of transferring a more or less reproducible configuration of lines from matrix to medium has been well understood since the advent of ancient seals, its practical negotiation as technology has proved a great deal more complex. Though undoubtedly complicated at its own inception around the turn of the fourteenth and fifteenth centuries, the printing of pictures and patterns from woodblocks was fairly well established, and even largely intuitive, by the mid-fifteenth-century rise of letter-press. Engraving, in contrast, represented a still-emerging technology. The first of the intaglio processes to be incorporated by the book industry, engraving employs a chisel-like burin to carve out grooves as it is pushed across a (usually copper) plate. Since the burin excises the metal from these cavities, rather than simply moving it aside, a clean groove without burr at its edges is formed. When it is time to print, the plate is covered with a greasy ink before its surface is wiped clean. The ink that has settled in the furrows created by the burin remains and, at this point, pressure is applied to draw that ink out of these grooves, imprinting lines upon dampened paper. This process is repeated for each print or impression.[3]

---

[1] For an introduction to the materials and processes of intaglio printmaking see Anthony Griffiths, *The Print before Photography* (London: British Museum, 2016), esp. pp. 38–49.

[2] For these claims see esp. David Landau and Peter Parshall, *The Renaissance Print: 1470–1550* (New Haven, CT: Yale University Press, 1994), p. 1; and Peter Parshall (ed.), *The Woodcut in Fifteenth-Century Europe* (New Haven, CT: Yale University Press/National Gallery of Art, 2009), pp. 9–10.

[3] For an excellent introduction to historical intaglio techniques see Ad Stijman, *Engraving and Etching, 1400–2000* (London: Archetype Publications, 2012), pp. 23–30.

Simple enough, as it goes. Yet, so much can—and often did—go wrong at every step in the process. Ink could be either too thick or not viscous enough, resulting in lines that are faint or that spread across the paper and merge. Copper is a soft metal, and the polished plate of the engraver is susceptible to scratches and cracks that can register as lines and even as an overall grey tone that obscures the intended image. Perhaps most importantly, the action of engraving with a burin has little relationship to the naturalized gestures of the draughtsman or scribe and correcting mistakes produced by this awkward process is time consuming. Francesco Berlinghieri's *Seven Days of Geography* (1482), one of the first books to incorporate engravings, provides a master class in how not to illustrate a printed book. Though the edition's thirty-one maps (Fig. 17.1) were based on decades-old conventional models, their translation into this new medium proved challenging. As with many early engravings, these maps can be difficult to read, their surfaces marred by an all-over greyness. So, too, surviving impressions are often uneven, an indication of the challenges faced by early roller presses in achieving consistent pressure across these nearly folio-sized plates, among the largest of the fifteenth century. More remarkable, though, is the fact that the engraver was unfamiliar with basic techniques like hammering and burnishing—in which copper is forced back into a groove and polished smooth to correct a mistake— and tools like letter punches. The upshot of all of this was that several thousand

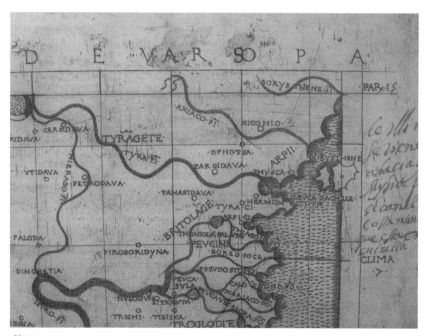

✦ **Fig. 17.1** *Ninth map of Europe (detail). Copperplate engraving from Francesco Berlinghieri, 'Seven Days of Geography' (Florence, 1482). Milan: Biblioteca Nazionale Braidense*

geographic labels had to be engraved free-hand and errant lines could not be erased. It is hard not to feel pangs of sympathy for the poor artisan when we look at the ninth map of Europe. Here, our hapless engraver mistakenly began by labelling his work 'ASIA'. Unable to remove these letters, 'EUROPA' was interposed between the previous title, producing an unintelligible jumble.[4]

The tools and techniques that might have prevented such glaring errors were known not just in northern Europe, but also considerably closer to the city on the Arno. So while our Florentine engraver was struggling, the German printer Conrad Sweynheym had already trained Roman craftsmen to perform precisely these kinds of corrections (Fig. 17.2).[5] The results were the maps of a splendid *Geography* which beat Berlinghieri's version to the market in 1478. In contrast to the Florentine version, Sweynheym's maps feature crisp lines against folia unmarred by cracks and scratches, and nearly flawless labels, the result of sharp metal-punches which freed the engravers from cutting each name painstakingly with the burin.[6] These maps exhibit a precocious sense of three-dimensionality, as in the world map's delicate mountain ranges, their slopes cast in shade formed by careful cross-hatching. The result is an unparalleled level of naturalism, barely approached, for example, by the schematic and flat, if highly legible, maps that accompanied the wood *Geography* printed in Ulm during these same years.

If Roman printers and engravers found solutions to some of the obvious visual hurdles presented by this new technology, a more fundamental barrier to engraving's incorporation within the book trade is driven home by another edition from the same Florentine print shop as Berlinghieri's *Geography*. Cristoforo Landino's commentary on Dante's *Divine Comedy* was published in 1481, intended as a luxury edition, and dedicated, in a copy printed on vellum, to Florence's government that same year.[7] Maps were incorporated into books by printing them on separate sheets and gathering these with text pages at the time of their binding. For this *Commentary*, author and printer sought instead to ambitiously combine illustrations for each of Dante's cantos directly on the first page of each section's text.[8] In conception, this might have seemed easy enough. After all, it had been done for decades using woodcuts. But woodcuts were printed using the traditional platen-type presses employed for type.

---

[4] Sean Roberts, *Printing a Mediterranean World* (Cambridge, MA: Harvard University Press, 2013), pp. 92–7.

[5] R. A. Skelton, 'Introduction', *Claudius Ptolemy: Cosmographia, Rome, 1478* (Amsterdam: Theatrum Orbis Terrarum, 1966), p. viii.

[6] Tony Campbell, 'Letter Punches: A Little-Known Feature of Early Engraved Maps', *Print Quarterly* 4 (1987): 151–4.

[7] See the newly discovered contract for this undertaking, published in Lorenz Böninger, 'Il contratto per la stampa e gli inizi del commercio del *Comento sopra la comedia*', in *Per Cristoforo Landino, lettore di Dante*, ed. Lorenz Boninger and Paolo Procaccioli (Florence: Le Lettere, 2016), pp. 97–118.

[8] Peter Keller, 'The Engravings in the 1481 Edition of the Divine Comedy,' in *Sandro Botticelli: The Drawings for Dante's Divine Comedy*, ed. H. Altcappenberg (London: Royal Academy of the Arts, 2000), pp. 326–33; and Palo Procaccioli, 'Introduction', *Cristoforo Landino: Comento sopra la Comedia* (Rome: Salierno, 2001).

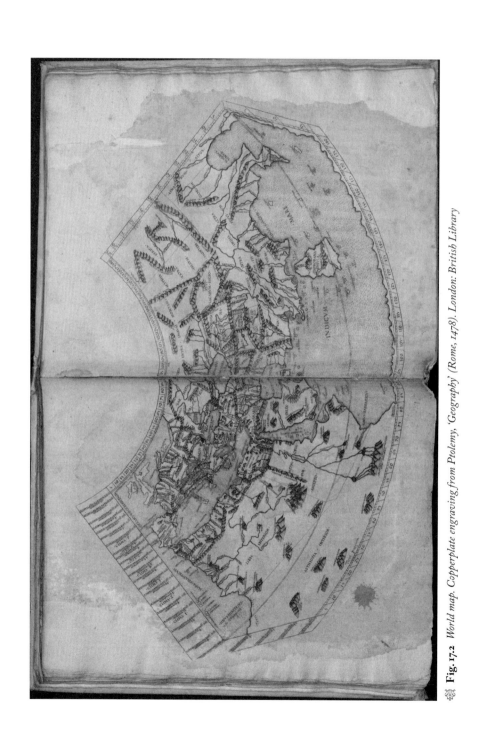

Fig. 17.2 *World map. Copperplate engraving from Ptolemy, 'Geography' (Rome, 1478). London: British Library*

In contrast, engraved plates required the application of significantly greater pressure, a problem generally solved by using a roller press. The *Commentary*'s publisher, then, faced an unexpected challenge in combining these media on a single page.

Initially (and overoptimistically) the printer attempted a two-step process. The text was printed first using the shop's usual platen press. These folia, with the spaces for their illustrations left blank, were then carefully lined up with the inked copper plate and passed through a roller press. Though effective in principle, this technique proved labour intensive, costly, and ultimately unsatisfactory. Any time a sheet needs to be run through a press twice issues of 'registration' arise. There is, in short, always a risk that without very careful attention the image will end up somewhere it should not be on the sheet. The challenges of this method are demonstrated nearly comically by the first page of canto three from a copy today in the Bodleian's collection.[9] Here, the engraved plate was placed both upside down and askew, producing a correspondingly off-kilter illustration (Fig. 17.3). Fearing, no doubt, that such mishaps would continue, a new strategy was adopted. The engraved illustrations were printed on separate folia using the roller press and these were subsequently cut out and pasted onto the finished letterpress pages. Even this proved organizationally difficult, and only a handful of copies survive with anything close to a full complement of the illustrations.

These false starts and jerry-rigged solutions tell us a great deal about the development of the illustrated book. First and foremost, they remind us that early modern printing practices were highly localized. Makers and printers relied upon tools and methods which were anything but evenly distributed throughout Europe. Engraving was, in its nascent stage, a completely new profession, combining skills employed by armourers, goldsmiths, painters, and printers who had previously worked with woodcut and letterpress. Yet localization was not only the result of organic growing pains. Rather, men like our Florentine and Roman printers—and the engravers they worked with—were entrepreneurs with a vested interest in protecting the most efficacious tools, recipes, and techniques as trade secrets.[10] And there is no question that the stakes were high. While the Roman Ptolemy was visually successful, it fared no better commercially than its Florentine counterpart. Experiments in this new medium were costly and the profit margins slim. Shortly after the *Geography*'s publication, Sweynheym and his business partners found themselves bankrupt and their operation was kept afloat only by a substantial loan from the papacy.[11]

[9] Oxford University, Bodleian Library, Auct. 2Q 1.11.

[10] Sean Roberts, 'Tricks of the Trade: The Secrets of Early Engraving', in *Visual Cultures of Secrecy in Early Modern Europe*, ed. Timothy McCall, Sean Roberts, and Giancarlo Fiorenza (Kirksville, MO: Truman State University Press, 2013), pp. 182–208. See most recently Christina Neilson, 'Demonstrating Ingenuity: The Display and Concealment of Knowledge in Renaissance Artists' Workshops', *I Tatti Studies in the Italian Renaissance* 19 (2016): 63–91.

[11] Skelton, *Cosmographia: Rome, 1478*, p. v.

Fig. 17.3 *Incipit of Canto III. Copperplate engraving and letterpress from Cristoforo Landino, 'Commentary on the Divine Comedy' (Florence, 1481). The Bodleian Libraries, University of Oxford. Shelfmark: Auct. 2 Q 1.11, f. Clv.*

Sweynheym's engravers utilized intricate hatching and precise control of line to develop a convincing sense of three-dimensionality, and to accommodate crisp, clean place names on these maps. The end result nonetheless shared with most early engraved illustrations one significant disadvantage when compared to their woodcut peers. Today, we almost universally associate printing with the aesthetic of the black line on the white page.[12] In contrast, early modern viewers, accustomed to manuscript illumination and faced with printed images that initially lacked a developed tonal system, expected their prints in living colour. If this preference was relatively short-lived regarding artists' prints, it long remained crucial for book illustrations that conveyed detailed visual information. Maps represent the most significant category of such technical images that required immediate and unmistakable distinction between figure and ground. Despite its obvious advantages, the density of engraved lines and their reliance on hatching to create tone tended to leave little negative space on the page for the semi-transparent watercolour usually used to add colour to early prints. Thus if books like the *Geography* produced in Ulm in 1482 could not compete with those of Florence and Rome in terms of either detail or naturalistic depth, their woodcut maps nonetheless offered large expanses of blank page which could be variously coloured without fear of scratches, cracks, or errant marks. Eventually, subtle hand colouring became both possible and, indeed, normalized as increasingly experienced engravers made careful allowances for such additions to their works. So too the increasingly common combination of traditional engraving with the chemical intaglio medium of etching—in which lines are created through the biting of acid on a copper plate rather than the direct force of a burin—allowed printmakers to substitute areas of subtle and graduated tone for colour.[13] And eventually, processes were developed for directly printing engravings in colour, such as the innovative two-colour system used for Cornelis de Bruijn's views of Egypt and the Middle East in his *Voyage to the Levant* of 1700.[14]

Many technical problems subsided as these methods came to be better understood and, in time, intaglio methods were as well understood as their relief predecessors. By the later sixteenth and early seventeenth century, these prints were increasingly produced by a professional class of trained engravers. These artisans, working in concert with draughtsman and publishers, were experts not so much in the arts of design as in translating visual ideas into a reproducible format. Still, some of these

[12] On the addition of colour to early prints by hand, see Susan Dackerman, *Painted Prints: The Revelation of Colour* (University Park, PA: Penn State University Press, 2002).

[13] Madeleine Viljoen, 'Etching and Drawing in Early Modern Europe', in *The Early Modern Painter-Etcher*, ed. Michael Cole (University Park, PA: Penn State University Press, 2006), pp. 37–52.

[14] From its very inception printers had, however, experimented with mechanized solutions to add colour to their works. See esp. Ad Stijnman and Elizabeth Savage (eds), *Printing Color, 1400–1700* (Leiden: Brill, 2015). For Bruijn see Benjamin Schmidt, *Inventing Exoticism: Geography, Globalism, and Europe's Early Modern World* (Philadelphia, PA: University of Pennsylvania Press, 2015), pp. 44–5.

early barriers would persist as defining characteristics of engraving's relationship to the book. The complexities of mixing relief and intaglio printing meant that engraving was best suited for the production of works like atlases in which images could be printed separately and bound with the finished product in sections. In other cases, including anatomical works and demonstrations of scientific instruments and models, engraving was used to produce what Suzanne Karr Schmidt has called 'sculptural prints'. Whether produced as single sheets or bound within books, these images were designed to be cut apart, assembled, and pasted together to produce objects that look very much like 'pop-up' books to modern eyes.[15] As Kelli Wood has shown, though these ephemeral objects are often lost today, engraved game boards represented a significant part of many printers' inventories. While these might be accompanied by letterpress treatises describing their rules, the boards were stand-alone objects rather than book components.[16] Likewise, many of the great projects for maps and views in the sixteenth and seventeenth centuries were not bound in books. Instead, they were sold as stand-alone projects like Mario Cartaro's pendant views of modern and ancient Rome of 1576 which enticed tourists and visitors to the eternal city.[17] In short, it may be considered a fair guess that the majority of early modern engravings were not produced, in any strict sense, as book parts.

Indeed, the relationship between the illustrated book and intaglio printmaking remained touch-and-go for much of the sixteenth century. Despite its potential, many of the most successful and influential editions continued to be illustrated by woodcut. When Giorgio Vasari sought to translate his portraits of Italy's artists into print for the expanded 1568 redaction of his *Lives*, he chose woodcut, even though this meant seeking a capable artisan in distant Venice. Preparatory drawings were thus sent north in batches so that blocks could be cut by a master craftsman. Proof impressions were likely pulled at this time and approved by the author's trusted agents. The finished blocks were then returned to Florence for printing.[18] The choice of woodcut was essential for the *Lives*, since these portraits had to be incorporated directly among the letterpress text at the start of each artist's biography. Likewise, despite its need for technical detail, Andreas Vesalius' *De Humani Corporis Fabrica* printed in Basel in 1543, relied upon woodcut. Vesalius' illustrated compendium of the dissected human body proved the most influential anatomical work of the period, unrivalled in its ubiquity until Henry Gray's eponymous nineteenth-century textbook. Vesalius'

---

[15] Susan Dackerman, 'Prints as Instruments', in *Prints and the Pursuit of Visual Knowledge* (Chicago, IL: University of Chicago Press, 2011), pp. 19–34; and Suzanne Karr Schmidt, *Interactive and Sculptural Printmaking in the Renaissance* (Leiden: Brill, 2017).

[16] Kelli Wood, 'The Art of Play', PhD dissertation, History of Art, University of Chicago, 2016.

[17] See esp. Jessica Maier, *Rome Measured and Imagined* (Chicago, IL: University of Chicago Press, 2016), pp. 143–51.

[18] Among the vast literature see, to start, Sharon Gregory, *Vasari and the Renaissance Print* (Farnham: Ashgate, 2012), pp. 83–114; and Laura Morretti and Sean Roberts, 'From the *Vite* or the *Ritratti*: Previously Unknown Portraits from Vasari's Libro de' Disegni', *I Tatti Studies in the Italian Renaissance* 21 (2018): 105–36.

demonstrations of the skeletal and muscular underpinnings of the flayed body tested the technical artistry of woodcut.[19] But what these illustrations might have lacked in precise, dense modelling, they more than made up for with one of woodcut's intrinsic qualities: its tremendous durability. The high pressure and relative pliability of copper meant that engravings wore down quickly with repeated printing.[20] In contrast, barring breakage of delicate details, wood blocks could be printed nearly indefinitely. The portrait blocks from Vasari's *Lives*, for example, were still being used nearly a century later, having migrated to Bologna where they illustrated a new edition in 1647.[21] The *Lives* and the *Fabrica* serve as reminders that a great many printed books—even those with illustrations of a technical or artistic sort—required the flexibility to integrate text and image and profited from the longevity of the matrix that woodcut provided.[22]

But for works that demanded especially intricate visual information which could be separated from the text—and whose potential readership justified the expense—engraving became indispensable and a mark of prestige. Professional engravers worked hand in hand with publishers in centres including Rome, and increasingly Antwerp, Amsterdam, and the cities of northern Europe to craft elaborate and impressive books.[23] By the last quarter of the sixteenth century, engraving was widely recognized as a technical marvel. Jan van der Straet (known as Stradanus), included the engraver's workshop among the ingenious new discoveries—*Nova Reperta*—heralded in a series of prints engraved by Jan Collaert and published by Phillips Galle. For Stradanus, engraving ranked alongside gunpowder and the compass as technologies that underwrote the modern world he and his patrons inhabited.[24]

Collections of maps were at the forefront of this trend. The Dutch humanist Abraham Ortelius chose engraving as the medium for his Latin geographical compendium, the *Theatrum Orbis Terrarum* printed in 1570.[25] Often considered the first true world atlas, the *Theatrum* drew upon the skills of Antwerp's first-rate engravers to provide readers and viewers with maps of unprecedented detail, clarity, and novelty (see Plate 6). Ortelius' world map remains a nearly flawless synthesis of breadth and

---

[19] For a summary of these developments see Domenico Laurenza, *Art and Anatomy in Renaissance Italy: Images from a Scientific Revolution* (New York: Metropolitan Museum of Art, 2012).

[20] Griffiths, *The Print before Photography*, pp. 50–61.

[21] Maria H. Loh, *Still Lives: Death, Desire, and the Portrait of the Old Master* (Princeton, NJ: Princeton University Press, 2015), pp. 20–1.

[22] See esp. Dackerman, *Prints and the Pursuit of Visual Knowledge*.

[23] See esp. Evelyn Lincoln, *Brilliant Discourse: Pictures and Readers in Early Modern Rome* (New Haven, CT: Yale University Press, 2014).

[24] See Alessandra Baroni and Manfred Sellink (eds), *Stradanus, 1523–1605: Court Artist of the Medici* (Turnhout: Brepols, 2012); Lia Markey, 'Stradano's Allegorical Invention of the Americas in Late Sixteenth-Century Florence', *Renaissance Quarterly* 65 (2012): 385–442.

[25] See Marcel van den Broecke et al. (eds), *Abraham Ortelius and the First Atlas* (Utrecht: HES, 1998).

depth of cartographic information, an epitome of geographical knowledge at the high point of the conventional age of discovery.[26] The viewer's eye moves seamlessly between the vast scale of the double-folio projection, spread across the opened pages, and its countless tiny cities, mountains, and rivers. Such details effectively blurred the boundaries between cartographic signs and evocative landscape, increasingly a hallmark of northern European naturalism. So, too, the full power of late Renaissance art is on display in the lavish ornaments and scrolls, sirens and putti, ships and sea monsters that populate the edges and blank spaces of this vibrant globe. And through careful planning, ample negative space was left between and around the geographic features of these maps to allow for uniform hand colouring that was highly responsive to the developing illusionism of the image.

The *Theatrum* rapidly took its place among the most successful printing projects of the early modern world, inspiring competition, imitation, and elaboration not only within Antwerp but across the continent. One of the most innovative examples of the creative spark the atlas provided may be seen in Georg Braun and Franz Hogenberg's collaboration the *Civitates orbis terrarum* (1572), which supplemented Ortelius' big picture with detailed views of the skylines, coastlines, and fortifications of the world's greatest cities.[27] Crucially, the modular nature of the *Theatrum* also meant that its engraved maps—far and away the book's most labour-intensive components— could be reused when the project was adapted for non-Latinate readers. Editions in Dutch, of course, but also in German and French rapidly followed the initial publication and proved cost effective and profitable. Engravings, in this sense, benefitted tremendously from their status as 'book parts', which remained nonetheless separate from the whole.

Even an entrepreneur on the scale of Ortelius could scarcely have imagined the heights which commercial, luxury engraving would reach in the following century. Building upon the success of several more limited endeavours, Johannes Blaeu introduced the world to the first volume of his so-called *Atlas Major* in 1662 (Plate 7). Printed in Amsterdam, by then arguably the centre of European publishing and drawing on the popularity of predecessors like the *Theatrum*, the *Atlas* would ultimately comprise eleven massive engraved volumes.[28] Still, Blaeu's ambitions far outstripped practical considerations, for he intended ultimately to also incorporate

[26] Tine Luk Meganck, *Erudite Eyes: Friendship, Art, and Erudition in the Network of Abraham Ortelius* (Leiden: Brill, 2017).

[27] Johannes Keuning, 'The "Civitates" of Braun and Hogenberg', *Imago Mundi* 17 (1963): 41–4; and Hillary Ballon and David Friedman, 'Portraying the City in Early Modern Europe: Measurement, Representation, and Planning', in *The History of Cartography*, 3, part 1, ed. David Woodward (Chicago, IL: University of Chicago Press, 2007), pp. 680–704.

[28] C. Koeman, Günter Schilder, Peter van der Krogt, and Marco van Egmond, 'Commercial Cartography and Map Production in the Low Countries, 1500–ca. 1672', in David Woodward, ed., *The History of Cartography*, Vol. 3 (Chicago, IL: University of Chicago Press, 2007); and Krogt 'The Atlas Maior of Joan Blaeu', in *Atlas Maior of 1665* (Köln: Taschen, 2005).

charts of the heavens and seas, providing a veritable spatial encyclopaedia. To an extraordinary degree, it was the spectacular graphic quality and scale of the *Atlas'* engravings rather than the distinctiveness of its geographic information that set these volumes apart. By the mid-seventeenth century, engraving was an art form characterized by increasingly breathtaking visual effects employed by specialized artists including the likes of Hendrik Goltzius and Claude Mellan.[29] On the pages of the *Atlas*, this technical mastery produced striking images like the double-hemisphere world map. Here state-of-the-art cartographic projection combines with powerful Baroque figures of the classical gods and goddesses and portraits of the geographers of the ancient world, all set amidst a painterly view of the heavens. Blaeu's *Atlas* was, among much else, the most expensive book available for purchase in the seventeenth century. In its most costly iteration it featured lavish hand colouring on each of its maps and has been estimated to have cost somewhere in the range of a skilled artisan's annual salary. Far more, of course, was at stake here than pride and artistic reputation. For its printer, this *Atlas* represented the latest and most powerful volley in an escalating commercial tug of war with the rival Hondius print shop. As was the case at its advent two centuries earlier, illustrated book engraving remained, at its heart, a risky, experimental, and technologically adventurous endeavour.

The subtlety, precision, and graphic density that engraving provided, especially when combined with the tonal effects of etching and hand colouring, meant that it remained, in many ways, the gold standard for deluxe book illustration for centuries. Indeed, for some image types, including the sorts of high-end atlases explored here, engraving held this pride of place until it was supplanted by offset lithography and the wide availability of commercial colour printing. Perhaps ironically, the virtuoso artistry of engravings like those included in Blaeu's *Atlas* were ultimately supplanted not by a radically new technology, but by the nineteenth-century revival of printing from wood, this time in the form of the dazzling and immersive wood engravings used by artists like Gustave Doré in his unparalleled illustrations for the Divine Comedy of 1882.

---

[29] Huigen Leeflang and Ger Luijten (eds), *Hendrick Goltzius 1558–1617* (Amsterdam: Waanders, 2003).

CHAPTER 18

FOOTNOTES[1]

---

[1] Jenny Davidson

The footnote bears a family resemblance to a host of other forms of annotation, some of them older not only than print but even than the form of the codex: these would include the Talmud, patristic commentaries on biblical texts, and copious manuscript glosses on authors both classical and biblical. Despite its title, this chapter will concern itself not just with footnotes but with the underlying principles that govern all forms of textual annotation; that said, the appearance of annotation at the foot of a printed page—as opposed to marginal annotation or alternately to the endnote—can be pinned down to northern Europe in the final years of the seventeenth century. Marcus Walsh points to French priest and biblical scholar Richard Simon (1638–1712) as a pivotal figure in the history of scholarly documentation.[1] Simon published his critical text of the Old Testament in 1680, stating outright in the preface that he would keep his citations in the text brief, so as not to bore his readers with lengthy testimonies; those minimalist marginal notations were matched to a fuller list of references printed at the end. The sequel volume on the New Testament (1689) hewed to a distinctively different form of documentation; certain people having complained that it was too much trouble to go and look up the relevant passages, Simon writes, he has decided to place them at the bottom of the page, 'où chacun pourra les lire dans toute leur ëtendüe, & dans la langue des Auteurs' ['where everyone will be able to read them in full, and in their original language'].[2] To publish any kind of critical edition of a scriptural text itself obviously represents a profound challenge to older forms of religious faith, and Evelyn B. Tribble suggests that the shape of the page often becomes 'more than usually visible' at periods when 'paradigms for receiving the past are under stress': '[i]n the early modern period, as models of annotation move from marginal glosses to footnotes', she observes, 'the note becomes the battlefield upon which competing notions of the relationship of authority and tradition, past and present, are fought'.[3]

The early years of the footnote were not tentative or partial. Almost as soon as the footnote came into existence, its tendency to proliferate and snarl up the printed page becomes evident, and some of the most baroquely ornate examples of foot-noting can be found in precisely these opening years of its existence. A floridly annotated page could offer an attractive way (at once cryptic and brazen) of mounting

[1] Marcus Walsh, 'Scholarly Documentation in the Enlightenment: Validation and Interpretation', in *Ancients and Moderns in Europe: Comparative Perspectives*, ed. Paddy Bullard and Alexis Tadié (Oxford: Voltaire Foundation, 2016), pp. 97–112.

[2] Richard Simon, *Histoire critique du texte du Nouveau Testament* (Rotterdam: Reinier Leers, 1689), as quoted in Walsh, 'Scholarly Documentation', p. 99.

[3] Evelyn B. Tribble, '"Like a Looking-Glas in the Frame": From the Marginal Note to the Footnote', in *The Margins of the Text*, ed. D. C. Greetham (Ann Arbor, MI: University of Michigan Press, 1997), pp. 229–44, 229.

an assault on contemporary religious orthodoxy, as it did in the case of Pierre Bayle's *Dictionnaire Historique et Critique*, first published in 1697 (the earliest English translation appeared in 1709) and subsequently expanded over many editions (Fig. 18.1). Consulting the four grand folio volumes of the sixth edition of 1741, for instance, we get a clear view of the fashion in which each page has become a quasi-Scriblerian tangle of commentaries, featuring multiple systems of annotation each with its own code of characters and numerals.[4] The influence of Bayle's style of annotation and the inductive method with which it was associated, which Lawrence Lipking has described as a mode of *'perpetual commentary*, in which the sequence of thought depends on reviewing all known sources of information', would become an organizing principle for a good deal of eighteenth-century criticism, including for Samuel Johnson in the *Lives of the Poets*, even when the critics' pages no longer bristled with annotation.[5]

Sixteenth-century humanists had developed new techniques for editing classical texts, and in the seventeenth century, biblical scholars adopted and adapted these for purposes along a spectrum that ranged from conservative to radically sceptical. *Circa* 1700, both biblical and classical textual editing had the highest possible stakes: political, cultural, intellectual, in other words all-encompassing. The practices of textual editing sat at the centre of Western European intellectual culture, its adherents identified (by their adversaries as well as themselves) as distinctively modern and associated especially with the British classical scholar Richard Bentley, but as the battle of ancients and moderns gained steam, 'straight' footnotes increasingly invited parody and elaboration, with Swift, Pope, and like-minded colleagues adopting the new form of annotation in order to comment on and critique modern ways of creating meaning. Put Descartes and Locke on one side of the balance and Swift, Pope, and assorted allies onto the other, and we can see very clearly the shape of a head-to-head battle between—on the one hand—a polemical modern position in which the human mind itself has become the prime object of inquiry, with ancient science and the received wisdom of an ancient literary tradition largely superseded, and—on the other hand—a deliberately backward-looking and self-consciously aristocratic (sometimes just 'gentlemanly') position, one that emphasizes continuity over breaks but that finds itself constantly tempted by the very modes of language and thought that it is determined to castigate. The introduction and development of footnotes as 'straight' forms of scholarly documentation, in other words, is matched simultaneously with their adoption as satirical tools for exposing the pedantry and self-involvement of so-called modern scholarship.[6]

---

[4] Pierre Bayle, *Dictionnaire Historique et Critique*, 6th edn, 4 vols (Basel: Jean Louis Brandmuller, 1741).

[5] Lawrence Lipking, 'The Marginal Gloss', *Critical Inquiry* 3, no. 4 (1977): 609–55, 625.

[6] This was not a new phenomenon. See Peter W. Cosgrove, 'Undermining the Text: Edward Gibbon, Alexander Pope, and the Anti-Authenticating Footnote', in *Annotation and Its Texts*, ed. Stephen A. Barney (New York: Oxford University Press, 1991), pp. 130–51, 134.

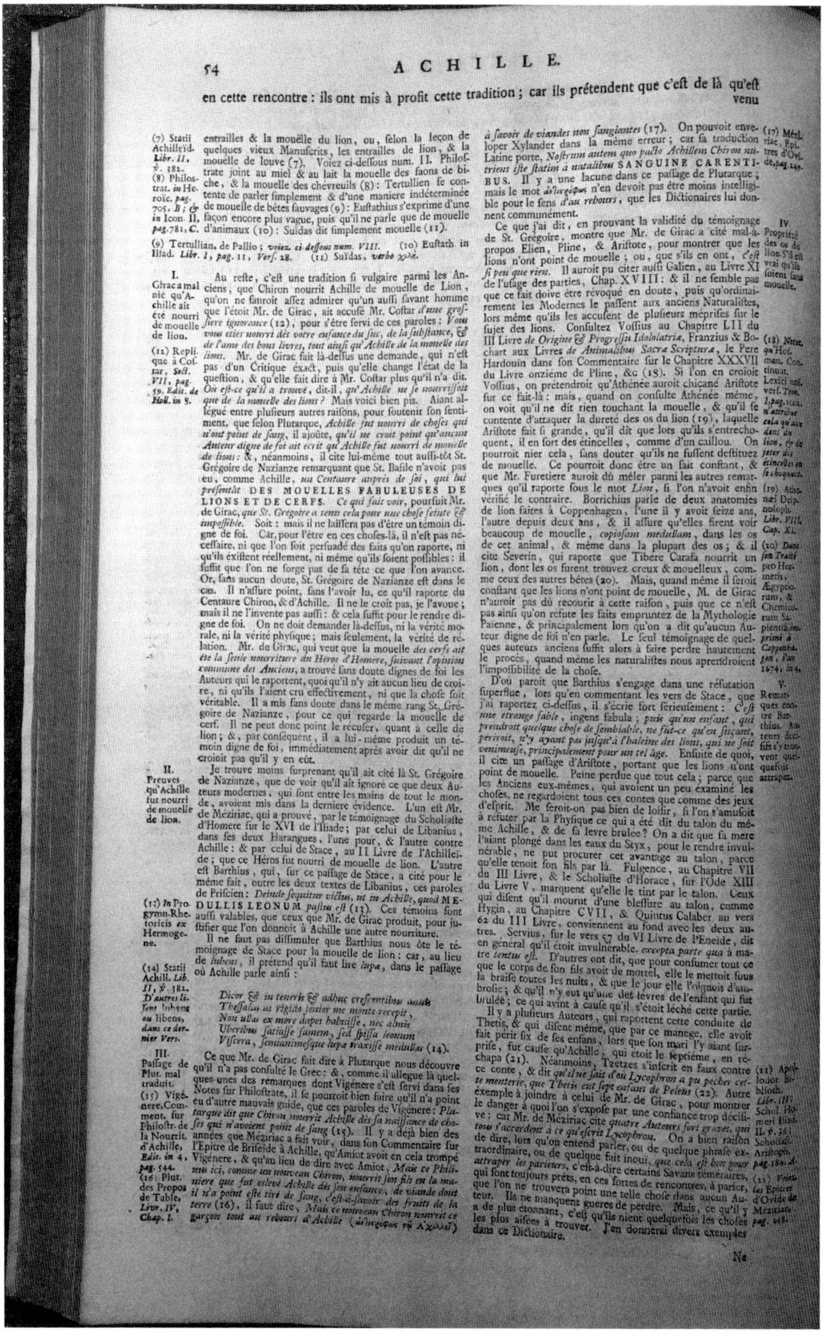
54 ACHILLE.

en cette rencontre : ils ont mis à profit cette tradition ; car ils prétendent que c'est de là qu'est venu

Fig. 18.1 *Pierre Bayle, Dictionnaire historique et critique, 6th edn, 4 vols (Basel: Jean Louis Brandmuller, 1741), entry for 'Achille', 1:54. In the collection of Harris Manchester College Library, Oxford (F 1741/2 (1–4)). Photo credit: Georgina Wilson*

Swift's *Tale of a Tub* provides another revealing moment in the early history of the footnote. For the fifth edition of the *Tale of a Tub*, printed in 1710, what had previously been only marginal glosses were supplemented with extensive footnotes.[7] Walsh notes that it wasn't 'the move in works of scholarship to footnotes as such' that mattered for Swift, and observes that it was Swift's bookseller Tooke rather than the author himself who argued for foot rather than endnotes: Swift objected rather to the new methodology in its entirety, and the parodic marginalia and footnotes of the *Tale* can be thought of as being 'part of an old humanism's anxious response to a new one'.[8]

Certain other explicitly religious modes of commentary (especially Protestant ones) must have fed into Swift's sense of annotation as a plague or an infection. Tribble observes of the early printed English bibles, many of whose pages are peppered with various forms of printed marginalia and annotation, that '[t]he humanist use of the page as a locus for consensus or community is thus turned on its head in a context which points up the importance of the printed page as a territory for ideological occupation'.[9]

It is the novel that we think of as the 'hungry' genre of this period—it picks up all of the topics and properties of the other discourses of print—but verse and prose satire are equally able to imitate and engulf practices more commonly associated with other modes of writing, and a great many of the literary works we still read from this period make use of the footnote as a tool for grounding, framing, or undermining the main text. Consider Pope's transformation of the *Dunciad* into an edition variorum, an edition that integrates prior editors' commentary at some length.[10] The character of textual editor Martinus Scriblerus had been jointly created by Pope, Swift, and a few others some years earlier, and the *Dunciad Variorum* represents the full flowering of the 'Scriblerian' page, where annotation swallows up and threatens to bury the main text.

One of Pope's formal targets in the *Dunciad Variorum* was Lewis Theobald, whose *Shakespeare Restored* (1726) had exposed the profound inadequacies of the editorial principles Pope applied in his edition of Shakespeare and who represented for Pope (stung by the personal tone of the attack) the worst excesses of modern textual

---

[7] Jonathan Swift, *A Tale of a Tub and Other Works*, ed. Marcus Walsh (Cambridge: Cambridge University Press, 2010), vol. 1 of *The Cambridge Edition of the Works of Jonathan Swift*, p. xxxiv.

[8] Swift, *Tale of a Tub*, pp. 105–6; the full text of Tooke's letter is given as an appendix at pp. 213–14. For a fuller history of scholarly documentation over the last few centuries, see Robert J. Connors, 'The Rhetoric of Citation Systems, Part I: The Development of Annotation Structures from the Renaissance to 1900', *Rhetoric Review* 17, no. 1 (1998): 6–48.

[9] Evelyn B. Tribble, *Margins and Marginality: The Printed Page in Early Modern England* (Charlottesville, VA: University Press of Virginia, 1993), p. 9.

[10] *The Dunciad Variorum. With the Prolegomena of Scriblerus* (London: A. Dod, 1729, rpt. Leeds: Scolar Press, 1966). I consider the transition from book 1 to book 2, at pp. 22–3, a plausible candidate for the most brilliant facing-page spread in all of eighteenth-century British literature.

criticism. The footnote would become a powerful expressive medium for editors of Shakespeare as the century progressed, Theobald (sharply learned) and Warburton (bullying and belligerent) among them, but Samuel Johnson's commentary on Shakespeare is surely the most collaborative and the most richly aware of the opportunity a variorum edition creates for conversation between readers who are not present in the same room or even perhaps alive at the same time, but whose proximity on the printed page brings the connection alive, reanimating voices and putting ideas and intellects into a mode of dynamic exchange. Johnson incidentally offers one of the century's most perceptive reflections on the trade-offs the annotator of the printed page is likely to encounter: 'Particular passages are cleared by notes, but the general effect of the work is weakened. The mind is refrigerated by interruption; the thoughts are diverted from the principal subject; the reader is weary, he suspects not why; and at last throws away the book, which he has too diligently studied.'[11] There is a profound ambivalence in Johnson as in many of his contemporaries about the form of the note itself and particularly the footnote, in the sense that it obtrudes itself on the reader's attention in a way that endnotes do not.

A focus on footnotes allows the critic to consider alongside one another a number of wildly different works that are not always thought of as participating in at all the same projects of creating meaning: Swift's *Tale of a Tub* and Pope's *Dunciad*, but also Richardson's *Clarissa* and its increasingly controlling use of footnotes to cross-reference and moralize in subsequent revisions, the self-annotation of mid-century poets such as Thomas Gray and James Grainger, and the apotheosis of the footnote in Gibbon's *Decline and Fall of the Roman Empire*. A number of great mid-century novels make interesting use of annotation at the base of the page, with *The Life and Opinions of Tristram Shandy, Gentleman* (1759–67) perhaps the best known in its borrowing of the apparatus of scholarship. But both *Clarissa* and *Tom Jones* (both 1748) make use of page-based annotation for purposes sometimes similar and sometimes profoundly divergent. Fielding will tend to use notes to augment (playfully and with an eye to the 'meta' qualities of his fiction) the parallels between the world of the novel and the real-life world onto which its scenes are mapped, not least by reminding the reader of the generic proximity of novel to newspaper, with its prolific advertisements. Referring in the text to 'the Agility and Strength of our Heroe', for instance, who is 'perhaps a Match for one of the First-Rate Boxers, and could, with great Ease, have beaten all the muffled Graduates of Mr. *Broughton*'s School', the narrator appends a footnote—'Lest Posterity should be puzzled by this Epithet, I think proper to explain it by an Advertisement which was published *Feb.* 1, 1747'—and proceeds to quote the entire text of an advertisement for Broughton's boxing

[11] 'Preface', *Johnson on Shakespeare*, ed. Arthur Sherbo, intro. Bertrand H. Bronson, vol. 1 of 2 (New Haven, CT: Yale University Press, 1968), vol. 7 of *The Yale Edition of the Works of Samuel Johnson*, p. 111.

academy in the Haymarket.[12] Richardson uses footnotes along loosely similar lines, although the effect is less of frame breaking than of direct advertisement: when Clarissa's sister tells her that 'Your drawings and your pieces are all taken down; as is also your own whole-length picture in the Vandyke taste, from your late parlour', a note earnestly observes: 'This picture is drawn as big as the life by Mr Highmore and is in his possession.'[13] More extensive and more problematic in *Clarissa*, though, is the managerial footnoting: attributable, for the reader who knows the novel's ending, to the actual person Belford, who is appointed Clarissa's literary executor, but also indistinguishable in many cases from Richardson's own voice, and enabled and elaborated by means of the unusual fact that he was the printer of his own books and possessed thereby an unusual degree of control over the book's format, including but not limited to the appearance of individual pages. Angus Ross notes that twenty-two 'omniscient' footnotes by the 'editor' were added by Richardson to the second edition and retained for the third, augmenting an aspect that was present in the first edition but greatly expanding it: 'Many of the notes act against the subtle process of unfolding the story in the letters, by brusquely pointing forward into the following narrative,' he adds, 'and the whole exercise must surely be seen as an attempt by Richardson to restore his control of the readers' interpretations of the novel letter-texts as well as story.'[14] The versatility of annotation's potentialities shows in the ways that subsequent generations of novelists would reinvent the footnote for their own purposes, and Claire Connolly offers a rich account of how the Irish novel in the Romantic period borrows from contemporary historiography many of the evidentiary protocols of scholarship and its apparatus of annotation: the role of footnotes in these novels, Connolly adds, is not just to serve as a device of alienation but 'to offer a mediated form of intimacy, bringing readers into proximity with a palpable community of knowledge, derived from an array of sources and preserved in print'.[15]

Another thing annotation can do is transform a contemporary poem into something that has some of the textual authority and *gravitas* of a classical exemplar, one dimension of Gray's self-annotation in certain editions of his own poems. When Gray annotated his famous 'Elegy Written in a Country Churchyard' for its republication in the 1768 collected poems, the footnotes he offers are not factual or verbal glosses, antiquarian contexts, or any of the other things that characterize his notes to poems he composed around the same time such as 'The Bard' or 'The Progress of Poesy'. Instead, they are quotations that serve as parallels, signalled obliquely in the text by way of allusion and then explicitly in the notes: as homage,

---

[12] Henry Fielding, *The History of Tom Jones, a Foundling*, ed. Thomas Keymer and Alice Wakely (London: Penguin, 2005), XIII.v, p. 617.

[13] Samuel Richardson, *Clarissa, or The History of a Young Lady* (1747–48), ed. Angus Ross (London: Penguin, 1985), p. 509.

[14] Richardson, *Clarissa*, p. 17.

[15] Claire Connolly, 'A Bookish History of Irish Romanticism', in *Rethinking British Romantic History, 1770–1845*, ed. Porscha Fermanis and John Regan (Oxford: Oxford University Press, 2014), pp. 271–96, 273.

as assistance to the reader, as a way of marking the poem's own gentility.[16] Gray's annotations to this poem proleptically call to mind Eliot's notes to *The Waste Land*, in that both poets share a cryptic, ambivalent orientation towards the practice of self-annotation, their notes working less to make the language more accessible than to obfuscate and lead astray.

'The Bard' was one of two Pindaric Odes first printed by Gray's close friend Horace Walpole on his new press at Strawberry Hill and then published more generally by Dodsley in 1757. The Pindaric ode is itself a cryptic, difficult form, ostentatiously learned and experimental in ways that are far from self-explanatory, so that both the form and subject matter of Gray's odes might pose difficulties of comprehension for readers then and now. There were no notes to either ode in the 1757 edition, and Lonsdale suggests that in the wake of the extraordinary success of the 'Elegy', Gray deliberately meant to be obscure; Walpole, in a letter to another friend written that year, sends the pair of poems with the comment 'they are Greek, they are Pindaric, they are sublime—consequently I fear a little obscure…I could not persuade him to add more notes; he says whatever wants to be explained, don't deserve to be.' Gray had written to Walpole a few months earlier, 'I do not love notes…They are signs of weakness and obscurity. If a thing cannot be understood without them, it had better be not understood at all.'[17] In 1768, though, Gray permitted the publication of two new editions (one printed in London by Dodsley, the other in Glasgow edited by James Beattie and printed by Robert and Andrew Foulis) with some pretensions to being complete works, and here the pair of Pindaric odes—both extensively footnoted—are preceded by an advertisement: 'When the Author first published this and the following Ode, he was advised, even by his Friends, to subjoin some few explanatory Notes; but had too much respect for the understanding of his Readers to take that liberty.'[18] Gray takes a rather injured tone on the question in a letter to his Scottish publisher:

> as to the notes, I do it out of spite, because the Publick did not understand the two odes…tho' the first was not very dark, & the second alluded to a few common facts to be found in any six-penny History of England by way of question & answer for the use of children. [T]he parallel passages I insert out of justice to those writers, from whom I happen'd to take the hint of any line, as far as I can recollect.[19]

---

[16] This account draws heavily on the superb headnotes provided by Roger Lonsdale in *The Poems of Thomas Gray, William Collins, Oliver Goldsmith* (London: Longmans, Green and Co., 1969).

[17] Quoted by Lonsdale, *Poems of Thomas Gray*, p. 158; ellipsis in the original quotation.

[18] *Poems by Mr Gray* (London: J. Dodsley, 1768). In the Glasgow edition, however, there is one significant difference: Beattie, probably, decided that though very light glossing could appear at the foot of the page, Gray's more extensive textual notes should be printed at the end of the volume rather than the foot of the page. See 'Notes by the Author, Now first published at the desire of Readers, who thought the PROGRESS of POESY, and the WELCH BARDS needed illustration', *Poems by Mr Gray* (Glasgow: Robert and Andrew Foulis, 1768), p. 59.

[19] Lonsdale, *Poems of Thomas Gray*, p. 180.

'The Bard' opens with a passage spoken by the bard of the title himself; it is marked as direct speech by way of an inverted comma at the beginning of each line, and the words possess the arresting minatory quality of prophetic speech and the performative qualities of a curse. But it is also a striking fact of the first ten lines, which are printed over two pages in this particular edition, that they are annotated not just with quotations ('Mocking the air with colours idly spread. *Shakespear's King John*') but also, comically I think to modern eyes at least, with details about the nomenclature and history of material culture: 'The Hauberk was a texture of steel ringlets, or rings interwoven, forming a coat of mail, that sate close to the body, and adapted itself to every motion.'[20] In some sense, this annotated 1768 version of 'The Bard' is camp, its sensibility owing something significant to Walpole's aesthetic as it was manifested in the design of Strawberry Hill and elsewhere. The poems have been 'distressed' or 'antiqued' by their author, their surfaces altered in order to create a quite different sense of the object's history and the ways one might interact with it.

The *Ossian* poems must have been one of Gray's immediate stimulants.[21] The new liking for extensive textural/textual annotation can be seen even more clearly in Chatterton's *Poems, Supposed to have been written at Bristol, by Thomas Rowley, and Others, in the Fifteenth Century* (1777); the ostentatiously annotated page there has a function that is at one sense decorative and powerfully performative, operating orthogonally to the ostensible purpose of glossing unfamiliar and obsolete terms. One aspect of the way this new kind of note creates meaning has been beautifully described by Christina Lupton, who writes that Gray along with his contemporary Henry Mackenzie 'work hard to make their printed texts appear as objects to which stories of accident and abandonment apply. This involves giving to print the identity of an object situated and vulnerable, as well as the feel of something that has arrived in our hands by accident.'[22] But the back-and-forth between Gray and his various correspondents, as well as the variety of appearances these passages and pages presented in their different editions, suggests a number of important points: there is no consensus as to what amount of annotation is the 'right' amount or how it should be presented on the page; printers rather than authors often determine the placement of self-annotation; finally, it is hard to take at face value what writers themselves state about their preferences and choices in this regard.

In his own history of the footnote, Anthony Grafton makes a striking claim:

> The historian who builds a literary house on a foundation of documents does not address the same task as the author of a religious, literary, or scientific work

---

[20] *Poems by Mr Gray*, pp. 53–4.

[21] Robert Crawford, *The Modern Poet: Poetry, Academia, and Knowledge since the 1750s* (Oxford: Oxford University Press, 2008), pp. 49, 51–2.

[22] Christina Lupton, *Knowing Books: The Consciousness of Mediation in Eighteenth-Century Britain* (Philadelphia, PA: University of Pennsylvania Press, 2012), p. 128.

who tries to fix the text's message unequivocally for posterity. The one explains the methods and procedures used to produce the text, the other the methods and procedures that should be used to consume it.[23]

There is rarely a hard and fast distinction between the two modes, though, and part of the appeal of the footnote is its versatility: it can walk and chew gum at the same time. Edward Gibbon's notes in *A History of the Decline and Fall of the Roman Empire* (1776–89), for instance, are capable not just of citing sources and offering commentary on the authority or lack thereof but making judgements about the quality of earlier scholarship, pointing out poignant parallels to contemporary life and allowing the narrative to take ceremonial leave of a given source as the history passes from one epoch to another—and these are only some of the multitude of purposes the history's annotation fills. *Decline and Fall* is famous for its footnotes—and yet the first edition of the first volume had endnotes, not footnotes. It was David Hume who wrote to his and Gibbon's mutual publisher Strahan to suggest a change for subsequent editions:

> One is also plagued with his Notes, according to the present Method of printing the Book: When a note is announced, you turn to the End of the Volume; and there you often find nothing but the Reference to an Authority: All these Authorities ought only to be printed at the Margin or the Bottom of the Page.[24]

Gibbon claims to have regretted this decision, annotating his praise in one draft of the memoirs for the Basel edition as follows: 'Of their fourteen octavo Volumes, the two last include the whole body of the notes. The public importunity had forced *me* to remove them from the end of the Volume to the bottom of the page, but I have often repented of my complyance.'[25] We can contextualize Gibbon's ambivalence with *The Printer's Grammar*, a text that displays mild hostility to overannotation: 'Hence we see in the productions of former Printers, that they delighted in seeing the pages lined with Notes and Quotations; which they enlarged on purpose, and contrived to encompass the pages of the text, that they might have the resemblance of a Looking-glass in a frame.'[26] Gray may have been readier to risk pedantry than Gibbon because he had more self-consciousness about his relatively low social origins and clung to his identity as an academic as protection against the vulgarity of being a popular writer, whereas Gibbon's desire to be thought of as a gentleman rather than a professional

---

[23] Anthony Grafton, *The Footnote: A Curious History* (Cambridge, MA: Harvard University Press, 1999), pp. 32–3.

[24] Hume to Strahan, quoted by Grafton, *The Footnote*, pp. 102–3.

[25] *The Autobiographies of Edward Gibbon*, ed. John Murray (London: John Murray, 1896), Memoir E, 339 n. 64.

[26] [John Smith], *The Printer's Grammar* (London: printed by L. Wayland and sold by T. Evans, 1787), pp. 124–5.

writer is part of what makes him ambivalent not about the facts of procedures of documentation, but about the ways they manifested themselves in the printed edition of the book.

Gibbon's sentences in the main text of the history roll one upon the other sonorously, with soothing regularity of rhythm. There is irony, but it is generally moderated, one might almost say 'baffled' in the literal sense by the sedate pacing of the prose, whereas the rhythms of the voice of the notes are more varied, punctuated differently (not least but also not only by the naming of authorities). The annotating voice sounds to me more intimate than the narrator of the main text—the Enlightenment historian, as opposed to the narrative chronicler in prose, is more present to us in many of the notes, and Gibbon does indeed reserve for the base of the page many of his most thought-provoking sociological or anthropological parallels. Not in all but in many of the footnotes, moreover, there is a sly ironizing wit that appears only selectively in the main narrative. Consider the history's account of what happened consequent upon Gordianus's son being declared emperor:

> His manners were less pure, but his character was equally amiable with that of his father. Twenty-two acknowledged concubines, and a library of sixty-two thousand volumes, attested the variety of his inclinations; and from the productions which he left behind him, it appears that the former as well as the latter were designed for use rather than for ostentation.[27]

These two sentences don't make sense to us until we read the footnote, in all of its playful malice: 'By each of his concubines, the younger Gordian left three or four children. His literary productions, though less numerous, were by no means contemptible.'

Readers' preferences for various forms of annotation may be difficult to pin down, not least because they will vary at different stages of the reading life and according to how and why one intends to consume a given text. When I read a novel that makes playful use of footnotes on a Kindle or similar electronic device—like Terry Pratchett's Discworld novels—I tend not to 'click' on the footnote, it being more economical of time and clickage to read all the notes at once at the end of the section. In an age when chunks of criticism are increasingly circulated via scanned PDFs, though, the footnote may have regained its immediate utility: remembering to scan the endnote pages as well as the chapter excerpted from a monograph is something that easily falls victim to human frailty, and the footnote's power to tether the underlying references securely to the main text is greeted with renewed appreciation in the digital age.

---

[27] Edward Gibbon, *The History of the Decline and Fall of the Roman Empire*, 3 vols, ed. David Womersley (London: Penguin/Allen Lane, 1994), chap. VII, n. 19, 1:195.

Marcus Walsh has emphasized the distinction, as eighteenth-century editors understood it, 'between the scholastic commentary, which they generally perceived and portrayed as self-obsessed, self-serving, parasitic, not seeking to explain the text but to replace it, on the one hand, and the explanatory commentary, designed to explicate and mediate, on the other.'[28] But it may be worth quoting Gérard Genette, in conclusion, on the editorial apparatus of Nabokov's great novel-in-the-form-of-commentary, *Pale Fire* (which uses endnotes rather than footnotes proper): 'A perfect example of textual appropriation, this *apparatus* is also an exemplary staging of the abusiveness and paranoia always found in any interpretive commentary, supported by the unlimited submissiveness of any text to any hermeneutic, however unscrupulous the latter may be.'[29] Even the most wishfully explicatory commentary, in other words, always threatens to become parasitic, florid, a tendency that comes through very clearly in major contemporary literary fictions of self-annotation like *The Mezzanine* and the writings of David Foster Wallace, and the threatening nature of such commentary is explicitly thematized in Mark Danielewski's *House of Leaves*.

[28] Marcus Walsh, *Shakespeare, Milton, and Eighteenth-Century Literary Editing: The Beginnings of Interpretive Scholarship* (Cambridge: Cambridge University Press, 1997), p. 25.

[29] Gérard Genette, *Paratexts: Thresholds of Interpretation*, trans. Jane E. Lewin, intro. Richard Macksey (Cambridge: Cambridge University Press, 1997), p. 342; see the entire chapter on notes, pp. 319–43.

ERRATA LISTS

Adam Smith

For "Chaptre" read "Chapter"
For "Adam Smith" read "Adam Smyth"

These are not misprints but beauties of my style hitherto undreamt of.

James Joyce, September 1922[1]

While historians of the early book can certainly point to astonishing feats of printing expertise—like the *Biblia Polyglotta*, printed at Christopher Plantin's shop in Antwerp between 1568 and 1572, in eight volumes, with parallel texts in Hebrew, Greek, Syriac, and Aramaic, and translations and commentary in Latin, a wonder of mise-en-page—it is also true that early modern books were awash with errors. 'Concerning *Mistakes* in the *Press*,' wrote Robert Croft in 1663, '[t]hey are not much vers'd in *Books*, that look for none.'[2] There were technical reasons why errors were so common—printing was difficult, particularly when dispersed across agents, presses, and print shops, with the pressures of deadlines and balance sheets—and it seems generally that authors, printers, publishers, and readers expected printed books to carry mistakes. Errata lists, or pages of 'castigata', were one mechanism of correction, alongside overprinting, stamped text, handwritten alterations, cancels, and pasted-in slips. One important difference between manuscript and print production was, as David McKitterick has noted, 'the removal of correction [in print] from *after* marking the page, to *before* it'.[3] But errata lists are evidence of this culture of correcting-before-printing breaking down. If most of the stages of correction and proofing are concealed in the final printed book, errata lists—one of the last parts of a book to be printed, after the process of composition, proofing, and the printing of the main text—capture some of the mistakes that were missed. As a consequence, the errata list can provide the reader with a glimpse of the pre-history of the finished text, and a sense of the flawed and human process of print shop labour. Alongside this story of book production, the errata list has another history, as a form full of satirical and literary potential.

Errata lists were one of print's innovations, and flourished from the early sixteenth century.[4] Sometimes they took the form of a note of a necessary global change

---

[1] *Letters of James Joyce*, vol. I, ed. Stuart Gilbert (New York: Viking Press, 1957), p. 187.

[2] Robert Croft, *The plea, case, and humble proposals of the truly-loyal and suffering officers* (1663), p. 12.

[3] David McKitterick, *Print, Manuscript and the Search for Order 1450–1830* (Cambridge: Cambridge University Press, 2003), p. 99. My italics.

[4] The most important scholarship on error and errata lists is McKitterick, *Print, Manuscript*, pp. 97–165; David McKitterick, *A History of Cambridge University Press* (Cambridge: Cambridge University Press, 1992), 3 vols, vol I, pp. 235–53; Ann Blair, 'Errata Lists and the Reader as Corrector', in *Agent of Change: Print Culture Studies after Elizabeth L. Eisenstein*, ed. Sabrina Alcorn Baron, Eric N. Lindquist, and Eleanor F. Shevlin (Amherst, MA: University of Massachusetts Press, 2007), pp. 21–40; Seth Lerer, *Error and the Academic Self: The Scholarly Imagination, Medieval to Modern* (New York: Columbia University Press, 2002), pp. 15–54; and

('Towards the midst, till the end of this Booke, for Getulia, alwaies reade Natolia'),[5] but more common was the litany of substitutions, pegged to page and sometimes line number—or, in one particularly careful instance, to 'quayre…page…[and] syde'.[6] For 'seede, reade feede'; for 'rake, reade take'; for 'annoynted, reade accounted'; for 'stayres, reade stories'; for 'miage, reade image'; for 'his armes, reade her armes'.[7] Certain kinds of early modern books produced particularly extensive lists of errata: mathematical works, in particular—both popular guides to reckoning, and also scholarly works—had a thematic concern with accuracy which combined with the difficulty of setting vertical calculations to prompt meticulous, lengthy litanies of errors and corrections ('D. ii. a. in the example, set 9, for 6, in the seconde rowe').[8]

The list of faults escaped was often accompanied by a brief, typically one paragraph, prose, or occasionally verse introduction or gloss: a usually anonymous passage of text written by author, publisher, or occasionally printer that presents a particular compound of humility, irritation, prescription, wit, and regret. This errata preface typically sought the reader's patience and forgiveness for the presence of the errors following; requested some variation of the formula 'Reader, Correct these Errors with thy Pen, before thou read the Book';[9] and noted that other errors not cited are to be ignored or corrected by the reader as they see fit. This errata preface is also often a space in which one agent involved in the production of the book (usually author or publisher, but sometimes printer) shifts responsibility for errors on to another agent (usually printer, but sometimes corrector, author (often blamed for supplying illegible copy), or translator). All of these functions combine in Johann Oberndorf's brief but generically orthodox final-page message in his *The anatomyes of the true physition, and counterfeit mounte-banke* (1602):

> Diuers faults haue escaped the Printer; which as they are easily discerned. So I entreat thee (friendly Reader) to amend with thy Pen, as thou goest along: and to pardon me, who by occasion of some Businesse, haue not looked so narrowly to them, as I should, and (otherwise) would haue done.[10]

The errata list often came near the start of the book, as the last item of prefatory material, or at the very end: the list hovered at the fringes, a supplement to, and not quite a constituent of, the central text, although, as we shall see, its rhetoric often

Alexandra da Costa, 'Negligence and Virtue: Errata Notices and their Evangelical Use', in *The Library* 7th series, 19, no. 2 (June 2018), 159–73.

[5] Emanuel Ford, *Parismus, Part 2* (1599), sig. A4v.

[6] Robert Record, *The ground of artes teaching the worke and practise of arithmetike* (1552), 'fautes escaped', sigs. a1v–a3v.

[7] Robert Chambers, *Palestina* (1600), 'Faults escaped'.

[8] Record, *The ground of artes*, 'fautes escaped'.

[9] George Mackenzie, *Aretina, or, The Serious Romance* (1660), sig. A8v.

[10] Johann Oberndorf, *The anatomyes of the true physition, and counterfeit mounte-banke* (1602), p. 43.

leaked into the body of the work. Errata lists were 'more often included in books in which blank pages were left', and so didn't incur any extra paper costs, their level of detail often reflecting the available blank space, rather than the actual extent of errors in the text.[11] Certainly, they are often squeezed into small spaces, or pasted in some (but not all) copies of a book, sometimes at different places in the text, or they might be included as a separate, loose insert: all of which creates the effect of an afterthought, a late arrival, a passage of text whose status is not clear.

These little confessional spaces look at first like emblems of a new culture of accuracy, and this is how earlier historians of the book have understood them: Elizabeth Eisenstein noted that 'the very act of publishing errata demonstrated a new capacity to locate textual errors with precision and to transmit this information simultaneously to scattered readers'.[12] But the errata list's relationship to error was paradoxical and sits uneasily amid these kinds of Whiggish histories of print. If a declaration of errors created the effect of book production diligence, books seeking to create the effect of accuracy did so by parading their mistakes. Was a short errata list more or less of a signal of an accurate text? Did a long errata list suggest print shop negligence or care? Errata lists are quite often subsequently augmented by further printed paste-in slips of corrections: a second wave of error spotting that both shores up, and weakens, the book's claims to accuracy. Sometimes errata lists themselves contained further errors—as was the case with Milton's *Paradise Regain'd*—often prompting further slips to be pasted on.[13]

Like other mechanisms of print correction, errata lists serve less to correct than to mark out error. They cast error as one of print's signature traits. And just as one overlooked consequence of print was the creation of huge numbers of books that were never read,[14] so the printing press was also a radical force for the dissemination of blunders. In Thomas Heywood's *An Apologie for Actors* (1612), the errata page has been narratavized into a general fuming at what Heywood calls the 'disworkeman-ship' of William Jaggard, who had (Heywood claims) printed his earlier book with mistakes: 'The infinite faults escaped in my booke of *Britaines Troy*, by the negligence of the Printer, as the misquotations, mistaking of sillables, misplacing halfe lines, coining of strange and neuer heard of words.'[15]

One model for a history of many of the paratextual forms considered in the present volume might propose a birth period (for errata lists, something like 1520–90) in which the conventions of the form are established through repetition, and then,

---

[11] Blair, 'Errata Lists', p. 26.

[12] Elizabeth L. Eisenstein, *The Printing Revolution in Early Modern Europe* (Cambridge: Cambridge University Press, 1983), p. 51.

[13] John Milton, *Paradise Regain'd* (1671), sig. P4r.

[14] Blair, 'Errata', p. 41, citing Hugh Amory.

[15] Thomas Heywood, *An Apologie for Actors* (1612), sig. G4r.

some time after, and once those conventions are known, a mature period in which the paratextual form could also be deployed for ludic, satirical, or literary effect. In some ways this is a helpful, if approximate outline, but it overlooks the fact that what we might call error discourse in print was always more than a merely textual concern. Errata lists emerged out of the heat of early Reformation polemic, and Seth Lerer has analysed the ways in which questions of textual accuracy were recruited into confessional debates during the early Reformation: thus, Thomas More constructs Protestant texts as books of error and elides typographical and moral mistakes as he presents himself as his own corrector, while William Tyndale educates the vernacular reader in using the errata sheet to become a diligent reader.[16] While some authors framed errors as expressive of technological challenges, others saw printed mistakes as eloquent markers of the fallen state of the world. In this sense, the errata list was a useful sign of the corrupted state of man, and a check on authorial pride. In *The Fall of Man* (1618), Godfrey Goodman framed his book's bountiful typographical blunders as not only the products of an error-fraught book trade (although they were that too), but also more fundamentally as a register of what Goodman calls 'a general corruption' of the cosmos: 'How happie was I to make choice of such a subiect, which seems to excuse all the errors of my Pamphlet?'[17]

If early modern writers saw an entwining of the textual and the moral, later writers deployed the errata list for more diversified effects. Often this meant blurring the boundary between text and paratext. The early, 1709 folio editions of *The Tatler* contained lists of errata written in the form of an intimate apology that sustained the register of the paper's essays: the separation of the author from the world of the print shop collapsed. Isaac Bickerstaff's explanations for the paper's errors produces vignettes of his writerly quirks: 'I always make Use of an old-fashioned e, which very little differs from an o', which explains errors such as 'those *for* these, beheld *for* behold, Corvix *for* Cervix, and the like'.[18]

The errata list's potential for satirical wit was also regularly exploited. A list of errors is already close to satire ('for killed, read kissed'),[19] and it only takes a gentle nudge to tip the errata list into something critical. John Taylor, poet and Thames waterman, used the form as one strand in his adventures in ludic bibliography. *Sir Gregory Nonsence His Newes from no place* (1622)—a text 'plentifully stored with want of *wit, learning, Iudgement, Rime and* Reason'—has a mock title page, a prefatory address 'To Nobody', and a Rabelaisian list of authors cited including 'Frier and the Boy', 'Boe to a Goose', 'Yard of Ale', and (Taylor's bibliographical wit) 'Proofes of OOOO'. Described approvingly by Robert Southey in 1831 as 'honest right rampant

---

[16] Blair, 'Errata Lists', *passim*; Lerer, *Error and the Academic Self*, pp. 23–9.

[17] Godfrey Goodman, *The Fall of Man* (1618), sig. [Ff7]v.

[18] F. W. Bateson, 'The Errata in *The Tatler*', in *Review of English Studies* 5, no. 18 (April 1929), pp. 155–66, 156.

[19] *The Mysteries of Love and Eloquence* (1658), 'Errata', sig A4v.

nonsense',[20] Taylor's text is in part a study in paratextual buffoonery, and also features a list of 'Faults escaped in the Printing' which offers a series of satirical jokes, including 'I[n] the 25. page. 44. line, for a *Friers mouth* read a *Pudding*', and 'In the 90. page, 27. line, for *friend* read *rare*'.[21] The errors are not actually present—there aren't even enough pages in the book—but Taylor dances across the conventions of the form. Moments like this, when a paratext's utilitarian function is left behind, or is folded into the literary project of the text, peak at times of satirical stress, including the late 1580s and 1590s, as witnessed in the Martin Marprelate pamphlets, and the writings of Thomas Nashe, and the 1650s, when Quaker Samuel Fisher uses the errata list in *Rusticus ad Academicos* (1660) to mock the idea that the Bible could be an error-free source of faith.

But the satirical potential of the errata list has a long history after the early modern. At the end of Samuel Taylor Coleridge's early radical pamphlet *Conciones ad Populum* (1795), in which the author condemned war with France and the Crown's recruitment of soldiers primarily from the poor, Coleridge added a mock-erratum note: 'Page 61, for MURDER read fight for his King and Country.'[22] And it was in the eighteenth century—perhaps the greatest period of paratextual wit—that the errata list was deployed more effectively for sustained satirical effect. Alexander Pope's *The Dunciad* (1728–43) is his *Aeneid*-shaped mock celebration of the goddess Dulness and her various earthly agents, and as Jenny Davidson notes in Chapter 18 of this present volume, the manipulation of conventions of annotation formed a key part of that project. The errata list becomes a potent space in which to mock what Pope saw as the pretensions, and self-aggrandizing apparatus, of modern textual critics such as Lewis Theobald, whose *Shakespeare Restored* (1726) had highlighted (to Pope's fury) 'the many errors, as well committed, as unamended, by Mr. Pope'. Written in the voice of Martin Scriblerus, Pope's revenging errata list suggests textual scholarship has descended into a pompous and unmoored over-reading of what are in fact often only printing slips:

> The *Errata* of this Edition we thought (gentle reader) to have trusted to thy candour and benignity, to correct with thy pen, as accidental Faults escaped the press: But seeing that certain Censors do give to such the name of *Corruptions of the Text* and *false Readings*, charge them on the Editor, and judge that correcting the same is to be called *Restoring* and an *Atchievement that brings Honour to the Critic*, we have in like manner taken it upon ourselves.

[20] *Lives and Works of the Uneducated Poets* (1831), quoted in Noel Malcolm, *The Origins of English Nonsense* (London: Fontana, 1997), p. 29.

[21] John Taylor, *Sir Gregory Nonsence His Newes from no place* (1622), sig. A5v.

[22] *The Collected Works of Samuel Taylor Coleridge*, Bollingen Series lxxv, 16 vols (Princeton, NJ: Princeton University Press, 1969–2001) I, p. 70, n. 2. Thanks to Seamus Perry for this point.

Scriblerus then offers the sort of overworked note Pope associated with critics such as Theobald and Richard Bentley. Bentley was regarded by later scholars, including A. E. Housman, as a crucial figure in the development of historical philology ('the greatest scholar that England or perhaps that Europe ever bred'),[23] but in the *Dunciad* he is a figure of wrong-headed pedantry whose 'unwearied pains / Made Horace dull' (Book 4, 211–12), and who ends his days as Master of Trinity College, Cambridge where he 'sleeps in Port':

> Book i. Verse 8. *E'er Pallas issu'd from the Thund'rers head. E'er* is the contraction of *ever*, but that is by no means the sense in this place: Correct it, without the least scruple, *E're*, the contraction of *or-ere*, an old *English* word for *before*. What Ignorance of our mother tongue![24]

In the twentieth century, a strikingly large number of poets have used the errata list as a rhetorical form creating literary effects. To read errata is to experience a particular combination of precision and abundance. One word, or phrase, is neatly substituted for another (for 'battering, reade bettering'),[25] and that seems unambiguous; yet we cannot but observe, imagine, laugh at, or worry about the relationships between the two, which means speculating on a causal link between mistake and correction—a causal link we know to be fictional, but which we have to at least entertain, if only to dismiss it. Notes of errata sometimes do what poets like to do: they yoke together unlike things; they switch suddenly between registers and worlds, between the quotidian and the transcendent: 'for *laughing*, reade, *languishing*'.[26] Certainly, poets have recognized the literary potential inherent in this form. Geoffrey Hill's *Triumph of Love* (1999) finds poetic resonance in the cadence of errata:

> Take out supposition. Insert suppository.
> For definitely the right era read: deaf in the right ear.[27]

Ian Hamilton Finlay's 'Errata of Ovid', cut into stones in Stockwood Park, Luton, casts classical myth as a series of printing errors, turning Ovidian metamorphoses into faults escaped in the press.

> for 'Daphne'
> read 'Laurel'
>
> for 'Philomela'
> read 'Nightingale'

---

[23] *A. E. Housman: Selected Prose*, ed. John Carter (Cambridge: Cambridge University Press, 1961), p. 12.

[24] *The Poems of Alexander Pope: The Dunciad (1728) and The Dunciad Variorum (1729)*, ed. Valerie Rumbold (London: Pearson Education, 2007), p. 311.

[25] Chambers, *Palestina*, 'Faults escaped'.

[26] Richard Bellings, *A Sixth Booke to the Countesse of Pembrokes Arcadia* (Dublin, 1624), sig. A4v.

[27] Geoffrey Hill, *Broken Hierarchies: Poems 1952–2012* (Oxford: Oxford University Press, 2015), p. 269.

for 'Cyane'
read 'Fountain'

for 'Echo'
read 'Echo'

for 'Atys'
read 'Pine'

for 'Narcissus'
read 'Narcissus'

for 'Adonis'
read 'Anemone'.[28]

Poems by Paul Muldoon and Charles Simic, among others, also explore the poetic possibilities of errata lists.[29]

If the errata list offers a particular kind of potential to poets, then to editors it offers an often paradoxical challenge. How should an editor respond to the errata list? Is the errata list part of the work, or outside it? Should an editor implement the prescribed changes in a text, or are the errors, and the list of corrections, authenticities that need to be maintained? Some of these complexities are caught nicely in Jerome J. McGann's 1980 edition of Byron's *Childe Harold's Pilgrimage*, which contains a list of six errors in the Greek and the note that '[t]he following examples of Byron's faulty Greek transcription were inadvertently corrected by the printer'.[30]

Robert Herrick's *Hesperides* (1648) offers another instance of the editorial problem of errata lists. Herrick's text includes four lines of verse by the author that introduce a list of printing errors and which shift blame for these misprints on to the printer:

> For these Transgressions which thou here dost see,
> Condemne the Printer, Reader, and not me;
> Who gave him forth good Grain, though he mistook
> The seed; so sow'd these Tares throughout my Book.

The errata list begins 'Page 33. Line 10. Read *Rods*' (where the book has 'Gods'), and itemizes sixteen corrections. It's not clear who compiled the list: given the blame the verse apportions, Herrick might be a plausible candidate. Whoever performed the work did an imperfect job; the list, typically for a publication of this period, fails to note a mass of further mistakes—sixty-nine in fact—that lie unrecorded in the book.[31]

---

[28] Ian Hamilton Finlay, *Selections* (Berkeley, CA: University of California Press, 2012), p. 190.

[29] Paul Muldoon, 'Errata', in *Hay* (London: Faber and Faber, 1998); Charles Simic, 'errata', in *Selected Early Poems* (New York: George Braziller, 2013).

[30] Lord Byron, *The Complete Poetical Works*, ed. Jerome J. McGann, vol. II (Oxford: Clarendon Press, 1980), 'Errata'.

[31] *The Complete Poetry of Robert Herrick*, ed. Tom Cain and Ruth Connolly, 2 vols (Oxford: Oxford University Press, 2013), vol. 1, p. 422.

Editors of Herrick haven't quite known what to do with this errata verse and list of corrections. Tom Cain and Ruth Connolly's 2013 edition enacts the sixteen changes—that is, they correct the errors the 1648 text tells them to correct—and so the errata list, while printed in their edition, no longer applies. Moreover, by paginating their edition differently from the 1648 text, while maintaining the original page and line numbers in the errata list ('P. 41 l. 19. R. *Gotiere*'), the list becomes impossible to use, like a broken online link. F. W. Moorman's 1915 edition follows a similar policy and adds the editorial note, 'The Errata have been corrected in the reprint. The page-numbers and line-numbers quoted above are those of the original text.' The 1921 version of this edition—'prepared, not for the scholar, but for the lover of poetry'— includes the four-line errata verse but omits the errata list, noting 'In the original text this address is followed by Errata, which have been duly corrected in this reprint.'[32] L. C. Martin's 1965 edition omits the four-line errata poem and the errata list but, bafflingly, includes reference to the poem in its index of first lines.

Herrick's errata is troubling for an editor, as a paratext that flickers on the edge of inside and out; as a text that calls for changes which, if implemented, produce a new text in which the errata list no longer has a rationale; and as an errata list that is explicitly literary and so makes claim for inclusion in Herrick's poetic corpus—a claim that some, but not all editors recognize. The errata verse and list here functions as a kind of textual pressure point: a way of gathering together some of the conflicting impulses that define the work of editing, a task that is always concerned with establishing the perimeter of a text (what is in, and what is out?), and that is often concerned with the tension between a desire to maintain a text according to its earliest manifestation (with errors in?) and an urge to modernize and correct (with errors out?).

What happens to the errata list when publications appear online? For most digital publications, the process of error correction is invisible to the reader due to the capacity of texts to be updated, after their first publication, with no material surface trace. Exceptions to this norm are conspicuous attempts to generate a sense of editorial and moral care: the *New York Times*, for example, provides a dated record of corrections at the end of an article, an effect of editorial diligence that is produced by resisting the digital's easy capacity to conceal past mistakes, a sort of moral supplement or excess in the face of the digital's legerdemain.[33] The future of attitudes towards online errors is not clear in a world of digital publishing where broader questions about credentialing, intellectual property, access, encoding standards, sustainability, and even what is known by the unlovely term 'link rot' remain uncertain.[34] It may be

[32] F. W. Moorman (ed.), *The Poetical Works of Robert Herrick* (Oxford: Clarendon, 1915), p. 4. F. W. Moorman (ed.), *The Poetical Works of Robert Herrick* (London: Oxford University Press, 1921), p. vi.

[33] For example, https://www.nytimes.com/2017/02/25/us/politics/trump-press-conflict.html.

[34] Paul Fyfe, 'Electronic Errata: Digital Publishing, Open Review, and the Futures of Correction', in *Debates in the Digital Humanities*, ed. Matthew K. Gold (Minneapolis, MN: University of Minnesota Press, 2012), pp. 259–80, p. 260.

that online publishing privileges speed, accessibility, and distribution over the labour of correction, and that mistakes are seen as a consequence-light casualty of this new order; it may be that the work of correction devolves down, or out, on to anonymous users possessed of varying literacies and expertise, a reliance (to put it positively) on what Clay Shirky calls the cognitive surplus of the web,[35] or (to put it negatively) a worrying gamble on the capacities and commitments of the crowd.

It is certainly true that whatever our commitment to accuracy, errata lists have proven to be generally ineffective as a means of eliminating mistakes in print, both in terms of their tendency to miss more errors than they catch, and in terms of the often negligible effect they seem to have had on subsequent editions. Although both James Joyce and Harriet Shaw Weaver each prepared a list of errata in 1917 for *A Portrait of the Artist as a Young Man*, most of the errors in the 1916 edition could still be found in printings at least as late as 1961.[36] And of the 110 'Faults Escaped in the Print' listed at the end of Books 1–3 of Edmund Spenser's *Faerie Queene* (1590), nearly half remained on the loose in the 1596 edition (an edition which itself introduced 183 new misprints), and subsequent editions of 1609, 1611–17, and 1679 paid little or no attention to the errata list. It was not until Thomas Birch's edition of 1751 that the 1590 errata list (which, it should be noted, contained its own errors) was read with any editorial care.[37] In this sense, the work performed by errata lists was often at least as much about a noisy rhetorical performance of error spotting as it was about implementing actual textual correctness; and those writers who saw literary and satirical potential in the errata list were not converting (naïve) utilitarian paratext into (sophisticated) ludic text, but were rather participating in a long history of the richness of errata.

[35] Fyfe, 'Electronic Errata', p. 269.

[36] Peter Spielberg, 'James Joyce's Errata for American Editions of *A Portrait of the Artist*', in *Joyce's Portrait: Criticisms and Critiques*, ed. Peter Spielberg and Thomas E. Connolly (New York: Appleton-Century-Crofts, 1963), pp. 318–28, p. 319.

[37] Toshiyuki Suzuki, 'A Note on the Errata to the 1590 Quarto of the *Faerie Queene*', *Studies in the Literary Imagination* 38, no. 2 (2005): 1–16, 1.

INDEXES

On the face of it, the index has much in common with the table of contents. Both are lists of labels with locators pointing to places in, or sections of, the main text. In the late Middle Ages, the two paratexts even go by the same array of names—register, table, rubric—making them indistinguishable without closer inspection.[1] When Chaucer's Knight briskly refuses to speculate on what happens to Arcite, one of the characters in his tale, after his death—'I nam no divynistre: / "Of soules" find I nought in this registre' (ll. 1953–4; in other words, 'I have no special insight: my register has no entry for "Souls"')—it is hard to know precisely which type of list he has in mind. Nevertheless, the two are quite distinct book parts—bookends straddling the main text, one before, one after—each with its own function and history.

Even without locators, the table of contents provides an overview of a work's structure: it follows the ordering of the text, revealing its architecture. We may glance at a table and reasonably conjecture what the overall argument is. To a degree, therefore, a table of contents is platform independent. It can still perform a useful function in a work that exists as a series of scrolls, for example, and as Joseph Howley has pointed out in this volume (Chapter 6), the table of contents has a history that stretches back into antiquity. By contrast, the index, a truly random-access technology, is an invention of the codex era. The sheaf of pages, folded and bound, that can be opened with as much ease in the middle or at the end, is the medium in which the index makes sense; and unlike a table of contents, an index without locators is as much use as a bicycle without wheels.

This is because the chief mechanism of the index is arbitrariness. Its principal innovation is in severing the relationship between the structure of the work and the structure of the table. The ordering of an index is reader-oriented, rather than text-oriented: if you know what you're looking for, the letters of the alphabet provide a universal, text-independent system in which to look it up. (We might say that most indexes are doubly arbitrary since the commonest locator—the page number—bears no intrinsic relationship to the work or its subject matter, but only to its medium.) 'The Middle Ages,' write Richard and Mary Rouse, 'did not like alphabetical order, which

---

[1] The term *index* is not commonly adopted until the seventeenth century. Regarding the vexed issue of the plural—whether *indexes* or *indices*—Henry Wheatley, in *What Is an Index?*, points to *Troilus and Cressida*, arguing that if the anglicized form is good enough for Shakespeare it should be good enough for us:

And in such indexes, although small pricks
To their subsequent volumes, there is seen
The baby figure of the giant mass
Of things to come at large. (I.iii.806–9)

Henry Wheatley, *What Is an Index? A Few Notes on Indexes and Indexers* (London: Index Society, 1878).

it considered the antithesis of reason.'[2] God had created an ordered and harmonious universe, and the work of the scholar was to discern and reflect this structure, not to ignore it. It would take a pressing need, then, for the divine usefulness of the index to outweigh its unholy arbitrariness.

The index emerges in the early thirteenth century as one of the many innovations in reading brought about by two new institutions: the preaching orders—the Dominicans and the Franciscans—and the universities. The requirements of preaching and teaching demanded a more efficient, more targeted way of reading than the old monastic mode of meditative memorization, and in the few decades either side of the turn of the thirteenth century the manuscript page took on a whole raft of meaningful features: 'running heads, chapter heads in red, initials in alternating red and blue, different sized initials, marked paragraphs, references, names of cited authors'.[3] A further key development, driven by the same shift in reading practices, was the division of the books of the Bible into chapters, by the English cleric Stephen Langton in around 1200. (Verses were to come later, in the mid-sixteenth century.) With Bible chapters as a suitable locator, the stage was set for the first great indexing milestone, the Bible concordance.

Begun between 1230 and 1235 and completed no later than 1247, the first Bible concordance was an astonishing feat of collective scholarly endeavour. Under the direction of Hugh of Saint Cher, it was compiled by the friars of the Dominican priory of St Jacques in Paris, on the left bank of the Seine just beside where the Panthéon now stands. The concordance lists about 10,000 keywords with roughly 129,000 locators between them. Essentially, every instance of every word (barring things like articles and prepositions) was logged and given a locator consisting of book, chapter, and an indication of how far through the chapter it appears (a letter from *a* to *g*, each chapter being notionally divided into seven equal parts). The whole was then retranscribed alphabetically so that it starts with the exclamation *Aaa*— or *A, a, a*—meaning *alas* (four occurrences) and ends with the Old Testament governor *Zorobabel*.

One of the remarkable things about the St Jacques concordance is its size. Arranging the material into five columns, abbreviating the names of the books of the Bible, and using very fine vellum, it was feasible to fit the whole thing into a pocket-sized format, as in the case of MS Canon Pat. Lat. 7 in the Bodleian Library in Oxford, only slightly larger than a mobile phone. But if portability was an advantage, it carried

---

[2] ['Le Moyen Âge n'aimait pas l'ordre alphabétique qu'il considérait comme une antithèse de la raison.'] Mary A. Rouse and Richard H. Rouse, 'La Naissance des index', in *Histoire de l'édition française*, ed. Henri-Jean Martin and Roger Chartier, 4 vols (Paris: Promodis, 1983), I, pp. 77–85, p. 80. For a comprehensive overview of the emergence of alphabetical order, see Lloyd W. Daly, *Contributions to a History of Alphabetization in Antiquity and the Middle Ages* (Brussels: Latomus, 1967).

[3] ['titres courants, têtes de chapitres en rouge, initiales alternativement rouges et bleues, initiales de taille diffé-rente, indication des paragraphes, renvois, noms des auteurs cités']. Rouse and Rouse, 'La Naissance des index', p. 78.

with it a significant drawback. If we take a term that appears on the first page, we can get a sense of the problem. Here are the first few entries for *abire*, to depart:

> Abire, Gen. xiiii.d. xviii.e.g. xxi.c. xxii.b. xxiii.a. xxv.b.g xxvii.a. xxx.c. xxxi.b.c xxxv.f. xxxvi.a. xliiii.c.d

That's sixteen separate references in Genesis alone. The full list runs to hundreds of entries across several columns, while entries like *deus* [god] and *peccatum* [sin] go on for pages. In cases like these—and they are not uncommon—the St Jacques concordance is not much use for locating specific passages since the amount of work still left to do—all that page turning and spotting the term within those broad chapter divisions—is still impracticable.

It was this failing in the first concordance that led to the creation of a second version, the so-called Concordantiae Anglicanae or English Concordance. The title of the work comes from the fact that it was compiled—once again at St Jacques in Paris—by a number of English Dominicans, among them Richard of Stavensby.[4] Appearing around the middle of the century, within a couple of decades of its predecessor, the innovation of the English Concordance is to add a passage of contextual quotation for each reference. It is what we would now call a keyword-in-context or KWIC index of the type seen in, for instance, the 'snippet view' on Google Books. Here's how the first few entries for *regnum* [kingdom] appear, the keyword appearing as a capitalized initial between two dots:

> Regnum
> Gen. x.c. fuit autem principium .R. eius Babilon et arach
> xx.e. quid peccavimus in te quia induxisti super me et super .R. meum peccatum grande
> xxxvi.g. cumque et hic obiisset successit in .R. balaam filius achobor
> xli.e. uno tantum .R. solio te precedam.[5]

As well as being told the book, chapter, and chapter section, we can now see at a glance the sentence in which it appears.

In producing the English Concordance, Stavensby and his associates had not simply taken Hugh's original and added context passages. The new work incorporated references missing from the first version, and corrected a vast number of errors. Nevertheless, there was one fundamental problem with the English Concordance. With a contextual sentence for each of its hundred-odd-thousand locators, what was

---

[4] Based on an assertion first made by Quétif and Echard in the early eighteenth century, it has traditionally been held that three Englishmen—Richard of Stavensby, John of Darlington, and Hugh of Croydon—prepared the second concordance. However, Rouse and Rouse find evidence only for Richard's involvement. Jacob Quétif and Jacob Echard, *Scriptores ordinis praedicatorum recensiti*, 2 vols (Paris, 1719), I, p. 209; Richard H. Rouse and Mary A. Rouse, 'The Verbal Concordance to the Scriptures', *Archivum Fratrum Praedicatorum* 44 (1974): 5–30, 13–15.

[5] Oxford, Bodleian Library MS Lat. misc. b. 18, f. 61.

formerly a masterpiece of miniaturism had now exploded into a huge, multi-volume format. Far from being the portable reference that its predecessor was, the English Concordance was cumbersome to an extent that would impose limits on its usefulness. There was a need, therefore, for another version, one which would keep the innovation of the context passages but which would make them far shorter.

Thus it came to pass that, by 1286, a third concordance, this time employing short contextual passages of two to five words, had issued forth from the monastery at St Jacques.[6] The Parisian Dominicans had been refining their original formula for around half a century, and like Goldilocks trying out chairs, the third version was neither too big nor too small, but just right. The Third Concordance is the model for the Bible concordances still in print, in many languages, today.

For all its exhaustiveness, however, a concordance will only tell us the location of specific terms. Its unit is the word, not the concept. We can see the limitations of this approach if we try to locate the parable of the prodigal son, that famous tale of forgiveness, using a Bible concordance: the parable does not contain the words *forgiveness* or *mercy*, or, for that matter, *prodigal*. But in 1230, just as friars of St Jacques were beginning their work on the concordance, in Oxford, the scientist and theologian Robert Grosseteste was devising and compiling a *topical* index, a forerunner of the modern subject index, which would reflect the encyclopaedic breadth of his reading. In order to marshal his vast learning, Grosseteste devised a system of annotation which would allow him to group subjects together, along with a set of references— essentially keywords—which could be used across disparate texts. Rather than being an alphabetical system, Grosseteste's *Tabula*, now preserved in the Bibliothèque municipale in Lyon, divides its subjects into nine categories, or *distinctions*, which are themselves divided into a varying number of subcategories, or topics. By way of example, the first distinction is entitled *de deo*, or *Of God*. Beneath this heading is a list of thirty-six topics each of which relates to its parent category: *that God exists, what God is, the unity of God, the trinity of God*, and so on. The first part of the *Tabula* is simply a list of these distinctions and topics, 440 of them. Alongside each, Grosseteste designed a symbol—simple but unique to that topic—so that, in the course of his reading, whenever a particular topic came up, he could quickly jot down the symbol in the margin for later reference. Sometimes the symbols have a clear relation to the topic—the trinity of God is represented by a triangle; the unity of God by a dot—but given the large number of topics in Grosseteste's system, it is no surprise that many are more arbitrary—and more complex—than this (Fig. 20.1).

The outline of the nine distinctions and their topics runs to five pages, three columns to a page, and it is immediately followed by the index proper. Here, each

---

[6] Most accounts follow Quétif and Echard in attributing the third concordance to Conrad Halberstadt. However, Rouse and Rouse show that it was already in circulation by 1286 when it appeared in the sales list of a Parisian stationer. This would likely have been too early for Halberstadt who was active in 1321. Rouse and Rouse, 'Verbal Concordance', pp. 18–20.

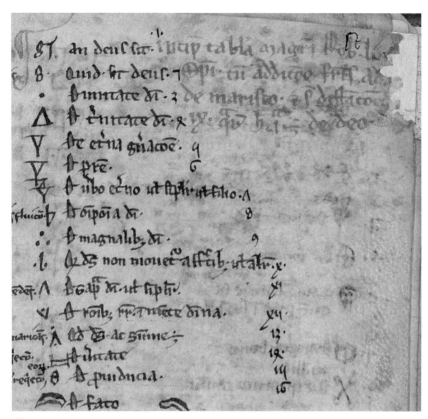

❦ **Fig. 20.1** *Detail of Robert Grosseteste's 'Tabula' showing topics and their symbols. Lyon, Bibliothèque municipale, MS 414 f.17r*

topic, along with its symbol, is listed again. This time, however, beneath the topic is a series of references, first to passages in the Bible which deal with the subject, then to the writings of the Church Fathers, and finally, in a separate column to the right, to Pagan or Arabic writers. So, taking the first topic from the first distinction—the proposition *that God exists*—we find Grosseteste's symbol for that topic followed by this set of references. Expanding the abbreviations we get the following (where *l'*—in Grosseteste's hand a crossed *l*—indicates *liber*, i.e. book):

ge· 1· a·
augustinus contra aduersarios legis et prophetarum· l'·1· De trinitate ·12· De libero· arbitrio· l'·1· De uera religione· epistola· 38· De ciuitate· dei l'·8· 10· 11· gregorius dialogi l'·4 ·27· Ieronimus· 13· damascenus· sentenciarum ·l'·1· c· 3· 41· anselmus prosologion· c· 2· 3· monologion·
[and in the right margin] aritstoteles methaphisice l'·1· [7]

---

[7] Robert Grosseteste, *Tabula*, ed. Philipp Rosemann, *Corpus Christianorum: Continuatio Mediaevalis* 130 (1995): 233–320, 265.

What this all means is that, should we wish to know more about the proposition *that God exists*, we should start by looking at the first chapter of Genesis ('In the beginning God created the heaven and the earth'). We might then look to various works by Augustine—Books 8, 10, and 11 of *City of God* (*De Civitate Dei*), for example—or Gregory's *Dialogues*, or Jerome, St John Damascene, or Anselm. And if we were prepared to go off-piste into non-Christian thought, we could try the first book of Aristotle's *Metaphysics*. If we follow one of these references up in Grosseteste's own copy of *De Civitate Dei*, now in the Bodleian Library in Oxford, we can turn to Book 8, and find the topic's symbol alongside the following section:

> Viderunt ergo isti philosophi, quos ceteris non inmerito fama atque gloria prae-latos uidemus, nullum corpus esse Deum, et ideo cuncta corpora transcenderunt quaerentes Deum.[8]

> [So these philosophers who, as we see, have not undeservedly achieved a glorious reputation beyond all others, perceived that no material body is God; and there-fore in seeking God they have gone above and beyond all material bodies.][9]

There is another sign, a little like a three-legged table, in the same section of the margin, annotating the same passage. This indicates *de videndo deum* [*On seeing God*], and sure enough, if we look this topic up in the *Tabula* the list of references includes *De Civitate Dei*, Book 8.

For the priest with sermons to write, or for the teacher in one of the newly founded universities, the value of works like the concordance or Grosseteste's *Tabula* is clear. Strictly speaking, however, neither are quite book parts. One is a book in itself, the other a kind of search engine to an entire library. In their wake, however, the small-scale index began to catch on. During the thirteenth century, readers started to annotate their books, writing indexes on the early leaves. The British Library, for example, holds a copy of William de Montibus's *Distinctiones* made in the mid-thirteenth century but which contains a bonus feature added a century later: a handwritten index on the front flyleaf.[10] The index is keyed to the pages of the book, numerals which were not there when the main text was written out, but which were added by the later scribe prior to compiling the index. The fact that de Montibus's *Distionctiones* is already an alphabetically arranged work was clearly not enough: the scribe here thought it would save labour if, knowing the entry you wanted to read, you could refer to the index then flip only the corners of the leaves until you found the page you needed.

---

[8] Oxford, Bodleian Library, MS Bodley 198, f. 31v.

[9] Augustine, *The City of God against the Pagans*, trans. David S. Wiesen, vol. 3 of 7 (London: Harvard University Press, 1968), p. 31.

[10] London, British Library, Royal MS 8 G ii, f. 1v.

The use of foliation, or page numbers, as locators here is a noteworthy expedient. Unlike the Bible or Augustine's *City of God*, not every work has widely recognized divisions into chapters or books, so what the compiler has done instead is to key this index to a physical feature of the book. But this means that the index is useful only for readers of this particular manuscript—it is *copy-specific*—due to the fact that, until the middle of the fifteenth century, all books had to be written out by hand, so pagination would almost always vary from one copy to another. With the arrival of printing, however, page numbering would become stable across an edition. A reader in Venice could be fairly certain that page 15 looked the same to him as it did to his friend in Prague. Thus, although the index had existed for centuries before, it is in the age of print that it really comes into its own.

If we look at some of the earliest printed books in English, we can get an insight into the index's novelty among the broadening readership of that period. We find that a book part which seems intuitive to us today once required instructions explicitly explaining what it was for and how to use it. Take, for example, William Caxton's edition of the *Legenda aurea sanctorum*, a book of saints' lives printed in 1483. The book comes with both an index and a table of contents, one after the other, and at the top of the two lists is the following explanation:

> And to thende eche hystoryy lyf & passyon may be shortely founden I have ordeyned this table folowyng / where & in what leef he shal fynde suche as shal be desyred / and have sette the nombre of every leef in the margyne.[11]

There are a few things of note here. Firstly, the quaintness of the printer explaining his inclusion of page numbers (or, rather, folio numbers; for more on these see Chapter 11 of this present volume), 'the nombre of every leef in the margyne'. Then there is the wonderfully pithy description of the tables' purpose: so that things might be 'shortely founden'—then, as now, time saving is the one criterion of a good index. But, most intriguingly, there is also that phrase, 'suche as shal be desyred'. It seems to cover all eventualities: *Whatever you're looking for, just look it up in the index and follow the reference.* There is perhaps a hint of the sales pitch here, mixed in with the How To guide. Hans Wellisch has noted how fifteenth-century printers saw an opportunity in the index: 'As readers increasingly came to appreciate the value of indexes, more finding aids were included by printers who quickly realised…that the provision of indexes helped to sell books.'[12] And yet, not every index of the period is accompanied by such an assurance of its comprehensiveness. The year before, Caxton had brought out an edition of Ranulf Higden's *Polychronicon* where the alphabetical index is introduced

---

[11] Jacobus de Varagine, *Legenda aurea sanctorum* (Westminster, 1483), sig. [pi]2r.
[12] Hans H. Wellisch, 'Incunabula Indexes', *Indexer* 19, no. 1 (1994): 3–12.

as 'a table shortly towchyd of the moost parte of this book'.[13] That phrase 'of the moost parte' doesn't exactly inspire the same confidence as 'suche as shal be desyred'. And Caxton's Cato of 1484 sounds an even clearer warning when its table concludes: 'And over and above these that be conteyned in this sayd table is many a notable commaundement / lernynge and counceylle moche prouffitable whiche is not sette in the sayd regystre or rubrysshe.'[14] Don't confuse the map with the territory, it seems to say: the index is *not* the whole book in miniature.

The history of the index through the sixteenth and seventeenth centuries is one of increasing sophistication and ubiquity, but it is also one in which this admonition—that the index is not a substitute for the work itself—is heard again and again. Erasmus introduces his *Brevissima scholia* (1532) with the quip that he had to write it in the form of an index because 'eos plerique solos legunt' ['many people read only them'],[15] while Galileo, a century later, bemoans 'that herd who...in order to acquire a knowledge of natural effects, do not betake themselves to ships or crossbows or cannons, but retire into their studies and glance through an index or a table of contents to see whether Aristotle has said anything about them'.[16] What these accounts tell us is that the index is becoming a victim of its own success: people, it seems, are really using them—a conclusion corroborated by the extent to which they begin to be trumpeted on title pages—but, alongside this, a suspicion is developing that scholars are using them *instead of* reading books all the way through. The index, more than any other book part (though others are certainly implicated), is taking the rap for an anxiety about what reading *should* be.

In England, this comes into sharpest focus during the 'Battle of the Books' at the turn of the eighteenth century, when the term 'index learning' is coined as a jibe against modern philologists like Richard Bentley. We find Alexander Pope sneering that 'index learning turns no student pale' (*Dunciad* [1743], I.279), implying that the connection between exertion and scholarship—burning the candle at both ends in the quest for knowledge—has been improperly broken by the convenience of extract reading. Jonathan Swift joins in the attack with a memorable dig against 'the Men, who pretend to understand a Book, by scouting thro' the *Index*, as if a traveller should go about to describe a *Palace*, when he had seen nothing but the *Privy*'.[17] But the best example of the 'Ancient' faction's contempt for 'alphabetical learning' comes itself in the form of an index: William King's 'Short Account of Dr Bentley by Way of Index',

[13] Ranulf Higden, *Polychronicon*, trans. John Trevisa (Westminster, 1482), sig. a3v.

[14] Cato, *Catonis disticha* (Westminster, 1484), sig. [pi]5v.

[15] Erasmus, *In elenchum Alberti Pii brevissima scholia per Erasmu[s] Rot.* (Basel: Froben, 1532), sig. m2r.

[16] Galileo Galilei, *Dialogue Concerning the Two Chief World Systems—Ptolemaic and Copernican*, trans. Stillman Drake, 2nd edn (London: University of California Press, 1967 [1632]), p. 185.

[17] Jonathan Swift, 'A Discourse Concerning the Mechanical Operation of the Spirit', in *The Tale of a Tub* (London: John Nutt, 1704), pp. 283–325, p. 315.

printed at the back of Charles Boyle's *Dr Bentley's Dissertations* (1698). The whole book is a caustic, *ad hominem* attack on Bentley for having the temerity to criticize Boyle's edition of the ancient Greek epistles supposedly written by Phalaris. Bentley's close textual analysis, drawing heavily on word lists for etymological details and datings, makes him the index-scholar par excellence, so an index is the perfect medium for a sarcastic character assassination pointing out, for example, his 'egregious dulness, p. 74, 106, 119, 135, 136, 137, 241', 'His familiar acquaintance with Books that he never saw, p. 76, 98, 115, 232', and, naturally, his 'Pedantry, from p. 93 to 99, 144, 216'.[18]

With this, King is widely regarded to have invented the satirical index, and a number of further examples, some by King himself, can be found in the decade that follows.[19] Ironically, however, in these subsequent mock indexes the object of satire is no longer index scholarship itself; rather, the index is finding favour, employed uncritically as a medium whose conventions offer a particular comic potential. As with so many other book parts, we find that the point at which they become exploited for comic purpose marks the beginning of their mature phase, the moment at which readers have become familiar enough with their codes to recognize when they are being abused.

The comical index is with us as much now as it was in Swift's day. The brevity of its subheadings can be used to skewer politicians, as in 'Aitken, Jonathan: admires risk-takers, 59; goes to jail, 60'; the arbitrariness of its ordering allows for surreal juxtapositions, viz.

> Holmes
> > Eamonn: 26n, 98, 152, 166n, 227, 230
> > Sherlock: 87-8;

while its distinctive backwards syntax means a punchline can be neatly set up at the end of a phrase: 'football, appeal to dunderheads: 167–9'.[20] We are still, clearly, well versed in index form. And yet, as a technology so intimately tied to the codex, the digital revolution poses a serious threat, and among the community of professional indexers, there is a strong sense of being embattled. Digital texts—whether web pages or Kindle books—frequently abandon the page number but remain, of course, highly searchable by other means. Nevertheless, our current digital search

---

[18] Charles Boyle, *Dr Bentley's Dissertations on the Epistles of Phalaris, and the Fables of Æsop, Examin'd*, 2nd edn (London: Thomas Bennet, 1698), sig. U2r–U3v. For more on King's index, see Dennis Duncan, 'Hoggs that Sh-te Soap, p. 66', *Times Literary Supplement*, 15 January 2016, pp. 14–15.

[19] See, for example, William Bromley, *Remarks in the Grande Tour of France and Italy*, 2nd edn (London: John Nutt, 1705); John Gay, *Trivia: Or, the Art of Walking the Streets of London* (London: Bernard Lintott, 1716); [William King], *The Transactioneer* (London, 1700).

[20] Francis Wheen, *How Mumbo-Jumbo Conquered the World* (London: Harper, 2004); Alan Partridge, *Nomad* (London: Trapeze, 2016); Charlie Brooker, *Dawn of the Dumb* (London: Faber and Faber, 2012). These examples are all taken from Paula Clarke Bain's indexing blog: http://baindex.org.

tools, whether the Google Books search bar or the Ctrl+f function in Word or Acrobat, are the inheritors of the concordance—the word index—not of the subject index, and share its limitations. And while publishers will always be eager to save money, the Society of Indexers continues to make the case that we are not yet, technologically, in a position to do without expertly compiled indexes. The future, for this particular book part, remains still to be contested. For now, however, the professional indexer, a figure who predates print by over a century, still has a vital role to play in the production of our books.

CHAPTER 21

ENDLEAVES

Sidney E. Berger

Part of the thrill of picking up an old book is in its ability to give us pleasure in its beauty. The beauty often lies in the materials that compose the volume. One never knows what will be discovered as the cover opens and the endleaves appear.[1] Plate 8 shows a remarkable pair of endleaves from nineteenth-century Spain, made of a cloth that has dozens of what look like miniature marbled squares, all different, in vibrant colours. Clearly, endleaves can be stunning, in their colour, and in the intricacy of their making. I was astonished when I opened this volume to discover a pattern I had never seen before. I still don't know how it was achieved. It has no relation to the text, but it does put one into a good mood to begin reading. Endleaves, as we shall see, are a necessary structural element of almost all books, and yet over time, like decorated covers, they have come to take on an aesthetic function, too. First, however, we must clarify terminology.

Endleaves (also called *endpapers* or *endsheets*, hyphenated or not) are leaves used by the binder to cover the inner boards and to connect the covers to the textblock. They are in two parts: the part of the leaf that is pasted onto the inside of the covers (called the *pastedown*) and the conjugate leaf that is loose (the *free endpaper*). The binder covers the outside of the boards with vellum, leather, cloth, paper, or some other material, pulling the part of the material that extends out over the three exposed edges of the board (the head, tail, and fore edge; the fourth edge of the board is covered at the spine) around the board and gluing those edges down to the inside of the board. These flaps are called *turn-ins*. Hence, the outsides of the boards (front and back) are usually covered, but the insides are covered only where the turn-ins are. The binder adds the endleaves, pasting one leaf down over the inner board, and leaving the conjugate leaf free. In a normal binding, the endleaves are the same size as the sheets of the book, so when the cover is opened, the edges of the free endleaf line up perfectly with the leaves of the text. The pastedown covers the full inner board and most of the turn-ins, covering up the relatively unsightly board and the often uneven edges of the turn-ins. The turn-ins are usually not covered completely; generally a small strip of them is left exposed on the inner edges of the boards. If the boards are covered with cloth, the exposed strips of the turn-ins at the head, fore edge, and tail of the book will show this cloth.[2]

The endleaves are not part of the *printing* of the volume, so they are not included in a collational formula in a bibliographical description. In such a description they

[1] Since paper is not the only material used, the term *endleaves* is preferred to *endpapers*. Some sources say that the free endleaf is sometimes called the flyleaf, but flyleaves are properly part of the printed part of the text and endsheets are parts of the binding.

[2] Often the turn-ins—especially on a leather binding—will be decorated, as with a gold-stamped pattern. They are then called *dentelles* (French, 'lace').

can be mentioned in the notes if they are significant: made of a distinct kind of paper or cloth, for example, or decorated, or containing writing or bookplates. Inexpensive books may contain no endleaves, a reflection of the book's status.

In binding literature, one will find the loose use of the word *endleaf* where a more scrupulous writer would use *flyleaf*, and vice versa. Strictly speaking, endleaves are the pastedowns and their conjugate free leaves; flyleaves are other blank leaves that are 'inside' these. David Pearson confuses the matter when he says that there are two kinds of endleaves, pastedowns and flyleaves.[3] This careless use of terminology is partly occasioned by the varying practices of binders using waste sheets to wrap around endleaves; to use printed or plain stubs; to leave the 'pastedown' unpasted and loose; to use vellum rather than paper as leaves or stubs; to use a pastedown with no conjugate free endleaf; to use a pastedown with no conjugate free leaf, to fold a stub and its full-sized conjugate leaf to form what is now the first flyleaf; to sew in endleaves rather than merely use paste; and so on. Nevertheless, we gain in precision if we restrict *endleaves* to pastedowns plus their conjugate free leaves.

In a laced-in binding, with the textblock attached to the boards with the same cords, thongs, or tapes that were used to sew the textblock, the endleaves are generally not viewed as a structural part of the binding. That is, they merely cover the exposed underside of the covers, and they do not hold the volume's parts together. However, Roberts and Etherington say:

> In hand binding the basic purpose of the endpapers is to take up the strain of opening the covers of the book, which [strain] would otherwise be on the first and last sections or leaves. This is of particular importance in the case of the upper cover and first section or leaf.[4]

So endleaves may perform a structural function in a laced-in binding.

In a cased-in binding, the endleaves are indeed structural, for the textblock is attached to the case by means of these leaves. The case, prepared separately from the textblock, has its boards and covering, with the standard turn-ins. The textblock is sewn or glued, so that all the leaves are now ready to be covered. The pastedown endleaves are attached to the inside of the boards, and the free endleaves are attached respectively to the first and last leaf of the textblock. The attachment between textblock and covers in this binding is as strong as is this bond between the two leaves, so the binding is considerably weaker than is that of a laced-in binding. But for the present purpose, the result is the same: a volume with endleaves, one pasted

---

[3] Pearson, *English Bookbinding Styles 1450–1800: A Handbook* (London: British Library; New Castle, DE: Oak Knoll, 2005), p. 31.

[4] Matt Roberts and Don Etherington, *Bookbinding and the Conservation of Books: A Dictionary of Descriptive Terminology* (Washington, DC: Library of Congress, 1981), p. 89.

down, the other free.[5] It is possible, however, that both endleaves in front and both at the back of the volume are not pasted down, and that another piece of material covers the turn-ins. That pasted-down leaf is not strictly an endleaf, but it can be part of the volume's decoration.

Also, to save time, it was not unusual for the binder not to paste down the 'pastedown'. In many volumes the leaf would be left unglued, and thus would be another 'free endpaper', and the turn-ins and the rest of the inner boards would be exposed. Often binders would use waste papers (printers' waste or other sheets that have no other use) to cover the inside of the boards. In library and edition binding using heavy cloth, it is common for the book and case to be held together by the endleaves alone.[6]

Paper has been the most common material used for endleaves, but they could also be made from vellum, satin or silk or other cloth, or any other material the binder chooses. If the endleaves are paper, they could be plain or decorated in many ways, as delineated below. One platitude about book design is that the design of the cover should prepare the reader for what is inside, in some thematic or aesthetic way. Not necessarily so for endleaves. Binders can adorn the volume with decorations at the endleaves that are not related to the volume's contents or even to the rest of the cover. If the aim of the volume is to give pleasure, then decorated endleaves can be ends in themselves. But as we shall see, many a volume does have endleaves that are related to the volume's text.

If the endleaves are paper, it is likely to be stronger and of a heavier weight than the paper used for the textblock. Endleaves made of simply folded pieces of paper will be 'unsatisfactory for a book that is to be consulted frequently', since only the thin line of adhesive holds the case to the book.[7] (A cloth joint, however, can mitigate the problem somewhat.)

Binders will probably want to use endleaves that are alkaline, and ones that are sufficiently sized that any adhesives used to adhere them to the volume do not cause them to cockle or allow the adhesive to penetrate the paper and discolour it. Cockled paper will distort the cover from the inside, and could then make the whole cover cockle or warp; and adhesive that penetrates the paper could cause the free endpaper to stick to the pastedown. In a carefully crafted binding, the grain of the endleaves' paper will ideally run vertical—parallel with the spine. And if the paper is water-marked, binders will prefer that the mark should be 'right-reading' when the paper is attached to the binding—in both parts of the leaf, the pastedown or the free

---

[5] Booksellers will abbreviate the term to FFEP (front free end paper).

[6] See Roberts and Etherington, *Bookbinding and the Conservation of Books*, p. 89.

[7] Roberts and Etherington, *Bookbinding and the Conservation of Books*; http://cool.conservation-us.org/don/dt/dt1192.html.

endpaper. Also, it is desirable that coloured endpapers be colourfast as well as the pigments used if the paper is decorated in any of the ways described below.

❧ 📖 ❧

The appearance of decorated papers in the West runs parallel to their use for covers and endleaves. They were first used in France in the first half of the seventeenth century.[8] Bookbinders were eager to learn marbling so they could decorate their books with this 'new' phenomenon, and by the end of the seventeenth century, and certainly throughout the eighteenth, binders could supply their own decorated sheets.[9] But the commodity became popular enough to engender a new trade, and by the beginning of the eighteenth century companies selling decorated paper were supplying binders with a broad array of decorated sheets, the most common of which in the eighteenth century were marbled, paste, and block-printed.[10] Germany, Italy, and France saw the greatest number of manufacturers of these papers, though they were available in other countries as well. By the nineteenth century, a tremendous industry of printed decorated papers supplied binders with an unimaginable number of such sheets.

Another phenomenon must be mentioned here, the doublure. This is usually a panel of a heavy material (usually backed silk or leather) pasted onto the inner covers of deluxe-bound books where one would expect to see the pastedown. Sometimes, the doublure is extended to the free endleaf. Doublures, frequently decorated, are almost always added by an owner to enhance the beauty of a volume—they are seldom the work of the original publisher. And since doublures add to the thickness of the textblock, new covers are generally necessary for the book. In many volumes, endpapers are bearers of information that help the reader, as with a volume that has maps of the geographical locations mentioned in the text. 'Some endpaper designs are integral to the narratives that they envelop, such as E.H. Shepard's map of the "100 Aker Wood" featured on the endpapers of A. A. Milne's 1926 *Winnie-the-Pooh*.'[11] The 1908 edition of *The Wizard of Oz* had for its endpaper a map of the 'Marvelous Land OZ' (see Plate 9).

[8] Pickwoad, email communique. See also Richard J. Wolfe, *Marbled Paper: Its History, Techniques, and Patterns, with Special Reference to the Relationship of Marbling to Bookbinding in Europe and the Western World* (Philadelphia, PA: University of Pennsylvania Press, 1990), pp. 14, 35; Pearson, *English Bookbinding Styles*, p. 39.

[9] See Wolfe, *Marbled Paper*, p. 14.

[10] This phenomenon is well covered by Wolfe and Haemmerle. See Albert Haemmerle, *Buntpapier: Herkommen, Geschichte, Techniken; Beziehungen zur Kunst* (Munich: Georg D. W. Callwey, 1961). A second edition was also published by the same firm in 1977.

[11] 'Under the Covers: A Visual History of Decorated Endpapers', catalogue to an exhibit at the Beinecke Library, Yale University, 18 January–31 May 2014; this statement can be found at http://beinecke.library.yale.edu/exhibitions/under-covers-visual-history-decorated-endpapers.

Endpapers can carry advertising for the publisher. The US version (published by Knopf) of Karen Brookfield's *Book* has a repeated pattern of a copying press and a quill; the British version contains images of other volumes printed by the publisher (Dorling Kindersley) in their Eyewitness series.[12] Other kinds of relationships can exist between endleaves and texts. In the first edition of the English translation of Vladimir Nabokov's *The Enchanter*, '[p]ortions of the original Russian typescript, with Vladimir Nabokov's handwritten corrections, appear as endpapers'.[13]

Owners, booksellers, and librarians may use the endleaves to record provenance information, dates of sales or acquisition, sources of purchase, prices paid or asked, or other information that could be tremendously useful to scholars. Owners may place inscriptions or dedications on endpapers. At the Phillips Library in the Peabody Essex Museum in Salem, Massachusetts, one seventeenth-century volume is signed on the front endleaves by two of its former owners, William Bradford (first governor of Massachusetts) and Cotton Mather (an important New England political and religious figure, famous for his writings and infamous for his support of the witchcraft trials in Salem, Massachusetts), while the rear endpaper is signed by another former owner, John Hancock, perhaps the most famous signer of the US Declaration of Independence.[14]

Some libraries, which rebind books for their own circulating collections, may have their own endleaves. Libraries at nine of the ten campuses of the University of California have their own endpaper—designed to identify the campus that owns an item. The information on the original endleaves can have such great research value that there is a data field in MARC (machine-readable cataloguing) records to record such information. If a book, especially one in a rare book or special collections department, is to be rebound, librarians are generally scrupulous to be sure the information on its endleaves is carefully saved.

In commercial bookmaking, endleaves are often reinforced by being laminated, or are specially produced papers slightly heavier than are the papers used for the textblock. One company, LBS, that specializes in the manufacture of endsheets, advertises as follows:

> Endsheets: the vital link between a book and its cover. We are the worldwide leader in the production and supply of reinforced endsheets.[15]

[12] In the British versions there are varying numbers of pictures of the Eyewitness books shown. As the publisher issued new Eyewitness volumes to the series, it included additional images to its endpapers. Some copies have pictures of 110 covers, some have 116, some 137.

[13] Dustjacket blurb, Vladimir Nabokov, *The Enchanter*, trans. Dmitri Nabokov (New York: G. P. Putnam's Sons, 1986).

[14] The book is Richard Rogers, *Seven treatises containing such direction as is gathered out of the Holy Scriptures*, 5th edn (London: Thomas Man for Richard Thrale, 1630).

[15] LBS: http://www.lbsbind.com/photo-books/endsheets/.

The production of endleaves, then, has become a small but significant sub-industry in the world of book making. The LBS website elaborately stresses the company's expertise with an extensive discussion on the quality of materials, exacting standards, the careful selection of the proper colours and weights of papers, the kinds of printing that can be done on the sheets, and much more. And it lists papers available for thirteen kinds of perfect-bound volumes, twenty-one kinds of sewn books, and five kinds of wire-stitched volumes, along with dozens of kinds of woven and non-woven materials from which the endsheets are made, with more than two dozen reinforcing materials.[16] From their humble beginnings, endleaves have become an industry in themselves.

With respect to the paper's surface, most common of all are unadorned, plain endpapers. Middleton calls them 'surface papers'—sometimes just plain or coated in a colour, and left as is or glazed.[17] He distinguishes one kind, 'Cobb Paper', which is dyed but otherwise unadorned.

Blank spaces call out to be filled. This impulse has led to a world of decoration in bookmaking, with covers and books' edges—the first parts of the volume one sees— the prime target for all kinds of decoration. In early manuscripts, the outer blank leaves were there purely for protection—preventing the writing or illumination of the text from being rubbed or defaced. They may not even have had a title or author written on them. But by the sixteenth century, with the coming of printing to the West, publishers and private collectors chose to add adornment to their volumes— on the covers and inside as well.

When one hears about endpapers, one almost automatically thinks of marbled sheets, since this is the most common form of paper decoration for these leaves. But there are other kinds of decoration, including paste papers, dutch gilt papers, and one of the most common decorated endpapers, block-printed sheets. Marbling, done by floating pigments on the surface of a size (a bath of water thickened with any of a number of agents such as gum tragacanth or Irish moss), manipulating them (or not), and then laying a specially prepared sheet over the surface of the bath to pick up the pigments, has been done in the West since perhaps the sixteenth century—though its actual origin is lost in the mist of time.[18] Certainly by the seventeenth century, marbled papers were being used for bookbindings, as cover papers or for endleaves.

---

[16] Ibid.

[17] Bernard C. Middleton, *A History of English Craft Bookbinding Techniques* (London: Hafner, 1963), pp. 37–8.

[18] For the pigments on the size to transfer and adhere to the paper, the sheet much be coated with a mordant— usually a smooth and invisible wash of alum, mixed in water—over the sheet's surface.

According to Richard J. Wolfe, '[w]ithout a doubt, the French were the first in Europe to use marbled paper as endpapers.... Sometimes they even applied marbled decorations to the edges of the books themselves.'[19] Wolfe neglects to give a date, but he seems to be speaking of the sixteenth century. Middleton claims that 'Marbled paper was in use in Holland by 1598, but the earliest English binding with it that has been noted by Mr Graham Pollard is dated 1655.'[20] Although this is in his chapter on endpapers, he does not say whether this use was for endpapers themselves, or for the covers of the volume.

Paper decorators learned early on how to comb the pigments into various patterns, but they also saw the attractiveness of stochastically dropped colours, so one will find Stormont (a splashing of random-distributed droplets of pigments), tiger eye, and Italian vein and other patternless distributions of the pigments on decorated endsheets. Other patterns were equally popular, with the colours combed into French snail, nonpareil, zig-zag, bouquet, Spanish wave, and many others.[21] Much more common are the patterns that can be made with simple combing of the pigments. Nonpareil was one of the most common—and easiest to make—patterns. A seemingly endless array of patterns have been used for marbled endleaves over the centuries.

Another kind of decorated endleaf, essentially a German invention, is paste papers, created from the late sixteenth century on. The process is simple: mix a coloured pigment into paste (for example, wheat starch or rice starch), brush or sponge it over a sheet of moistened paper, and manipulate the paste into a decoration of some kind. A simple 'pattern' is created when a sheet, so spread with the coloured pigment, is folded in half over itself, with the two pasted surfaces touching, and then the two leaves are pulled apart, creating what is called a 'pulled pattern'.[22] If the facing leaves are pressed in a variety of ways while they are still touching, the paste will be pushed in whatever ways the sheets are pressed (as with fingers, say, making a circular or spiral motion), so that the 'repositioned' paste will show that 'pattern' when the leaves are pulled apart (see Plate 10). Either way (with or without the manipulation of the leaves while the wet leaves are still touching), the effect can be quite beautiful, and such papers were used as endleaves in countless volumes.

More common, however, is simply brushing on the coloured paste and manipulating it, while it is still wet, with fingers or tools. However the paste is touched, there will be a disruption in the pigment that exposes the leaf under it. An endless number

---

[19] Wolfe, *Marbled Paper*, p. 14.

[20] Middleton, *A History*, p. 34.

[21] A host of marbled patterns (even the non-patterned marbled papers) have names, and still untold numbers of others—the work of imaginative artists—are idiosyncratic to a single marbler and may not be named. See Wolfe, *Marbled Paper*.

[22] Of course, the effect can be achieved, also, with two pasted sheets rather than one that is folded in half. This produces two full-sized sheets with a near-identical 'pattern'; the word is in quotation marks because there really is no 'pattern' per se, but a configuration of striations on the sheets.

of tools can be used: combs of various kinds, graining tools, bottle caps, rubber stamps, potatoes with patterns carved onto their cut surfaces, corks, pastry-crimping tools, and on and on. The artist is limited only by her imagination. More than one colour of paste can be used, either in a single operation or in a second one after the first layer of paste has dried, and accomplished artists can create amazing patterns (spirals, circles, geometrical, repeated, or otherwise) or pictures of people, flowers, landscapes, trees, furniture, animals, and an almost infinite array of other images.

Paste papers were used mostly for cover papers, but they also appear as endpapers from the seventeenth century on.

A third kind of decorated paper became tremendously popular in the nineteenth century: block-printed papers. This technique actually goes back to the end of the sixteenth century, when wood blocks were cut to produce decorated papers, and these sheets were common throughout the seventeenth and eighteenth centuries, usually in geometric patterns, but also with pictorial images. In the nineteenth century, companies like Remondini and Rizzi in Italy and others in France and Germany produced lovely one-, two-, and three-colour block prints (sometimes using even more than three colours) to create thousands of patterns of sheets, used for book covers and endleaves.[23] But in the nineteenth century, machine printing led to a tremendous proliferation of printed papers, and untold numbers of patterns were produced throughout Europe and were used in millions of volumes as endleaves. In one city alone, Aschaffenburg, Bavaria, paper mills in the nineteenth century produced thousands of decorated papers (Plate 11).[24] The call for such papers for endleaves was great, and companies like those in Germany answered the call.[25]

Above I mentioned the remarkable ingenuity of the artist who created the end-leaves of the Spanish publication shown in Plate 8. An equal level of astonishment is elicited by the Aschaffenburg catalogues. Page after page of these sample books reveals decoration of every kind: variations in colours (of papers and inks and colour combinations), textures (smooth, ribbed, textured, pebbled, embossed), finishes (matte, semi-gloss, shiny), materials (like metallic surfaces and inks), printing tech-niques (block printing, lithography, serigraph, relief), and pattern (by the thousands, many of which are printed in a variety of colour combinations). Papers are made to look like metal, translucent plastic films, fabrics, and several kinds of leather and

[23] See Tanya Schmoller, *Remondini and Rizzi: A Chapter in Italian Decorated Paper History* (New Castle, DE: Oak Knoll, 1990). In England such artists as Walter Crane, Enid Marx, Paul Nash, Sarah Nechamkin, Diana Wilbraham, Edward Bawden, and Eric Ravilious created many printed patterned papers that were used for endleaves, the last six named for the Curwen Press.

[24] The Aschaffenburg companies issued many sample books, many of which contained over 1,500 different paper samples.

[25] Douglas Cockerell warns that simple printed patterns may work well for endleaves, 'but over elaborate [sic] end papers [sic], and especially those that aim at pictorial effect, are seldom successful' (pp. 83–4). See Cockerell, *Bookbinding, and the Care of Books: A Text-book for Bookbinders and Librarians*, 4th edn (London: Sir Isaac Pitman & Sons, 1937).

vellum. There are literally thousands of patterns: geometrics of all kinds, figurative, floral, animal and mineral, objects of all kinds, forms of transportation, implements, and on and on. The artists who created these papers were imaginative beyond measure. Linen-finished papers look like real cloth, vellum and leather papers are realistic substitutes for the original materials, and machine-made papers are created to look like paste papers and marbled sheets—with no indication that they are not the real thing. Almost all of these were used as endleaves in books, from their first appearance in the nineteenth century through most of the twentieth. Publishers easily added touches of elegance to their books with such papers without adding more than a fraction of a cent to their cost.

Many other kinds of decorated papers were used as endleaves, but one last one is worth mentioning here: dutch gilt papers. From the end of the seventeenth century to the beginning of the nineteenth, mostly in Germany but also in Italy, this kind of adorned sheet was popular. The term comes either from the word *Deutsch* ('German') or from the fact that in Western Europe, where they were used, much of the supply outside of Germany came from the Netherlands since the Dutch got them from the Germans. The paper usually had a wash of coloured paste brushed or sponged over the surface (as with paste paper; and the paste could be a single colour or several, stencilled on in a geometrical pattern), and the gold image would be stamped over that. The foil was not real gold but some golden metal, sometimes mixed with copper to give the pattern a reddish/coppery cast. A silver foil was also used. The patterns were stamped onto the sheets with metal or woodblocks, and the technique was truly a relief process, for in many sheets one can discern the debossing that such printing yields. There were many patterns: geometrics; animals; birds; natural scenes; people doing all kinds of things; professions; alphabets; trees, plants, and flowers; scenes from legends and tales; soldiers; saints (particularly popular); brocades; mythological beasts; and many others (Plate 12). The paper has many uses, including, for our purposes, endleaves.[26]

It is hoped that this chapter, while necessarily brief, has nonetheless introduced that blend of the aesthetic and the utilitarian that often defines the endleaf, and has shed light on the specialized labour performed by bookbinders and paper decorators as they produced this particular book part.

---

[26] See Sidney E. Berger, 'Dutch Gilt Papers as Substitutes for Leather', *Hand Papermaking* 24, no. 2 (Winter 2009): 14–16.

CHAPTER 22

'BLURBS'

ABIGAIL WILLIAMS

In 1936 George Orwell announced with characteristic éclat that 'the novel is being shouted out of existence. Question any thinking person as to why he "never reads novels", and you will usually find that, at bottom, it is because of the disgusting tripe that is written by the blurb-reviewers.'[1] Two years later, Holbrook Jackson, author of *The Printing of Books* (1938), would take an equally extreme view in the opposite direction: 'The historian of the future may yet learn more of our period from book-jackets and blurbs than from the novels whose flamboyancies [they] are designed to sell.'[2] Both men identify a symbiotic and competitive relationship between novel and blurb, interdependent texts which make different kinds of claims upon their readers. The blurb occupies a peculiar space in the history of the book: not traditionally part of descriptive bibliography, it is often physically separated from the work it accompanies through the removal of the dust jacket in research libraries (see Chapter 2 of this present volume).[3] Studies of the history of the jacket tend to privilege the graphic design of the cover, rather than the text upon it, and digital image collections of jackets often omit the back cover.[4] The blurb lacks history, definition, and archival record—yet is at the same time a fundamental element of the modern book.

THE HISTORY OF THE BLURB

Although the term blurb itself, and the advent of printed external covers, date only from the late nineteenth and early twentieth century, the use of supplementary commentary as a form of textual promotion has a much longer story. When Thomas More asked Erasmus to write a recommendation for *Utopia*, Erasmus buttressed his friend's prose work with a statement of his own intellectual repute: 'I see that all learned men unanimously subscribe to my opinion and admire the man's superhuman genius.'[5] The 1598 title page of Shakespeare's *1 Henry IV* offers a different kind of

---

[1] George Orwell, 'In Defence of the Novel', *New English Weekly*, 12 and 19 November 1936, reprinted in *The Collected Essays, Journalism and Letters of George Orwell*, ed. Sonia Orwell and Ian Angus (London: Secker and Warburg, 1968).

[2] Holbrook Jackson, *The Printing of Books* (London: Cassell, 1938), p. 252.

[3] For bibliographical debates about book jackets, see G. Thomas Tanselle, *Book-Jackets: Their History, Forms and Use* (Charlottesville, VA: Bibliographical Society of the University of Virginia, 2011), pp. 24–40.

[4] The Bodleian Library's digitized collection of book jackets from the John Johnson collection generally includes only the front cover and spine. On image over text in studies of the jacket, see Thomas S. Hansen, *Classic Book Jackets: The Design Legacy of George Salter* (Princeton, NJ: Princeton Architectural Press, 2005).

[5] Erasmus to John Froben, 25 August 1517, preface to Thomas More, *Utopia*, in *The Complete Works of St. Thomas More*, ed. Edward Surtz, S. J., and J. H. Hexter (New Haven, CT: Yale University Press, 1965), vol. 4, p. 3.

recommendation for the play, invoking not an external expert, but the promise of the entertainment value of the play's beloved comic knight: 'with the humorous conceits of Sir Iohn Fastalffe'.[6] As these examples suggest, we might reasonably recruit other elements of the book as proto-blurbs: the title page, the dedication, the preface have all played a part in this more extensive history. But the thing that has come to be known as a blurb, a separately printed endorsement or a precis on the outside cover of a work could only come into being once books had printed cloth covers or jackets. The introduction of publishers' cloth from the 1820s onwards marked a sea change in the potential for the outside of a book.[7] As other contributors to this volume have noted, because loose sheets or books in boards had previously been bound by owners or booksellers, up until this point, the book cover had essentially made a statement about ownership rather than marketing. As we have seen in Chapter 2, even after the advent of the book in covers, nineteenth-century examples of printed book covers have a plainness suggesting that for most of the century, the external jacket was seen as a protective device, rather than as a form of advertising.[8] It was not until the 1890s that comments were specifically written to promote the book within the jacket.[9]

The speed with which the blurb became established is evidenced by the fact that within less than two decades it was possible to satirize the form. In 1906 the American critic and writer Gelett Burgess published a sixty-page prose work entitled *Are you a Bromide?*, a satire on conventional thinking, originality, and cliché (see Fig. 22.1). The following year, B. W. Huebsch, the publisher, distributed it at the 1907 convention of the American Booksellers' Association in jackets printed with 'YES, this is a BLURB! All the Other Publishers commit them. Why Shouldn't We?'.[10] Yet although outrageous claims and brazen marketing were mocked almost from the inception of the blurb, it survived this and all subsequent attacks on its credibility. It has remained an essential part of the modern book, and the hyperbole that operates as currency within its world is still legal tender. As we can see from the Burgess example, a comic self-consciousness dates right from the birth of the form. The depersonalized voice of the commendatory text is clearly being mocked in Charles Divine's collection *The Road to Town* in which paragraphs on the front and back are headed 'The Author Writes His Own Blurb'.[11] Ninety years later, the same strategy of both parodying and exploiting the form is evident on the cover of Gabriel Tallent's novel *My Absolute Darling* which bears a neon banner with the statement from the

---

[6] Q1 title page, 1598, reproduced in *King Henry the Fourth Part I*, ed. David Scott Kastan (London: Arden, 2002), p. 107.

[7] David McKitterick, 'Changes in the Look of the Book', in *The Cambridge History of the Book in Britain, Vol VI, 1830–1914*, ed. David McKitterick (Cambridge: Cambridge University Press, 2009), pp. 75–116, p. 99.

[8] See McKitterick, 'Changes to the Look of the Book', pp. 102–4.

[9] Tanselle, *Book Jackets*, p. 15.

[10] Tanselle, *Book Jackets*, p. 16. Two copies of this jacket are in the Rare Book division of the Library of Congress.

[11] Charles Divine, *The Road to Town: A Book of Poems* (New York: T. Seltzer, 1925).

YES, this is a "BLURB"!

All the Other Publishers commit them. Why Shouldn't We?

MISS
BELINDA
BLURB

IN
THE ACT OF
BLURBING

ARE YOU A BROMIDE?

BY

GELETT BURGESS

Say! Ain't this book a 90-H. P., six-cylinder Seller? If WE do say it as shouldn't, WE consider that this man Burgess has got Henry James locked into the coal-bin, telephoning for " Information "

WE expect to sell 350 copies of this great, grand book. It has gush and go to it, it has that Certain Something which makes you want to crawl through thirty miles of dense tropical jungle and bite somebody in the neck. No hero no heroine, nothing like that for OURS, but when you've *READ* this masterpiece, you'll know what a BOOK is, and you'll sic it onto your mother-in-law, your dentist and the pale youth who dips hot-air into Little Marjorie until 4 Q. M. in the front parlour. This book has 42-carat THRILLS in it. It fairly BURBLES. Ask the man at the counter what HE thinks of it! He's seen Janice Meredith faded to a mauve magenta. He's seen BLURBS before, and he's dead wise. He'll say:

This Book is the Proud Purple Penultimate ! !

✻ **Fig. 22.1** *Jacket for Gelett Burgess, 'Are You A Bromide?' (New York: B. W. Heubsch, 1906). Library of Congress, Rare Books and Special Collections Division, Printed Ephemera Collection*

horror writer Stephen King: 'The word "masterpiece" has been cheapened by too many blurbs, but *My Absolute Darling* absolutely is one.'[12] Recognition of the hackneyed nature of blurb praise is also evident in the occasional deployment of negative comment on a book cover. This counter-intuitive advertising strategy can gesture to the controversial or challenging nature of the work: Iain Banks's 1984 novel *The Wasp*

[12] Gabrielle Tallent, *My Absolute Darling* (London: Fourth Estate, 2017).

Factory was republished in 2008 with a string of review comments ranging from 'a mighty imagination has arrived on the scene' (*Daily Mail*) to 'Rubbish' (*The Times*) and 'The literary equivalent of the nastiest kind of juvenile delinquency' (*Times Literary Supplement*).[13]

The nature of the blurb is determined by the genre and market positioning of the work it accompanies. In contemporary genre fiction there is traditionally more emphasis on summary description. Mills and Boon romances bear only the plot summary, while mid-market fiction tends to combine plot description with quoted opinion about the author: 'Paige has only a few vivid memories of her mother, who abandoned her when she was five,' accompanied by a critical comment: 'She is a master of her craft…Humanity is what Picoult does best.'[14] Literary fiction may offer greater contextualization through the reputation of the author: the author photo on the back cover of the hardback of Martin Amis's *London Fields* is accompanied by a statement by John Carey: 'He has a style as quick and efficient as a flick-knife, and a gift for the grotesque that makes other people's nightmares look like Victorian watercolours.'[15] Within modern editions of literary classics, the job of the blurb is often to situate the work within a universalizing rhetoric, enabling a text of the past to speak to the modern reader. Although such editions commonly feature introductions authored by a named editor, the blurbs themselves are anonymous. In the 1971 Penguin Classics Chaucer's *Troilus and Criseyde*, 'Chaucer is meditating on the nature of love, and on human love in particular.'[16] The 1977 Collins edition of Virginia Woolf's *The Waves* 'invites us to examine our own sense of being'.[17] At times the jacket copy aims for multiple forms of recommendation: we might usefully distinguish between endorsement blurb and précis blurb, and both forms can be present at the same time. *The Missing Miniature*, published by Knopf in 1937, bears on the front the anonymous instruction 'Those who read for pleasure will find plenty of it in this rare combination of joyous comedy and wildly exciting mystery.' The front flap buttresses this with the personal opinion of William Lyon Phelps: 'it is an absolutely enchanting book. The ingredients of mirth and excitement are perfectly mingled. The humor is fine, spontaneous, graceful, delicate!' And then, for the reader who wants to know what it's actually about, 'For a fuller description of this happy tale see the back of the wrapper.'[18]

---

[13] Iain Banks, *The Wasp Factory* (London: Macmillan, 1984, repr. Abacus 2008).

[14] 'Eight years ago Logan Tate had broken Marianne Conway's heart…but in all those years she had never stopped loving him.' Lilian Peake, *No Second Parting* (London: Mills and Boon, 1977); Jodi Picoult, *Harvesting the Heart* (London, Hodder, 2011).

[15] Martin Amis, *London Fields* (London: Jonathan Cape, 1989).

[16] Geoffrey Chaucer, *Troilus and Criseyde*, ed. Neville Coghill (Harmondsworth: Penguin, 1978).

[17] Virginia Woolf, *The Waves* (London: Collins, 1989).

[18] Erich Kastner, *The Missing Miniature* (New York: Knopf, 1937).

AUTHENTICITY AND ATTRIBUTION

As these examples suggest, one of the distinctive features of the blurb is its changeable use of voice. Within endorsement blurbs, the attribution of promotional statements to notable critics, authors, and publications has long been a hallmark of the genre, the name of the authority operating as an imprimatur for the work within. Erasmus's letter prefacing More's *Utopia* provides an early precursor, as do the praise poems printed before the text in early modern works. William Barnes's lines in celebration of John Tatham's *The Fancies Theater* (1640) frame the work which follows within a vocabulary of pleasure:

> How sweet and delici'ous to the taste:
> How pleasing to the eye, how trim'd, how chaste;
> And where thy Fancy hits upon a crime,
> Thy Verse doth mask it, suting with the Time.[19]

The modern endorsement has moved outside the work, to its cover, but it plays a similar role. It frequently offers insights into the perceived status of individual commentators: the role of the blurb compiler is to determine whether the pull of the named authority or the named publication is the greatest. As such, the attribution of these comments operates as an index of critical reputation. So, in the case of Hanif Kureishi's *The Buddha of Suburbia*, a list of comments from the *Daily Mail, Financial Times, Evening Standard*, and *Independent on Sunday* are cited with no indication of authorship; but we are given 'Angela Carter, *Guardian*' and simply 'Salman Rushdie' for the two final quotes.[20] Graham Swift's *Last Orders* cites comments from the *Times Literary Supplement, Guardian, Sunday Times, Daily Mail, Observer*, and then, individually named and in a league of his own, again, Salman Rushdie.[21] The blurb exposes the stratification of literary reviewing, the fact that not all praise is equal. It is ripe ground for network theory: gesturing towards the symbiotic relationships between authors and reviewers, patterns of mutual praise that underlie the promotion of literary fiction and trade publication. Satirical columns such as 'Logrolling in Our Time' in the American satirical magazine *Spy*, or, in Britain, *Private Eye*'s 'Order of the Brown Nose', have exposed habits of reciprocal reviewing between writers. The relative positions between reviewer and reviewed can, of course, shift. T. S. Eliot wrote numerous blurbs for Faber and Gwyer, later Faber and Faber, in his role as editor, and in the *Hand-List of the Literary Manuscripts in the T. S. Eliot Collection*, there is a record of three Faber catalogues marked by the poet to indicate his authorship

---

[19] William Barnes, 'To his friend M. Io. Tatham on his Fancies Theater', prefacing John Tatham, *Fancies Theater* (London, 1640), A2v.

[20] Hanif Kureishi, *The Buddha of Suburbia* (London: Faber and Faber, 1990).

[21] Graham Swift, *Last Orders* (London: Picador, 1996).

of book-jacket material.[22] Eliot wrote promotional material as part of his day job at Faber: his comments were published anonymously. There is an irony in the fact that he was invisible as the creator of these words, yet would become the kind of name that authors could only dream of having as an endorsement on their book, a reminder that that the dynamic between book, blurb, and celebrity endorser changes over time. Surveying Ernest Hemingway's decades of promotional commentary, usually attributed, one is struck by the gap between the literary giant's subsequent status and the stature of the relatively minor authors on whom he lavishes praise.[23] He declares of a novel entitled *The Professional*, 'the only good novel I've read about a fighter, and an excellent first novel in its own right'.[24] *Cuba: Isla de las Maravillas*, a travel guide to the island, is emblazoned with a replica of a statement in Hemingway's hand: 'This is an excellent book. It is well written and the illustrations are good. It should be read by every visitor to Cuba.'[25] The representation here of the material form of the endorsement—in this case an image of a handwritten note—to convey authenticity is not unusual. The blurb on the front dust jacket of *The Chink in the Armour* by Marie Belloc Lowndes displays a replica typewritten letter signed by Hemingway and two other writers, Alexander Woolcott and Edmund Pearson:

> It is lamentable that 'THE CHINK IN THE ARMOUR'—that uncanny masterpiece of dread and suspense—should be so little known in this country and virtually unobtainable here. We beg you to publish it so that we may get it when we want it and give it to our friends.[26]

The inclusion of the 'petition' implies no off-the-peg endorsement but a sincere, personal plea from the three writers. In a similar vein, the jacket for Sallie Hovey's *The Rehabilitation of Eve* displays a facsimile of a complete letter of 11 June 1924 from Eugene O'Neill to Hovey congratulating her on her book.[27]

This use of 'private' documents to convey genuine praise is not a new phenomenon: from the very inception of the novel, the use of a privacy effect to convey authenticity signals an awareness of the potential cynicism of the published recommendation. Samuel Richardson's epistolary novel *Pamela* (1740) was met with an enthusiastic, but contested reception amongst eighteenth-century readers. As the story of a young

[22] *A Preliminary Hand-List of the Literary Manuscripts in the T.S. Eliot Collection bequeathed to King's College Cambridge* (Cambridge: King's College, 1970). Tanselle argues that words in a blurb are often the only iteration of those words and so should be part of the author's bibliography. Tanselle, *Book Jackets*, p. 19.

[23] *Hemingway and the Mechanism of Fame: Statements, Public Letters, Introductions, Forewords, Prefaces, Blurbs, Reviews, and Endorsements*, ed. Matthew J. Bruccoli with Judith S. Baughman (Columbia, SC: University of South Carolina Press, 2006).

[24] W. C. Heinz, *The Professional* (New York: Harper, 1958).

[25] Ernesto T. Brivio, *Cuba: Isla de las Maravillas* (Havana: Luis David Rodriguez, 1953).

[26] Marie Belloc Lowndes, *The Chink in the Armour* (New York: Longmans, Green, 1937).

[27] Sallie Hovey, *The Rehabilitation of Eve* (Chicago, IL: Hyman-McGee, 1924).

servant girl who virtuously resists her master's advances, only to be rewarded by marriage to the man at the end of the novel, it was variously read as a heartfelt and honest incitement to virtue, or, as an encouragement to young women to flirt coyly with their employers with the hope of attaining social mobility. In order to convey the novel's intended moral purpose, Richardson prefaced it with two letters emphasizing the place of the book in reinforcing Christian conduct.[28] And when he revised for the second edition, he added more. The dramatist and poet Aaron Hill had written to him in praise of his novel, and in the second edition, Richardson included Hill's letters as a form of endorsement: 'I have done nothing but read it to others, and hear others again read it, to me, ever since it came into my Hands; and I find I am likely to do nothing else.'[29] While it was fairly common within eighteenth-century printed texts to include a letter from the author addressed to a dedicatee or patron, it was less usual to introduce personal correspondence into the prefatory pages of a fictional work. The apparatus of the letter, like the quotation marks around endorsements, signifies a more personal form of approval, the private document or the individually spoken word. Both gestures signal the way the blurb has been, and continues to be framed within a sense of its own hackneyed emptiness, a form of writing which has sought to transcend its own genre, to gesture to the cliché it represents, whilst being trapped in its norms.

FROM TITLE PAGE TO BLURB

The blurb is a marketing tool of the moment: its tone, content, and role are intended to address a historically specific readership, framing the text in the ways that will speak most powerfully to the intended buyer. Like the design, the blurb is produced after the book, but is read before it. As a form of writing designed to lure potential purchasers, it is both an invitation and an introduction. So how might this relationship between blurb and book evolve over time? If we take as a case study Daniel Defoe's *Moll Flanders*, we can start to see how changing reading contexts have reshaped the promotional description, and we can map the way in which the descriptive blurb has moved around the book's form. *Moll Flanders* was first published in 1721, the fictional autobiography of a woman who lived as a prostitute and thief, before her final repentance. The novel is notable for its provocative title page, which provides a summary of the most salacious details of Moll's life story:

> Who was born in Newgate, and during a life of continu'd Variety for Threescore Years, besides her Childhood, was Twelve Year a Whore, five times a Wife (whereof once to her own Brother) Twelve Year a Thief, Eight Year a Transported

[28] Samuel Richardson, *Pamela: Or Virtue Rewarded*, ed. Albert J. Rivero (Cambridge: Cambridge University Press, 2011), pp. 4–8. The letters are from Jean Baptiste de Freval and the Rev William Webster.

[29] Aaron Hill to Samuel Richardson, preface to the second edition of *Pamela*, reproduced in Rivero (ed.), p. 464.

Felon in Virginia, at last grew Rich, liv'd Honest, and died a Penitent, Written from her own Memorandums.[30]

In an era before printed book jackets, flaps, or publicity departments, this is a blurb. It is both descriptive and titillating, designed to sell stock. But it is also at odds with everything that Defoe later says about how his novel ought to be consumed. In the preface to *Moll Flanders*, he states that

> This Work is chiefly recommended to those who know how to Read it, and how to make the good Uses of it, which the Story all along recommends to them, so it is to be hop'd that such Readers will be much more pleas'd with the Moral than the Fable, with the Application than with the Relation, and with the End of the Writer than with the Life of the Person written of.[31]

Yet as we have seen, like the blurbs of modern genre fiction, the original title page of *Moll Flanders* sells the book on the promise of personal revelation, sexual scandal, and true crime, anticipating its readers' interest in precisely the kind of hermeneutics Defoe had outlawed, namely the fable, the relation, and the life. From the very inception of the novel form in Britain, there is a clear tension between the moral or aesthetic complexity of the fictional work, and the demands of the promotional text.

Like many other novels of the era, Moll Flanders went on to have a vigorous afterlife in the form of abridgements and chapbooks.[32] The text got considerably shorter, down from 366 pages in octavo in 1721, to seventy-two, twenty-four, sixteen, and even eight pages within a century.[33] Yet it is noticeable that although the novel itself became shorter, the title page blurb got longer, and it continued to be revised even when the chapbook text remained the same across editions. The seventy-two-page early nineteenth-century duodecimo abridgement entitled *The History and Intrigues of the Famous Moll Flanders* offers additional details:

> debauched at the Age of Eighteen by one Brother, and afterwards marrying the other; Twelve Years a Whore with Different Persons; Four other Times married (once to her own Brother;) was Eight Years with another Husband, transported to Virginia, where she grew rich; returned to Ireland, lived honest, and died truly penitent in the Seventy-fifth Year of her Age.[34]

---

[30] Daniel Defoe, *The Fortunes and Misfortunes of the Famous Moll Flanders &c*, 2nd edition (London, 1722).

[31] Defoe, Preface to *Moll Flanders*, p. iii.

[32] Pat Rogers has argued that *Moll Flanders* survived only in these truncated forms. Pat Rogers, 'Classics and Chapbooks', in *Literature and Popular Culture in Eighteenth-Century England* (Brighton: Harvester, 1985), pp. 162–82, p. 178.

[33] Pat Rogers, 'Moll in the Chapbooks', in *Literature and Popular Culture in Eighteenth-Century England*, pp. 183–97, p. 184.

[34] *The History and Intrigues of the Famous Moll Flanders* (London, printed and sold by J. Hollis, Shoemaker Row). 72p. Long duodecimo. Bodleian Library, Oxford, Harding A 57 (11).

The revised and extended title page amplifies the shock value of the description. She commits incest with two brothers, not just one; her twelve years a whore is said to be 'with different persons'; another husband is introduced into the summary. This additional detail is not unique to this abridgement. In the even briefer twenty-four page chapbook *The Fortunes and Misfortunes of Moll Flanders*, published between 1760 and 1780, we are told more about geographical locations.[35] Moll

> was born in Newgate, and during a life of continued Variety for sixty Years, was 17 Times a Whore, 5 Times a Wife, whereof once to her own Brother, 12 Years a Thief, 11 Times in Bridewell, 9 Times in New Prison, 11 Times in Wood-Street Compter, 14 Times in the Gatehouse, 25 Times in Newgate, 15 Times whipt at the Cart's Arse, 4 Times burnt in the Hand, once condemned for Life, and 8 Years a Transport in Virginia. At last grew rich, lived honest, and died a Penitent.

A good part of this description is not even true: there is no burning or whipping in the original novel, and no mention of 'the Cart's Arse'. The role of this particular summary is to give local detail to the punishment and imprisonment undergone during the course of the novel.[36] In the case of one of the later versions of this chapbook, *The History of the Famous Moll Flanders*, the description is followed by a quatrain upon the story, which is both blurb and epigraph:

> READER, observe the sudden turns of fate,
> And from her fortune thy sure omen date;
> Thro' all degrees of life you plainly see,
> Man's fate is order'd by God's just decree.[37]

The moralizing lines are not entirely appropriate for the narrative they are supposed to be interpreting. Moll's story is about ingenuity, punishment, repentance, and redemption, a humanly driven course of action rather than the turns of the wheel of fate, as is suggested here.

Looking across these and later iterations of *Moll Flanders* it becomes clear that the blurb can travel around the book. It begins in 1722 on the title page, but in various editions of the twenty-four-page chapbook version, *The History of the Famous Moll*

---

[35] *The Fortunes and Misfortunes of Moll Flanders* (London, printed and sold at no. 4 Aldermary Church Yard). 24p. Long duodecimo. Bodleian Library, Oxford, Harding A 63 (18). According to Rogers's study of chapbook versions of the novel, this edition, produced by the Dicey family's chapbook firm, formed the main line of descent for all other chapbook versions—yet across all these versions, the title page is regularly revised.

[36] This text recurs in the title pages of *The Fortunes and Misfortunes of Moll Flanders* (London, printed for and sold by J. Pitts, no. 14, Great St Andrew Street, Seven Dials), 24p. Long duodecimo, Bodleian Library, Oxford, Douce adds. 275 (11) and a Scottish imprint, *The History of the Famous Miss Moll Flanders* (Edinburgh, printed by A. Robertson, opposite the foot of the Assembly Close, 1791). Bodleian Library, Oxford, Harding A 73 (1), 24p., Long duodecimo. ESTC T300469.

[37] *The History of the Famous Miss Moll Flanders* (Edinburgh, 1791). ESTC T300469.

Flanders, the blurb has been replicated, or sometimes moved, so that it is at the end of the volume. The narrative finishes:

> Twelve years a whore,
> A wife unto thy brother:
> And such a thief,
> There scarce could be another:
> Unwearied trav'ller,
> Whither dost thou roam?
> Lo! in this place remote
> To find a tomb?
> Transported hence,
> To heav'n, 'tis hoped, thou'rt sent,
> Who wick'd livd,
> But dy'd a penitent.[38]

The verses take the title page summary, and project them beyond the end of the novel, and beyond the end of Moll's life, offering us a picture of the heroine's future transport into heaven (perhaps). This didactic spin is not unique to eighteenth-century editions of the novel. A large print 1991 edition uses the text of the first edition title page on its own title page, and has the following description on the back:

> She soon recognizes, however, that a *good* husband is necessary for her survival and she resumes her search for a protector...Her touching conversion in the shadow of the gallows earns her a reprieve, and she endeavours to spend the remainder of her life in sincere penitence.[39]

For this potential readership, some moral gloss was provided to mediate the seamy detail of the original plot summary. The original title page has continued to operate as a blurb in other modern editions. The back cover of the Oxford World's Classics 1981 edition, edited by G. A. Starr, reproduces the same text, followed by: 'Racy, ironic, rich in realistic sociological detail, it is also a romance, with Moll in her quest for a familial paradise its charmed heroine.'[40] Here the role of the blurb is to sell the novel for its story and period detail, rather than its didactic function. In the Corgi edition of 1960, the novel acquires a subtitle: '*Moll Flanders: The story of a wanton.*' The back cover copy in this case is a mid twentieth-century version of the first title page, a description designed to titillate for the 1960s:

---

[38] *The History of the Famous Moll Flanders* (Falkirk, printed and sold by T. Johnston, *c.* 1798–1810), ESTC T300506. p. 24. Long duodecimo. Bodleian Library, Oxford, Douce PP 165 (6).

[39] Daniel Defoe, *Moll Flanders* (Isis Clear Type Classic; Oxford:,Clio, 1991).

[40] Daniel Defoe, *Moll Flanders*, ed. and intro G.A. Starr (Oxford: Oxford University Press, 1981).

As the years passed by uncounted, Moll Flanders began to mature and to exhibit a beauty which left no doubt as to what her future would be…and in the gutters and tawdry rooms, she irrevocably debased her mind and body. This classic novel tells the tragic, shockingly true-to-life story of Moll Flanders written with all the vigour and pace and narrative genius that has made the author world-famous in two centuries of changing literature.[41]

The Corgi blurb appeals to the sentimental and the erotic and the canonical all at the same time, reminding us that there are often competing impulses within the promotional statement: the need to sell, to make a claim for literary or canonical status, to describe what the book is about, to relate the particulars of the fiction to a universalized model of human existence.

As this account has suggested, the long and shorter history of the form demonstrates the way in which the blurb frames the tensions between telling and selling in epitome. Or alternatively: 'in tracing the evolving role of the printed endorsement, this article offers a searching examination of the self-authorizing nature of the literary text and the powerful interconnection between literary and market value'.

---

[41] Daniel Defoe, *Moll Flanders: The Story of a Wanton* (London: Corgi/Transworld, 1960).

SELECT BIBLIOGRAPHY

PARATEXTS AND PARTS

Gérard Genette, *Paratexts: Thresholds of Interpretation*, trans. Jane E. Lewin (Cambridge: Cambridge University Press, 1997)

Jonn Herschend and Will Rogan (eds), *The Thing the Book: A Monument to the Book as Object* (San Francisco, CA: Chronicle, 2016)

Kevin Jackson, *Invisible Forms: A Guide to Literary Curiosities* (New York: Picador, 1999)

Marie Maclean, 'Pretexts and Paratexts: The Art of the Peripheral', *New Literary History* 22, no. 2 (1991): 273–9

Helen Smith and Louise Wilson (eds), *Renaissance Paratexts* (Cambridge: Cambridge University Press, 2011)

DUST JACKETS

Mark Godburn, *Nineteenth-Century Dust Jackets* (New Castle, DE: Oak Knoll, 2016)

Charles Rosner, *The Growth of the Book Jacket* (London: Sylvan, 1954)

Martin Salisbury, *The Illustrated History of the Dust Jacket: 1920–1970* (London: Thames and Hudson, 2017)

G. Thomas Tanselle, *Book-Jackets: Their History, Forms and Use* (Charlottesville, VA: Bibliographical Society of the University of Virginia, 2011)

FRONTISPIECES

Margery Corbett and Ronald Lightbown, *The Comely Frontispiece: The Emblematic Title-Page in England 1550–1660* (London: Routledge and Kegan Paul, 1979)

Alastair Fowler, *The Mind of the Book: Pictorial Title Pages* (Oxford: Oxford University Press, 2017)

David Piper, *The Image of the Poet: British Poets and Their Portraits* (Oxford: Clarendon, 1982)

W. Pollard, 'A Rough List of the Contents of the Bagford Collection', *Transactions of the Bibliographical Society* 1st series, 7 (1902–4): 143–59

Volker R. Remmert, '"Docet parva picture, quod multae scripturae non dicunt": Frontispieces, Their Functions, and Their Audiences in Seventeenth-Century

Mathematical Sciences', *Transmitting Knowledge: Words, Images, and Instruments in Early Modern Europe*, ed. Sachiko Kusukawa and Ian Maclean (Oxford: Oxford University Press, 2006), pp. 239–70

TITLE PAGES

Margery Corbett, *The Comely Frontispiece* (Chicago, IL: University of Chicago Press, 1979)

Alastair Fowler, *The Mind of the Book: Pictorial Title Pages* (Oxford: Oxford University Press, 2017)

Ronald McKerrow, *Title-Page Borders Used in England and Scotland 1485–1640* (Oxford: Oxford University Press, 1932)

A. W. Pollard, *Last Words on the History of the Title-Page* (London: Nimmo, 1891)

Margaret Smith, *The Title-Page: Its Early Development 1460–1510* (London: British Library, 2000)

IMPRINTS, IMPRIMATURS, AND COPYRIGHT PAGES

Peter W. M. Blayney, *The Stationers' Company and the Printers of London, 1501–1557*, 2 vols (Cambridge: Cambridge University Press, 2013)

John Carter and Nicolas Barker, *ABC for Book Collectors*, 8th edn (London: British Library; New Castle, DE: Oak Knoll, 2006)

Primary Sources on Copyright (1450–1900): http://www.copyrighthistory.org

Michael F. Suarez, S. J., and H. R. Woudhuysen (eds), *The Oxford Companion to the Book*, 2 vols (Oxford: Oxford University Press, 2010)

TABLES OF CONTENTS

A. Doody, *Pliny's Encyclopedia: The Reception of the Natural History* (Cambridge: Cambridge University Press, 2010)

R. Gibson, 'Starting with the Index in Pliny', in L. Jansen (ed.), *The Roman Paratext* (Cambridge: Cambridge University Press, 2014), pp. 33–55

Georges Mathieu (ed.) *La Table des Matières. Son histoire, ses règles, ses fonctions son esthétique* (Paris: Classiques Garnier, 2017)

A. Riggsby, 'Guides to the Wor(l)d', in J. König and T. Whitmarsh (eds), *Ordering Knowledge in the Roman Empire* (Cambridge: Cambridge University Press, 2007), pp. 88–107

Bianca-Jeanette Schröder, *Titel und Text: zur Entwicklung lateinischer Gedichtüberschriften* (Berlin: De Gruyter, 1999)

ADDRESSES TO THE READER

Randall Anderson, 'The Rhetoric of Paratext in Early Printed Books', in *The Cambridge History of the Book in Britain. Vol. IV: 1557–1695*, ed. John Barnard and D. F. McKenzie (Cambridge: Cambridge University Press, 2002), pp. 636–44

Wayne Booth, *The Rhetoric of Fiction* (Chicago, IL: University of Chicago Press, 1961)

Michael Saenger, *The Commodification of Textual Engagements in the English Renaissance* (Aldershot: Ashgate, 2006)

William H. Sherman, 'The Beginning of "The End": Terminal Paratext and the Birth of Print Culture', in *Renaissance Paratexts*, ed. Helen Smith and Louise Wilson (Cambridge: Cambridge University Press, 2011), pp. 65–87

Linda Simon, 'Instructions to the Reader: James's Prefaces to the New York Edition', in *The Critical Reception of Henry James* (London: Boydell and Brewer, 2007)

ACKNOWLEDGEMENTS AND DEDICATIONS

Terry Caesar, *Conspiring with Forms: Life in Academic Texts* (Athens, GA: University of Georgia Press, 2010)

Dustin Griffin, *Literary Patronage in England, 1650–1800* (Cambridge: Cambridge University Press, 1996)

Richard A. McCabe, *'Ungainefull Arte': Poetry, Patronage, and Print in the Early Modern Era* (Oxford: Oxford University Press, 2016)

Valerie Schutte, *Mary I and the Art of Book Dedications: Royal Women, Power, and Persuasion* (New York: Palgrave Macmillan, 2015)

Franklin B. Williams, *Index of Dedications and Commendatory Verses in English Books before 1641* (London: Bibliographical Society, 1961)

PRINTERS' ORNAMENTS AND FLOWERS

Mark Arman, *Fleurons: Their Place in History and in Print* (Thaxted: Workshop, 1988)

Christopher Flint, 'In Other Words: Eighteenth-Century Authorship and the Ornaments of Print', *Eighteenth-Century Fiction* 14 (2002): 621–66

K. I. D. Maslen, *The Bowyer Ornament Stock* (Oxford: Oxford Bibliographical Society, 1973)

John Ryder, *Flowers and Flourishes* (London: Bodley Head, 1976)

P. Spedding, 'Thomas Gardner's Ornament Stock: A Checklist', *Script and Print: Bulletin of the Bibliographical Society of Australia and New Zealand* 39 (2015): 69–111

Ad Stijman, *Engraving and Etching, 1400–2000* (London: Archetype, 2012)

CHARACTER LISTS

Tamara Atkin and Emma Smith, 'The Form and Function of Character Lists in Plays Printed before the Closing of the Theatres', *Review of English Studies* 65 (2014): 647–72

Matteo Pangallo, '"I will keep and character that name": Dramatis Personae Lists in Early Modern Manuscript Plays', *Early Theatre* 18 (2015): 87–118

Gary Taylor, 'The Order of Persons', in *Thomas Middleton and Early Modern Textual Culture: A Companion to the Collected Works*, ed. Gary Taylor and John Lavagnino (Oxford: Oxford University Press, 2007), pp. 31–79

PAGE NUMBERS, SIGNATURES, AND CATCHWORDS

Rebecca Bullard, 'Signs of the Times? Reading Signatures in Two Late Seventeenth-Century Secret Histories', in *The Perils of Print Culture: Book, Print and Publishing History in Theory and Practice*, ed. Jason McElligott and Eve Patten (Basingstoke: Palgrave, 2014), pp. 118–33

Richard Rouse, 'Cistercian Aids to Study in the Thirteenth Century', in *Studies in Medieval Cistercian History II*, ed. J. R. Sommerfeldt, Cistercian Studies 24 (Kalamazoo, MI: Cistercian Publications, 1976), pp. 123–34

Paul Saenger, 'The Impact of the Early Printed Page on the History of Reading', in *Bulletin du bibliophile* (1996): 237–301

Margaret M. Smith, 'Printed Foliation: Forerunner to Printed Page Numbers?', in *Gutenberg-Jahrbuch* 63 (1988): 54–70

Eric G. Turner, *The Typology of the Early Codex* (Philadelphia, PA: University of Pennsylvania Press, 1977)

CHAPTER HEADS

Ego Dionne, *La Voie aux chapitres: Poétique de la disposition Romanesque* (Paris: Seuil, 2008)

Aude Doody, *Pliny's Encyclopedia: The Reception of the* Natural History (Cambridge: Cambridge University Press, 2010)

Johanna Drucker, 'Graphic Devices: Narration and Navigation,' *Narrative* 16, no. 2 (2008): 121–39

Laura Jansen (ed.), *The Roman Paratext: Frame, Texts, Readers* (Cambridge: Cambridge University Press, 2014)

Bianca-Jeanette Schröder, *Titel und Text: zur Entwicklung lateintscher Gedichtüber-schriften* (Berlin: de Gruyter, 1999)

EPIGRAPHS

Janine Barchas, *Graphic Design, Print Culture, and the Eighteenth-Century Novel* (Cambridge: Cambridge University Press, 2003)

Ann Ferry, *The Title to the Poem* (Stanford, CA: Stanford University Press, 1996)

Ellen McCracken, *Paratexts and Performance in the Novels of Junot Díaz and Sandra Cisneros* (Basingstoke: Palgrave Macmillan, 2016)

Kate Rumbold, *Shakespeare and the Eighteenth-Century Novel: Cultures of Quotation from Samuel Richardson to Jane Austen* (Cambridge: Cambridge University Press, 2016)

STAGE DIRECTIONS

Philip Butterworth, *Staging Conventions in Medieval English Theatre* (Cambridge: Cambridge University Press, 2014)

Sarah Dastagheer and Gillian Woods (eds), *Stage Directions and Shakespearean Theatre* (London: Bloomsbury, 2018)

Alan C. Dessen, *Elizabethan Stage Directions and Modern Interpreters* (Cambridge: Cambridge University Press, 1985)

T. H. Howard-Hill, 'The Evolution of the Form of Plays in English during the Renaissance', *Renaissance Quarterly* 43 (1990): 112–45

Linda McJannet, *The Voice of Elizabethan Stage Directions* (Newark, DE: University of Delaware Press, 1999)

RUNNING TITLES

Fredson Bowers, 'Notes on Running-Titles as Bibliographical Evidence', *The Library*, 4th series, 19 (1938): 315–38

Matthew Day, '"Intended to offenders": The Running Titles of Early Modern Books', in *Renaissance Paratexts*, ed. Louise Wilson and Helen Smith (Cambridge: Cambridge University Press, 2014), pp. 34–47

Charlton Hinman, *The Printing and Proof-Reading of the First Folio of Shakespeare*, 2 vols (Oxford: Oxford University Press, 1963)

Malcolm B. Parkes, 'The Influence of the Concepts of *Ordinatio* and *Compilatio* on the Development of the Book', in *Scribes, Scripts, and Readers: Studies in the Communication, Presentation, and Dissemination of Medieval Texts* (London: Hambledon Press, 1991), pp. 35–70

Edwin E. Willoughby, 'A Note on the Typography of the Running Titles of the First Folio', *The Library*, 4th series, 9 (1929): 385–7

WOODCUTS

Antony Griffiths, *The Print before Photography: An Introduction to European Printmaking, 1550–1820* (London: British Museum, 2016)

Edward Hodnett, *Five Centuries of English Book Illustration* (Aldershot: Scolar, 1988)

Sachiko Kusukawa, *Picturing the Book of Nature: Image, Text, and Argument in Sixteenth-Century Human Anatomy and Medical Botany* (Chicago, IL: University of Chicago Press, 2011)

Ruth S. Luborsky, 'Woodcuts in Tudor Books: Clarifying Their Documentation', *Papers of the Bibliographical Society of America* 86, no. 1 (1992): 67–81

Matilde Malaspina and Yujie Zhong, 'Image-Matching Technology Applied to Fifteenth-Century Printed Book Illustration', *Lettera Matematica International Edition* 5, no. 4 (2017): 287–92

Christopher Marsh, 'A Woodcut and Its Wanderings in Seventeenth-Century England', *Huntington Library Quarterly* 79, no. 2 (2016): 245–62

ENGRAVINGS

Susan Dackerman (ed.), *Prints and the Pursuit of Visual Knowledge* (Chicago, IL: University of Chicago Press, 2011)

Anthony Griffiths, *The Print before Photography: An Introduction to European Printmaking, 1550–1820* (London: British Museum Press, 2016)

David Landau and Peter Parshall, *The Renaissance Print: 1470–1550* (New Haven, CT: Yale University Press, 1994)

Evelyn Lincoln, *Brilliant Discourse: Pictures and Readers in Early Modern Rome* (New Haven, CT: Yale University Press, 2014)

FOOTNOTES

Claire Connolly, 'A Bookish History of Irish Romanticism', in *Rethinking British Romantic History, 1770–1845*, ed. Porscha Fermanis and John Regan (Oxford: Oxford University Press, 2014), pp. 271–96

Anthony Grafton, *The Footnote: A Curious History* (Cambridge, MA: Harvard University Press, 1999)

Evelyn B. Tribble, *Margins and Marginality: The Printed Page in Early Modern England* (Charlottesville, VA: University Press of Virginia, 1993)

Evelyn B. Tribble, '"Like a Looking-Glas in the Frame": From the Marginal Note to the Footnote', in *The Margins of the Text*, ed. D. C. Greetham (Ann Arbor, MI: University of Michigan Press, 1997), pp. 229–44

Marcus Walsh, 'Scholarly Documentation in the Enlightenment: Validation and Interpretation', in *Ancients and Moderns in Europe: Comparative Perspectives*, ed. Paddy Bullard and Alexis Tadié (Oxford: Voltaire Foundation, 2016), pp. 97–112

ERRATA LISTS

Ann Blair, 'Errata Lists and the Reader as Corrector', in *Agent of Change: Print Culture Studies after Elizabeth L. Eisenstein*, ed. Sabrina Alcorn Baron, Eric N. Lindquist, and Eleanor F. Shevlin (Amherst, MA: University of Massachusetts Press, 2007), pp. 21–40

Alexandra da Costa, 'Negligence and Virtue: Errata Notices and their Evangelical Use', in *The Library* 7th series, 19, no. 2 (2018): 159–73

Paul Fyfe, 'Electronic Errata: Digital Publishing, Open Review, and the Futures of Correction', in *Debates in the Digital Humanities*, ed. Matthew K. Gold (Minneapolis, MN: University of Minnesota Press, 2012), pp. 259–80

Seth Lerer, *Error and the Academic Self: The Scholarly Imagination, Medieval to Modern* (New York: Columbia University Press, 2002)

David McKitterick, *Print, Manuscript and the Search for Order 1450–1830* (Cambridge: Cambridge University Press, 2003)

INDEXES

Lloyd W. Daly, *Contributions to a History of Alphabetization in Antiquity and the Middle Ages* (Brussels: Latomus, 1967)

Mary A. Rouse and Richard H. Rouse, 'La Naissance des index', in *Histoire de l'édition française*, ed. Henri-Jean Martin and Roger Chartier, 4 vols (Paris: Promodis, 1983), I, pp. 77–85

Richard H. Rouse and Mary A. Rouse, 'The Verbal Concordance to the Scriptures', *Archivum Fratrum Praedicatorum* 44 (1974): 5–30

Hans H. Wellisch, 'Incunabula Indexes', *The Indexer* 19, no. 1 (1994): 3–12

Henry Wheatley, *What Is an Index? A Few Notes on Indexes and Indexers* (London: Index Society, 1878)

ENDLEAVES

Sidney E. Berger, 'Dutch Gilt Papers as Substitutes for Leather', *Hand Papermaking* 24, no. 2 (Winter 2009): 14–16

Douglas Cockerell, *Bookbinding, and the Care of Books: A Text-Book for Bookbinders and Librarians* (London: Sir Isaac Pitman and Sons, 1937)

David Pearson, *English Bookbinding Styles 1450–1800: A Handbook* (London: British Library; New Castle, DE: Oak Knoll, 2005)

Tanya Schmoller, *Remondini and Rizzi: A Chapter in Italian Decorated Paper History* (New Castle, DE: Oak Knoll, 1990)

Richard J. Wolfe, *Marbled Paper: Its History, Techniques, and Patterns, with Special Reference to the Relationship of Marbling to Bookbinding in Europe and the Western World* (Philadelphia, PA: University of Pennsylvania Press, 1990)

BLURBS

Matthew J. Bruccoli and Judith S. Baughman, *Hemingway and the Mechanism of Fame: Statements, Public Letters, Introductions, Forewords, Prefaces, Blurbs, Reviews, and Endorsements* (Columbia, SC: University of South Carolina Press, 2006)

Mark Davis, 'Theorizing the Blurb: The Strange Case at the End of the Book', *Meanjin* 53, no. 2 (1994): 245–57

David McKitterick, 'Changes in the Look of the Book', in *The Cambridge History of the Book in Britain, vol. VI, 1830–1914* (Cambridge: Cambridge University Press, 2009), pp. 75–116

G. Thomas Tanselle, *Book-Jackets: Their History, Forms and Use* (Charlottesville, VA: Bibliographical Society of the University of Virginia, 2011)

INDEX

Note: Page numbers in italics indicate figures.